THE ART OF
RESTORING ANTIQUES

Professional Secrets For
The Amateur

THE ART OF
RESTORING ANTIQUES

Professional Secrets For
The Amateur

MICHEL DOUSSY

Translated from the French by
PATRICK EVANS

Times
BOOKS

First paperback edition September, 1978

First British edition published 1973 by Souvenir Press Ltd,
95 Mortimer Street, London W1N 8HP
and simultaneously in Canada by J. M. Dent & Sons
(Canada) Ltd, Ontario, Canada

Library of Congress Cataloging in Publication Data

Doussy, Michel.
    The art of restoring antiques.

    Translation of Guide des secrets de l'antiquaire.
        1. Antiques—Conservation and restoration—
Handbooks, manuals, etc. I. Title.
NK1125.D6513 1978   745.1'028   78-18003
ISBN 0-8129-6302-4

To my father, an art-craftsman
To my son, who takes after him

Illustrations and Acknowledgements

Giraudon:

Musée des Arts et Traditions populaires, Paris (Photo J.-L. Charmet):

Roger-Viollet:

Musée du Bardo:

Musée des Arts décoratifs:
Drawings by P. Ballanger.

French National Museums: (Bibliothèque Nationale), (A.T.P.) (B.N.) (B.N.) (B.N.) (B.N.)

Photo P. Guillet:

Photo Subra:

Contents

Preface

THIS book by Michel Doussy eludes the clutches of literary criticism or art criticism; it is not in their province. It bobs gaily and humorously along; it is akin to the works of practical information which have been appearing ever since the late 15th century, when the Florentine Cenino Cenini, to combat boredom while in prison for debt, wrote a treatise on the painting and restoration of pictures.

Some of Michel Doussy's ancestors were *compagnons du Tour de France*—craftsmen who, after completing their apprenticeship, had travelled the country plying their trade and increasing their knowledge; his undertaking reflects something of their simple, almost naïve, attitude. It is as if he had been commissioned to restore the objects collected by *le facteur* Cheval, the postman and *amateur*, whose eccentric hoard is now on the way to fame—and had felt impelled thereafter to turn instructor. Specialized craftsmen may smile at his summary treatment; in a few pages he gives directions for repairing a piece of furniture, nursing its veneers and pegs, restoring its gilding. In the same way, collectors of bronzes, or lovers of jewellery or Renaissance ceramics, will look down their noses at an author who in a few short chapters presumes to expound the various cuts of rock crystal, or the repair of faiences and porcelains.

The fact remains that this is a well-informed book. Michel Doussy knows his subject and his easily applied recipes will restore the bloom to many a jaded *bibelot*. Here is encouragement for youthful amateurs, many of them with slim purses, to venture out into the provinces and try their luck among the small antique dealers, seeking that beauty and delight which are the reward of a successful discovery. Unfortunately, the low market value of many of these finds prevents the amateur from entrusting them to an expert craftsman for repair. With the help of this book he will learn—like a family which has adopted a child—how to look after them, nurse them in sickness, protect them from the maladies which attack wood, bronze and other materials. He will not only save money on costly repairs; he will give himself the extra pleasure of becoming intimately acquainted with his purchase, and of imbuing it with the aura of his own passion.

Finally, it is to be hoped that this book will awaken in a few readers a vocation for the restoration of *objets d'art*: a fascinating profession which demands years of apprenticeship but, quite rightly, is among the best-paid of all categories of manual work. Specialists in these lines charge high fees; the monthly income of a front-rank craftsman is in many cases equal to that of a higher civil servant, or someone at middle management level.

The book is largely instructional in character. The author knows how to teach by entertaining; he hops merrily from one subject to another and, by means of an apparent disorder which is in fact perfectly deliberate, holds the reader's attention. This is something which the qualified expert, with his specialized approach, does not always find easy to achieve.

MAURICE RHEIMS

Foreword

THERE are dynasties of antique dealers, just as there used to be dynasties of cabinet makers or painters. Does this mean that personal aptitude is a matter of genetic inheritance? Our own opinion is that the transmission, from generation to generation, of techniques and knowledge—including 'secrets', naturally—has been of great value to the descendants of truly creative individuals. But where does art fit into this process? The question can be answered only by someone capable of formulating the relationship of art to technique, and of telling us how much either owes to the other.

Why do I put antique dealers in the same category as the cabinet makers and painters—the artists? Simply because everything ends up in the antique dealer's shop; not only the artists' material creations but also a thorough knowledge of technique; *all* the techniques. We can hardly quarrel with the antique dealers for jealously guarding what they know. Familiarity with old furniture and other objects of value requires a mass of observation and experience, built up on a foundation of genuine culture. An accumulation of knowledge presupposes an ally: time. And this, in turn, means predecessors.

It is true some antique dealers are self-taught, but would they themselves claim that they had never regretted the absence of an expert guide in the early stages? His presence would have enabled them to bypass a forest of mistakes and hesitations.

It was with all these thoughts in my mind that I set out to write the book. While planning and putting it together I saw myself in imagination confronted by a Dutch or Spanish cabinet, with the lid open and a multitude of drawers all empty, awaiting use. In each of them I was to place a few particles of knowledge, guided by my own experience, my likes and dislikes, my personal inquiries, and finally to check the whole by consultation with qualified specialists.

Having brought my manuscript to an arbitrary close—otherwise it might never have reached the public—I left the imaginary cabinet open, with its compartments more or less filled but some of them still empty. Why? There's a first time for everything, and while I am aware that none of the drawers will ever be completely full I can at least claim credit for having tried.

Not everyone is going to thank me.

A well-known dealer told me what his father used to impress on him: 'When a customer comes in, shake hands with him but don't say anything—because, you see, in our trade, by just saying "Good morning" you've already said too much.'

This secretiveness and love of mystery have, for many years past, constituted the armour-plating round the financial well-being of a small, select profession. Today, however, the trade has 'come down into the market-place'. Census figures show a total of 3000 antique dealers and junk dealers in Paris and about 7000 in the provinces, and the clientele too has democratically broadened out and diversified. Today's 'young Turks' no longer gamble on the customer's ignorance; on the contrary, they like their customers to be well-informed, to understand what is being offered to them, and not to grudge paying a fair price for it. So 'secrets' are out of date; their time has run out.

But in watching one profession develop, we are also witnessing the irrevocable death of another: that of the restorer of antiques. Marc Roy, founder of the Guide Emer, the Bible of antique and curio dealers all over France, states that the youngest restorers are all over sixty and that most of them are between seventy and eighty-five. What is worse is that they are alone, without apprentices to carry on after they are gone. Every time one of them dies it is like the destruction of capital; his knowledge dies with him. A few specialists, however, have undertaken the essential task of composing a methodical survey of the arts of restoration. The most skilful of them all is

probably André France-Lanord, founder of the Laboratory of
Archaeological Research at the Musée Lorrain in Nancy. It
was he who reconstituted the crater of Vix, saved the horses of
St Mark's in Venice, and achieved the improbable feats of
restoring the statue of Pacatianus at Vienne (Isère) and the
clothes and jewellery of the Merovingian queen Arnegonde,
whose body had lain under the flagstones of the church of
Saint-Denis from the 6th century to our own day. He, if
anyone, is aware that unless restorers get together and exchange information, an incalculable number of relics from the
past will be lost for ever.

In his opinion, this exchange should be executed
systematically: after every repair, the details should be noted
on a record-card which will thereafter accompany the piece on
its journey through space and time. Thus, whenever a great
craftsman dies only his own marvellous touch and skill will go
with him; his technique, substantially, will remain with us.
What is doubtful is whether all the craftsmen will be easy to
convince of the need to communicate their knowledge; and
equally, whether we can educate the public sufficiently, so that
they can apply first-aid themselves whenever they have a piece
which they cannot afford to entrust to a specialist. A badly
repaired piece is surely better than none at all.

In this book we have attempted to draw the line at which do-
it-yourself repairs should halt, and to prevent a number of
mistakes. There are certain time-honoured but unscientific
procedures we did not feel obliged to disclaim; many of them
are both effective and safe. There are picturesque recipes, some
of which seem highly fanciful, but which, empirical though they
are, rational analysis has not condemned. It took a forger, van
Meegeren, to discover that Vermeer painted his canvases with
oil of lilac; deterioration in *Le Moulin de la Galette* revealed
that Renoir did not know how to prepare a canvas; and only
when the ceiling painted by Chagall for the Paris Opéra began
steadily coming away was it discovered that the painting of his
predecessor, Jules Lenepveu, which Chagall had used as a
ground for his own, had been executed with a beeswax base to

armour it against the fumes from the gas-lights of the principal
chandelier.

In an age like ours, can we really tolerate having to learn the
'secrets' of art the hard way, or by chance?

This book sets out hopefully to fill the gap, and to initiate a
dialogue between those who know and those who seek.

PART ONE

AMBER

Evocative Amber

AMBER is simply the resin of fossilized conifers. Highly prized in the Near, Middle and Far East and throughout Islam, the *elektron* of the Greeks originates in the Baltic Sea. It is known with certainty that, from the earliest epochs of mankind, amber has been used as a currency and, of course, for personal adornment. According to a belief still widely held today, even in France, it possesses therapeutic and antibiotic qualities in every kind of illness or emotional disturbance. Necklaces made of bits of unworked amber threaded on silk ribbon are placed round the necks of newborn babies and little children because, or so it seems, this ensures teething without tears. To the end of his days, Sacha Guitry ostentatiously wore a necklace of large beads of amber, and frequently informed his family of his conviction that this long, voluminous necklace possessed the virtue of recharging his energy. Such are the beliefs which have attached themselves to amber.

The Far East, in particular, has always carved figures of members of its philosophical and religious pantheon in blocks of amber, and is still exporting them via Hong Kong.

At this point we must warn the amateur to be very much on his guard: amber is rarely, practically never, absolutely pure; as we have indicated, it consists of the resinous exudations from giant conifers which perished in the geological upheavals of the Tertiary Period. Hence vegetable fragments and fossil insects of several hundreds of species were embedded in it. One naturally raises an eyebrow when being shown carved figures, sometimes as much as 20 in. (50 cm.) high, of perfect transparency and purity, in which the most careful examination can find no flaw. The vendor will perhaps try to make out that the piece is worth a lot precisely because of its 'exceptional' purity; but don't be too trusting; this is one of the many fields in which a precious material is tending to be replaced by plastics.

Moreover, there is nothing to stop anyone who has mastered the technique of casting with synthetic resins from incorporating insects or vegetable fragments; though, as it happens, this is something that fakers have not attempted—yet.

More widespread, but equally dubious, is a practice which the Chinese have developed with astonishing perfection: melting the stuff down. From amber chips, which are worth little, they produce blocks of considerable size and absolute purity. Sometimes they produce a decorative piece by casting and then dexterously touching it up.

HOW TO RECOGNIZE AMBER

Most amber comes from the southern shores of the Baltic. Small quantities are also found in Spain, Italy, Sicily, Syria, Poland and European Russia. Only by chemical analysis can the differences be formally established, and even then not altogether. It has been found that Baltic amber contains a higher proportion of succinic acid than that from elsewhere.

From the earliest times, two varieties of amber have been recognized: *light*, which is the colour of honey or beeswax (the *elektron* of the Greeks), and *dark*, which is reddish brown, like caramel (*suali ternicum*). This distinction indicates nothing about provenance; both kinds are found in the same deposits.

To tell whether a specimen of amber is real or imitation, the first thing to check is whether it possesses that power of electrical attraction, so mysterious to the ancients, which has always astonished the onlooker and to which our language owes the word 'electricity' (from *electron*). On rubbing the amber with a piece of dry woollen rag, it will be seen that the turbulences of the resulting static electricity attract dust or tiny bits of paper.

It is true that some kinds of plastic have the same property, but if you sniff the amber after rubbing it you will notice a definite aroma rather similar to that of pine resin.

REPAIRING AMBER

Whatever the shape of the object to be repaired, whether it be a statuette or merely a bead, there is a very simple method which is perfectly successful. Daub the broken surfaces with wet caustic soda or caustic potash, press the two (or more) parts together with elastic bands, sticky tape or a weight, and leave for twenty-four hours. The join will then be found to have taken place.

To *clean* amber is perfectly easy. Use alcohol. Immersion, where possible, is the best method for articles which have got very dirty, such as cigarette-holders. The alcohol will dry almost without trace. If it leaves a thin white deposit, rub the amber with a piece of chamois leather.

RENOVATING AMBER

Several things can render amber opaque, the most important of which are time, neglect and exposure to damp. Very ancient pieces, brought to light by excavation, are usually in a state of degeneration and have a dull, dead appearance.

This is how to 'refresh' amber and restore it to its pristine transparency:

Never wash the object. If it is dusty, brush it.

Before starting treatment, make sure the object is perfectly dry. If necessary, leave it in a warm room for a few days (but be careful: do not expose it to direct heat. It is enough to keep it in an atmosphere which is warm and above all dry).

In a suitable vessel, prepare the following mixture:

4 parts rectified turpentine
1 part alcohol (96 per cent)

Suspend the object *above* the liquid and close the vessel, making sure that it is absolutely airtight. After twenty-four hours the amber will have completely regained its transparency.

Amber pieces of venerable age deserve to be protected and 'fed'. This will necessitate acquiring some dammar gum, a hard natural gum obtainable from cabinet makers' supplies merchants. Mix one part powdered dammar gum with three parts turpentine; add 2 per cent of pure beeswax (mixed in cold, not melted). This mixture is the basis of a series of dilutions which must be carried out successively.

The mixture will be further diluted with turpentine at each stage of the treatment, the proportion of turpentine being decreased by 5 parts each time, yielding 15 parts of turpentine, then 10, then 5. The final proportion is three parts.

The treatment you are embarking on will take a long time, but the results are spectacular. At each stage, immerse the article completely for two hours, then dry it for three days in a warm dry atmosphere; do this four or five times, always allowing the full drying-out period. In the final bath (three parts turpentine), carry out three or four immersions, with the usual drying-out periods between.

As you see, the treatment is simple but takes about a month to complete. Bear in mind that the results far outweigh the trouble; this method enables one to rescue pieces of great value.

After a fairly lengthy interim (not less than a fortnight), during which the article can be put back on display, you may polish it gently with a soft, supple chamois leather.

Note that amber can be efficiently protected by giving it a thin coat of cellulose varnish, which will be invisible after application. Varnish should only be applied after reconditioning as described here.

PART TWO

SILVER

The Glories of Silver

IN ancient Egypt, as early as 3500 B.C., silver was rated considerably superior to gold as a precious metal: its value was twice that of its weight in fine gold. Although there appear never to have been any silver mines in Egypt, a certain amount of silver was extracted from Nubian gold, which had a silver content of between 9·7 and 24 per cent. This process was very imperfect, and one of the so-called silver war trumpets found in Tutankhamen's tomb can be classified as 'white gold', i.e. gold with a high proportion of silver in it.

Early in the third millennium, silver from the mines of Anatolia probably supplanted the gold obtained from mines farther to the east. Archaeological sites at Ur and Susa have yielded a few examples of goldsmith's work; however, silver, unlike gold, suffers heavily from oxidation and the results of excavation are modified accordingly.

In Europe, silver was known as a precious metal two thousand years before Christ, but argentiferous deposits were scarce and metallurgists were compelled to extract silver from lead, which in the raw state always contains varying amounts of silver. Six centuries before Christ, the Greeks achieved a stable process and minted the earliest known silver currency.

The mining, smelting and working of silver on a large scale, however, may have originated on the coast of Peru about 500 B.C., or on the high plateaux of Colombia. The conjecture is forced on us by the fact that the metal was not much esteemed under the pre-Colombian civilizations; possibly because they had not mastered the technique of extracting it. Not until the 13th century of our own epoch, under the Incas, do we find a large number of useful, precious or ornamental objects made of a silver and copper alloy. The one certain fact is that the world's main silver-bearing deposits are in Central and South

America. The *conquistadores*, having failed to find Eldorado but succeeding in pillaging the natives' gold, had thereafter to make do with silver, which they dispatched in large ingots in their famous galleons. This made it so plentiful that it was used for common everyday objects, at least by the well-to-do. Previously, gold had held pride of place on rich men's tables. The inventory of Charles V's possessions, in his will, lists seven dozen large gold dishes, followed by one hundred and thirty-eight silver dishes, evidently regarded as small fry by comparison.

After the time of Charles V the Spaniards caused silver to become commonplace all over Europe. Silverware, in the modern sense, dates from then.

Nevertheless, there were powerful Western countries— France and England in particular—which for the preceding two centuries had sought to protect the standard of silver by strict control. In the 13th century, in both countries, there emerged guilds or *jurandes* whose hallmarks were accepted as official standards by all. Later, silver became coin of the realm; and authority, whether royal, imperial or republican, jealously protected itself against counterfeiters, as authority always does. Since Charles V's time, every government has laid down standards for the various grades of silver and has kept production under surveillance. It seems that Henri III was the first French ruler to tax precious metals, imposing the *droit de remède* in 1579. Calling a tax a 'remedy' sounds fairly quaint, but the problem was in fact to 'cure' precious metals of a vexatious tendency to sink below the value of the official coinage, which was subject to regular depreciation (yes, even then!). Louis XIV, after the setbacks which marked the later stages of his reign, doubled the existing tax (which was three *sous* per ounce of goldsmith's ware, one ounce being 31 grammes). In 1723 the tax on silver rose to 10 *sous* 6 *deniers* per ounce. The Revolution swept these constraints away and silver was set free—which in effect meant freedom to adulterate it, so that control was re-established as early as the 18th day of the month *brumaire* in the year VI (9 November 1797). And of course a few taxes were added at the same time.

The official system of standards and hallmarks was changed in 1838. Private owners were allowed four and a half months within which to come and have the new marks imposed alongside the old ones, without charge.

This continuous official participation in commercial transactions involving silver makes it at once simple and more complicated to identify antique silverware and the metal of which it is made. The minuteness of the regulations (for instance, the

'Collation prepared in a garden'; engraving after a painting by Gillot

fact that the position of the hallmark is laid down according to the type of article), *plus* the fact that we possess a complete knowledge of all the hallmarks, *bigornes*, marks and countermarks which have obtained since the regulations began, make it possible to fix the period and general origin of any piece, and the standard of the silver, with perfect certainty. On the other hand, the huge number and variety of these marks, their meanings, their countries of origin (every country has its own), compel both the serious amateur and the most experienced professional to refer to the excellent specialist works in which all the hallmarks and regulations are classified and described.[1]

HOW TO RECOGNIZE SILVER

As the reader has understood, officialdom's guarantee is expressed by the hallmarks indicating the standard, that is to say the pure silver content, of the piece on which the marks are impressed. In the course of business, however, pieces sometimes crop up which have somehow eluded official control. Moreover, when visiting a curiosity shop or an antique dealer you may find that superficial examination or the absence of information leaves you dubious about the metal itself, in the case of a piece whose dirty or oxidized condition renders it open to question.

In a case like this you can hardly resort to tests based on chemical reactions, unless you make a practice of carrying the necessary kit with you!

Experienced dealers have two very simple methods on which they rely. The first consists of testing by hand; feeling the weight of the article. Silver, like any other metal, has a specific gravity. Experts claim to be able to recognize silver simply by appreciating its weight in the hand. They may be right; but how does one acquire this virtuoso ability, which is partly inborn anyway?

The second way is by smell. This is more in the amateur's line. Silver, if vigorously rubbed with a piece of woollen rag (or the cuff of your jacket) or the palm of the hand (spit on your hand first, if you like), gives off a highly characteristic smell. You can easily familiarize yourself with this smell and index it in your olfactory memory (one of the most accurate, retentive components of the faculty of memory as a whole) by training

1. TARDY, *Les Poinçons de garantie internationaux pour l'argent*, 'Annuaires d'horlogerie-bijouterie', 18 rue des Volontaires, Paris. (*Poinçon* means hallmark.)

yourself at home, practising on a piece which you know to be genuine.

HOW TO CLEAN SILVER

The air of towns and cities, which contains sulphuretted hydrogen, rapidly spoils silver. Eggs and cabbage both turn silver black because of the sulphur in them. But however glaring this oxidation may be, it never goes deep and is easy to remove.

Commercial polishing pastes, whether sold for copper, brass, silver, aluminium, tin or pewter, are a little too abrasive to be recommended for frequent use.

However, you may find them extremely serviceable for pieces which have lain neglected over a period of time, perhaps exposed to harmful effluvia, and which have grossly deteriorated. We would like to persuade lovers of silverware that the finest lustre is often obtained by much gentler methods:

(1) Lukewarm soapy water, stirred to a good froth, is very effective for cleaning silver which has merely turned black through use. A small amount of a powder detergent in very hot water will produce the same result without any danger to the metal.

After a thorough rinsing in hot water, vigorous polishing with a chamois leather will achieve the desired brilliance.

(2) Alcohol is a perfect cleaning agent for all precious metals. With the addition of a few pinches of whiting (Spanish white) it becomes a cheap, simple mixture for reviving the brilliance of tarnished silver, even if the surface is slightly scratched (as is frequently the case with household utensils and with bracelets and rings, all of which are liable to take a knock now and then).

(3) Cyanide of potassium dissolves the oxides of silver, but is much too poisonous to be considered for ordinary use.

(4) Silverware hardly ever turns up in excavations, and when it does its care always constitutes a special case. It is regarded

primarily as a piece of archaeological evidence; its appearance is a minor consideration. Only coins are usually cleaned in depth, to display their original brightness in numismatic collections. To achieve this result with grossly dirty items, sulphuric acid (vitriol), diluted with water, should be used, in the proportion of one part of acid to ten parts of water (add the acid to the water, not the other way round). Immerse the pieces in the liquid for a few minutes, watching the effect carefully.

(5) Perfectly genuine silver sometimes shows traces of verdigris, resulting, of course, from long exposure to a corrosive atmosphere or from having lain buried underground. There is a straightforward reason for this peculiarity: silver is almost always alloyed with a certain percentage of copper in order to give it the mechanical properties, including hardness, which pure silver does not possess.

Silversmiths in their workshop; engraving from Diderot, *Encyclopédie*

The method for completely removing this surface copper is a trifle drastic, but very easily controlled.

Heat the article red-hot (but be careful: silver melts at 960 °C. = 1760 °F., so don't use a powerful gas or propane torch; the ordinary domestic gas supply is quite adequate for the purpose; better still, use a barbecue stove). Whatever source of heat is used, the article will quickly turn black because the heat oxidizes the copper. At this point, *boil* the article in sulphuric acid diluted as for cleaning coins (one part acid in ten parts water). The copper will disappear and the surface will be pure silver, which you can polish with chamois leather and whiting.

FOR THOSE WHO LIKE FOLK RECIPES

Here are a few ancient dodges, in the old-wives' category; they work excellently, and are picturesque enough to tempt anyone to try them.

Powdered red ochre

Ordinary ochre, as used by house painters, bound with a little soap or vegetable oil, makes a very bland polishing paste for ordinary use.

Cuttlefish bone

If you go to the seaside for your holiday, pick up the cuttlefish bones left by the tide on the beach. Cage birds love having them to peck at, but that isn't why we are recommending them. You will pound them to a fine dust (which is easy) and use it for polishing your silver. The results are surprising.

Sour milk

Or, to be precise, skim milk. This provides a painless way of restoring the brilliance of any silverware item which is suffer-

Phoenician coins (Museum of Le Bardo, Tunis)

ing from mild neglect. Immerse the object in skim milk for a few minutes; when you take it out don't rinse it but let it dry on its own, then rub it up with a rag or chamois leather.

DO YOU WANT A PATINA?

The blackening of silver, nicely controlled, makes an effective contrast for heightening the effect of relief or intaglio. Professionals use a liquid whose basic ingredients are alcohol and

Silver tureen, 18th century (Musée des arts décoratifs)

antimony. This darkens the silver; the parts in relief can then be rubbed with a commercial polish or a little silk-fine pumice, to produce the light and shade that some amateurs particularly cherish.

Another very simple method: expose your silver to sulphur vapour. This will quickly turn it black. Alternatively, warm the article and then dip it very briefly in strong bleach, which will achieve the same result.

PART THREE

WOOD

Pegs and What They Tell Us

LOVERS of antiques who like to think they know it all, invariably pass an absent-minded finger over an imperceptibly protruding peg, or turn a chair upside down to inspect the state of the rails—and, of course, the pegs—as a guarantee of age and authenticity.

Fairly often, someone has got there before these enthusiasts and anticipated their scrutiny. This 'someone' is the antique dealer. In dealers' back-shops, pegging goes on with might and main: the public having discovered this infallible criterion of age, there is a natural anxiety not to disappoint them. Pegs are driven in all over the place; until, eventually, it dawns on the disconsolate customer that the 'infallible' criterion means precisely nothing. Nevertheless, the evolution of the peg as an aspect of the furniture maker's art represents a touchstone of particular interest. Moreover, I must point out that pegging is not an end in itself but a means to an end, namely that of fixing two pieces of wood rigidly together, and in order to avoid giving this chapter an artificially over-specialized bias I shall try to show how the technique of construction has developed and changed with the passage of time. The fact that pegging became obsolete is in itself a useful pointer.

THE MIDDLE AGES

We must take this rather vaguely delimited period as our starting point, despite the fact that its furniture is not exactly abundant in dealers' showrooms. The point is that in Gothic furniture, from start to finish and even during the Renaissance, the peg was used *as a nail*. Of course we find it holding a tenon in a mortise; but we also find it securing the crosspieces on the underside of the lid of a chest, or fixing a table top to the central upright. Carvings are often attached to a piece of furniture by this means; they are literally nailed on with a peg. When a panel consists of two or three sections, don't look for a chamfer or a tongue-and-groove; pegs will have been used, in some cases driven in obliquely.

During the 17th century the technique of pegging, though already very satisfactory, underwent a slight improvement. In table tops and chest lids, and in every cabinet making operation requiring several boards to be joined together in a plane, countersunk fillets (*pigeons*, in French) were introduced. Mortises are cut in the underside of the boards and a thin piece of wood, fitted flush, is pegged in to secure the flat assembly thus obtained. Sometimes, in a table top, you can see the pegs, usually in a circular formation, straddling the join. Don't be puzzled: this is not some cabbalistic secret sign but simply a '*pigeon*'.

'Pigeons' in the lid of a chest

Form follows function in the shaping of the peg, which is long and slim, tapers to a point and is thickest at the head. Usually it is of the same kind of wood as the piece as a whole. As you are never likely to take a piece of furniture to pieces and therefore to extract the pegs, these details are somewhat academic. Still, pegs sometimes work their way out spontaneously; you will then be able to verify our information and your own knowledge. It should be noted that pegs were usually made from square dowel, which is why the butt-end, or 'head' if one can call it that, is square.

Putting new pegs in a chest. Here, a peg is being whittled to shape with a flat chisel

In the 18th century, cabinet making was further refined and perfected. Dovetail joints were much used and mitred construction made its appearance (this is supposed to have been invented in the 16th century, but did not become current practice until much later). Marquetry became widespread under Louis XIV; so did gilded furniture. Pegs were masked by veneer or by gilding. It was the beginning of the end for the peg—a device regarded as technically necessary but aesthetically displeasing. However, it remained indispensable throughout the 18th century. Craftsmen producing furniture for the people made no bones about it, but those working for the aristocracy concealed their pegs with carvings (especially on chairs, etc.), or with veneers, which by this time were ruling the roost, or with lacquer, which was a novelty.

Commodes and *semainiers* were even sent out unfinished to China, where local craftsmen completed them. In 1748 two brothers, Frenchmen by the name of Martin, invented a process which was described at the time as producing varnishes '*façon de Chine*'. Today, Martin's varnishes are famous (and are known in English as well as French as *vernis Martin*). All these advances in decoration tended towards greater refinement in both form and technique.

The Louis XVI style, in its elegance and proportion, represents the culmination of the trend. Simultaneously, there was developing in England a school of cabinet making whose first great creative figure was Chippendale, succeeded however by artists like Robert Adam, Thomas Sheraton and (pre-eminently) George Hepplewhite, all of whom underwent the influence of the French stylists. The goal towards which they strove was an almost excessive lightness of design, carried to such a pitch that the joints then commonly used would have been out of place in their armchairs with airily soaring backs, and their slender chairs with threadlike limbs. Sheraton refined the joints and avoided ordinary pegging as far as possible; he used grooved pins, and moreover perfected the art of gluing by using the toothed plane, a complete novelty at the time. The blade of this type of plane cuts a number of triangular grooves and thereby doubles or trebles the area of contact and, in consequence, the holding power of the glue.

The way the plane works is perhaps made clearer if we add that it cuts regular furrows in both surfaces, and that the two surfaces then fit each other perfectly and are secured by gluing.

The 19th century was to sound the death knell of the peg. The Empire style juggled it away out of sight under a mahogany veneer; or, when it did tolerate its presence, insisted that it be small. The peg was gradually but inexorably suppressed. However, under Louis-Philippe and even later, during

the Second Empire, it was accepted provided it was invisible. It
can be found in the woodwork of chairs upholstered all over,
and frequently in the rails of chairs and armchairs, but only
when the rails are covered up out of sight. The firmness of the
backs and arms of chairs was obtained by means of glue, the
famous 'strong glue' (see the chapter on glues), a bone glue
which was kept simmering, in a pot with a water-jacket, in
every workshop.

In high-quality work an excellent device, wedging, in the
special form of a foxed tenon, is used. A saw-cut is made in the
end of the tenon and a small wooden wedge, slightly too long, is
inserted in it; the tenon is then driven home in the mortise, the
wedge being thus brought flush with the end of the tenon and
causing it to expand, so that the joint is solid for keeps. It can
never be taken apart, the only way to undo it would be to break
and destroy it.

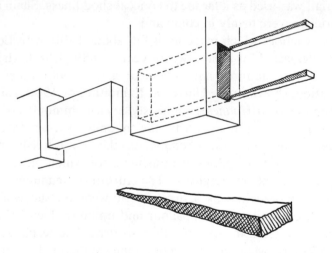

During the second half of the 19th century the cabinet
maker's craft developed towards a technical perfection which
robbed it of freshness and stifled the creative urge under a
feather pillow of academicism. Imitation—of the Louis XVI
style, and of medievalism—was the order of the day; alas, if

only the craftsmen had contented themselves with straightforward copying! Ossified decorative preferences, and technical difficulties, were promiscuously combined. Craftsmanship ruled triumphant; it had become an end in itself, instead of
existing to serve art.

High-quality furniture was transmogrified into 'masterpieces', in the craft sense of that term: that is to say, the piece
was regarded as an opportunity for the craftsman to show off
all his knowledge and cunning at one go, without consideration
for the general aesthetic effect. Artistic subtlety was ousted by
craft virtuosity—and the next step was the industrialization of
cabinet making, with all that followed from it.

The old tenon-and-mortise was almost completely replaced
by dowel joints, it being easier to drill holes than make mortises. Screws were another short cut. Veneer was no longer an
adornment but a device for reducing cost. Wood, that noble
material, was used as a façade to conceal shoddiness. Sham and
historicism were firmly in command.

The reaction, which made itself felt about 1900, with Louis
Majorelle, lasted for a bare twenty years (1889–1909). Majorelle was both admired and ridiculed: a desk with water-lily
decoration, shown in the Universal Exhibition of 1900, gained
him the *Legion d'Honneur*, but his style was commonly defined
by various unflattering epithets: the 'noodle', 'garter', 'Métro'
or 'eel' style and even *rastaqouère*, the 'bounderish' style
(implying a certain species of raffishness for which there is no
exact equivalent in English). The furniture manufacturing
industry ignored him as a dreamer; it went on successfully
churning out imitation Pompadour and imitation Henri II and
was not interested in anyone with new ideas. The result is that
the trademark 'Majorelle' has entered the pantheon of the great,
along with such masters as Jacob, Boulle, Cressent and
Riesener.

For, despite appearances to the contrary, the pliant vegetable
forms of the 'modern style' (as it was also called) are conceived
in a spirit of profound rigour. The joints are the sound,
traditional ones, with extra support to carry the projections and

overhangs produced by Majorelle's very free designing. Beautiful furniture is never badly made, though it does not necessarily follow that well-made furniture is beautiful. By concentrating on a single technical aspect, namely pegs and joints, and casting a few brief glances at the history of cabinet making from this point of view, we have been able to watch the development of an art. Every material has a logic of its own; this naturally imposes the techniques employed in the use of that material, in conjunction with the development of tools and equipment from one period to another.

After the first look at any piece of furniture comes the detailed examination. It requires no particularly expert knowledge to realize that:

the regular markings left by the modern band-saw make one a little suspicious of a supposed Louis XIII piece, even though it be efficiently pegged (sometimes newly so!);

the slightly wavy texture left by machine planing indicates either a modern fake or a clumsy piece of restoration;

the head of a peg which is lighter than the object as a whole implies that the pegs were added later and are therefore spurious;

pegs, even if much coated, as if by age, mean nothing if other features point to modern mass production (rear panels made of plywood; screws; carvings added to complete the effect, etc.);

excessively thin veneers are always an indication of cheap mass production;

nails (unless hand-forged) and screws are foreign to genuine antique furniture which has been well looked after;

finally, to end a list which might go on indefinitely, checking the measurements of a piece of furniture is frequently enough to put the intelligent observer on his guard. In France, prior to the 19th century, the units of measurement were the foot (0·33 m.) and the inch (27·07 mm.). The dimensions of furniture were in terms of these units, not of the metric system.

Stripping Cottage Furniture

MOTORING on holiday, you fall in love with a rustic piece of furniture that you come across in the shop of a likeable dealer. You agree the price and buy the thing without examining it very closely. It's pretty dirty; the dealer says he found it in a chicken-house.

On closer inspection you find it is covered with that fearful dark brown paint of which the recipe seems to be known only to village painters; and the bottom rail and the feet are badly worm-eaten. To cap it all, the patina which you mistook for some kind of craftsman's finish is just a thick layer of dirt, polished by long use. So perhaps you feel disappointed. But why should you? A piece, whether it be furniture or anything else, remains dead or comes to life according to the amount of interest bestowed on it. How often have you not found that an object which looked like nothing at all in a dealer's window increases its value tenfold in your own home?

GET THE DIRT OFF FIRST

The preliminary to all stripping is cleaning. Until you have got the superficial dirt off you can't tell much about what lies underneath it: the paint or varnish which you intend to remove.

Use a powder detergent and warm water, in the proportion of 50 grammes to a litre, or $1\frac{2}{3}$ oz. to $1\frac{3}{4}$ pint. 50 grammes or $1\frac{2}{3}$ oz. is roughly a handful.

The things you need for any sizeable job of stripping are: a packet of washing powder for cleaning, some caustic soda or caustic potash for stripping, a soft brush, a wire brush for clasps, locks, hinges, etc., a putty knife for grooves, the interstices of carvings and so on.

Using a sponge, moisten the entire surface with the washing liquid (diluted as above). Leave it to work for a few seconds, then repeat, using a larger amount of liquid. Dirty carvings, if any, will defeat the sponge. This is where your soft brush comes in. As you will see, it will be useful in various other ways before you have finished.

The washing liquid must be given a chance to 'bite'. Only prolonged contact will enable it to do so. Soak a large rag, such as an old apron or flannel, in the liquid, clap it on and leave it long enough for the active principles of the liquid to take effect. A much-used device is to add flour to the liquid so as to make a flour paste; this sticks to the vertical parts of the piece and allows the cleansing to go on for as long as you want.

STRIP FURNITURE CAUTIOUSLY

Stripping with potash is very spectacular, but *dangerous* to the eyes and to sensitive skins. Certain precautions are necessary; don't neglect them. The first is simply: Be careful. Don't pour

out too much of the stripping agent at one time. Wear spec-
tacles and plastic gloves (not rubber—the potash will soon
begin breaking it down). If possible work out of doors, near a
water supply. The potash should be diluted with warm water;
in what proportion, will depend on the resistance of the paint
(start by trying about two wineglassfuls of potash to a litre,
about $1\frac{3}{4}$ pints of water). Abundant froth is the sign that the
potash is working. Don't rinse off the froth as fast as it appears,
leave it to work. You will find that any carvings will have to be
stripped in a horizontal position, so that the stripping agent can
get into the crannies; so lay the object flat on its side or back.
In places where the soft brush is not man enough for the job,
for example if the paint is too thick, use the putty knife.

It may be that your chemist or drugstore has no potash; in
that case, a satisfactory substitute is any of the products sold
for unblocking a washhand basin. These products usually come
in crystal form (the size of the crystals varies from one brand
to another). Sprinkle the crystals over the surface of the piece
(dry), ensuring good coverage everywhere; then pour very hot
water over them. Use a watering can with a fine rose; too
powerful a stream would sweep the crystals away. The instantaneous result is a violent effervescence, and on rinsing down
you will see that all traces of paint have vanished.

We repeat our safety warning. These products are powerful
and effective but must not be handled carelessly. Splashes can
be dangerous. Don't let children or pets come near you when
you have a piece of furniture to strip.

After these successive applications, copious rinsing is indispensable. If you neglect this, the potash will 'bloom' in the
form of minute crystals on the surface of the wood. The jet of a
garden hose will enable you to get at the trickiest places.

Don't let the piece dry off yet, there is something very
important still to be done. Potash, like a number of other
substances, including ammonia, has the property of causing
chemical reactions which make some kinds of wood turn
darker in colour—it does it to oak, for example, and Spanish
chestnut; cherry, on the other hand, turns red. *So the colour of*

the wood, denatured by the potash, must be lightened. This is very necessary: if you were to wax-polish your piece of furniture at this stage the result would be a gloomy, greyish, matt tone, without gloss. There are several ways of restoring the colour to its natural lightness. Cabinet makers' suppliers sell peroxide (120 volumes), which is a powerful bleach (watch out for your fingers and clothes); an older method is to use an oxalic salt, which comes in the form of a white crystalline powder. Dust this on the piece while it is still damp. The salt acts almost immediately. To help it dissolve, so that the active principle can penetrate the wood, pour on hot water from a kettle.

A few minutes later, rinse copiously. The job is now done. The wood has gone back to its natural colour. The article can be left to dry (you will, of course, have taken the opportunity of cleaning the interior, such as drawers or shelves).

It is worth noting that one of the cabinet maker's recipes for lightening the colour of wood is to use hydrochloric acid, which makes oak produce a rather beautiful golden glow.

In Praise of Fine Cabinet Making

REALLY fine furniture, with or without inlays or marquetry, has not always eluded the over-enthusiastic paintbrush or the efforts of the would be improver. There are many reasons for this, some of them almost unbelievable, and it is never a bad thing for a lover of antiques to pause for a second glance at some piece whose surprisingly elegant design is contradicted by a superficial appearance which might discourage further examination. I have seen a genuine Louis XV table of remarkable purity of style being used as a laundry bench by a country washerwoman. To make it slope she had partially amputated two of the legs; a piece of wood had been nailed on to provide a ledge for her soap; and the whole had been carefully painted white, 'to be nice and clean'!

This desire for so-called cleanliness is one of the worst enemies of neglected, unloved furniture.

Undoubtedly, the refrigerators, washing machines and gas or electric cookers or ranges which have invaded country kitchens in recent years are out of harmony with traditional furniture, which therefore often gets dumped in an outhouse. Sometimes it gets exchanged for items with Formica tops by travelling furniture dealers, shrewd operators well aware of being on to a good thing. Alternatively, these antique pieces may simply be given a good coat of enamel and garnished with 'contemporary' handles, etc., and be allowed to keep their place because they are useful. However, their disfigurement is not irrevocable.

A further cause of these bizarre expedients is the ravages of time. Bits of inlay that have come unglued and got lost, lacquer cracking or flaking, scars from burns: any or all of these may provoke misguided repairs, usually in the form of camouflage. And camouflage means paint, of course, often with a pseudo-genteel finish in view, such as graining or imitation marble.

THAT DREADFUL BLACK PAINT

This panorama of faulty taste and the crimes of ignorance would of course be incomplete if we omitted the faults engendered by fashion. In the bourgeois, narrow-minded atmosphere of France under Louis-Philippe (who reigned from 1830 to 1848), dark furniture was in favour. Ebony being expensive, anything which looked like ebony was accepted as a substitute. So everything was painted black; and, at least, one is forced to admit that the paint was of such good quality that the furniture of that period is as lustrous today as when the paint was put on.

But the treatment was not confined to the output of contemporary cabinet makers; it was conscientiously applied to the furniture of earlier periods (though it is interesting to note that Empire furniture, on the whole, escaped; it was already solemn enough, being made of dark mahogany).

Louis XVI furniture, on the other hand, came under heavy tribute; large numbers of delightful chairs, couches, commodes and loo-tables were thrust into perpetual mourning. Respectable people, the *bien-pensants*, who plumed themselves on their principles, had even found a moral justification for this assault on the fine furniture of the late 18th century: furniture, they said, should wear mourning for the *Roi Martyr*! They did not demand the same of the reigning monarch, Louis-Philippe, whose father, Philippe Egalité, had voted for the death of Louis XVI.

Today this black paint is the despair of many lovers of antiques, especially when they encounter it on a piece of furniture which a dealer says was not like that 'from birth'.

REMOVING 'LOUIS-PHILIPPE' BLACK

This substance's tenacity, which we have often come up against, impressed us so much that we asked a technical laboratory to analyse it. We were told that it is not really a paint at all but a *lacquer varnish*, whose brilliant surface was obtained by the methods described in our chapter on French polishing.

Hence it is sometimes responsive to alcohol (but not highly so), and can always be removed by a stripper containing acetone.

These strippers are easy enough to buy. They are put on with a brush but almost always need washing off afterwards. Can this always be done?

If you venture on the dangerous experiment of stripping a chair, armchair or some other kind of seat, at the same time protecting its upholstery, washing down is out of the question. Scraping is the only answer; and, as we shall see, it is the answer in most other cases too, however slow and boring a business it may be.

If you use a cabinet maker's scraper for removing paint or varnish it will probably soon get clogged and become blunt. To restore a perfect edge to a scraper demands a knack few amateurs possess. Moreover, the broad, flat blade of the conventional tool is useless in grooves, flutings, carvings and suchlike recesses, especially those found on chairs, etc. A razor blade is at once too flexible and too brittle and is always a hazard. Use a piece of broken glass. You may think it an amateurish makeshift. We disagree. Antique dealers and cabinet makers use it constantly.

Anyone who went to a French primary school remembers the annual ritual of desk-scraping. Graffiti and ink spots were defenceless against these improvised scrapers.

To ensure making a neat job of it and not scoring the wood, use plenty of bits of glass and throw the old one away as soon as it gets dirty. Use very light pressure. You will soon find that the paint comes off very easily if the angle of attack is right. A few minutes are enough to acquire the knack. The only hazard is 'writer's cramp'; the glass is held between two fingers and fatigue inevitably sets in sooner or later.

After scraping, rub down with the finest grade of glasspaper you can get, leaving the surface absolutely smooth and even. Don't press too hard on the marquetry, you may go right through it, especially if it is loose or has risen (see the chapter on 'Repairing Marquetry').

Last of all, use steel wool. You can get rolls of it from hardware dealers who specialize in cabinet makers' tools and supplies. Failing this, use ordinary household scouring pads. They produce a fine polish, especially on curves and mouldings.

THE STORY OF 'TRIANON GREY'

In 1687 the Grand Trianon replaced a small, one-storey pavilion which had a façade of five bays covered in blue and white faience, and was known, incorrectly, as the *Trianon de porcelaine.*

Louis XIV in person supervised the building of this stone and marble palace 'in the Italian taste', with flat roofs surrounded by balustrades. He wanted a place to which he could escape now and then from the vast, oppressively majestic rooms of the château. His architects, Mansart, succeeded by his brother-in-law, Robert de Cotte, set themselves to satisfy his wishes under the direction of Louvois, who combined his functions as Prime Minister with those of Minister of Works and Buildings.

The king paid frequent visits to the workshop. One day he pointed out to his minister that a window was slightly out of true. Louvois was quite capable of standing up to the king and would sometimes turn stubborn without good reason, and he refused to agree; as far as he was concerned there was nothing wrong with the window.

The king seized a rule, proved himself right and spoke sharply to his minister. Saint-Simon relates in his *Memoirs* that

Louvois, 'returning to his offices, gathered his colleagues about him and informed them of his disgrace: "I have lost the confidence of the king," he said, in the depths of distress, "and am no longer the *homme nécessaire* of the kingdom." "Become it once more," whispered a counsellor; "declare war!"' The war against the League of Augsburg began a few days later.

The conflict made disastrous inroads on the royal coffers and some of the finishing of the Grand Trianon was carried out on the cheap. The woodwork destined for gilding was left in the preparatory stage, covered with an undercoat consisting probably of white lead, *blanc de Meudon* (a kind of extremely fine plaster) and sifted ashes. The mixture of white lead and ashes, though bright white when first put on, changed colour as time went on and produced that light grey with a tinge of blue which posterity christened *gris Trianon* and came to associate with the Louis XVI style, in which indeed it was copiously used.

Veneers and Marquetry

VENEERING consists of sticking a thin sheet of fine wood over the surfaces of a piece of furniture made of some more ordinary variety of timber.

Marquetry consists of decorative or ornamental compositions added to the veneer by inlaying.

These definitions are not superfluous, because there is a tendency to treat the two terms as synonyms.

There is no question here of expounding the complicated technique of veneers and marquetry, which demands not only special materials but also a manual skill which can be acquired only from good teachers and after much experience.

Our aim is to enable you to repair the commonest kinds of damage or deterioration which disfigure the furniture one loves. Perhaps, however, we shall not be over-ambitious if we simultaneously attempt to initiate you into the development of the art, and to tell you how to recognize the successive periods through which it has passed.

Ever since man started using wood for more than immediate, utilitarian purposes, he has contrived to adorn it with incrustations of bone, ivory or horn, and, of course, with other species of wood, which he quickly learnt to differentiate in terms of quality.

André-Charles Boulle is sometimes credited with the invention of both marquetry and veneer. But this is wrong. As early as the 16th century and probably before, the Italians had occasionally used the technique. Under Louis XIII, ebony veneers were used on the cabinets for which the fashion had spread to France from Italy and Spain. Nevertheless it was the famous French cabinet maker who was responsible for the triumph of veneer and marquetry. Curiously, André-Charles

Marquetry commode with the cipher of Marie Antoinette (Musée du Louvre)

hardly ever used wood in his marquetry: his usual materials were mostly brass and tortoiseshell, sometimes pewter. It is said (and a few examples exist to confirm it) that Boulle always made two of every piece of furniture, and that whatever parts of the marquetry were tortoiseshell in one, were of brass in the other. The explanation of this interesting fact is that the cutting-out of a marquetry motif was effected in a single operation; a sheet of brass was placed on top of a leaf of tortoiseshell, and because the two materials were cut together the resulting shapes fitted each other perfectly and could be combined in a single inlay. The offcuts from one also fitted the offcuts from the other, but the other way round, so that the ornamentation for the second piece of furniture was automatically to hand. (In English, the two sets are sometimes known as Boulle—or Buhl, which is a corruption—and counter-Boulle.)

After Boulle there was a return to a more massive style of

furniture, but not for long. The Compagnie des Indes, under the Regency of Philippe d'Orléans (1715–1723), introduced new species of timber into France, satiny and coloured varieties whose advantages the cabinet makers were quick to see and exploit. One of the first to do so was Charles Cressent, who appears to have been the originator of the commode as we have since known it. Before him, the commode had been more or less an offshoot of the chest. It can certainly be said that he lightened its forms, gave it longer, slenderer legs and was the first to use those crossbow-shaped bottom rails, *traverses* '*en arbalète*', which are part of the distinctive character of the Régence and Louis XV style.

Here let us pause momentarily in this brief historical outline and explain what marquetry and veneer consisted of at this period.

Wood for veneering is obtained in either of two ways: cross-cut and unrolling.

The first consists of cutting a thin, flat film of wood from the seasoned trunk; like a plank but only a few tenths of a milli-metre thick, and of course with its width limited by the diameter of the trunk.

The second, as its name implies, consists of 'unrolling' or, as one might more suitably say, 'peeling' a trunk by rotating it about its long axis; the width of the resulting sheet depending on the circumference of the trunk. This is the method now used industrially.

In the 18th century, only the first of these two methods was practised. As far as can be seen, high-quality timber was sawn into sheets as thin as the essentially manual nature of the operation permitted. Guessing a little, we may say that un-finished sheets of a thickness of 2 mm. were obtained (as compared with $\frac{4}{10}$ mm., the usual thickness of veneers today). Planing and sanding would bring the thickness down to about $1\frac{1}{2}$ mm. This purely technical reason accounts for the fact that genuine 18th-century furniture always has thick veneers; even considerably later, under the Empire, when the process was developed further, it was impossible to achieve veneers as thin as those which infallibly point to the industrial era.

Curved surfaces were the reason why, in the 18th century, veneers had to be as thin as possible. It would have been asking for trouble to try to stick an insufficiently flexible sheet on a convex or concave surface. But though a continual effort was made to reduce the thickness the craftsmen rarely managed to get it below 1·2 mm.

It may be that the cabinet makers of those days could have gone further had they dared, refraining not so much because of any technical impossibility as out of respect for the

Marquetry depicting musical instruments (Musée des Arts décoratifs)

material. Excessive sanding might have produced a lower-quality veneer.

Eighteenth-century veneer, we emphasize once again, *is comparatively thick*. This is an important criterion for the amateur.

Let us now glance at the technique involved in marquetry. As we have seen, Charles Boulle used to cut out both background and motifs in a single operation. His method was dropped; his successors' practice was to cut spaces in the background for the motifs, which were prepared separately. This is a highly important fact, because it enables one easily to distinguish 18th-century work from that of the 19th, when improved equipment made it possible to revive Boulle's technique and apply it to veneer.

Slight but perceptible irregularities are, in fact, typical of 18th-century marquetry. Joins are more prominent, tiny chisel-marks give evidence of retouching, and asymmetry in the motifs is almost universal.

These little things, which sound unfavourable to the cabinet makers in question, are, on the contrary, just what confers outstanding life and vigour on the marquetry of the period. One recognizes the presence of the craftsman's hand throughout. The perfection of Napoleon III marquetry, for instance, has an utterly disembodied character, a mindless frigidity totally unrelieved by the different tones of the woods used, well chosen though they are.

This leads us to ask a question which is more important than it sounds; one which promotes our understanding of the forms fashioned by truly creative artists, and the intentions under-lying their work. Is there any reason why perfectionism should be the guiding principle of all human endeavour? To discover whether technique is a means, an end or an accessory would not carry us much farther towards an answer. The great creators invented such techniques as would serve their imagin-ation; the opposite process—imagining forms to fit an existing technique—is something which occurs rarely, if at all. A humorous reflection you can sometimes hear from the best restorers, on the subject of the cabinet makers of the past, is that 'they didn't make a religion of the plumbline'. Which is

true enough; though one should remember that the plumbline is not much used in cabinet making anyway, and that judgement is objectively difficult in connection with furniture which has been subject to the assaults of time, the movement and shrinking of the wood, and normal wear and tear. However, what gave me the answer was not the restorers' observation but something an old craftsman let fall while I was watching him execute a bit of precision work. I noticed he hardly ever referred to the drawing and commented on this. 'I know,' he said, carrying on with his work meanwhile, 'but then the drawing is just a diagram on the flat. In making a piece of artistic furniture to specification, what matters is *pleasing the eye.*' Surely that is the real perfectionism? What other criterion have we on which to base our love and pursuit of the beautiful?

REPAIRING 'BLISTERS'

'Blisters' are the swellings, large or small in area, which come up in a veneer. They are mainly caused by damp, or by insufficient gluing when the piece was made.

The simplest policy is to try to reheat whatever glue may still exist under the blister, and to apply pressure so that the veneer sticks down again. How is this achieved? Use an electric iron, such as is now possessed by every home. But proceed with care. If your iron has an adjustable thermostat set the pointer at 'Silk'. If not, guess the temperature as best you can; it does not need to be very high. Protect the varnish with a piece of cardboard or anything else suitable, and apply the iron with a slow movement, using a good deal of pressure. The moment will come when you sense that a slight, tacky adhesion has occurred; this is an indication that the glue has softened. Now let the iron cool down; if necessary, replace it with some heavy metallic object (which, obviously, should be flat). It will be advisable to allow several hours for drying. Failure is always possible, especially if the initial cause was inadequate gluing. In that case, a slit must be made in the blister with a razor blade or a very sharp chisel. Make sure the slit goes *with* the grain, not across it, otherwise the repair will always remain visible. The slit enables you to put in the glue. For preference, use the same kind of glue as the old cabinet makers did: bone glue, melted in the old-fashioned glue-pot with a water-jacket. The best procedure is to press down on one side of the blister; this makes the other side come up, so that the slit conveniently gapes open for you to pour in the glue. You then do the other side in the same way, and stroke the area of the mend with your finger so as to squeeze out the superfluous glue. It remains only to put the blister under pressure with the help of one or more cramps.

Warning! The piece of wood you put between the cramp and the blister may get stuck on to the veneer if any more glue comes out of the slit. So put on a sheet of tissue paper first. After drying, it can easily be removed with a fine scraper or a razor blade.

VINYL GLUE—AND WHY NOT?

Bone glue is not commonly sold nowadays; modern cabinet makers use vinyl adhesives, which are more satisfactory from every point of view. There are two methods open to you. The first is that just explained; simply use a vinyl glue instead of the old-fashioned kind, and apply pressure.

The second method is a particularly neat one; it does the trick without any special equipment, and moreover is easy to control.

Work the glue in as already described, squeeze out any excess, and leave it to dry for twenty minutes. The next step is to lay tissue paper over the blister and iron it with a warm iron, set to 'Silk', as before. Press hard for as long as is necessary to ensure adhesion. Then switch off the current to your iron but leave the iron in position; as it gradually cools the glue will do the same, giving perfect adhesion without recourse to a cramp.

AND WHAT ABOUT NEOPRENE?

Modern technology has given us an adhesive specifically intended for laminates. This is neoprene (see the chapter on 'Glues'), which is a contact adhesive. As the term implies, mere contact between the two surfaces to be joined, each of which is previously coated with the adhesive, suffices to produce perfect adhesion, without pressure. Cabinet makers, however, seem rather slow to welcome it. Is this just traditional conservatism? Anyway, the contact adhesive in question can be enormously useful to both professionals and amateurs, provided they always observe the condition that *both* surfaces must be coated with it. The two things to be stuck—the veneer and the carcase—should both be given a thin, even film of adhesive (use a scraper, or any suitable object with a straight edge, to obtain a smooth covering). Leave them to dry until tacky, so that they no longer stick to you when tested with finger-tip pressure. Then bring the two surfaces together and smooth them over with a piece of board, the flat striking-face of a hammer or any other flat, smooth object. In this way you should be able to achieve an impeccable piece of veneering.

Warning: if you have put on a veneer in this way, never try to take it off again. It's practically impossible. And if you did succeed you would leave a very awkward surface for subsequent veneering.

A method which is sometimes worth trying but is a good deal of a gamble is to use a cork pad. Rub the blister vigorously, with a steady to-and-fro motion, with a cork pad; the heat produced by friction sometimes does the trick. The chief advantage is that the pad cannot damage the varnish.

CRACKS

A veneer displaying a network of hair-cracks does not necessarily demand repair; cracks of this kind are just a sign of venerable age. If a piece of veneer has deteriorated so badly that you are compelled to replace it, you may also decide to age it artificially so that its appearance doesn't stick out like a sore thumb. We can give you a few tips for this, but it is up to you to pick whichever method suits your purpose.

Before applying adhesive, thoroughly wet the new piece of veneer. Then iron it with a very hot iron. This sometimes produces tiny cracks and slightly browns the surface.

Hot sand (really hot) has always been an item in the cabinet maker's arsenal. It is used for giving a patina to the background parts of a carving, and for darkening marquetry. Hold the new piece of veneer in something suitable (such as eyebrow tweezers) and dip it in very hot sand, which can be in a saucepan on a gas-ring. Always remember to wet the veneer first, so as to avoid scorching or burning it. Leave it in the sand just long enough and no longer.

Finally, you can seal the grain of the wood (see the section on French polishing), an operation which is a preliminary to varnishing and which, in this instance, will be carried out not only with pumice (which is neutral in colour) but with an admixture of umber, which will emphasize the delicate network of the medullary rays of the wood.

REPLACING A MISSING PIECE

Every case is a special case; hardly ever is a missing fragment merely the equivalent of a lost piece from a jigsaw puzzle. Sometimes a hole has been made by the veneer's being gradually worn away, causing what in French workshops is called *une perce*. Sometimes the glue has failed and one day, by mischance, the cleaning duster has torn out a splinter; the fragment was carefully kept for a time, then lost. Or there was an accident; a hard knock, something digging in and tearing the veneer. Or a cigarette burn or the like; or some elusive, quite unexpected cause.

We shall suggest remedies for as many of these special cases as we can.

Popular engraving: carpenters at work

HOLES

We start with these because they are undoubtedly the hardest of the lot. After being sanded and revarnished a few times the veneer wears away, but very unevenly; when a perforation develops it is usually where there is something slightly uneven, such as a blister which was left untreated.

Simply letting in a new piece won't work, because the new veneer, being as yet of its original thickness, would be 'proud' (protruding) and would be practically impossible to reduce to the level of the surrounding surface. Here is the professional craftsman's solution.

It requires care and skill, but as far as we know it is the only real answer. You remove the veneer (see the section on this); the area taken off should be two or three times greater than that of the perforation. Trim the edges of the latter a little, not so as to give them sharp, regularly-shaped edges but in order to get rid of any wood that is too thin. Then make a slit along the grain (as directed in the section on repairing blisters). By means of this slit, insert a piece of veneer slightly larger than the hole, having first made sure that you have chosen a wood whose grain and character are as similar as possible to those of the object under repair.

Centre the piece carefully and fix it down (for example by sticking a needle through it); then, with a pencil, mark the approximate outline of the hole.

Remove the new piece and thin it down gradually from the pencilled line outwards towards the edges, using for this a very sharp wood chisel, glasspaper, a fine file, etc.

Now apply glue and put the piece in position, taking care that all excess glue is removed, and place under pressure. A trick of the trade which cabinet makers find useful is this: between the new piece and the flat piece of wood (really flat and true) which takes the pressure of the cramps, put two or three thicknesses of rubber obtained by cutting up an inner tube. This distributes the pressure evenly and causes it to be applied with a good 'touch'.

When the glue has finished setting, sand carefully to equalize the different thicknesses and achieve a rigorously flat surface.

A final warning! When putting on the new piece, make sure the grain is pointing the right way. A repair with the grain running crossway would be hideous.

PERFORATED BOLLS

'Burrs' or 'bolls' in elm, arbor vitae and other timbers give rise to interesting effects in veneer. Striking examples of this can be seen in the furniture of the first *Restauration* period in France (the restoration of Louis XVIII, April 1814–March 1815. The second restoration lasted from July 1815 to July 1830 and included the reign of Charles X, the last Bourbon monarch in

France). Perhaps you already know what a boll consists of. You must have noticed, on tree trunks, round, rough bulges; these excrescences are the bolls. In the sawmill, their fibres are found to lie in swirling, curly, shimmering patterns which have a decided decorative quality. Unfortunately the resulting veneer is somewhat capricious and unreliable. The grain flickers about in any direction and in many instances contains holes caused by tiny knots, as when a branch began to grow but failed to develop; and by scars, and so on.

When a hole in a veneer is caused by a boll, the trouble has usually developed in the first place from one of these minute knotholes. Even when the furniture was being made there were probably some which the cabinet maker or polisher was obliged to fill. Follow his example. He is certain to have used shellac. This is easy to buy from firms catering for cabinet makers and such-like; it comes in slabs, like bars of chocolate, in a wide range of shades, from which you can choose the one which suits whatever you are doing. It looks exactly the same when you buy it as it will after being put on; so don't be alarmed at any change in its appearance while you are working with it.

Shellac is comparatively hard and melts when heated. The secret of successful in-filling is to observe a few simple rules. Never melt the shellac over a flame; use a hot bar of iron.

Avoid getting the shellac too hot and making it boil; this will create bubbles, which cause weak points and may show up as holes when it comes to sanding.

Shellac shrinks on cooling, so always use a little more than is necessary. Superfluous shellac, once it has set hard, can be removed with a chisel and then given a perfect surface by sanding.

A MISSING PIECE

The policy for this is always the same: treat the problem as one of marquetry. If the piece is regular in shape, you reproduce it as exactly as possible. If it is irregular, try to give it a logical shape (i.e. not just a formless-looking patch); whenever possible, make it something like a parallelogram (*en sifflet*, 'whistle-shaped', that is to say with the ends cut obliquely, like the mouthpiece of a whistle), in all cases where what needs mending is a smooth panel (such as a table top or the top of a commode, the front of a drawer, or suchlike). If an insertion shaped *en sifflet* is not practicable, try to make use of the outer limits of a motif or of a prominently-marked area of grain. Your own taste must be your guide to the shape of the repair, in your attempt to effect an 'invisible mend'.

In achieving this ideal shape you will inevitably have to remove a certain amount of the old veneer. Depending on the size of the repair, you will use either a chisel or a very fine-toothed saw (if you possess a veneering saw, so much the better; if not, a small tenon saw will do perfectly). As a guide for the saw you can position a ruler along the line of cut and hold it in place with a couple of cramps. Don't saw deeper than the veneer. A saw-cut in the carcase would create a line of weakness just where you do not want it, along the join. Thoroughly clean off all old glue from the exposed surface of the carcase. Then make a template of the exact shape of the new piece of veneer. For this you will need some thin, stiff cardboard, nicely matching the replacement (if you can, go to a bookbinder for some, which in France is called *carte de Lyon*; it is $\frac{1}{10}$ mm. thick, very stiff and just right for the job). Make sure your template is perfectly accurate. Before sawing the veneer, use the template to find the best orientation, so as to marry the veins and grain of the new veneer with those of the old to maintain uniformity.

The veneer must be not only sawn flat but forced to remain flat while being sawn; if necessary, cramp it between two pieces of plywood.

Another method, excellent in every way, consists of placing the veneer over the site of the intended repair before trimming the edges of the latter. Then cut both at once; this ensures that, after tidying up any mess left by the old veneer, the new piece will be a perfect fit. (The method does not, however, apply in cases where the outline contains any angles, causing the saw-cuts to intersect.)

The cardboard template method is particularly useful in establishing the outlines of pieces missing from a marquetry pattern.

Gluing is carried out along the lines already described. But it should be noted that if the piece of veneer being replaced is large, any surplus glue may produce disastrous results by causing bulges. It is therefore advisable, when cramping-up, to begin at the middle of the new piece, thus forcing the glue outwards and enabling the surplus to come out round the edges.

AN IMPORTANT POINT: THE THICKNESS OF THE VENEER

Any veneer you can get through ordinary commercial channels is most unlikely to be of the same gauge as the piece requiring replacement. As was pointed out at the beginning of this chapter, the old veneers and marquetry were substantially thicker than those of our own time. Don't let yourself be discouraged by this irritating problem. Professional cabinet makers encounter it too and find it just as troublesome. In workshops specializing in the restoration of valuable furniture the tiniest offcuts of veneer are saved and hoarded like fine gold, only to prove valueless—the wrong thickness or texture—when it comes to using them.

Here are two ways of getting round the difficulty:

1. *If the difference is minimal,* say between 0·1 and 0·3 mm.: before gluing, cut a piece of tissue paper to the necessary shape, saturate it with glue and apply it to the carcase. Let it dry before proceeding to glue up by one of the methods already described. The thickness of the paper, carefully selected for the purpose, will make up the difference. And the resulting repair will be just as strong, provided that the glue has really penetrated the paper, consolidating its fibres.

2. *If the difference is larger,* simply use two pieces of veneer,

one on top of the other. This expedient may bring howls from the purists, but it is indispensable. Moreover it will enable you to achieve a high-precision result, because modern veneers are made in several gauges between 0·4 and 0·6 mm. The right combination of these will solve the problem.

DENTS IN VENEER

The cause is always an impact of some kind, usually that of a sharply pointed object: the corner of another piece of furniture, or a crate carelessly handled by removers' men, or a marble sculpture whose position had to be altered, or the projecting angle of a wall. Repairing dents is a trying business; there is no single, simple answer. Sometimes the damage, on examination, proves to be slight: the veneer is a bit crunched but the carcase is intact. The dent can be eliminated by applying steam; this makes the fibres of the wood swell up and resume their proper position. Take a piece of rag of just sufficient size to cover the damaged area, soak it well, and place it in position. Apply a really hot iron, so as to produce a copious amount of steam. Don't keep it there too long: the aim is to penetrate *only the surface* of the wood, without affecting the glue or spoiling the varnish. Repeat several times. You will see the wood recovering its original shape, which it will retain after drying out.

A harder blow, denting not only the veneer but also the carcase, is more serious. You will find that the forcible bending of the veneer has broken it across. Using a very thin tool of some kind, detach the damaged part of the veneer and fold it back a little way; to manage this you will probably have to split it along the grain. Any pieces that break right off should be carefully saved if they look usable. The carcase, usually made of softwood like pine or poplar, will be deeply marked.

The simplest solution is to use plastic wood, obtainable until recently only in tins but now also available in tubes. Plastic wood, which is a soft, pliable paste, must be allowed to dry out very thoroughly before the veneer is put back on. The solvent

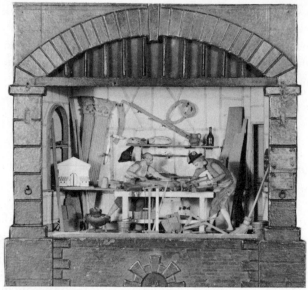

Automaton, French Revolution period: a carpenter's
shop

used in plastic wood is alcohol in some brands, acetone in
others; it must have time to evaporate completely if it is not to
cause trouble after gluing. Apply the plastic wood with a
spatula or palette knife, like mastic. If you find it has cracked
or shrunk during drying, put on some more and allow that to
dry out too. After that you can sand or rasp or otherwise work
on it, just like ordinary wood.

A quicker method is to use shellac. Directions for this have
already been given: heat it with a hot bar of iron, never over a
naked flame. The veneer can then be glued on to this new
support, which will first have been made perfectly smooth in
the way fully described above. The repair will probably have to
be completed by sanding and revarnishing.

A SPLIT IN THE CARCASE

Damage of this severity may well demand more repairing than
the amateur's skill and tools will run to. However, for com-

pleteness, let us explain briefly that the whole of the veneer on the split panel has to be removed. The causes of the split are then investigated; this implies a deep knowledge of wood, especially as the veneer, despite having given way to some extent, has nevertheless curbed the movement of the split portion of the carcase, which may, therefore, produce further movement. What is the correct solution? To close the split by inserting thin fillets secured by glue? To strengthen the panel by small crosspieces at the back (a method also much used in repairing paintings on wood panels that have split)? Some cabinet makers favour canvas straps, glued on, to hold the panel together. And a point which must always be reckoned with is that the split may have been caused by deformation in the whole structure, in which case general reconstruction will be necessary.

There are some things it is always better to hand over to the expert.

REPLACING VENEER ON A ROUND OR CONVEX SUPPORT

A contact adhesive will serve you best in cases of this kind; it lets you out of the difficulty of using cramps on round or convex places in a piece of furniture. Special problems like this are only to be solved by using a special substance, correctly applied. However, here are a few tricks of the trade which are much used by craftsmen and may help you too.

The plaster mould method

This means using plaster of Paris, not as an adhesive but to make a mould which exactly copies the contours of the piece of veneer to be stuck on. This constitutes a former which holds the new veneer in place with absolute precision. Mix your plaster in the normal way (remember: add plaster to water, not water to plaster). When you sense that the plaster has begun 'working', apply it to the part to be reproduced (if you like, mix some plumber's tow with the plaster first; this makes it less elusive to handle and also acts as an armature to hold it together while it is setting). As soon as the mould has set hard, which takes only a few minutes, remove it and put it aside to dry.

The sandbag method

This is by far the easiest method of all. You make a flat bag, only a little larger than the piece of veneer to be pressed on. Fill the bag with sand (until recently, it was the custom to heat the sand first so as to soften the bone glue then still used). Put a flat piece of wood on top and apply pressure with cramps or weights. The sand moulds itself to the convex surface and distributes the pressure evenly.

The strap method

This is a time-honoured method which you may find useful, particularly on round components (such as the feet of some pieces of furniture, though as a rule these are not veneered). It consists simply of tightly binding the part in question with a woven strap. The strap is well wetted first, so that it stretches and is thoroughly supple. When the buckle is done up the strap is drawn tight and exerts strong pressure. Incidentally, some of the straps now available, made of synthetics, have special buckles on the wire-strainer principle, which exert extra high tension.

REMOVING VENEER

We have said plenty about *sticking*—how to glue a piece of veneer on. But what about *unsticking*—taking a piece of veneer off? We shall not dodge this; there are some repair jobs in which it is essential.

The old-fashioned glues present no great difficulty. They

respond to heat and humidity. Use a dishcloth and a hot iron, taking care to wet the cloth as often as may be necessary. Everyone has his own pet method for speeding the result. Some recommend a pinch of bicarbonate of soda or washing soda in the water; others, a well-stirred mixture of alcohol and hot water (in which case the cloth and hot iron are not required). All these recipes are effective.

Modern glues present a more complex problem.

Vinyl adhesives can be softened by heat, using an electric iron set at 'silk' or 'cotton'. But mechanical help is also necessary. Have a suitable flat tool ready to hand, which can be inserted under the veneer to prise it up as the glue softens. Contact adhesives also react to heat but are most sensitive to solvents, such as acetone, benzine, benzoline, trichloroethylene, etc.

THE CHAIN METHOD OF AGEING

One form of damage found in veneered furniture is an indication that the work is faked; the damage was added to make it look genuine. Light blows have been inflicted, leaving

The marks of 'ageing' with a chain can be clearly seen on the lower part of this chest

marks about the size and shape of a grain of rice. Their uniformity, and the fact that they make the wood darker than the rest, render them easily recognizable. The practice is sometimes known in the trade as thrashing. The faker uses a length of ordinary chain and thrashes the piece with it, more or less at random but particularly on sharp edges, the resulting marks being just what you might expect a chain to produce. A little common sense and alertness will suffice to arouse your suspicions. A similar effect can be obtained by tapping with the flat end of a hammer.

BANDS AND OTHER BRASS ORNAMENTATION

Furniture is not infrequently embellished with brass ornamentation, emphasizing the general lines of the design. Some of these embellishments are bands fitting snugly in half-round grooves on the legs of a table, or, occasionally, the uprights, glazing bars or applied mouldings of a glazed cabinet.

It is most irritating when these ornaments loosen in the course of time, especially as they are not easy to stick back in place. Worse still is the nightmare of having to replace them altogether when time or moving house has caused their loss.

Let us take the easier case first, that in which the ornaments are neither broken nor distorted but have simply come off.

If you have a small soldering iron of the kind used by electricians, you can use it to heat the brass strip before pressing it firmly back into its groove. The heat will soften the glue and fix the ornament in place. Another method you can try is to make the head of a hammer really hot (but take care not to burn the handle).

If these methods fail, try to clean off the old glue on the strip with a file, keeping the strip flat on a true surface while doing so. The groove can be cleaned out with a tiny flat chisel or mortise chisel (these can be bought in sizes from 2 mm., or approximately $\frac{1}{12}$ in., upwards). Then use a contact adhesive on both surfaces.

Brass strips which are twisted, broken or stretched must be replaced with new ones. Shops which specialize in materials of this kind sell them by the yard. You may be able to fix them yourself, following the directions given here, but in most cases you will do better to take the job to a qualified craftsman. Attaching brass strips, bands and ornamental mouldings requires a skill born of many years' practice.

Giving Furniture the Right Patina

WHAT SORT OF SURFACE DO YOU LIKE?

THERE are some words we use so often that we forget what they really mean. People blithely confuse patina with dirt; a dangerous error. The fact is that the shining film, not to say crust, which confers rustic charm on some piece of furniture discovered in a farmyard may well prove disappointing when transferred to a town apartment; even, when strongly lit, somewhat repellent. And the dull, opaque coating hastily brushed on by a junk dealer has nothing in common with the slow, discreet ripening which only time can give. In any case, different woods have their own ways of ageing; do you know what these are? Oak and walnut are capable of actually losing their pigmentation over a period of time. Most Gothic furniture—if genuine—is pale, hardly even golden. Beech changes colour little or not at all; the reddest cherry-wood turns blond; elm and chestnut darken slightly, especially in the soft parts between the grain; so does ash, though its tendency to deviate from its original colour is on the whole very slight.

All of which is a long way from the kind of patina which can be put on with a brush!

Patina is a caress. This is no mere metaphor but a reality, a fact at once tangible and even technical. A caress for the sense of sight, which discovers the true contours of a piece of furniture and sees their saliences reinforced by subtle differentiations not of colour but of light. And a caress for the sense of touch. No faking, no sanding or artificial signs of wear can ever take the place of the polished smoothness created by long use. So true is this, that a genuinely antique piece can be stripped with powerful chemicals, washed, thoroughly rinsed and allowed to dry, and will immediately regain its shine at the touch of your rag or cloth, without needing any wax or other polishing material at all.

All you have done is to restore the effect of long years of care, the maintenance patiently applied by generations of devoted, loving ownership.

It is true that many pieces, when new, were given a coat of stain to bring out the inherent decorative qualities of the material. But the stain used in such cases was a decoction of vegetable origin, in other words made with water; hence it penetrated the wood only for a short distance. It was utterly different from the atrocious brews daubed on with such frenzy by professional prettifiers. After staining came polishing—with beeswax, that golden natural substance which, in time, builds up a translucent deposit for which there is no substitute.

However, we do sometimes find ourselves compelled to reconstitute a patina which has been destroyed by neglect or by exposing furniture to the weather, or to harmonize restored portions with the whole. Various products are available for the purpose and it is not for us to discuss their relative merits. Some of them are combined stains and polishes. Our own advice, given below, is to use natural methods, though we also suggest ways for accelerating the effects which are normally created only by the lapse of time.

HOT WAXING

The first treatment to give to a piece of furniture, after cleaning or stripping it, is a coat of liquid wax. You can either use one of the high-quality standard brands of furniture polish, diluted with turpentine, or mix your own by melting a cake of beeswax in a water-jacket and adding turpentine, stirring continuously meanwhile. The right proportion is 250 grammes of beeswax to 1 litre of turpentine (nearly 9 oz. beeswax to $1\frac{3}{4}$ pints turpentine). Be careful not to let the liquid catch fire; have a lid ready to extinguish a flare-up if it occurs.

The diluted wax is applied with an ordinary brush, care

being taken to cover every detail. The aim of this initial operation is to nourish the pores of the wood, which will have been scoured empty by cleaning.

An 18th-century *caquetaire* (Musée des Arts décoratifs)

Leave the work to dry out thoroughly. Absorption will be total. The piece is then ready to undergo the highly important operation of hot waxing.

Arm yourself with a cake of wax, a brazing torch or blowlamp with a flat (fishtail) burner, and a suitable brush or two. You will soon acquire the requisite knack.

Soften the wax slightly and rub it on the wood, rapidly but

with plenty of pressure. You will find that a little wax is deposited on the surface by each movement to and fro. Pass the flame of your torch over these deposits. They will melt, sink deeply into the wood, close the pores and spread out over the surface. If there is too little wax anywhere you simply put on more and run over it with the flame—tactfully, of course, so as to avoid blackening the wood or setting the wax alight. If there is too much wax anywhere it is easily removed by energetic polishing with a stiff brush; not having had time to harden completely, it comes off easily. The effect is spectacular and almost instantaneous. Undiluted wax dries quickly and the brush eliminates any irregularities; a brilliant surface appears at once. On carvings and mouldings, use a burnisher—and don't be frightened off by this technical term, the tool is one you can easily make yourself. Take a small piece of hardwood and cut one end of it to a sharp bevel edge. With this you can scrape the protuberant details without fear of damage, such as a metal tool would certainly inflict.

You have now made the wax sink well into the wood, impregnating it for keeps. Maintenance is no trouble; an occasional rub with a soft rag or woollen duster restores the brilliance.

Some cabinet makers use a hot iron instead of a blowtorch. This avoids the risk of scorching and darkening the wood, but we find it makes the wax go too runny so that all of it sinks into the wood instead of sealing the superficial pores correctly. Here again, touch is all.

There is another method which has the attraction of producing a high gloss, but which, in our opinion, is rather artificial. It consists of using a liquid wax and following it up with a coat of copal varnish dissolved in alcohol. This is more akin to French polishing than to hot waxing.

There are plenty of recipes for 'miracle' polishes. One of them is a mixture of stearine or spermaceti with beeswax; paraffin (kerosene) wax is also sometimes used. Many excellent polishes are now available commercially, based on highly successful formulae whose ingredients include very hard vegetable

Doors of a 15th-century buffet

waxes which, when dry, give a tough durable finish; examples are 'carnauba' wax from South America, and wax extracted from palm leaves.

SHOE POLISH

Though comparatively expensive, shoe polish has always been one of the cabinet maker's most valuable allies. It is used for heightening the details of carvings. Coloured polish, not the transparent neutral kind, is of course what you want. You put it on with a small brush (this provides your discarded toothbrush with a second career). Leave the polish to dry for a few hours, then rub the carving with a stiff brush or wooden burnisher; the parts in relief turn lighter, the undercuts will stay dark because the brush or burnisher can't reach them.

In France, one famous manufacturer of shoe polish has brought out an excellent product designed specially for cabinet makers, suitably coloured for different varieties of wood.

MECHANICAL AIDS

In recent years the accessories available for use with portable electric drills have included a polisher, usually made of lamb's wool. In practice this produces rather disappointing results, although in principle it looks like a sound method for obtaining in a minute or two the effect of decades of maintenance by hand. The cause is a simple one: portable electric drills run at 2500 r.p.m. or even more; some of the two-speed drills run at 1400 and 900 r.p.m. At speeds like these the wax melts and is dispersed by centrifugal force. Even the varnishes in normal use disintegrate because the friction generates more heat than they can stand. So it is no use expecting to polish a piece of furniture by this means. However, a special mechanical polisher has been designed and put on the market; it works on the same principle but runs at only 400–500 r.p.m., the threshold beyond which the wax breaks down. The polishing attachments provided are either brushes of different degrees of stiffness, or a sheepskin roller. Another item of equipment, which deserves to be better known than at present, is a disc made from a material directly derived from that of which scouring cloths are made. These discs are invaluable. Although their action is gentle they are just as effective on wood, which they polish to perfection, as on bronze or iron.

A restoration carried out with new wood can be given an exemplary patina after treatment with these discs, which are available in various grades to provide different degrees of abrasion. The same discs can also be used for straightforward cleaning; handled judiciously, at a speed from 500 to 1000 r.p.m., they leave the wood clean without making circular grooves or scratches.

SPECIAL CASES

All the woods commonly used in cabinet making, such as oak, walnut and wild cherry and other fruitwoods, can be treated in the manner described here. So can mahogany, although most people prefer it varnished.

Cuban mahogany, which is very dense in texture, would gain nothing from being hot-waxed; the same applies to South American rosewood, ebony and lignum vitae. These are outstandingly hard, close-grained woods, which are virtually without pores to be sealed.

Teak, at one time used exclusively for exotic furniture, has been domesticated into household use by the talent of Swedish designers. It is a wood whose oily exudations protect it from deterioration, so that it practically looks after itself. If it ever does need cleaning, use plenty of trichlorethylene on a clean rag. When it has dried, use teak oil; this special liquid is far more suitable for the purpose than wax. After that, rub with a cloth in the ordinary way.

RESINOUS WOODS

These take very kindly to hot waxing and equally so to an undercoat of wax and turpentine, with which, of course, they have a natural affinity. However, there is a time-honoured recipe which has been used ever since the early Middle Ages and which can be recommended on several counts; its results are remarkable. This is *linseed oil*. Use it as hot as you can and go on applying it until the wood rejects it, that is to say until you can see the oil staying on the surface instead of sinking in. Let it become part-way dry, then wipe off the excess and leave until drying is complete; this will take several days, even in hot, dry weather. This is the only drawback with linseed oil.

The final step is to polish with a brush or cloth, producing a bright, lasting gloss. A considerable advantage is that even the softest wood is made perceptibly harder by being impregnated with linseed oil, which is therefore suitable not only for resinous woods but also for poplar and lime, which are rather sad and colourless in themselves but, after treatment, display a delightful golden radiance.

Local Customs

DESPITE being radically opposed to all spurious 'patinas' which violate the nature of any species of timber—and for the genuine *amateur*, the division of woods into 'noble' and 'base' is meaningless—we have to admit that certain local or regional customs do seriously modify the character of the wood. Here are some examples from different parts of France.

In Brittany, cupboards, panelled beds and oak coffers are frequently found whose colour, without being exactly black, reminds one of coffee grounds. Any attempt to lighten it would be hopeless. It is true that the Breton oak is particularly rich in tannin; it is called 'black oak' and coopers would have nothing to do with it, because it gave too dark a tint to brandy. They preferred 'white' oak from Dordogne or the Limousin. But there is more to it than this. For centuries, wood was seasoned by immersion in water. After felling and barking, the trunks were trundled into ponds or meres and left there almost indefinitely, or at any rate for a very long time. It seems likely that the practice originated in Flanders; the Flemish cabinet makers frequently used wood which had spent a considerable period of time in water. Possibly they also used ships' timbers.

A revealing piece of evidence comes to us from Burgundy (which was not so remote from Flanders as might appear: that province was part of the empire of Charles the Bold). The accounts of the abbot who commissioned the building of the Hôtel-Dieu at Tonnerre (Yonne) record the abbot's own justification of his outlay for the timber frame. He says, in effect: 'I wavered long between two lots of timber. The first had been seasoned for only [only!] five hundred years; the other, for six hundred. It was dearer, but more suitable for serious building.'

It is astonishing to realize that, in the 15th century, timber was being used which dated from the time of Charlemagne.

Drawing of a carpenter's shop, 14th century

Contemporary documents make it clear that seasoning consisted of prolonged immersion; so long, in fact, that the oak became as if petrified.

Coming back to Brittany, we find that immersion was widely practised but with a significant difference. The trunks were cast into the sea, and we know beyond doubt that it was the custom to bury them deep in the mud. This was a time-honoured procedure. It has always been known that wood rots only in the air. Under water or buried in mud, it loses its sap, is penetrated by mineral salts and undergoes a transformation not unlike petrification. Much of the Breton furniture is made from timber which spent some time in the sea. Not long ago we saw an old cabinet maker burying in the sand of the seashore the components of a piece of furniture he had just made; he told us it would stay there for about a year. Well, he knew what he was doing.

A tip well known to cabinet makers is that when you have to use a piece of new wood in restoring an old piece of furniture, you can make quite sure of its not warping by soaking it in brine for a week. Presumably it has to be thoroughly rinsed on being taken out, otherwise an unwelcome efflorescence of salt crystals would appear later on its surface.

Woods which have been water-seasoned can be recognized by certain peculiarities. Among these is the one which we pointed out first, which forms the subject of this chapter: their dark colouring. Oxides from the water, and tannin in the oak itself, combine to colour the oak very strongly, right to the heart. Another characteristic is that the wood is hardly ever a prey to woodworm and other pests. In a few cases they may manage to penetrate soft places, especially in the sapwood, if any of it has been left (usually it has not). Finally, these timbers pass the cabinet maker's acid test: when he planes them they yield no shavings; the blade removes a cloud of short, broken fibres.

In the Basque areas, it is not unusual to find coffers which are extremely dark. When we open them we find that the inside has the natural colour of the wood, which is generally chestnut. Careful inspection of the outside quickly reveals the presence of a thick, durable coat of something or other. Tradition has it that this is ox-blood, and chemical analysis has proved tradition right. Painting with ox-blood serum has been studied by a Spanish scientist, Dr Carbonell. It was hailed as a sensational discovery in the late 18th century and was used at that time for painting every public building in Madrid, including the interior of the royal palace, with a 'paint resembling stone', according to Dr Carbonell's account of his own process, 'obtained by mixing lime, only just slaked, with ox-blood serum'. It is clear beyond doubt that, in the countryside, ox-blood had long been used as paint, without separating its constituents. We have come across pieces of furniture which date from much earlier than Dr Carbonell's account, and which are coated with ox-blood; it has the property of turning black with time and, what is more striking, of resisting wind and weather and of becoming shiny, like varnish.

It should be recalled that a mixture of ox-blood and sawdust used to be used for making figurines which looked rather as if made of ebony.

In Vendée, Loire-Atlantique and, even more so, in Brière, the same tradition is found. In the museum of the castle of Anne of Brittany, in Nantes, there can be seen several reconstructions of regional interiors in which furniture painted with ox-blood figures prominently.

Death to Stains!

THE most precious piece of furniture can be disfigured by ordinary carelessness: a wet glass, an upset inkpot, spilt perfume, grease, a cigarette burn. The blemish becomes a perpetual reproach, you see only it and not the cherished furniture itself. However, the case is never hopeless; the most unsightly stain can be conquered.

STAINS FROM DAMP

The foot of a glass or the bottom of a bottle, or the base of a vase of flowers which has not been properly wiped, leaves a white ring on a polished surface. This is not a serious matter in cases where contact was reasonably brief. Let the mark dry thoroughly, then rub with plenty of turpentine, letting it soak in, and apply fresh polish. If this fails, which it sometimes does on woods that are light in colour, rub in a pat of butter until it is completely absorbed.

On stained furniture (i.e. those that have been given a coat of stain), the wetness removes the pigment. The only thing to do is to give the affected part a new coat of stain. If this scares you, try wetting the whole of the surface of the piece with a sponge dipped in a mixture of strong detergent and water (one or two small teaspoonsful say to a litre, $1\frac{3}{4}$ pints, of water); this slightly lightens the colour of the whole and may make it homogeneous.

ALCOHOL

Glasses put down carelessly on your furniture are the main source of this, but it can also come from a bottle being upset, or scent, medicine and so on getting spilt. On polished surfaces alcohol leaves a mark like that of ordinary wetness, and the treatment is the same. But the damage is decidedly worse on varnished furniture, because most of the varnishes in common use are soluble in alcohol. Light sanding with flower paper (very fine glasspaper) is the first step; then build up the surface again (see the chapter on 'French polishing').

GREASE, FATS AND OILS

Whether the marks they make are only on the surface or sink in deeply, fatty or oily substances, animal, vegetable or mineral in origin, sometimes pose annoying problems. In theory, benzoline will cope with them, and so will benzine and trichlorethylene; when all else fails, highly refined cigarette-lighter fuel will succeed; ether, too, is highly effective except when the mark goes deep in, in which case it is too volatile.

The drawback of solvents is that they attack glue and loosen veneer. But on any furniture not veneered they work like a charm.

Another very effective method, with the advantage of being harmless to marquetry and veneer, is to use talc. Spread a thick layer of it on the spot and warm it very gently with a hot iron protected by several thicknesses of tissue paper. Both the talc and the paper will soak up the grease. Start again with a fresh lot of talc and paper, and repeat until the spot disappears. Fuller's earth can be used instead of talc.

In some cases where a piece of furniture has been rescued from a dreadful fate it has been used as a bench, and is disfigured by oily swarf having fallen on it. The methods just described will answer very well, but only in the second stage of rehabilitation. The first stage consists of loosening the oil marks by applying some other kind of oily or greasy substance, appropriately chosen, and rubbing it in; this may succeed in removing the marks, and can then itself be removed, as directed above.

INK

There are numbers of recipes for removing ink spots from furniture, which is in itself an indication that the problem has never really been solved. We have got no further with it today than people had done a hundred years ago; with this difference, that ink is no longer much used, even by schoolchildren.

So we are more often challenged by old ink stains, on escritoires, tables, secretaires and the like, than by recent ones.

Here are a few methods which undoubtedly work very well but which may be defeated by one kind of ink or another; so you may have to try each in turn.

A fresh ink stain

Wash with water, then use lemon juice.

An old ink stain

First sand lightly to get rid of extraneous substances and expose the surface of the wood. Place a cottonwool pad over the stain and pour sulphuric acid on to the pad—this prevents the acid from running about; after two or three minutes, inspect for results to see whether you are on the right track. Repeat with a fresh pad. Not many inks can withstand sulphuric acid, which possesses the advantage of not damaging the wood.

Oxalic acid, diluted with warm water, is also highly effective; so is muriatic acid, that well-known household specific.

Inks used to be made from 'oak apples' (oak galls, also known as nut galls), ferrous sulphate, copper sulphate and a decoction of logwood. When steel nibs came in and quill pens went out, the copper sulphate, which corroded the nibs, was omitted, but otherwise the recipe stayed much as before. It contains no ingredient which is not easily conquered with one or another of the acids now in common use and easy to obtain.

Red ink is often more recalcitrant. It is essentially vegetable in composition, being made of an infusion of wood from a species of Brazilian tree (*Caesalpina echinata*) in vinegar, *plus* madder, indigo (from the 17th to the 19th century), alum and gum arabic. Oxalic acid, well diluted with warm water, is the answer. Or muriatic acid can be used instead, heavily diluted with warm water to which a few drops of hydrogen peroxide have been added. When treating a really venerable red ink stain you may see it turn dark, even black, but don't worry: carry on, the treatment does work.

Plane (Musée des Arts et Traditions populaires)

If you can find a chemist or drugstore willing to supply you with potassium hyperchlorate, you can use it in the same way as the specifics already mentioned, heavily diluted with warm water.

WINE

Wine, like fruit juices, can make peculiarly tenacious stains on wood. However, we can take comfort from the fact that they hardly ever go very deep. Clean the surface by light scraping or sanding, then use muriatic acid diluted with lukewarm water. While the area is still wet with acid, put a few drops of hydrogen peroxide on it.

Sulphur fumes readily decompose the pigments in wine and those in any fruit juice or vegetable sap. But exposing the affected part of a piece of furniture to these fumes is an awkward business. This is how to manage it. Place a saucer beside the stain, with a stick piece of cardboard under it to insulate the wood against heat, and burn some bits of sulphur candle of the kind used for purifying barrels, hogsheads, etc. The fumes will rise vertically; now place a paper cone, like a dunce's cap, or, even better, the lid of a cheese dish, over the stain and the saucer. The fumes will completely fill this confined space and plentifully 'bathe' the surface of the wood.

BLOOD

This, too, is a more frequent cause of stains than might be thought. It is the origin of some of the otherwise unaccountable stigmata that one finds on furniture which has been through a long career of vicissitudes.

Bloodstains are easy to take out with ordinary hydrogen peroxide. If the stain proves stubborn, ask your chemist or drugstore for some sodium thiosulphate diluted to 5 per cent. Dab the stain with it, in the confidence of ultimate victory.

BURNS

These are wounds of a mechanical order, not stains. No natural or artificial chemical can ever remove the discoloration of wood that has been burnt by a hot iron carelessly put down, or a forgotten cigarette or cigar. Only by deep scraping or sanding can such marks be mitigated or removed.

A Delicate Technique: French Polishing

TO give a permanent lustrous coat to a whitewood piece, or to obliterate scratches and grazes from a valuable antique commode, demands a certain basic knowledge combined with the manual skill we associate with the lifelong craftsman.

However, modern preparations are continually tending to facilitate the work of both the professional and the amateur. It is now possible to say that French polishing is something anyone can do, with the sole reservation that there is no one universal answer: every case must be studied on its merits and treated accordingly. We shall try to show how to do this.

BRIEF REVIEW OF THE VARNISHES NOW AVAILABLE

One needs to acquaint oneself with the characteristics both of the traditional and of the most modern varnishes, so as to know exactly how to apply them and, what is equally important, which is the right one for a given job. Hence this rapid review.

Oil-based varnishes

We are including these merely for completeness; they are not applied with a pad, which is the 'French' polisher's primary tool. They consist of copal resin boiled up with linseed oil or imported oils. The nature of the ingredients makes them slow to dry, but the final result is usually very good provided every coat is allowed to dry out thoroughly before the next is put on. Note that they cannot be thinned with alcohol, but with turpentine (if natural turpentine is not to hand, you can, at a pinch, use white spirit, which is synthetic turpentine; but never mix turpentine and white spirit).

It is possible by means of these oil-based varnishes to build up a good foundation for French polishing, but is it really desirable to mix two techniques in this way? Whenever using a varnish of this type it is essential to remove any traces of oil or grease from the surface of the wood, otherwise the varnish does not 'take' securely; a preliminary washing-down with petrol or trichlorethylene is always advisable. By sanding carefully with pumice powder between coats—lightly after the first, more vigorously after the second—an effect exactly like French polishing can be obtained.

Cellulose varnishes

These are the commonest kind. They consist chiefly of shellac and cellulose dissolved in alcohol. Their remarkable transparency and ease of application cause them to be preferred to all others for French polishing properly so-called. They are very hard. The only snag to watch for is to avoid using them on any wood you suspect of being less than perfectly dry.

One of the advantages of a cellulose varnish is that it is a quick drier, making it possible to complete the job in a short time, without much delay between coats.

Alkyd varnishes

These are very tough and durable but have the disadvantage of drying slowly, which makes them vulnerable to airborne dust. However, they also possess undeniable advantages. They play no part in French polishing but are so widely used today that we cannot omit them here. They are put on with a brush, and as their consistency is usually fairly thick it is advisable to draw out each coat as thin as possible and put one coat crosswise over another, avoiding runs and 'fat edges'. Thorough sanding with glasspaper after every coat is essential. Or flower paper, which should be wetted first, can be used.

'Plastic' varnishes

All these have a tremendous future: the epoxy resins, polyesters and polyurethanes, the ureaformaldehyde and phenolic resins and so on. As a rule they are presented as two separate substances, the plastic varnish itself and a catalyst, the hardener.

The only 'plastic' varnishes which are relevant here are the polyesters. They supersede all the traditional methods of varnishing furniture. Their advantages, aesthetic as well as practical, outstrip everything previously known. Finally, they completely cut out the conventional preliminaries such as sanding, sealing and so on. They are put on with a gun, and for this reason are perhaps outside the range of the genuine amateur. To achieve perfect results one needs the proper equipment, sufficient experience to acquire the delicate knack of using the gun and, finally, a dust-free work space.

AND NOW, WHAT ABOUT FRENCH POLISHING?

This quick run-down on the current varnishes brings us to the main subject of this section: 'French' polishing, the pillar of traditional cabinet making.

The basic ingredients are of the simplest: copal, shellac and other imported resins, dissolved in spirit (alcohol). Of course everyone has his own way of making them up, some special additional substance which he claims is an improvement on the original mixture. You should perhaps take care to get special varnishing spirit, which is obtainable from any specialized merchant, rather than methylated spirit, which can be bought from most hardware stores, chemists and so on. In fact, though the latter is quite safe to use, people say the adulterant added to it spoils the varnish; but don't worry about this, it is one of those professional fads which have more to do with ancient tradition than contemporary fact.

WHAT *IS* FRENCH POLISHING?

In principle, French polishing is a technique of varnishing in which a cloth pad is used instead of a brush.

But this, as we shall see, is a thoroughly inadequate description.

For, in fact, the pad does various things which no brush could ever do. It acts as a reservoir of varnish, enabling a whole surface to be treated without stopping to refill. It regulates the release of varnish, avoiding the runs and fat edges which are the varnisher's bugbear. It is a direct extension of the hand, sensitively transmitting the subtlest variations of touch. Its fibres keep the varnish evenly mixed; the latter's ingredients do not separate out. Finally, it serves not only for varnishing but also for polishing, and for the preliminary sealing of the pores of the wood with powdered pumice, which it withholds or releases automatically, as the surface may require.

LEARNING TO MAKE A PAD

The pad should always be of the shape and size of a nice, large egg. Vary its volume to suit your own hand if you like, but that is all.

You will need not one pad, but two.

The *first* should be fairly coarse, for sealing the grain. A piece of fine hessian filled with rags of various kinds will do very well. Always take care to see that the rags are clean and that no colour can come out of them. We cannot utter this warning too strongly: *the spirit your pad soaks up may loosen any dye in the rags and make stains on the wood.*

The *second* should be *finer* in texture and very supple. Cotton jersey or mutton cloth is ideal provided it is not new, in which case it will shed bits of fluff. An old jersey and old knitted underwear (not of the cellular or string vest type) are excellent.

The stuffing of these pads should be other kinds of highly

absorbent rags with plenty of spring in them, such as knitted woollens, shoddy or woollen rags. White cotton waste, which is easy to buy, is very suitable. The outer cover of an egg-shaped pad requires a piece of fabric no larger than from 12 to 15 cm. square (about 5 in. or 6 in. square). But you will have to use twice as much because, in order always to be working with a clean pad, you will constantly need to turn the outer cover inside out. So make sure the cover is large enough.

PRELIMINARY OPERATIONS

One should never set about French polishing before making the surface of the wood absolutely smooth. The first operation is always thorough sanding, using finer and finer glasspaper and working along the grain, not across it. After this, remove all traces of dust and hold the freshly sanded wood up to the light—natural light from a window or glazed door—and look along it at eye level to make sure it really is smooth.

Another essential is to work in a warm room, at 15–16 °C. (about 60 °F.). At higher temperatures (20 °C., 78 °F.) the spirit evaporates too fast.

Sealing the grain

Most species of wood have tiny hollow veins, known aptly enough as 'pores', which are in fact the medullary canals through which the sap of the tree circulates. These 'pores' are more or less marked in different species. It is essential to close them. If the wood is painted they are simply covered up. But in varnishing (which is what French polishing really is) we cannot do this, since the objective is precisely to bring out the decorative beauty of the wood. So we use pumice powder. This is available at low cost from specialized merchants; but you may find that in particularly delicate work you cannot use it as it is but must sift it through a fine sieve.

The medium which is to carry the powder is spirit (alcohol).

Soak your pad in this, but not too much. Then dip it in the pumice powder and coat the surface of your work with the mixture, using small circular movements at the start and gradually increasing the radius so that each movement covers as much of the surface as possible. In this way you traverse the grain *in every direction*. To avoid accentuating the pores, don't bear down on the pad; the operation of filling them is not intended to result in a renewed sanding. Shake out your pad as soon as it gets dirty; do not let it become encrusted.

And don't overdo the spirit; if you use too much it will soak into the wood, loosen the veneer (if any) and cause swelling, followed by shrinking, thus jeopardizing smoothness. To make the pumice powder hold well, add a few drops of polish (see below) to your pad as soon as you have acquired the knack of the correct movement. But take care not to use too much. French polishing is an *art of moderation*.

Squint along your work, as you did after sanding it, to check results. The moment will come when filling seems complete: a smooth surface meets your gaze. Pause for a few minutes while the work dries. After a while you will see that some degree of shrinking has occurred: the pores are showing again, though less prominently. You must repeat the filling operation, but already you can use a more liberal allowance of polish.

We urgently advise you not to polish continuously, and to disregard the impression of instantaneous drying-out produced by the evaporation of the spirit. With a little patience you will see that your polish is 'working', as craftsmen say. That lovely, glassy surface you thought you had achieved is no longer so perfect, it needs several hours in which to dry.

Polishing is performed with a constant mixture of 50 per cent varnish to 50 per cent spirit. It is out of the question for you to make up your own polishes, as is done by professional cabinet makers who have been in the trade all their lives. Nor should you try to choose a varnish yourself from among the various makes on the market. Get advice from someone who really knows. All you have to tell him is what kind of wood you are working on and what effect you are aiming for; he will recommend the appropriate brand.

Mix your varnish and spirit in a bottle and shake it well every time you put some on to your pad. Having damped the pad with the polish—never excessively—apply it to the wood

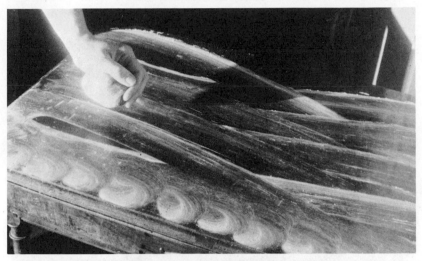

The combination of movements in French polishing: circles of various sizes for filling, elongated figure 8's, without pressure, for polishing

in a series of more or less elongated figure-8 movements. Examine your work against the light to make sure that you have gone evenly everywhere, without runs or patches. Work with a light hand. Never let the pad get soiled with dust, pumice powder or anything else. Turn the outer cover over from time to time, so as always to work with a clean pad.

Every pass with the pad leaves a thin film of polish, i.e. dilute varnish, and the instantaneous evaporation of the spirit immediately produces a dry surface. By making several passes in succession you can progressively add to this film. But stop in time to give the polish a chance to dry out properly, in depth.

When it has done so you will discover flaws: places where

the varnish has sunk, built up too thick, or contracted into wrinkles. The remedy is buffing—virtually a combination of sanding and polishing. There are various methods of buffing; the simplest is to use flower paper (sometimes known as 'wet and dry') wetted with water; but the best answer is to use the finest grade of flower paper obtainable, with a little Vaseline instead of water. You can use a sanding pad, but take care it is

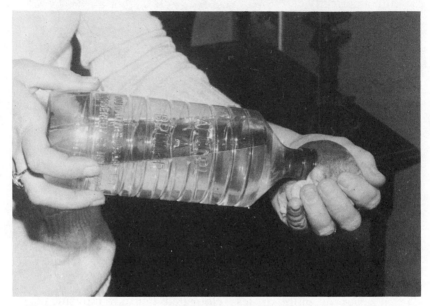

The pad can always be freshened up with spirit when it starts to get sticky

not too soft and supple, otherwise it may catch on the rough places and raise the surface instead of reducing it. This is impossible with something harder, such as a cork pad; better still is a wooden block with bevelled edges.

Before you carry on again with your polishing, clean the work carefully to remove any dust or lubricant left after buffing. Thorough wiping may be enough, but it will do no harm to go one better and polish the surface with a chamois leather or a sponge—a natural sponge, *not* a plastic one.

Continue applying polish as before, and if necessary, buff

again after the second coat. The great essential, if you want
first-class results, is to let your work dry thoroughly every
time.

Finally, after a twenty-four hours' drying period, you can,
if you feel sufficiently sure of yourself, 'make the final
movement', as the expression goes.

This is a very simple process but demands a delicate touch.
With a perfectly clean pad of very closely woven stuff, dipped in
spirit alone (special finishing spirit is obtainable), go over your
work for the last time, *very* quickly and lightly, using figure-8
movements at first and straight passes forwards and backwards
to finish off. The object of the final movement is to impart the
ultimate perfect gloss. The unmixed spirit must not be given
time to dissolve and soften the dry polish but should just coat
the surface, so that, on drying, the polish is perfectly equalized
and shows no traces of the movements of the pad. When drying
is complete, you can if you wish polish the work with a
chamois leather wetted with a very little of your polish mixture,
taking care not to shake or stir it this time, so that the varnish
at the bottom, which is very slightly abrasive, does not mingle
with the liquid on top.

A TIME-SAVING METHOD

New products are continually tending to cut out long, tiresome
processes and difficult, skilled operations. Sealing the grain
with pumice powder, which is the key to successful French
polishing, can now be by-passed by using a *hard base*, a ready-
made liquid seal; followed by careful sanding, this produces a
fairly good result. It is fair to add that products such as this are
always being improved, and it will not be long before they
entirely supersede the conventional methods. On the foundation provided by a liquid seal the polish can be successfully
built up either with a pad or with a brush; in the latter case the
polish will be one of the alkyd varnishes, whose consistency
renders them self-equalizing—they spread out smoothly of

their own accord after application, and hardly shrink at all in drying.

SPECIAL PROBLEMS: A FEW HINTS

Stained wood or stained polish?

The beauty of French polishing lies mainly in its transparency, hence it should be as nearly as possible colourless. Tinted polishes should be used with great circumspection. It is much better to stain the wood to the desired shade before polishing. The stains available for the purpose are either water stains or spirit stains.

Water stains are made either of a natural colouring agent, vegetable or mineral in origin, or else of aniline (a coal-tar extract), dissolved in water.

If the shade you want can be achieved with a natural colouring agent, such as walnut juice or logwood, you can be quite sure of getting a fast colour, whereas some of the aniline colours are sensitive to ultra-violet light.

Spirit stains are usually made from aniline.

Water stains take a certain time to dry and have the drawback of bringing up the grain. You will therefore have to sand *after* staining, which of course may alter the colour a bit so that you have to put on more stain. At the same time, sanding after staining has the advantage of emphasizing the decorative quality of the grain.

Spirit stains dry almost instantly, so that you do not have to wait long before polishing. The only risk is that the colour may deteriorate if the piece is much exposed to sunlight.

We hasten to add that colouring agents are being improved all the time, and some makes bear the word 'Permanent' on the container, meaning that they do not react to light.

Scratches on French polish

The polish must be renewed over the affected area. Everything depends on the seriousness of the damage. To treat an ordinary scratch, sand lightly to equalize the surface and try to soften the old polish with spirit. If it dissolves and goes tacky, spread it out with a pad on which you have placed a little fresh polish. Proceed exactly as for normal polishing but avoid overloading the frontier of the sanded area. Sand lightly between coats.

How to clean French polish

Plenty of preparations are sold for this purpose, but not many of them are both effective and safe. The famous 'popotte'[1] beloved of antique dealers, has never been superseded. Merely rub on a little with a soft cloth and wipe carefully afterwards. The effect is usually excellent.

French polish to which a wax furniture polish has been applied: furniture which was originally French-polished has sometimes been subjected to treatment with furniture polish at a later date. These useless accumulations can be removed with the aid of petrol (gasoline).

To renew 'tired' French polish: even if not actually scratched or flaking, French polish sometimes loses its brilliance after many years. A pad dipped in polish will quickly rejuvenate it.

1. A mixture of beeswax and linseed oil, with a little turpentine.

Learn How to Dismantle a Cupboard

ARE you moving to another house? No doubt your family furniture includes grandmother's monumental cupboard— vast, heavy, the Immovable Mass, as you are only too well aware. Nevertheless you have made up your mind to give it a place of honour in your new home. Don't worry; it can be taken to pieces; not a particularly hard job.

You will need help; the separate pieces, though not very heavy, will be awkward to handle. The first stage is to remove everything that comes apart easily, without special measures.

Usually, the cornice is a sliding fit, with nothing but gravity to hold it in place, and in most cases the top of the cupboard is fixed to it; so that removing the two together is just like taking off the lid of a box. In some cases, the doors are mounted on invisible pivots known to joiners and cabinet makers as pivot-hinges. These are small metal plates let into the top and bottom rails and fastened with screws. By taking out only *one*, the top one, you can lift out the entire door.

Undo the two or three screws holding it and wobble the door to and fro to make the top plate slide in its groove. In re-assembling the cupboard you will perform the same operation in reverse order, getting the plate into position first and putting the screws in afterwards, guided by the existing screw holes.

Hinges of the visible type present no problem. Open the doors at right angles and raise them so as to lift them off the pins.

Having got the doors off, take out the shelves. If they are a tight fit they can be loosened by a smart blow from underneath near one end, with the flat of the hand. Always take out a shelf by raising one end; the other can then be lifted from the cleat supporting it.

We now come to the tricky part of the job: *taking out the*

pegs. Pursuing our comparison with a box, we can say that each main component of the cupboard is a complete entity: (1) the top, (2) the doors (already removed), (3) the sides and (4) the bottom. Never take the pegs out of these components themselves but only out of the pieces connecting them, namely (*a*) the top and bottom side rails, and (*b*) the rails of the back of the cupboard. Usually each bearer has two pegs, giving a total of eight pegs for the sides and from eight to sixteen pegs for the bottom.

Something you cannot do without is a drift or a punch, 4 or 6 in. long (10–15 cm.), with a diameter slightly less than that of the pegs, say $\frac{1}{4}$ in. or $\frac{3}{16}$ in. (5 or 6 mm.). Joiners and cabinet makers frequently use a large nail with the point sawn off.

You will drive the pegs from *inside* to *outside*. Sometimes they protrude slightly on the inside. Tap them sharply to start them, taking care to hit straight. Then take hammer and drift to get them out.

In practice, it is unusual for all the pegs to respond to the drift; some refuse to budge at all, others break up *in situ*. The only thing to do with these is to drill them out. You simply drill a hole exactly in the centre of the end of the peg, using a bit of exactly the same diameter as the peg; the peg turns into sawdust and its hole is left clean.

The conventional $\frac{3}{8}$-in. (8-mm.) twist bit, which is the right size for pegs, does not act well when used with end grain. Moreover, if not accurately centred it leaves bits of the peg sticking to the sides of the hole. Use a plain gouge. This simple tool acts on a different principle from other types of bit, and centring occurs automatically through contact with the sides of the hole, thus leaving nothing behind. Not everyone is aware of the existence of gouge bits, which are intended precisely for this purpose. They can be purchased from any well-stocked hardware store.[1]

1. If you prefer using an electric drill, don't try using a gouge bit. Begin by using a drill with a much smaller diameter and make a starting hole as a guide, about $\frac{1}{4}$ in. deep; then drill out the peg with a drill of exactly the same diameter as the peg. Incidentally, make sure first that your electric drill has a big enough chuck; the smallest electric drills are not quite big enough for this job.

After removing the pegs, take off the whole side of the cupboard, starting at the top. Use a wooden mallet, or failing that a hammer, and a piece of wood to prevent marking. Tap, or hit, all over the part being removed.

The first components to come away will be the top rails. It is a good thing to hold them in place while dismantling; if they are allowed to fall out the leverage may well result in snapping off a tenon inside its mortise. This precaution applies particularly to the top front rail; the rear ones are held in place by the panels. After removing the top rails, deal with the bottom ones in the same way.

Because the cupboard is about to lose one of its sides and will therefore be in danger of toppling over, prop it from underneath with telephone directories, a small stool or any other suitable object. This is a vital precaution.

The back, which may be in two parts and constitutes the final operation, is unlikely to give trouble. A long or medium cold chisel will help you to lever it apart. A useful precaution is to make marks with chalk or a pencil so as to know which part corresponds to which; this is never a waste of time. Nothing is more annoying, when reassembling, than to find that the screw holes don't line up. And of course this always happens just at the end!

Reassembling consists of repeating the dismantling operations in reverse order. The old pegs, without exception, will have to be replaced with new ones. You can buy good oak pegs but they have one defect: they are four-sided; in other words, square in section, which would look rather crude on a fine piece of furniture. But don't make too much of a business of rectifying their shape; just take a flat chisel and smooth off their sharp edges. They will then be octagonal in section, which is quite good enough. After putting them in, cut them off flush with a panel saw or combination saw, smooth them (on the outside) with fine glasspaper, stain them to match, then wax them to seal the grain and give them the same patina as the rest of the cupboard.

A FEW HINTS

Suppose you have finished reassembling your cupboard and find that the doors don't close quite as they did before. Either they stick at top or bottom, or, on the other hand, have a tendency to swing open of their own accord. This is a matter of levelling. Experiment with thin blocks under the feet of the cupboard until you get the level right.

The doors and the cornice are the parts most likely to get knocked about in transport. Put the doors together with a blanket or a sheet of corrugated cardboard between them, and their inner sides facing outwards. Remember to take out the key and to remove any protruding metal fitments. Pad the cornice with corrugated cardboard and protect its corners with corrugated paper tied on with sisal string.

To reassemble a cupboard whose joints are a close fit and don't want to go together again, lay it on its side. You can then forcibly re-insert any tenons which are obstinately too tight. Rubbing them with a lump of pure beeswax or paraffin wax will make your work easier.

Gilt on Wood

GILDING—whether encountered on picture frames, carved panels, console tables, armchairs or pier-glasses—commands our interest both by its intrinsic decorative value and by the distinction it is capable of adding to an *ensemble*. On the other hand, nothing plumbs the nadir of vulgarity so surely as gilding carried to excess. In connection with gilding as with everything else, the lover of antiques, including antique furniture, is always discovering afresh that good taste is born of moderation.

The keynote of gilding is preciosity, which characterizes the material itself, its handling and the preparations for its use. The application of gold leaf demands a skill most amateurs can never hope to acquire. It would be pointless to present the reader with the recipes and procedures of the few remaining practitioners to be found in the Faubourg Saint-Antoine in Paris and a handful of old-world workshops elsewhere. There is nothing mysterious about the technique and we shall include a summary account of it, but manual skill is incommunicable and is not to be acquired from printed directions; it demands time, observation, practice and, if it is to be raised to the level of an art, the heavenly gift of talent.

IN GILDING, 'LESS IS MORE'

Fortunately, furniture or carvings, or an antique piece of any kind, or some motif forming part of it, can be re-gilded by others besides specialists. You can certainly undertake minor repairs and rescue operations, or enhance the brilliance or character of some small item picked up cheaply. We can help you here—*provided* you remember that repairing gilded pieces

Gilding: engraving of a workshop scene, one of the illustrations in
the *Encyclopédie* (1751–66)

should never degenerate into a kind of outrageous face-lift. The
age of a piece is part of its very essence and generates much of
its charm. If, in the worn patches, the reddish foundation under
the ancient gold leaf is glimmering hazily through, don't feel
obliged to slosh the thing with gold all over and give it a
brilliance which, so far from resembling the splendour of its
youth, will be a meretricious parody. Always use gilt sparingly.
This is the counsel not of economy, but of taste.

GOLD LEAF

As we have pointed out, it would be a mistake to attempt
gilding with gold leaf in accordance with a technique which is

many centuries old and which is still carried on by a few craftsmen; only a specialist is capable of this slow, minute, complex work which, as described in 1772 by M. Watin in a volume of instructions regarded as a Bible in the trade, requires no less than seventeen separate operations! A daunting prospect.

People have always been looking for new tricks of the trade in order to bypass some of these operations, and above all, for a satisfactory substitute for gold. We shall enumerate these in passing. But the worst difficulty of all, in our opinion, lies in building up the foundation (undercoat) before putting on the gold leaf. Cutting a long story short, it is a matter of mixing parchment size or hide size with whiting (very fine plaster—known in France as *blanc de Meudon*) and Armenian bole (a kind of ochreous clay) and applying several coats of this mixture to the carvings or mouldings, using a very fine brush; each coat must be sanded and polished and the details re-carved. As can easily be imagined, the thickness builds up unevenly—in the hollows, for instance—and has to be corrected. As soon as a coat has been applied, the gilder taps the back of the piece so as to spread the mixture by vibration. After drying—which takes a number of hours—the whole business of re-carving, sanding and polishing has to be done again. The actual gilding, after such preliminaries, might seem to be a mere formality; but this is far from the case.

Do not attempt to renew the gilding on a frame, for example, unless the foundation is in good condition and the carving simple. There is no need to resort to any complicated recipe; specialized firms can supply you with a ready-made preparation, a gilding base or sealer. Give the frame a careful cleaning, then apply this mixture with a very fine brush. It is absolutely essential to give it time to dry. Let it have at least forty-eight hours.

When the surface is well and truly dry, put on the actual gold. Gold leaf is sold in books, each leaf separated from its neighbours by a thin sheet of paper. The leaves are usually square (84 × 84 mm., or about $3\frac{1}{2}$ in.^{2}) and $\frac{1}{1000}$ mm. thick (if 'thick' is the word). This extreme delicacy accounts for the ease with which the material adjusts itself to the minutest details of a carving, and its readiness to adhere almost automatically to the foundation. A simple but necessary precaution is to eliminate draughts in the room where you are working; otherwise your gold leaf will curl up into a useless, crumpled ball. Professional gilders use calfskin pads (with the flesh side outwards; in bookbinding and most other things it is the hair side which is outermost) made from the skin of a stillborn calf (which is peculiarly fine in texture), of perfect quality and protected by a thin frame. You can either procure one of these for yourself, or improvise a substitute. The fact that the gold leaf is supplied in books makes it easier to handle because each leaf is stuck to its protective sheet of paper and consequently holds more securely.

CARVED AND GILDED FRAMES

Apply the gold leaf, with no further preparation, straight on to the freshly applied 'mixture' and dab it gently with a cotton-wool pad held between finger and thumb (the old craftsmen always used a hare's foot—possibly for luck!). Smooth the leaf down with little or no pressure; tap it with the fleshy part of a finger-tip if you like; a sable brush is useful for intricate details. Put on the gold leaves one after the other, with a slight overlap at the edges. Always do the smooth parts first, then those in relief.

Proceed gently: gold leaf is the easiest stuff in the world to fray or tear. If you have to shift a piece after putting it on, slip a piece of card under the edge or, better still, the tip of a gilding knife. If you need to use a small bit of leaf, say on a detail or a join, it is a simple matter to cut it with the knife and transfer it sticking to your finger-tip, which you can make sufficiently damp and greasy by first rubbing it on your forehead (this is what the professional invariably does).

When finished, your gilding will look far too new and

uniform; it will need to be given a patina—'browned', as the professionals say. Their recipe is to use fine agate, but you will be most unwise to imitate them. Be content to protect your gold with a thin coat of varnish. Choose a varnish with a slightly brown tint; when the first coat is dry put on a second, concentrating particularly on the hollows so as to heighten the parts in relief.

SOME USEFUL EXPEDIENTS AND VARIANTS

Genuine gold is expensive, but various copper alloys provide acceptable substitutes; most 'gilded' mouldings sold commercially are produced this way.

If you find the gold leaf not sticking down properly, try slightly damping the surface of the mixture; but do this very cautiously and never moisten the area of more than one leaf at a time. Use a very pure mineral water, such as Evian, freshly opened.

To keep costs down, in the 18th century and for some time thereafter recourse was had to a stratagem which is interesting for more than one reason. Silver leaf was used instead of gold leaf. The work was then given a coat of brown varnish, or of a preparation based on shellac, which made it look like gold. There were lots of workshop 'secrets' of this kind. Among the most interesting is a preparation which was known as *vermeil*. The recipe is not easily translated into contemporary language, although all the ingredients can still be found in the highly specialized shops of the Faubourg Saint-Antoine in Paris: *rocou* (a red dye), 2 oz.; gutta percha, 2 oz.; vermilion, 1 oz.; dragon's blood (a resin used in making varnishes), $\frac{1}{2}$ oz.; *cendres gravelées* (lees of wine, calcined), 2 oz.; the whole to be boiled with water until a syrupy consistency is attained. Directly before use, gum arabic water (4 oz. of gum to 1 pint of water) is added. (1 oz. = 30 grammes; 1 pint = 0·93 litre).

However antiquated this mixture may sound, it does give a fine warm glow to the 'gilt', even when the latter is silver! We have not quoted the procedure in such detail in order that amateurs should become fakers; far from it. But, for one thing, it is well that lovers of antiques should increase their knowledge. And, for another, every time we have seen an example of this silver 'gilding' we have been struck by its genuine beauty; it has a character of its own, and we sincerely believe it has been mainly handicapped, and restricted in use, by its reputation as a substitute, an 'imitation', whereas it is really a highly decorative material in its own right.

To end this rather specialized section, it is worth mentioning a fairly blameless stratagem which was frequently used by professionals. Gold leaf was applied only to one half of an object—chandeliers and church ornaments in particular—the remainder being given a matching coat of ochre. This expedient was of course confined to pieces intended to be seen from one side only.

GILDING FOR EVERYMAN

Take a brush . . .

How much easier it is to do it this way! You merely buy a pot of gold paint from a hardware shop and brush it on. But if you opt for this solution, choose your gold paint with due care. And to make assurance doubly sure, don't put it on straight away; make two or three trials of your paint on something else before setting about your delicate task. Different shades of gold paint are procurable: old gold, dark, pale, glossy, matt; choose the one best suited to the piece.

When the paint has dried, polish it with a little beeswax on a soft rag or piece of cottonwool.

Remember that for good results you will need at least two brushes, the smallest being for the carved parts.

There are various treatments you can apply to gold paint if you want to. When it has dried it looks too new and artificial, and different ways of giving it a patina leap to the mind. A brown varnish is the obvious answer. It always accumulates more in the valleys and less on the raised parts, giving rise to intriguing contrasts. You can also amuse yourself with an ageing varnish or a cracking varnish (see the chapter on Pictures).

Varnish gilding

After thoroughly cleaning and drying a piece that requires gilding you can apply a special *vernis à colle d'or*; failing this, use an ordinary varnish, either clear or pale brown.

Use a small flat brush and avoid accumulations of varnish in the hollows. Then take a fat pinch of gold dust between forefinger and thumb and blow it at the varnished surface, to which the airborne gold will duly adhere. Only a little breath is needed, otherwise the gold will fly all over the place. Alternatively, you can use a paper tube or a squeezer-dispenser of the sort made for insecticides. Despite being rather unorthodox the method produces remarkably good results. When you have achieved an even covering of gold, leave your work to dry; when it has done so, give it a coat of melted paraffin wax with a soft brush. The finishing touch, when the wax has cooled and hardened, is to polish it with a ball of cottonwool screwed up into a pad.

Removing gilt from a woodcarving

Stripping the gilt from a carved piece also entails removing the various undercoats.

To a bowl of very hot water add bicarbonate of soda and detergent powder (between 10 and 20 grammes per litre of water). The detergent is indispensable: among its properties is that of reducing the surface tension of liquids and hence of increasing their power of penetration.

Stir the solution well, dip a sponge into it and rub the old gilding. This will have to be repeated several times. The ideal method would be to immerse the object completely in the liquid, but of course this is hardly practicable.

Finish off by scrubbing with a stiff brush to remove the last particles of gilding from the crannies of the carving. It is amusing to glance at the dictionary of chemistry of Cadet Gassencourt, presented before the Academy of Sciences in the late 18th century, in which the author analyses the best ways of removing gilt from wood and concludes that it is sufficient to plunge the article into a cauldron of water on the boil. Which leads one to the reflection that chemistry began with the invention of hot water!

LOOKING AFTER GILDED WOOD

Cleaning gilded wood is almost no problem, because gold is not subject to corrosion and any dirt coming into contact with it is confined to the surface.

As already mentioned, good results are obtained with soapy water, applied with a small brush to penetrate the details of mouldings and carvings. Ordinary alcohol (such as methylated spirits) is also an excellent agent, perhaps the best, for the care of gilt; it should be followed by polishing with a chamois leather.

One can also use one of the workshop recipes of the professional gilder. After brushing all the dust out of the surfaces, add a few drops of bleach to the white of an egg and beat until thoroughly mixed. Apply the mixture with a flat brush; the resulting film, when dry, can be picked off like scales, taking any dirt with it. In another version of the recipe, a handful of salt is used instead of the bleach.

At all times, avoid any cleaning process which might get out of hand once the original undercoat is laid bare. This—the layer of whiting and parchment size—needs nothing stronger than water to dissolve it.

There are a few popular recipes which are amusing to try and, as we know from personal experience, safe.

Onion juice, or grated onion, can be put on with a brush and will brighten but not damage the gold, which should then be washed with water and polished with a soft cloth or chamois leather. If the gilt is very dirty a satisfactory result can be obtained by rubbing it with a sponge dipped in undilute vinegar, and then washing it with water.

PART FOUR

BRONZE

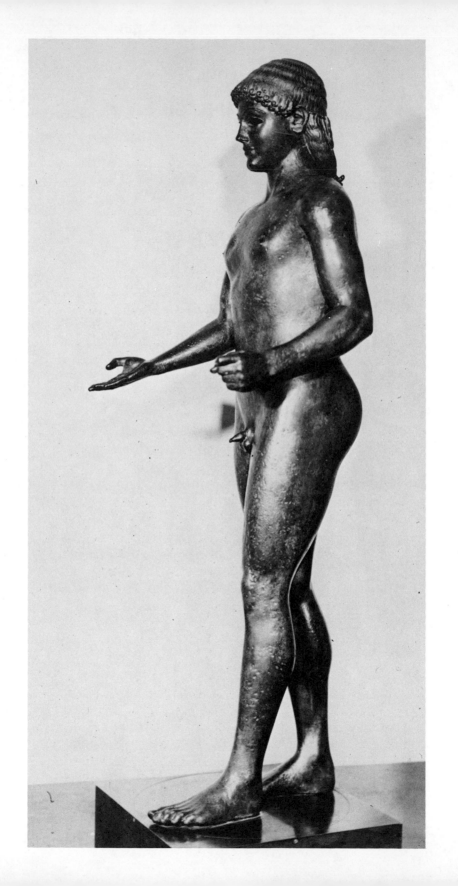

Bronze, the Universal Metal

BRONZE has been known to man from remote antiquity, as can be seen from the modern name for a major division of prehistory, the Bronze Age. It probably emerged as a chance discovery, since in those times the ores of copper and tin were mixed together and smelted directly. The 'tin' of the ancients was produced in this way. The art of bronze-founding, which was developed in Mesopotamia and Egypt some three thousand years before Christ, was flourishing in Crete by about 2000 B.C. As yet, archaeologists have discovered only small figures (statuettes) in Crete, which implies that large ones were the exception. The big classical bronzes, such as the Zeus of the Artemision and the ephebus of Anticythera, are few, but there are a great many small figures, reliefs and domestic utensils, which were finished with the chisel and embellished by the addition of gold or silver.

The Western World, discovering Far Eastern art in the 19th century during the Empire period in France, became aware for the first time of the exceptional quality of Chinese, Korean and Japanese bronzes, and of their antiquity: bronze vessels have been found as far back as the Chang dynasty (15th century B.C.). In Japan, however, it was only towards the 3rd century A.D. that works of art in bronze appeared in abundance and variety: vessels, mirrors and drums, including the famous drums in the temple of Karagor. The Japanese sculptors went on to achieve an art of infinite refinement in their colossal figures; the most celebrated example is the *Trinity* of Kodo.

As for the Romans, they summoned to their aid the best artists in Greece, who, among other things, embellished the Circus in Rome with more than three thousand statues. Today, in Naples Museum, there are one hundred and fifteen bronze sculptures and a large number of articles of furniture, excavated from the ruins of Pompeii.

Information about the bronze-founders of the Middle Ages is scanty. The few known names include those of Jean de Dinant, who signed the lectern in the cathedral at Tongres, in Belgium, and Laurent Urim, who cast Louis XI's tomb.

It is stated, not altogether correctly, that the knowledge of the master bronze-founders of antiquity had perished by the Middle Ages and that there was no longer anyone capable of casting the colossal statues which were the pride of ancient Rome. The Renaissance, with its love of architectural ornament, made many attempts to rediscover the lost art. France, however, seems not to have been interested in this reawakening; under François I there were two foundries in the kingdom but their function was purely military—they cast nothing but artillery pieces. Anecdotal tradition maintains that Benvenuto Cellini achieved the masterly rediscovery of the forgotten skills and presented them to the world by casting his celebrated figure of Perseus. This rather overlooks his most famous predecessors, such as his master, Michelangelo, and Verrocchio and, in the Middle Ages, the anonymous Mosan bronze-founders to whom we owe the door at Hildesheim and the cathedral door at Gnesen, those incomparable bronze monuments cast in a single pour in each case, as long ago as the 10th and 11th centuries.

French national pride can console itself with the thought that the leading figure in the revival of bronze-founding at the Renaissance was a Frenchman, Giovanni di Bologna, whose real name was Jean de Boulogne and who was born at Douai. It was not until the 17th century that bronze began appearing as a component in furniture, with the advent of Charles-André Boulle. The 18th was the century *par excellence* of the adaptation of bronze to furniture making: bronze, in the form of handles, rings, locks and mouldings, became the indispensable partner of exotic woods. It was also used in the ornamentation of clocks and candelabra. Artists abounded, masters of their period as well as their art: Caffieri, Duplessis, August Galliène,

Mantelpiece with pilasters in the form of quivers. Marie-Antoin-
ette's boudoir. Bronzes by Gouthière

Leblanc, Saint-Germain, Martincourt and Gouthière, perhaps the most famous of them all.

In the last century, bronze sank into the decadence common to all the decorative arts.

Today, bronze is being rediscovered by a few artists. But is it really a modern material? Is it not too strongly reminiscent of the admirable works of the past? How rare is the talent which can devote itself to such a tradition yet have nothing to fear from the inevitable comparisons! Still, our confidence is strengthened by these contemporary artists and their attempts to create new forms in their chosen material. For them, as for the ancients, bronze remains the symbol of the immortality of art.

Genuine or Fake?

TECHNIQUES can be so perfected, and the experience accumulated in a traditional craft can become so great, that imitations of the highest quality become possible. We ourselves have seen this happen and in some instances have admired the results. Moreover, we hasten to add that bronze-founders in the artistic field do not use their skill and knowledge to deceive anybody—it is rather their customers who not infrequently do that!—but in order to render faithfully the forms handed down from the past. For in this context, as in some others, the painful observation has to be made that we are living on the creativeness of earlier centuries and that our own period, apart from a few novel adaptations, will go down as having produced nothing new. From this summary judgement, however, we must exempt figure sculpture, and, for the record, an attempt by Diego Giacometti to rejuvenate certain aspects of the use of bronze in connection with furniture design.

Imitation, be. it said, is subject, even when carried to the pitch of genius, to certain inherent limitations. We admit that these are elusive, and that to recognize them on sight doubtless demands a deep familiarity, born of experience. But that familiarity, that certainty, is precisely what we prize. In a piece of knitting, a single loose stitch is enough to unravel the whole; and in a work of art a single clue, however tiny, is enough to give the game away, no matter how skilfully it has been played. Nor should instinct be underrated. May not the instinct which attracted us to certain objects or forms in the first place also be capable of alerting us in the presence of the factitious, the artificial? In any case, we are convinced that instinct frequently amounts to nothing more than common sense. People are deceived only if they want to be. There is no masochism in this; it is, rather, the dreamer's capacity to abandon himself to his dream. In the ultimate analysis, the lover of beautiful things who lets himself be taken in might well lay out his time and money to worse advantage. The object he acquires, after all, is the fruit of others' skill. What is to be avoided is not so much being wrong, as committing an error of taste.

Imitation need not find us completely helpless. For a start, we can appeal to our visual memory. If you find yourself tempted to buy something, it is wise to analyse the feelings which attract you to it. Perhaps their cause is commonplace— the object conveniently fills a gap in your decorative scheme; it is, let us say, the very chandelier you were looking for, or just that item of door furniture (as certain metal fitments are called) required to put the finishing touch to your front door; in which case there is nothing more to be said. On the other hand, it may have given you that slight, but unmistakable, 'shock of recognition' which characterizes the presence of a work of art; and this brings us to the heart of the problem. What gave you this sense of recognition, what buried mechanism was activated by the object's appearance? Were you reminded of a similar object which you had seen illustrated in specialized journals or books, or admired in a museum or a friend's collection? Reflect a little; in some instances the resulting mental images will tell you that your response was engendered not by your instinct for a work of art but merely by memory and familiarity, just as in a crowd one sees a face one thinks one knows yet cannot be quite sure whether to speak or pass on. Sometimes the image will be sharp enough for you to identify it exactly. This is the moment at which to compare it with the object itself. Absence of the creative spirit is what shows up the fake. A faker *imitates*, he never innovates; if he did he would not be a faker. The most dangerous species of faker is no doubt the *pasticheur*, the man who is an adept at turning out an article 'in the manner of' some great master, but it should be remembered that, while a work of high quality is always harmonious and approaches perfection, pastiche is essentially the *accentuation of faults*. Most fakes are imitations of something well known, because it would not pay the faker to imitate anything else.

Until the end of the 18th century, bronze ornaments on
furniture were always conceived as an integral part of the
whole piece, formally speaking. But during the Directoire and
Empire periods, decorative motifs became something applied to
the piece; they were impeccable in execution, as before, but an
army of nuts and bolts was necessary to fix them on. Every
element had become a separate creation. Mechanical aids crept
in, such as lathe turning and the grinding wheel. Whatever the
work gained in the way of exactness and symmetry was more

Gilders at work; an engraving from the *Encyclopédie* (1751–66)

than offset by the loss of vitality and freedom. Nevertheless, bronze-workers continued to constitute an élite among craftsmen.

Is it a simple matter to tell modern work from antique? Yes, in our opinion; the difference consists not so much of skilful or clumsy workmanship as of higher or lower cost. Any bronze piece, fresh from the mould, is only a rough approximation to the finished article. It has yet to be worked up on the lathe, trimmed, chiselled and polished. But just how is this tool work done?

At the present day, accurate reproduction work, using the old methods, is perfectly feasible; there are craftsmen who, in work of the highest quality, employ the same techniques of chiselling and mercurial gilding as their predecessors in the *Grand Siècle* (the age of Louis XIV). But commissions of this kind are exceptional; not many customers can afford them.

You would have to acquire first-hand knowledge of the bronze-worker's tools in order to detect signs of them on the motifs: the chiselling, chasing and pearling, the beadings and delicate acanthus leaves and so on all have their own special tools, usually made by the craftsman himself to suit his own requirements.

Not having this knowledge of the craft, content yourself with examining all the bronze parts for traces of hand-tools and for any slight asymmetry. Tooling is in itself a sign of quality, even if the craftsman has abandoned his hand-tools in favour of mechanical aids. Conversely, distrust any bronze work in which the hollows and crannies have been left rough, as they came from the foundry, only the parts in relief and any smooth accessible surfaces having been polished, of course by machine; what you are looking at is undoubtedly an industrial product, mass-produced or thereabouts.

If possible, scrape the reverse side of one of the dubious bronze mounts. Examine the colour of the metal thus exposed and think of what is said in our chapter on 'Different kinds of bronze'; this will enable you to gauge the quality of the material.

Check on the patinas. Consult the chapter on 'Bronze and its patinas'; you will not take long to distinguish an artificial patina from a natural one.

Finally, there is the question of gilt bronze. Three techniques have been used. Mercurial gilding: this was the only method known to the ancient world; and no other was used before the end of the 18th century.

For completeness, mention should be made of *gold nitrate gilding*; and finally there is gilding by *electro-plating*, which employs electrolysis to cause molecular deposition. This is the method used industrially. It produces excellent results but, unlike mercurial gilding, makes it possible to deposit a very thin layer of gold, which will wear away sooner. To tell the difference between the two is a delicate matter, virtually impossible unless one has some mean of gauging the thickness of the gilt. But there is this consolation, at any rate: gilded bronze means quality. We need hardly add that this applies only to art bronze; we are not referring to the vast output of anodized industrial products ranging from bathroom fittings to cocktail trolleys. But we trust the reader needs no prompting from us to make such a distinction.

Different Kinds of Bronze

A KNOWLEDGE of bronze and its states of conservation, enabling one both to judge it and to take care of it, will be acquired more easily if we examine some of the names and the numerous varieties of the alloy to which they are applied.

As most people know, bronze is an alloy of copper and tin.

Bronze has been much used both for artistic purposes and for the manufacture of articles useful in everyday life; this is a result of its properties, namely its low melting-point (1083 °C., 1981 °F.), suitability for casting, hardness, mechanical strength, sonority, brilliance when polished, and, above all, its colour, closely resembling gold. Bronze is made by adding tin to molten copper, the surface of the liquid metal in the crucible being protected by a layer of charcoal and a deoxidizer, usually cupro-phosphorus.

The proportion of copper to tin in the class of alloys known generally as 'bronze' has always been thoroughly haphazard, and is so still, in our opinion, where the manufacture of bronze for artistic purposes is concerned.

However, some attempt has been made to standardize the proportion in terms of the various uses for which the alloy is intended. Here is a brief review of these proportions.

For making medals and coins from flat sheet, 3–8 per cent of tin. These malleable bronzes are hard-wearing and keep their polish and colour well. They are also produced in bars (flats, squares, rounds, etc.) and wire, the latter being much used in jewellery.

8–12 per cent tin for machine parts, gears and anything exposed to sea water or certain other chemically aggressive media (some automobile parts, at least at one time; taps and other plumbing components, etc.). This would be of no interest to us here were it not that the Greeks and Romans made their bronze in this proportion.

13–20 per cent tin for high resistance to friction (bushes, bearings). At the present day, 83 per cent copper to 17 per cent tin is the ratio used for bronze destined for casting works of art.

20–30 per cent tin for casting bells and cymbals. Bronzes in this range have a low capacity for damping their own vibrations, hence their sonority.

30–40 per cent of tin is found in the bronze mirrors of antiquity. Bronzes in this range are hard, brittle and white. They polished exceptionally well and were thus highly suitable for their purpose.

67 per cent copper to 33 per cent tin is the ratio used at the present time for domestic purposes.

The colour of the bronzes mentioned so far varies according to the tin content and ranges from pink through greenish yellow to greyish white. The colour of any bronze object is a trustworthy criterion.

We shall indicate in due course the ways in which differences in period can be detected by observing differences in the metal. The composition of bronze displays a certain development down the centuries. As we have indicated, the amount of tin in bronze manufactured for a given purpose was far from constant; as time went on, moreover, other metals were added in an attempt to embody their special characteristics in the alloy, the most attractive of these being doubtless their cheapness.

An admixture of zinc, which is cheaper than either copper or tin, makes casting easier. Lead, similarly, makes the bronze easier to machine and also increases its plasticity, so that bronze containing from 5 to 30 per cent lead is used for moving parts in machinery. The same type of bronze also occurs fairly frequently in Roman coinage.

These bronzes containing tin and lead are those most commonly used on account of their comparative cheapness and their suitability for machining. In theory, this range contains from 5 to 8 per cent tin, from 2 to 5 per cent zinc and from 1 to 5 per cent lead. But this classification is not very meaningful: when bronze of this type is used for a work of art, as is sometimes the case, the chief qualities aimed at are easy casting and a particular shade of colour, and the aim is pursued in a throughly empirical manner.

Modern founders often use bronze provided by the scrap-metal industry, and I hope I shall not be accused of denigrating certain contemporary works of art if I point out that they owe a good deal to the plumbers, who by supplying old taps and gas-mantle burners for melting down have made themselves very useful to the bronze founders. In such circumstances, it is obviously impossible to specify the exact composition of the alloy produced.

To complete our review of the bronzes now in use, and the names of some of them, we mention:

'Paris bronze', *le bronze parisien*: an alloy of 88 per cent copper, 10 per cent zinc, 2 per cent lead. 'Bronze' is a mis-nomer in this case; the metal is brass with a little lead in it. Because of its pinkish golden colour and its working qualities it is much used for making jewellery, ornaments and trinkets, the so-called *articles de Paris*, whence its name.

The quest for cheaper bronze resulted in alloys containing as much as 25 or 30 per cent zinc, during the last century and more particularly in the first part of this one. There must be a multitude of clocks, hanging lights and small sculptural figur-ines which were made of this metal and are still in good condition, despite the brittleness of the material.

For clock making, which demanded very delicate castings and complicated assemblies, the founders rejected orthodox bronze, preferring an alloy consisting of exactly 80 per cent copper, 4 per cent tin, 14 per cent zinc and 2 per cent lead; a compromise between bronze and brass.

White metal is used industrially for its low coefficient of friction; it consists mainly of tin, with small quantities of copper, antimony and lead. An alloy similar to it, but not identical with it, was used in large quantities during the early part of this century as an imitation bronze for manufacturing cheap ornaments, such as allegorical or rustic ornamental mantelpieces.

This 'white metal', wrongly so called, was usually zinc thinly coated with bronze by means of galvanoplasty, or else a mixture of zinc and lead. The fracture of this alloy is characterized by the brilliance of the metallic crystalline structure. 'White metal' objects are usually regarded as worthless. But everything is grist to the mill, and some antique dealers will have a 'white metal' article polished up, rendering it shiny and somewhat similar to pewter. One use for such things is to turn them into lamps, sometimes with quite happy results.

WE END OUR SURVEY WITH

'*Zamac*', and escape from this tangle of genuine and spurious alloys through the back door, as it were; that is, by turning to the subject of fakes. '*Zamac*' was not developed by fakers but is frequently used as a substitute for bronze, despite resembling it neither in properties nor in appearance. It is an alloy of zinc and lead which casts easily, has about the same specific gravity as bronze, is cheap, readily accepts different patinas and is easier to carve or chase than genuine bronze. But why should the amateur concern himself with all this?

Simply to avoid being taken in. Some unscrupulous dealers, telling rather less than a half-truth, may offer to sell you pieces which they say are made of 'Zamac bronze', *bronze de Zamac*, whereas the officially authorized name is *fonte zamac*, 'zamac alloy'. Quite a difference!

Bronze and Its Patinas

PATINA is not, in itself, a guarantee that a supposed antique bronze is either old or genuine. Present-day bronze craftsmen claim to be able to reproduce any patina by chemical means. Collectors say it can't be done. Whom is one to believe?

In the chapter on 'Bronzes from excavations' we shall discuss what constitutes a patina and what does not, in cases where time and the atmosphere have wreaked some degree of destruction. In the present chapter we shall not go so far back but shall glance briefly at bronze in its normal states of maturity.

Velvet black

This patina is specially typical of Far Eastern bronzes. As its name indicates, it is a fairly deep black; sometimes it has a bottle-green sheen. The finest velvety patinas of all are said to be produced by stroking with the human hand.

Green

Bronze from the ancient world (see 'Bronzes from excavations') exhibit many different shades of green, particularly blue-greens. All are caused by copper oxide mingled with extraneous substances.

'Embugadon'

This name is applied to a reddish-brown patina common to many Eastern and Far Eastern pieces (including Indian); sometimes it is as deep in colour as wine-lees.

Commode in the *salon des jeux de la reine*, Château de
Fontainebleau

Medallion black

Fairly dark, with glints of brown; almost matt; perfectly smooth; found on medals and on Egyptian bronze figurines.

Renaissance rose

Sixteenth-century bronzes have a very beautiful patina, usually brown, but on the parts in relief the metal shows through —a very characteristic pinkish-yellow ground (typical of Florentine bronzes).

Domestic articles of the 16th and 17th centuries exhibit various patinas, many of which recall the 'black velvet' patina of Far Eastern bronzes on a ground of light yellow with a cool gleam.

Of course all these different shades, named or unnamed, depend wholly on approximate appreciation; they are subjective. In most cases they are the direct outcome of the composition of the alloy, the treatment to which it has been subjected and in some cases the use to which the article has been put, and the substances with which it has come into contact.

'ARTIFICIAL' PATINAS

Workshop secrets for the treatment of bronze abound, according to traditional craftsmen. They may or may not be right.

Bronze having formed part of industrial manufacture for the last one hundred and fifty years at least, it must be difficult to shroud any of the stock techniques in secrecy. Certainly every craftsman may have his own special skills, or a favourite chemical recipe—probably not much different from the next man's—but that is as far as it goes.

BAIN DE BARÈGES OR *PIERRE DE BARÈGES*

It is not exactly known what this substance, *pierre de Barèges*, 'Barèges stone', owes to the Pyrenean spa from which it takes its name; probably something to do with the sulphur in the waters. In any case, 'Barèges stone' is a colouring matter which forms the basis for several patinas. The bronze is first thoroughly cleaned, preferably with mild acid (such as vinegar), coated with a special varnish or with 'ageing' oil and rubbed with *pierre de Barèges*, which is available in various suitable colours for use on bronze.

Polish

The piece to be treated is strongly heated and then given a coat of ordinary wax. The liquid constituents of the wax evaporate and the colouring matter is left on the metal. After drying, the piece is rubbed with a cloth to shine it up and brighten the parts in relief.

A 'natural' patina

Here is a much-used method which gives a fairly natural-looking patina. The piece is well heated and plunged into clean mineral oil. The bronze instantaneously loses the brand-new appearance which it inevitably possesses as it comes from the craftsman's hand, and acquires a warm colour.

'Antique' green

This can be produced with *pierre de Barèges*; another way is to use sulphuric acid, somewhat diluted. The resulting oxidation can be fixed with varnish or beeswax.

The most convincing 'antique' green of all can be attained by a method anyone can use, with the co-operation of an obliging chemist or drugstore. To 100 grammes of acetic acid, add 10 grammes of ammonium carbonate, 10 grammes of bay salt, 10 grammes of potassium tartrate diluted with a little water. Coat the bronze with this mixture and leave it exposed to the air for two or three days, by the end of which time it will have turned a beautiful green. Tidy up the oxidations with a brush and apply a coat of wax.

Deep black

Here is a common device which works like a charm on bronze furniture mounts that look glaringly new. A quick dip in ammonia gives them a blue-black gleam. Ammonium carbonate blackens them completely. All you have to do is to complete the patina with a little wax, or a mixture of Sienese earth and turpentine, and polish up the articles slightly so as to emphasize the relief.

THE CARE OF ANTIQUE BRONZE

The patina of a bronze must be respected, there can be no argument about that; one should never reduce bronze to the brilliance of well-polished copper or brass. It is generally agreed that bronze should retain the imprint of time which adds to its character.

A bronze in good condition can be cleaned with soapy water and a soft brush which will penetrate the detail. After rinsing, it should be dried in dry air (on a central-heating radiator or an electric radiator), then hot-waxed with melted beeswax. When the work has cooled completely, remove excess wax with a brush and rub with a woollen duster.

The Care of Bronze Mounts on Furniture

BRONZE on genuine antique furniture has in most cases been gilded. Metal polish would merely have the effect of wearing the gilding away and eventually eliminating it. At first this appears not to be so, because the brightness of the bronze looks like gilding, but in the long run the discoloration of the metal will draw attention to the difference. Admittedly the gilding will be worn away only on the raised parts and will remain intact between them: on the other hand, the accumulated residues of polish, wax and dust in the hollows will prevent the gilding from being seen.

FIRST STAGE: CLEANING

A soft brush (preferably of vegetable fibres) and some soapy water (with the possible addition of a little detergent) will enable you to get rid of the encrusted deposits which have accumulated in the details of the bronze motifs. Persevere until everything is completely clean. You will then see at once whether any gilding is left. Gold does not corrode and is therefore bound to regain its brightness directly it is cleaned. Rinse and dry the parts you have washed.

To prevent water from running over the rest of the piece, keep a sponge handy or else protect the surface with a sheet of plastic held down by adhesive tape.

IF ANY GILDING IS LEFT

Bring your bronzes back to their original state of polish by rubbing with a chamois leather. Don't use a polishing paste; it

Metal-gilders in their workshop

contains abrasives. At most, use tripoli or some similar harmless powder, applying it dry and working with a light hand; then dust the motifs with a soft brush.

IF NO GILDING IS LEFT

This gives you a free hand; you can't damage what isn't there.

Thoroughly clean the bronze parts and then shine them up with any of the established metal polishes used for brass. But at all costs avoid accumulations of polish in the crannies; on drying out they turn white. So remove them with a brush before shining up.

A few time-savers

On clean bronze, whether gilded or not, apply a 1 : 1 dilution of nitric acid. The metal shines immediately. Rinse, and rub with a soft cloth or a chamois leather.

Another mixture, which is slightly more complicated but gives excellent results, is 20 grammes of nitric acid in 80 grammes of water, with the addition of a little aluminium sulphate.

Cabinet makers pressed for time use concentrated nitric acid to which they add a little common salt and a little lamp-black.

Whenever possible, bronze mounts should be removed before cleaning; most of the preparations used for cleaning or stripping them are harmful to wood or varnish.

The preparations mentioned here will work most efficiently if the items to be cleaned are first heated to about 100 °C. (212 °F.).

To remove the mounts you can pull out the nails with a pair of electrician's pliers or pincers, using a piece of cardboard for them to bear against so as to avoid marking the bronze or the wood. Sometimes the mounts are fixed by screws, in which case take care to use a screwdriver of the right size.

Once clean and shiny again, the mounts can be protected against tarnishing by means of a clear varnish.

Bronze Sculpture and Its Editions

BRONZE sculptures, provided they are not of monumental size, have everything to attract the collector: a profusion of forms and styles, *plus* famous signatures and the interest of the different 'editions'. Demand is continually rising for short runs (small editions) dating from the late 19th or early 20th century, particularly of the works of Rodin, Pradier and Maillol and of the *animaliers* (animal sculptors) such as Barye, Rosa and Isidore Bonheur, Pompon, P.-J. Mène and others.

This increased demand obviously invites forgeries, especially as most of the works concerned are old enough to be no longer subject to copyright. There is, however, one peculiarity which unmasks the fakes. The faker naturally needs a genuine work from which to make his copy; this is called *surmoulage* (there seems to be no specifically corresponding term in English). In principle this ought to yield a perfect replica, but in practice there is always a definite though varying degree of shrinkage; we can take it as being about 10 per cent of the original volume. There are several reasons for it, all simple, the main one being the expansion of the molten metal and perhaps of the mould as well. Another is that the original went through the usual finishing process, it was tooled and polished; the same will apply to the replica and this means a further reduction in size.

So be careful when buying a *bronze d'édition*. Demand a certificate of genuineness or consult a specialist, unless you are gifted with an intuitive eye for size and, moreover, are familiar with the dimensions of the original.

On the first edition it is usual to find a second signature. This is the founder's stamp; examples are Hébrard for the bronzes

of Daumier, Barbedienne for some (but not all) of those of
Barye, Mène, Fratin, etc.[1]

This second signature, though not an absolute guarantee, is a
valuable indication.

The goddess Bastet (bronze). Egyptian, Saïte period

1. A peculiarity of the last-named is that the signature on his original
bronzes has the N of Fratin the wrong way round (И). Forgers have taken it
on themselves to correct the supposed mistake and so have given the game
away.

Bronzes from Excavations

BRONZES from excavations, whether Oriental, Greek, Roman, Etruscan or Gaulish in origin, speak with the voice of the past. Usually small, they are figurines or other objects which time and conditions underground have attacked in a greater or lesser degree, though we hasten to add that bronze is highly resistant to deterioration of various kinds. It has been found that after an initial phase of surface oxidation a buried object becomes stabilized; deterioration slackens and becomes gratifyingly slow. The oxides cause chemical reactions in the surrounding soil and mineralize it. The real danger comes with disinterment: corrosion springs to life again. The chlorides that have eaten into the bronze absorb water vapour from the atmosphere, and ignorance of the real nature of bronze and hence of the correct precautions and treatment can result in nothing being left on the shelf of a display case but a mound of green dust, a derisory monument to an object now defunct.

BEWARE OF OAK

Roman coinages were subject to frequent devaluation: sometimes they were minted in more or less base metals, and there was a whole numismatic period, about 500 B.C., when currency was manufactured from lead bronze. Not all collectors are able to house their treasures in cabinets lined with plush or velvet; sometimes they use an ordinary cupboard— not realizing that an oak drawer may be fatal to their choicest finds. Oak, in fact, gives off exhalations of acetic acid which combine with lead and transform it into a carbonate. The first symptom of this chemical attack is the presence of a greyish dust on the surface of the object. Don't wait for further developments, re-house your collection.

EGYPTIAN BRONZES

It is hard to lay down general rules for these figurines and other objects; the alloys are pretty haphazard and some are short of tin, that metal having been very scarce in ancient Egypt. Most contain lead. The dry, hot climate of the banks of the Nile has had a strongly preservative effect on the pieces that have come down to us, and the Cairo Museum has the reputation of providing the most salubrious environment in the world for the fruits of excavation. It is observed, however, that the oxidation of bronze, and in particular the agglomerations of copper salts on the surface of the object, have picked up silica in varying amounts. There is general agreement today that Egyptian bronzes should be cleaned, their concretions removed and the original colour of the metal brought to light.

There is an important question of principle here: ought the oxidations coating the majority of excavated bronzes to be removed or not? For many years it was held that the green colour produced by copper salts was like a signature authenticating ancient bronzes. Today the preference, whenever possible, is to restore the object to its original appearance. There are two arguments to suggest that this course is not arbitrary. Careful cleaning has often revealed details (chisellings, encrusted decoration, gilt and even inscriptions) which would have remained hidden under the layer of mineralized oxides. Again, it is dangerous not to know what reactions are going on beneath that layer; whereas if the object is clean it is easy enough to tell whether the surface is active or not. A covering of alien substances might delay detection until too late.

BRONZES FROM GREECE, ROME, GAUL AND ELSEWHERE

A good quality of alloy was used for many of these, the tin content being the very correct one of from 8 to 15 per cent. Their state depends on their age and the conditions surrounding them at the time of discovery. Don't hesitate to clean them; real concretions are very hard and only those foreign bodies which are loosely attached will come off, a desirable result from every point of view. The contemporary doctrine on conservation is to remove everything which is 'exterior' to the form and leave what is 'interior'. Just what does this mean?

An object from an excavation has undergone molecular changes; oxidation is not specifically a superficial phenomenon but coincides with zones of weakness in the metal, microscopic fissures. It is therefore largely interior. The copper salts, as we have mentioned, colonize their environment and eventually effect a mineralization which engenders stable substances: nitrates and carbonates such as malachite and azurite. This mineralization is, by definition, *exterior*, at least as regards its visible part. It is the proof of the genuineness of the object; some of it, therefore, should be left undisturbed provided it does not ruin some harmonious line or volume.

These indications are a guide in exposing fakes. No fabricated 'patina', no deterioration artificially contrived with acids or other chemicals is capable of marking the very substance of which the faked piece is made. Experts are well aware of this and can test the genuineness of the piece merely by passing a hand over it.

HOW TO CLEAN BRONZES FROM EXCAVATIONS

We must preface our directions by counselling moderation. Anything which might damage an object or diminish the signs of its authenticity must be rigorously avoided. On the other hand an ancient bronze, if it is to be preserved at all, does require a certain amount of treatment. In prescribing it, we must adhere consistently to the principles and methods we have assembled for your benefit.

An object still covered with soil, etc., should be gently brushed. When its general outlines have become recognizable the brushing can be assisted by a scalpel which will loosen identifiable extraneous substances.

Provided you can see nothing abnormal—notably a tendency on the part of the object and the matter clinging to it to come away in pulverized form—wash the bronze in a bath whose composition must be *strictly* as follows:

> *To every $\frac{1}{2}$ litre of water*: 90 grammes of sodium or potassium tartrate (*sel de Seignette*); 30 grammes of caustic soda; and a little hydrogen peroxide.

Any chemist or drugstore can provide the ingredients.

Place the object in the mixture. It is of course a sensible thing to try a little of the mixture on part of the object first. After ten minutes, take the object out and examine the effect. In theory, all foreign bodies will have dissolved except the mineralized accumulations. Help things along by brushing. If no reaction has occurred, reimmerse the object for another thirty minutes or, at the most, one hour. If you notice any change of colour on the part of the object, particularly a reddish tinge, take the object out and rinse it, then place it in water to which 5 per cent of sulphuric acid has been added. This completes the washing process, though you can supplement it if you like by a rinse in a mineral water of high purity, such as Evian, which may produce a beneficial effect by dissolving any chlorides remaining in the fissures of the surface. At this stage in the cleaning there is an essential check to be made, namely whether these chlorides are present or not, because the accelerated oxidation observed in objects from excavations depends in fact on the presence or absence of chlorides in their molecules. How are you to tell whether there are any chlorides there and, if so, how do you get rid of them?

CONCEALED CHLORIDES

Facilities exist in specialized museums for making scientific analyses to detect and chemically identify these chlorides. This is something you can't do, and it doesn't matter that you can't.

Your method is as follows: it is exactly the same as that used by the restorers employed by the museums in question.

After washing the object, get it absolutely dry.

In doing so, *never* heat it above 100–120 °C. (212–248 °F.); at any higher temperature expansion would produce new microscopic cracks and open the door to further chemical attack. Use an infra-red lamp, an electric fire or a hair drier; in other words, a source of *dry heat*, free of noxious combustion products like those of gas.

Improvise a 'damp chamber': any sort of container which can be tightly closed, in which to place some water and the object to be tested; the latter, of course, not being in contact with the water. The humidity will soon show up in chlorides; they will become visible in a few hours. You will recognize their presence by droplets of water on the surface of the object, characteristic tiny globules, slightly cloudy, sometimes with a 'skin' on them, like blisters on the patina. If you dry them with blotting paper they will re-form in a few hours.

It is an excellent omen if the phenomenon is only slight; a small amount of chlorides is easy to neutralize, as we shall shortly show. If, on the other hand, the drops are prominent, special treatment will be necessary. Complicated and highly complicated processes exist for eliminating chlorides, notably by ultrasonics. *The effectiveness of the process suggested here is equalled only by its simplicity.*

Prepare a mixture by dissolving some gelatine in 1 litre of water at boiling point; add 2–3 grammes of agar-agar and 6–10 grammes of glycerine.

Here again, all the ingredients are in common use and can be found in your chemist or drugstore.

Cover the object with the mixture as thickly as possible; the coating should be 2 or 3 mm. deep. Wrap it in thin aluminium foil (chocolate 'paper' or cooking foil), place the parcel in the damp chamber and leave it. After a few hours you will be surprised to see that the aluminium is being corroded; it will have a hole in it somewhere, or several holes. Wash the wrapping—with the object still inside—being specially thorough at and round the holes; put on a little more of the gelatine mixture and cover the holes with pieces of foil.

Continue the process until the foil wrapping is used up; you can then thoroughly clean the object, apply another coat of the mixture and put on a new wrapping.

When all the chlorides have migrated from the bronze to attack the aluminium, you will see that the 'blisters' which previously disfigured the object have disappeared, leaving a clean surface. Finish off with thorough rinsing, followed by brushing and drying.

PRESERVATION OF BRONZES

Do not let the object cool after drying; it would absorb humidity. On the contrary, this is the moment to dip it in melted wax (60 °C., 140 °F.), a mixture of natural beeswax and 5 per cent of carnauba wax (a very hard vegetable wax with the comparatively high melting point of 110–120 °C. (230–248 °F.), which can be obtained from specialized firms which deal with cabinet makers. It is worth noting that some high-quality furniture polishes contain carnauba wax).

When the object has cooled and the wax has set you have only to polish it up with a soft cloth. The same very simple method is applicable to bronzes in good condition or only slightly affected. It has the advantage of neutralizing the chlorides by isolating them from the humidity of the atmosphere. You will do well, however, to take the precaution of adding a fungicide to the wax (a few drops of formaldehyde, for example), so as to protect it from the possibility of attack by micro-organisms.

ANOTHER METHOD, AND SPECIAL CASES

An object which is actively crumbling, becoming powdery, must not be subjected to washing, which would probably be fatal. Certain factors have caused the tin in the alloy to become dissociated. The only possible course is to consolidate the surface by impregnating it with cellulose varnish. The first coat should be heavily diluted (five or ten times more solvent than varnish), the others less so. If possible, apply the varnish by dipping.

CAN BRONZES BE REPAIRED?

This is too specialized a question for us to deal with it at any length. Every case must be studied separately. However, plastic resins have now opened up huge possibilities which cannot be better utilized than in repairing antique bronzes, especially as some of these resins can be coloured so accurately as to merge perfectly with the whole.

BRONZES FROM EXCAVATIONS

France has a greater wealth of metallic objects brought to light by archaeology than any other country in the world. These collections, scattered in some nine hundred museums, represent a total of at least 150–200 tons!

To restore all the objects deposited in these museums would take three thousand years. But the matter possesses a yet more serious aspect. It is thought that an object which has survived fifteen hundred years underground may totally disintegrate in fifty or a hundred years when exposed on a shelf in a display case.

PART FIVE

ADHESIVES

ADHESIVES: TABULATED INFORMATION

Materials	Adhesives recommended	Points to watch
All species of wood. Carcase wood, joints, ply, insulating board, compressed wall-board	Vinyl adhesives Fish glue Casein	Cramp parts together Beware of damp For rough surfaces, oily woods, low temperatures. May stain wood
Wide areas of contact in any material. Fibre board, veneers. Laminates.	Neoprene contact adhesives	Coat both surfaces and allow to dry for a few minutes before contact
Plastic tiles, mural sheets, plastic floor coverings. Anti-damp coverings (insulating or foil-backed board)	Acrylic adhesives	Same technique, but position of parts can be adjusted after contact, before adhesive sets
Joints intended to resist humidity, water or hydrocarbons	Resorcinol adhesives and plastic resins	Temperature not less than 15 °C. (59 °F.) Follow makers' directions closely; they vary, but are always essential to produce the required chemical reaction Don't use resorcinol adhesives on porous surfaces. If necessary apply a second coat after the first has dried
Polyvinyl Polyethylene Plastic floor tiles	Solvent-based adhesives	Coat both surfaces thinly; allow to dry before contact Avoid bubbles or air pockets
Expanded polystyrene	Special mastics Synthetic resins	Apply in blobs These behave like neoprene but do not dissolve expanded polystyrene

Materials	Adhesives recommended	Points to watch
	Certain vinyl adhesives	Ask manufacturers about the characteristics of these
Glass, enamel, metal, faience, marble	Epoxy resins	Use in atmosphere of not less than 15 °C. (59 °F.). Coat both surfaces and let them partially dry Remove superfluous resin with alcohol before it sets N.B. There is a one-part contact variety
Textiles	Latex adhesives	Contact only required
Wallpaper, cardboard	Starch adhesives Cellulose adhesives	Dissolve in water Dissolve in water; allow to stand for thirty minutes before use

Modern Adhesives are Revolutionizing Traditional Skills

O F all the numerous discoveries placed at the disposal of antique restorers in recent years those of the adhesives industry, with its plastic resins and special solvents, are undoubtedly the most astonishing. But technical progress, it should be remembered, is always a matter of specialization. Grandad's famous old glue, his stand-by for everything from joinery to marquetry to bookbinding, has been ousted not by one product but by ten.

The following outline of the principal uses of modern adhesives may therefore not be out of place.

WOOD

For all ordinary joints—tenon-and-mortise, butt joints, dovetail, half-lap joints, etc.—*vinyl adhesives*, as a rule, will be found appropriate.

These are white or transparent liquids with a pleasant smell and a long shelf life (which makes them practical for occasional use). They stand up to moisture pretty well but are unhappy at low temperatures, which cause them to dry slowly and stick badly.

Many manufacturers have improved their vinyl glues by adding special ingredients which (or so they tell us) result in producing a completely all-purpose adhesive, suitable for concrete, leather, plastics, laminates and so on. We shall come back to this when reviewing these materials individually; for the moment we shall confine ourselves to general guidance. Vinyl adhesives are very powerful when used thinly. They cannot be recommended for joining irregular surfaces requiring a thick layer of glue. Some of them set quickly, others take

longer, but as a general rule it is advisable to apply a reasonable amount of pressure to the joint so as to ensure a thin,
strong film.

Never prematurely subject a joint to the load it is going to have
to bear; it is always safer to wait for twenty-four hours.

Warning! Beware of vinyl glues which separate into several
layers; they are usually badly balanced emulsions and in any
case deficient in vinyl and owe their viscosity to the addition of
talc, which naturally tends to sink and form a deposit. Glues of
this nature lack the quality required for decent work.

Fish glue: provided the material to be stuck is wood, cannot
be overlooked. It has one grave defect: it does not stand up to
damp. It smells unpleasant but holds well; however, its day is
really done now.

Casein glues, on the other hand, are an old-fashioned
adhesive which is still far from obsolete for certain special
purposes, notably for working in cold weather and for use on
oily varieties of wood. You may not know that most of the
exotic woods, such as teak, lignum vitae, South American rosewood and hickory, produce oily exudations which interfere with
adhesion (before gluing or painting any of these, clean the
surface with trichlo or white spirit). Some resinous woods,
such as red pine and yew, have the same peculiarity. Casein
destroys the exuded substance and is therefore valuable in
making it possible to use these woods. Moreover, casein is
effective on irregular surfaces, because it does not shrink when
drying and keeps its strength when put on thickly, even on
badly made joints. Cramps should therefore be only lightly
applied. so as to avoid squeezing out the glue; their only
purpose is to hold the members in contact.

Drawbacks of casein: it is vulnerable to damp, and some
kinds of wood, such as oak and mahogany, are discoloured by
it.

Wood responds well to every type of glue, but special cases
frequently occur.

Let us take a quick glance at one such case: the question of fibreboard or compressed wallboard panels, which you certainly won't encounter in old furniture but which you may want to use for lining a cupboard, for example. A good general rule is to stick them with a vinyl adhesive, laying it on a little thicker than usual to allow for the porosity of the material. Alternatively, neoprene glues—'contact' adhesives as they are called, because cramping is unnecessary—are very suitable. The pieces being joined become totally inseparable the moment they are brought into contact. To obtain this effect, *both* surfaces must be glued: each is given a very thin film of adhesive and allowed to dry until it will no longer stick to the fingers. Only then are they brought together; adhesion is ensured by striking here and there with a hammer, of course with a piece of wood to mask the blows and prevent marking; and that is that, the job is done.

Neoprene is indicated for numerous purposes but is best suited to sticking large surfaces which give its limpet-like quality full scope. The following are its main uses:

1. Fibreboard panels.

2. Laminates (superimposed on wood).

3. Veneering; neoprene makes this much easier, particularly on curved surfaces. The bulky old veneering presses—specialized equipment indeed!—are now totally unnecessary. Traditional cabinet makers distrust neoprene but this may be merely lack of familiarity (see the chapter on marquetry).

4. Finally, the very special case of surfaces which are damp themselves and are going to be exposed to damp after covering with another material. The highly volatile solvents incorporated in neoprene adhesives evaporate on coming into contact with water and make it possible to apply the covering material in conditions which would defeat any other type of adhesive.

Another class of special cases: Resistance to fresh or salt water and, in some circumstances, to hydrocarbons (as in the moulds used in boatbuilding); a field which calls for *resorcinol* adhesives or for *plastic resins*, both of which usually consist of two separate substances.

Plastic resins are cheaper than resorcinol. They are usually in the form of a powder (ureaformaldehyde) and a catalyst. Some manufacturers specify their being mixed with water, others with a special solvent. The resulting joint is of almost mineral hardness. The physical and chemical reactions of the resin or resorcinol demand certain conditions, laid down in the manufacturer's directions. These should be followed to the letter; we cannot give them here.

The observation most frequently made is that these adhesives require a certain degree of warmth—not less than 15 °C. (59 °F.)—in order to 'take' properly.

Another observation from experience is that the joints on which adhesives of this type are used should be very exact or else should not be subjected to movement and stress. The film, which, as already indicated, is very hard, may also be brittle, especially if it is thick.

To avoid making this chapter over-specialized, and omitting to specify some of the modern types of adhesive on the ground that they are of no interest to the restorer, we have drawn up a comprehensive tabulated summary (pp. 159–60) of these products, experience having taught us that no limits can be set to the technical needs which may arise in the physical rehabilitation of a work of art.

HOW TO STICK PLASTICS

There is no need to emphasize the part played in our lives by plastics for wall coverings, floorings, household articles and so on. The difficulties encountered in exploiting these new materials have demanded the creation of special adhesives: some solvents 'burn' some plastics or, alternatively, simply inhibit adhesion.

Every kind of plastic covering will accept neoprene glue (a thicker grade is used for this). But *acrylic adhesives* should not be overlooked: they have one advantage over neoprene, namely that surfaces stuck together with it can be shifted about while the drying (which is not instantaneous) is still incomplete. Thus one has a few minutes' grace in which to rectify an error when using plastic tiles, for instance, or even porcelain tiles.

On *polyvinyl* and *polyethylene*, solvent-based adhesives are very suitable. Spread the adhesive thinly on both surfaces, leave it for a few minutes while the solvent evaporates and then bring them together, avoiding air pockets. Finish off by rubbing vigorously.

Be careful with expanded polystyrene: it is the odd man out in the plastic family. Most solvents attack it. It is fixed either with a special mastic put on in blobs about the size of a walnut or hazel nut (at the four corners of a sheet about 30 cm. × 30 cm., for example), or with synthetic resins. The latter 'take' instantly, like contact adhesives.

Glass, *enamel*, *metal*, *faience* and *marble* are best suited by epoxy resins. These are expensive but will stand up to just about everything, including temperatures of 300 °C. (572 °F.) and considerable mechanical strain.

We recommend double gluing (i.e. coat both surfaces), and partial drying before contact. Any dribbles of adhesive squeezed out of the join should be carefully wiped off with spirits while the resin is still liquid (see the various chapters in which this type of adhesive is mentioned, with full details of how to use it).

TEXTILES

These have entered interior decoration in a big way, as tapestries and wall hangings. Latex adhesives, one of the adhesive industry's most successful creations, are just the thing for instant hemming, attaching edgings, repairing canvases or putting on patches. Usually supplied in handy dispensers, they stick at once, by contact alone. It no longer makes sense to use the old-fashioned methods now that we have latex adhesives (which also stick leather).

Finally, the best adhesives for *paper* and *cardboard* are still *starch* glues (soluble in water), or *cellulose* glues (which should be dissolved in water and left to stand for half an hour).

PART SIX

CRYSTAL

The Matchless Transparency of Crystal

LEGEND has it that, in some remotely ancient period, a party of merchants who had landed on the coast of Phoenicia used blocks of saltpetre to prop up their cooking pot, and that the saltpetre became fused with sand from the shore to create a hitherto unknown substance: glass.

In reality, glass was known in the countries of the East certainly not later than 3000 B.C. The custom of burying glass objects in tombs appears to have been common both to Southern Egypt and to Assyria.

For readers who like literary references one may quote Aristotle, who mentions that in Greece there were 'glass mirrors lined with polished metal'. Our own 'silvered' mirrors could hardly be better described.

The Latins, who were better at copying than inventing, began by importing glass from Egypt; later, in Nero's reign, it was manufactured in Rome. A large number of glass factories sprang up in 'the capital of the world'; it is even thought that, by 210, there was a glassmakers' quarter, a neighbourhood in the city exclusively occupied by them. Glass was turned on the lathe; it was also carved, like silver. It was used for covering interior walls in houses, probably in the form of mosaics. Everyday Roman glassware consisted of drinking cups, perfume bottles, perfume jars and so on. In the catacombs, objects known as 'Christian glassware' have been found which are engraved with religious scenes and symbols.

In the 10th century of our era the most highly esteemed glass was imported from the East by the Venetians; early in the 13th, Venice herself became the largest Western centre of glassmaking. In France it was not until the early Renaissance period, under François I and Henri II, that the glass industry made an appearance and the first royal workshop was set up at

Saint-Germain. Colbert, in 1665, created the first royal glass factory. But it was not until the 19th century that the industry developed on a large scale and reached a huge public as a result of significant technical improvements such as the Siemens furnace; another result was the rediscovery of lost secrets, for example those of iridescent glass and spun glass.

This was the period which saw the establishment of the chief French makers of crystal and cut glass (at Saint-Louis and Baccarat, 1819; and the firm of Daum at Nancy, 1875).

It has often been asserted that these establishments are concentrated in eastern France not because of the deposits of potash, a necessary ingredient in the composition of crystal, but because the vast woodlands of the Vosges supplied fuel for the furnaces. Anecdotal sources confirm that, in those days, every glass factory had more woodcutters than glassworkers on its payroll. An odd fact, worth underlining, is that the siting of a glass factory has never been conditioned by that of the raw material. Venice, for instance, imports sand from which to make its famous crystal; and this sand comes from Fontainebleau!

The working temperature for crystal is its melting point, between 1200 °C. and 1400 °C. (2192–2552 °F.). The glass-blower picks up the right amount of molten crystal with his blowpipe and transfers it to a cast-iron mould. The mould is hermetically closed; he applies his mouth to the other end of his blowpipe and blows, to make the crystal conform itself snugly to the interior. When it has cooled, he will have obtained the cup of (let us say) a wineglass. He then takes more molten crystal and draws it out to the required length to form the stem; after which he takes another lot of crystal and flattens it to make the foot. From these three he puts together the embryonic wineglass.

This is passed on to the grinder for trimming. Every grinding operation is specifically conceived for its purpose. The speed of rotation will depend on the fineness or coarseness of the wheel selected, which in turn depends on the effect required. A carborundum wheel will be needed for the first trim. For cutting, a wheel of Alsatian grit-stone (*grès d'Alsace*) will be sufficient. Corundum, a porcelain agglomerate, is another material used for grinding-wheels.

Next, the piece will be polished on a wheel made of wood, and another of natural or compressed cork; after which it will be engraved with little cutters tipped with grit-stone, sand or emery, very like a dentist's drill. The finished glass, in its inimitable transparency, is now ready to take its place on your table or in your collection.

This technique produces perfectly uniform shapes. But there is nothing to stop you preferring the less stereotyped forms produced by master glassblowers who reject moulds and multiple polishings in favour of greater freedom, in the high tradition of the great craftsmen of the past. The piece is shaped by blowing and by an ingenious and variable combination of movements in the air and of rotating it on a smooth surface (the 'marver', a metal or marble plate). Of course the result is imperfect, in a sense. There will be bubbles in the glass, the contours will be a little irregular, and there is no chance whatsoever of your being given a complete service consisting of identical pieces. But does that matter? If you really love crystal or glass, you will be content to allow the material to impose its own laws on the technique, not conversely (and rigidly). What a pleasure it is to lay a table on which every *couvert* preserves, amid the general harmony, its own individuality and life instead of servilely duplicating its neighbours!

IDENTIFYING GLASS AND CRYSTAL

The criteria which make it possible to tell crystal from ordinary glass are quite unreliable unless backed up by considerable training. Wetting the rim of a glass and rubbing it with a finger to make it vibrate and sound a musical note, is merely a parlour trick. People say that genuine crystal produces a pure note, but in fact this frequently depends on the shape of the wineglass, cocktail glass, tumbler, vase or what have you. Common glass is sometimes delightfully sonorous.

The main thing to realize is that crystal is much stronger than glass (it contains lead, whereas glass contains barytes) but, as a result of its composition, less elastic, more brittle.

Crystal and glass, in fact, are like dogs and cats: there are various breeds, any individual specimen can be described in terms of its origin, appearance and ancestry, and the price varies too. Luckily, however, crystal and glass have their own official studbook, as it were: legal standards have been set up by which to classify them. In France, the *norme* NF B-30004 differentiates them precisely in terms of their refractive indices. (The refractive index expresses the angle through which light rays are 'bent' by passing through glass. The higher the index, the greater the degree to which light is trapped by reflection and caused to 'play' within the refracting medium.)

Let us explore the characteristics of crystal and glass.

Lead crystal is required by law to contain 24 per cent of lead. Its metallic sonority (caused by its high lead oxide content), and its brilliance, clarity and density make it the noblest material in the whole range. French master craftsmen, admired the world over, create true works of art in this medium.

Crystal contains less than 24 per cent lead but is none the less a noble material. Its refractive index is high and its purity, brilliance and sonority enable models of great beauty to be obtained from it. Crystal vessels, deeply and richly cut, contribute to the most refined of tables a charm and elegance acknowledged by all.

Crystalline has a lower refractive index but is a sonorous, brilliant and very pleasing material. Finely cut and elegantly shaped services, with decorative elements, are made from it.

Glass, with the lowest refractive index, is also the cheapest of these materials. Clear or coloured services can be produced in it, whose simple or elegant design gives pleasure in daily use.

To end our list, let us denounce an impostor. What is often called *demi-crystal* is a kind of glass intended to imitate crystal; its name is incorrect and illegal.

If we are to believe the craftsmen, crystal is above all, a feminine taste.

Glass basket by Sébastien Stosskopf (Strasburg Museum)

Crystal can only be produced by craftsmen and, in our mechanical age, is bound to be expensive. It is worth reflecting, as you sip your Saint-Emilion or Riesling, that the glass containing it may well have undergone a hundred and twenty different operations—details of which we forbear to give, yet could not leave wholly unmentioned.

IRIDESCENT GLASS FROM EXCAVATIONS

The Mediterranean basin—Egypt, Mesopotamia, Palestine, Greece and Rome—has yielded up a number of objects which fascinate collectors and are in some instances of great antiquity; they include flasks, tear bottles, *alabastres* and the like. For the most part they are small, iridescent, elegantly shaped receptacles, not very transparent. In origin they are generally funerary; this explains their miraculous state of preservation, for they are fragile for more reasons than one.

As always, the faking industry has set itself to copy them: these fakes are manufactured in Venice, the Balearic Islands, Syria and probably wherever glassblowers are still to be found.

Luckily the fakes are fairly obvious. They are always heavier than the genuine thing, whose extreme lightness is always immediately impressive. Moreover they are blown in a single operation, whereas very ancient glass was fashioned by a different technique. A core of clay was coated with molten glass; when the glass had cooled the core was washed out of the vessel built up round it. Sometimes the core was held in shape by a jacket of fine gauze. Traces of this device appear in the result, especially as the glass was applied in successive layers. This is the cause of the highly characteristic leafy tracery exhibited by this species of glassware. The inner surface of the vessel often displays concretions, usually calcareous, and these deposits are rather unskilfully reproduced by the fakers. Genuine examples, because of the long, slow process by which they were built up in successive layers, show variations in thickness and colouring; the fakes do not. The faker uses the same colouring matter throughout; usually a mixture of whitewash and ochre.

Later, almost certainly in the last two centuries of the pagan era, and probably in Greece, the technique of glassblowing was discovered. But the extreme lightness of the results, and the nature of the concretions, none the less provide a sound pointer to the age of any given piece.

ROCK CRYSTAL

The glassblowers' crystal must not be confused with rock crystal. The latter is a natural chemical compound, a variety of quartz, substantial quantities of which occur in a few deposits in the Alps, Brazil and Madagascar. Rock crystal is appreciably harder than its near namesake; it can be worked only with special diamond-faced grinding wheels. There is, indeed, an interesting degree of resemblance between diamonds and rock crystal: the sites where they are found are geologically similar, and the refractive index of both substances is high.

Rock crystal has been used from very early times for making precious objects like jewellery and amulets; it occurs in medieval reliquaries; later still, it was the material preferred for the costliest lighting assemblies—candelabra, chandeliers and ornamental candlesticks. Specialists with a great deal of experience can recognize rock crystal at a glance and do not mistake it for crystal. One can, in fact, on looking through rock crystal, detect a 'freckled' effect, presumably caused by its crystalline structure. In default of many years of practice, simply examine it in the light of common sense. Rock crystal is always worked by means of abrasion. You should therefore be able to find traces of this treatment not only on edges, motifs and facets but also on flat surfaces: though perfectly polished, they will present very slight departures from flatness here and there.

REPAIRING GLASS AND CRYSTAL

There is no proper technique for this; only expedients. Of course you can make permanent repairs by sticking broken pieces together again with two-part epoxy resin adhesives, but the join will always be visible (see directions for mending faience and porcelain).

In some cases a break can be evened out by grinding, for example on the edge or foot of a glass, but this is a craftsman's job; you are unlikely to have the necessary equipment. Metal bands can be used to repair a really valuable piece which you want to rescue from oblivion. The foot of a stemmed cup which has been snapped clean off can be stuck on again and the repair concealed by a metal band. Fine work of this kind can also be applied to the neck or handle of a carafe. Very few craftsmen are capable of such work; in France at the present time we are aware of only one restorer who regularly undertakes it.

However, there is one piece of advice which the amateur will find useful. When a piece is kept in a cabinet and never gets wet it can be simply and almost invisibly mended by using white of egg as an adhesive. This works well. Moreover, a one-stage (as against two-part) contact adhesive has recently been developed.

It takes only ten minutes to reach maximum hardness, a single drop will cover 6 cm.², and because it has the same refractive index as glass it is invisible even when used for a large repair.

LOOKING AFTER GLASS AND CRYSTAL

Crystal, being so fragile, must be looked after with great care. Its greatest enemies are dust and, if we may say so, clumsy housewives.

So the care required, though simple, is minute. There is always the danger of scratches, hence crystal should never be dusted when dry. It is always safe to remove dust by washing in lukewarm water, not by dipping in a bowl but by holding under a tap. A glass or other vessel should never be placed upside down on a hard surface, such as a draining board, without first covering the latter with a cloth or a sheet of foam rubber. This avoids chipping the rim. For drying, use a very soft cloth or a chamois leather.

PART SEVEN

COPPER AND BRASS

Copper's Rustic Glow

THE leading interior decorators have an unjustifiable prejudice against copper. True, one does all too often encounter those pseudo-countrified displays which, headed by the inevitable copper kettle and running through a line of saucepans of different sizes, crown a mantelpiece or some other favourite position; the whole effect, at once vulgar and hackneyed, essaying to mimic Ye Olde Worlde Hostelrie. Surely, however, a few necessary distinctions can be drawn?

In France, people blithely confuse copper with brass because the same word, *cuivre*, is used indiscriminately for either instead of being reserved for the reddish or orange metal in its pure state, namely copper. This very widespread material has been used for making innumerable articles of daily use such as kettles, saucepans and warming pans. It is unusual to encounter it in objects with a decorative as well as a functional role, such as candlesticks, candelabra, ewers and so on. It is not easy to be certain why; probably it was because brass looks something like gold and was preferred for items with a status above the purely practical. This is one of the few cases in which our ancestors' logic was at fault; it was well known and always had been that copper was poisonous, especially in contact with organic substances such as fat and oil. Its toxicity, though exaggerated by the ancients, made it essential for the inside of kitchen utensils to be tinned.

Brass is an alloy of copper and zinc. The Gauls are thought to have been familiar with it after the Roman conquest, and to have distinguished it clearly from bronze. It seems that the great civilizations of the Mediterranean and the Middle and Far East were unacquainted with it, producing it only by accident when making bronze.

What is certain is that, in northern Europe, the cradle of the brass industry was Dinant in Belgium and the region of Namur. The word *dinanderie* was the generic term for everything made of brass from the early Middle Ages to the Renaissance. This localization is chiefly to be explained by the abundance of zinc ore (calamine) in the valley of the Meuse, though it was not until the 16th century that the metal itself was isolated and named by Paracelsus.

Until then, the ore was regarded merely as an additive which lightened the colour of copper. And it was only in the 19th century that a chemist in Liège, the Abbé Daniel Dony, invented a rational method of extracting zinc from calamine (zinc carbonate), Napoleon I having granted him the concession of the mine at Moresnet (near Liège and Verviers).

Thus for centuries copper and zinc were combined in an alloy empirically, the nature of one of the ingredients remaining substantially unknown. Contemporary documents show that brass was manufactured at Dinant in the 11th century. But that town did not long retain the sole privilege: Lyon, Beaucaire and Paris manufactured *dinanderies*. So did certain centres in Auvergne. The Belgians' technique reached Italy and Milan had a very active community of *dinandiers*; likewise some of the German states. It is curious to note the present-day survival of the art of the coppersmith and brassworker among certain gipsy tribes of Spanish origin, now scattered in considerable numbers all over Europe. In France, members of that people are to be found at Saint-Ouen, the home of the *Marché aux Puces*, the celebrated 'Flea Market' of Paris. A specially interesting point is that in Spain coppersmithing is one of the *artes flamencos*, Flemish arts. Does this indicate a connection between the dinanderies of Flanders and the gipsies of Iberia?

COPPER ANCIENT AND MODERN

Old and modern copper are easy to tell apart. In the past, all work in copper was achieved by patiently hammering an ingot on a former. As the metal was gradually drawn out by the

hammer it was heated from time to time, to restore its malle-
ability by annealing. The article thus produced was not uniform
in thickness.

Moreover, not all utensils could be shaped in one piece; pots
and pans could, but urns, narrow-necked ewers and so on could
not, and were made by joining several pieces together. The
joins are always visible. The brazing metal employed for copper having usually been brass, the line of the join is easy to
detect and, incidentally, is seen more often than not to be
crenellated, thus extending the area of contact.

Modern copper articles are made from sheet copper
produced by a rolling mill. They are of uniform thickness
throughout. The old coppersmiths always made the bottom of
the utensil thicker than the rest, both as a precaution against
wear and in order to hold the heat, especially in the case of
cooking vessels. These features are absent in modern copperware—its manufacturers know perfectly well that it is purely
decorative in function.

But the traditional coppersmiths, such as the afore-
mentioned gipsies, while readily availing themselves of industrially manufactured copper stock, still braze their work in
the old way.

Distrust any article in which the join consists of a seam

(which is made by turning the metal back on itself and hammering the two parts together to make all tight and secure). The technique itself is not new, but it represents an easy way out which you are more likely to find in a modern piece than an old one. Finally, the following points to watch are as important as those we have already given:

Copper vessels soldered with tin should usually be rejected, with occasional exceptions in the case of objects not intended for use on the fire, such as watering cans and urns. In the latter, which are very decorative and possess great charm, only the tap and the knob on the lids should be soldered, not the body of the urn (except in the case of repairs). The coppersmiths of bygone periods made and brazed and soldered this class of objects with special care. You should also beware of any ostentatiously beautiful repoussé work—*fleurs-de-lis*, in particular. The old craftsmen did sometimes embellish their pieces with repoussé but usually engraved these motifs as well, and foliage and stylized flowers are encountered more often than elaborate coats of arms or the *fleur-de-lis*, the emblem of the French monarchy.

Reject without argument anything on which the hammer marks are absolutely regular; this is a sign of machine production for the cheap trade. Even articles whose hammering, though obviously done by hand, is too prominent, should be shunned; someone has been trying too hard! The fact of the matter is that craftsmen in the old days accepted hammering as their technique because it was necessary, but always did their best to let it show as little as possible.

If you find an article with one or more tubular handles, check for the presence of a longitudinal join in each of them. If there is none the article is modern: the maker has availed himself of a piece of copper pipe, like those used in plumbing. Here again, the choice of the easy way out, in the form of industrially produced materials, lets the cat out of the bag. It is the same with iron handles: if hand-forged, they are slightly irregular; if mass-produced, perfect.

For a variety of reasons, part economic and part technical—notably the irregular thickness which distinguishes antique copper—modern copperware is perceptibly lighter than the genuine article.

The Gipsies as Tinkers

THE most convincing hypothesis concerning the origin of the gipsies, those perpetual wanderers, is that they came from India, their migration westwards having begun about when prehistory ended. They are traditionally supposed to have brought the use of bronze to the countries round the Mediterranean. As late as 1332, the Englishman Simon Worcester made the first historical mention of these wandering tribes, at which date they were in Cyprus and appear to have been established there since much earlier. Not until 1427 is their presence recorded in Paris and, more especially, at nearby Saint-Denis (where they have been ever since) and Pontoise. Harried wherever they went, it was only in northern Europe, or to be precise in Poland, that they were given rights (and also obligations). They were allowed to follow three trades, of which

Coppersmiths at work

they held a virtual monopoly: those of the farrier, the locksmith and the tinker. This tolerance spread to the princely courts of Germany, where their skill was esteemed, and for some unexplained reason the same situation arose in Turkey, where to this day they are in almost exclusive control of the trades, and the premises, of the brass-founder, the tinker and the farrier.

BRAZIERS (BRASS-WORKERS)

By a kind of unspoken convention, the work of the coppersmith and tinker is always thought of separately from that of the brazier. While there is no conclusive justification for the distinction, it serves to underline the higher value, and in some cases the greater antiquity, of certain work in brass.

Broadly, the division is as follows. The coppersmith or tinker was responsible for kitchen utensils: pots, kettles, preserving pans, stewpans, saucepans, cake moulds, dishes, ladles and the like, urns (sometimes ornate) and warming pans. The brass-worker was concerned with what are now antique forms of lighting: candlesticks, candelabra and lanterns; and with such work as bordered on the province of the goldsmith: ewers, including the small kind for hand washing (aquamaniles), censers and so on.

The objection to this rigid classification is that, in practice, coppersmithing covered all work done by forming and drawing out a sheet of metal, whether copper or brass.

The real technical difference between the coppersmith and the brazier was that between hammering and casting. It is clear at a glance that many antique lighting devices, and even some receptacles, were made in moulds. This applies to most candlesticks prior to the 18th century; the so-called 'Dutch' candelabra; *coquemars* (a kind of kettle); the 'Beaucaire' kettles, characterized by their having two spouts and by the leonine or grotesque heads with which the hinges of the handle are ornamented (despite the name, Beaucaire was not the only place where they were made); and some other things. The techniques were often combined: the pillar or stem of a candle-stick would be cast, the base hammered, and the whole finished and polished on the lathe. Details on candelabra were heightened with the chisel. Hollow forms were frequently used to avoid unnecessary weight; the two halves were beaten to shape and joined like the halves of a shell. Some people dog-matically assert that the brass-workers always stuck to a single, specific technique, but this is not tenable. We have seen examples of cast brass, others which were hammered to shape on a former, and yet others produced by stamping, a method akin to forged ironwork. Some amateurs nevertheless scrutin-ize brass candlesticks for signs of brazing or soldering as a visible sign of antiquity. We must point out that such signs are not always present and that nothing is proved by their absence.

Certain subsidiary indications, of a purely technical charac-ter, will tell you more.

Kettle from Beaucaire

Screw threads

Really antique candlesticks are usually in two parts, the column (stem) and the base. In some cases the spindle on which the socket (candleholder) and sconce (disc or cup for catching grease) are mounted is screwed directly into the base. All the various parts are held together by screw threads, which, in

antique work, have a characteristic form. The 'lands' of the thread are a bit rudimentary, have no sharp edges and are rather stout; the grooves between them are broad and flat bottomed. Take a good look at the threads on any antique piece of established authenticity, and you will always be able to recognize them thereafter. They also occur on 'Dutch' candelabra, to fix the sconces to the branches.

Structure of candelabra

The 'Dutch' candelabra, a triumph of Flemish art, have had an exemplary career. Their design remained virtually unaltered and was uneclipsed for at least four centuries, and it is sometimes extremely difficult to date them with any certainty. However, here is an attempt at classification.

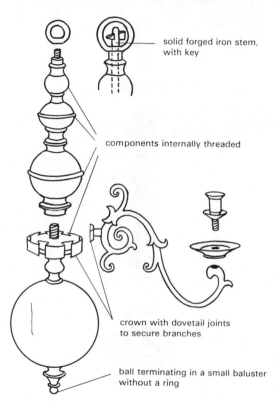

solid forged iron stem, with key

components internally threaded

crown with dovetail joints to secure branches

ball terminating in a small baluster without a ring

Prior to the 18th century:

the components are joined together either by large threaded portions cut in the main body of the metal, or are pierced by a solid forged iron stem and held in place by a key or cotter which is a force-fit in a key-way in the stem and secures the upper ring;

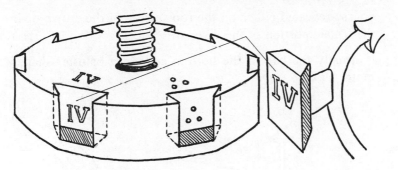

the branches are removable, being simply dovetailed into
sockets in the crown which supports them. Sometimes their
position is marked with a Roman figure engraved with the
burin, or drawn with punchmarks, the same figure being of

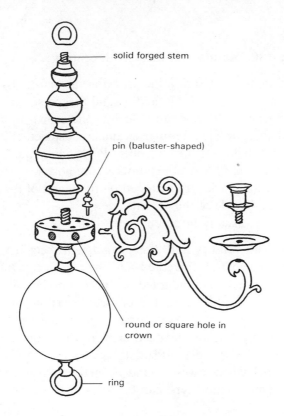

solid forged stem

pin (baluster-shaped)

round or square hole in
crown

ring

course repeated either on the top surface of the crown or in the female portion of the dovetail;

usually the ball at the bottom ends in a baluster-shaped motif, *with no ring*.

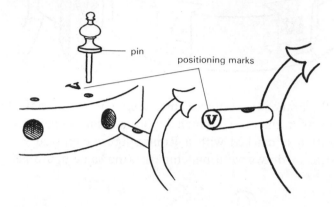

In the 18th century and early 19th century:

the components are joined together as before, by internal threads in the main body and a solid forged stem;

the arms, still removable, fit into the crown by means of round holes or square mortises and are fastened to it by little keys like balusters or ninepins. Positioning marks are as before, except that Arabic numerals are now sometimes used and that the marks are stamped on the tenon of the arm and on the underside of the crown;

a ring is usually fitted under the ball.

In the 19th century and after, candlelight became obsolete; gas lighting had been invented and the classical 'Dutch' candelabrum design was adapted to accommodate it. Hollow branches, to supply gas to the burners, were an unavoidable innovation; their shapes were gradually softened and adulterated, departing further and further from the original. Holders with clips (claws) were added, to accommodate the opaline globes. The branches were round in section and in some cases had taps. No common type can be defined:

Different combinations, unrelated to those preceding them, developed simultaneously. However, it must be admitted that the materials used were still of good quality (the brass was cast and polished). Some models are more felicitous than others and give evidence of care in design and construction.

Further development arose with the coming of electricity. Branches became solid again, and sconces, as if for candles, returned. These candelabra were adapted for electricity by means of wires with transparent insulation, *glued* to the branches and unobtrusively hugging their curves. The sconces were fitted with imitation candles and 'flame' bulbs. The branches were of course no longer dovetailed or keyed to the crown but were usually held by screws from the inside of the crown, and the whole assembly was mounted on a tubular rod. Some of these adaptations were fairly satisfactory.

Copies of genuine candelabra exist, and are tending to become commoner in the stock of dishonest antique dealers. Careful examination, with no guide other than common sense,

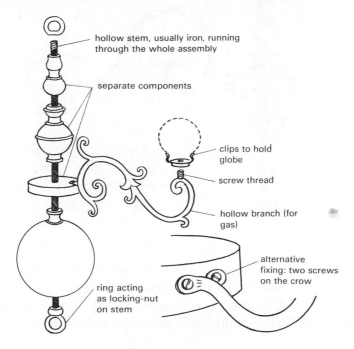

will soon put you right about them. It is enough to remember that a candelabrum which is several hundreds years old has seen a good deal of service, will have been polished innumerable times and is bound to show signs of its past.

FURTHER REMARKS

A dolphin with another dolphin's tail in its mouth, or several such pairs, are a motif often found on the branches of 'Dutch' candelabra (other motifs, notably foliage, are also found, but dolphins are the most common).

Mosque lamp. The ring supports
a coloured glass in which a wick
is arranged to float on oil

An interesting comparison for the curious who may care to pursue it is that between dolphins on the arms of candelabra and the well-known 'devouring monsters' which figure so largely in Viking culture. It is natural to wonder whether there is a decorative tradition common to the Low Countries and Scandinavia.

'Dutch' candelabra frequently display one or more specific symbols. The one most frequently found is an eagle with out-spread wings, either on each of the branches or, which is more usual, at the top, just below the ring. These symbols are simply the emblem of the Hanseatic towns, of which Dinant was one. In various other centres where candelabra were made, the motif was repeated for purely decorative reasons.

dolphin motif

foliage motif (baroque; late)

The Virgin and Child, especially in the Gothic period (the Middle Ages), are another motif occurring in 'Dutch' candelabra, at the top.

You may come across a candelabrum of 'Dutch' type whose arms are simply let into mortises in the crown, and in which the brass has been left rough from the file instead of being polished. Usually there is no ball and sometimes no sconces. Each arm ends in a ring. This type is an Oriental variant known as a 'mosque lamp'. The ring holds a coloured glass, in which a wick is arranged to float on oil.

Lovers of copper and brass will be well advised to look at Flemish painting—which in any case is magnificent in its own right—from Van Eyck to Vermeer; the many interior scenes depicted often include copper or brass objects, treated with such accuracy and detail as to be of great documentary value.

Cleaning and Preserving Copper

GROSSLY OXIDIZED COPPER

IMAGINE yourself to have rescued some antique copper vessel whose form and one-time function charmed your eye and mind. Nobody loved it; you found it abandoned in the corner of an attic or a barn, or plucked it off a heap in a scrap dealer's yard like a brand from the burning. Whatever it happens to be—a kettle, an ancient alembic, a watering can, a hand pump, a warming pan, a jug—it is thick enough with verdigris and dirt to discourage the stoutest heart.

There are various mixtures, all much alike, for resuscitating ancient copper; our own recipe is the following:

Dissolve some potassium oxalate crystals in water in the proportion of one-third crystals to 2 litres of water. If you can't get potassium oxalate, use hydrochloric acid in the same proportions but in this case make sure the water is very hot. If possible, immerse the copper article. If it is too big, wet some cloths in the mixture and wrap them round it. The effect usually occurs quickly; as soon as the bare metal appears, rinse, then polish with any good commercial metal polish.

Strong bleach in boiling water is also very effective, providing the object to be stripped can be immersed in it.

Severe oxidation will certainly not be completely removed by any of these recipes. You must tackle it with pumice powder or a metal scouring pad (used cautiously), before repeating the above treatment.

Here is a folk recipe which has been found satisfactory by generations of housewives. Put a handful of sea salt in a saucer and pour over it a little less than enough boiling vinegar to dissolve all of it. Rub the copper with this mixture but do not let the mixture run down. You will see the oxidized patches progressively brightening and will have perfect control over the stripping.

Washing soda crystals or an ordinary detergent powder (two handfuls to a litre of water) produce a deep, thorough cleansing action.

The best method for using this recipe is to take a receptacle large enough to allow complete immersion of the article to be treated; place the article in it and fill up with the liquid; then bring to the boil, watching the effect from time to time. Follow this by thorough rinsing, then polish.

HOW TO MAKE COPPER REALLY BRIGHT

If you are determined to make up your own polishing mixture, here are two recipes which can be recommended with confidence. Either should be used only on badly tarnished copper, not on anything which has been regularly polished.

Recipe 1: make a paste with tripoli and water to which about 20 per cent of oxalic acid has been added. Rub your copper items vigorously with this; finish off with a clean rag.

Recipe 2: mix 30 grammes oxalic acid with 100 grammes water. Add 40 grammes charcoal, 30 grammes alcohol (90 per cent) and 20 grammes turpentine. This results in a blackish paste which is excellent for restoring badly tarnished copper to its proper colour.

THE SECRET OF LASTING BRILLIANCE

This consists of perfect polishing, whose stages are described below, *plus* a technical trick.

'Cleaning the copper' used to be a regular annual ceremony in every bourgeois household; it was carried out in late spring, in accordance with a well established ritual which has our entire approval.

The first stage consisted of cleaning all the articles with

CLEANING AND PRESERVING COPPER   197

liquid metal polish and giving them a good rub. Next, they were polished with dry tripoli. Finally, the polishing was finished with Spanish whiting to produce a dazzling brilliance.

But this was not all. To coax a warm gold glow from brass, and to 'fix' the brilliance of copper, all the articles were exposed for a few hours to the sun.

The effect was magnificent. With a little determination you can achieve it yourself, provided you have a garden or a sunny balcony.

The best manufactured polishes in the world can never replace this series of operations. Public Enemy No. 1 for copper and brass is carbonic acid, and hence the carbon dioxide mixed with the humidity of the atmosphere. A rough measure of the increase in atmospheric pollution is provided by the frequency with which copper articles now need polishing, especially in urban surroundings; a few decades ago, once a year was quite enough.

Today, you can keep your copper and brass items permanently bright by giving them a coat of transparent colourless varnish, obtainable either in small tins or bottles or in atomizer dispensers; the latter are by far the best for applying an invisible uniform film.

Note: All the methods for polishing and burnishing pewter are also applicable to brass and copper, and the reader is referred to the chapter in question.

PART EIGHT

TORTOISE SHELL

The turtle's greatest gift to man: its shell

T HE visitor to the castle at Pau can view the cradle of that popular monarch, Henri IV, which consists of the carapace of a tortoise, upside down. To us today it seems merely unusual but in the 16th century it was an object of beauty and luxury. It seems, in fact, that tortoise shell was an unknown material to the craftsmen of the Western world until the late 15th century. This noble substance was introduced into Spain, Portugal, Italy and, subsequently, France, by the world navigators whose newly invented magnetic compasses had enabled them to push back the frontiers of the unknown.

Apparently, however, the ancient Greeks and Romans had not only been familiar with tortoise shell but had probably used whole carapaces for making musical instruments—lyre, lute or cithara. But this is not altogether certain; in all likelihood what they employed was the shell of the land tortoise, which is common in all the Mediterranean countries. The marine turtle is the only kind that concerns us here, the source of tortoise shell as we know it, that precious and noble substance. The Renaissance cabinet makers used it a great deal for encrusted decoration on cabinets and small chests; after falling rather out of fashion in the early 17th century it reached its peak in the 18th, achieving fame for all time. In the reign of the *Roi Soleil* (Louis XIV) André-Charles Boulle created an authoritative style with his furniture embodying brass-and-tortoise shell marquetry. It is no exaggeration to say that this was an official style, one whose florid ornamentation was perfectly adapted to the Versailles of Louis XIV. Tortoise shell also emerged in a triumphant profusion of such things as *boîtes à mouches* (little boxes for containing beauty patches), fans, combs, snuffboxes, frames—a burst of popularity which was also the signal for the appearance of the earliest fakes. Powdered tortoise shell was bonded with gelatine or bone glue to look very like the real thing, a practice encouraged by the fact that moulded copies of the forms in vogue could thus be produced in large numbers. However, this may not have been intended to deceive. It is a reasonable supposition that craftsmen were still groping for the technique of working in tortoise shell; it was not until much later, in the Second Empire period, that they discovered how to weld it (joining it by heat, as described below), a process apparently unknown in the 18th century.

A number of famous collections contain genuine 18th century pieces which are simply powdered tortoise shell stuck together with gelatine. This fact does not lower the value of the pieces in question; but it does impose on us the need to be highly circumspect in the matter of restoration.

After being slightly neglected in the opening decades of the 19th century, tortoise shell recaptured public favour when, under the Third Empire, the colonialist fever took hold of France, though the advent of celluloid soon brought severe competition.

Today, the subtle transparencies of tortoise shell are imitated with unprecedented perfection by the plastics industry.

But this does not destroy the refined pleasure a collector feels in the possession of objects whose value is known to himself alone.

THE MARINE TURTLE

This creature is a native of the warm seas of the world. Though widely distributed in the Atlantic, Pacific and Indian Oceans, it is in the Caribbean that it supports large-scale operations, notably in the Bahamas, which yield the celebrated pale tortoise shell. The animal is by no means a marine monster—it weighs at most 50 kilos (about 110 lb). The 'caret' turtle, which is very common, is perceptibly different; its scales are what is called tuilées and are browner, sometimes almost black, and coarser in texture. Their market value is almost exactly ten times less than that of 'blonde' or 'demi-blonde' tortoise shell. But they are much heavier: a '*caret*' turtle may tip the scale at 200 kilos (440 lb) or more.[1]

There is no satisfactory way of removing a turtle's carapace. The natives in the South Seas surprise the reptile when it is busy laying its eggs on a sandy beach, turn it on its back and light a fire over it. This makes the scales easy to detach. It must be pointed out that the turtle's carapace, though rigid, is not all in one piece but is an articulated structure.

The back is composed of thirteen principal scales with a border of subsidiary scales of a different shape; the belly, which is almost smooth, is always relatively thin. Fire has the drawback of damaging the carapace to some extent, and the method preferred when possible is to place the animal in boiling water. The death throes of the marine turtle are dreadfully long, few creatures in nature being endowed with such tenacity of life. The details are not for the squeamish: in the fisheries of the Seychelles, Madagascar and the Bahamas, which manufacture the famous turtle soup and sell it all over the world, the turtles are disembowelled and the meat is cut out in lumps from the natural receptacle formed by the carapace; and until the last moment, when the last pound of flesh has been extracted, the heart, in a horrifying pool of blood, continues to beat and flutter. Only a reflex, perhaps; but how do we know? It is a pity that turtles are not as appealing as baby seals—which (especially if one presses the comparison home) they decidedly are not. Some skilled practitioners in the Caribbean even manage to strip the turtle without killing it; they throw the naked reptile back into the sea, and provided no barracuda, shark or other predator snaps it up, it grows a new shell. Experts are not deceived by this spare tyre, as it were, whose quality never equals that of the original. One cannot help thinking that, for such a comparison to have arisen, some of these poor creatures must have undergone the same treatment several times.

1. Pale tortoise shell may fetch 600 or 700 francs a kilo; ordinary brown tortoise shell, only 50 or 70 francs.

IDENTIFYING TORTOISE SHELL

The material varies too much in appearance to be fully described, nor can any reliable standards be given for identifying it and distinguishing it from plastic imitations. It varies in quality from black to pale.

Comb by Lalique

Mediocre grades are rather opaque and are brown or black with lighter, translucent veins. An intermediate quality is 'cherry', in which the marbling is unobtrusive and the colour comparatively homogeneous. A whole gamut of different marblings can be observed as the colour range passes through medium-pale to pale; in the latter, the most valuable and highly sought after, the marblings usually coalesce into a tint whose wonderful transparencies recall the varying nuances of amber. As for deciding whether a piece of tortoise shell is real or imitation, only your eyes, carefully used, will tell you anything. Without special training, no one can claim the ability to pronounce whether the piece is genuine. The imitations are astonishingly close, virtually identical. Heating an object to detect whether it is made of plastic is unreliable (because some plastics don't melt), and may cause pointless damage. The only rational recommendation is not to buy tortoise shell except from a specialist.

REPAIRS TO TORTOISE SHELL

Tortoise shell is a living substance which has the surprising quality of being susceptible to contact welding. We shall see how this is done.

Tortoise shell has often been compared with plastics, and the comparison is not a bad one. Like synthetic resins, it is softened by heat. The craftsmen of the last century used to plunge it into boiling water to which they had added a glassful of olive oil. This method still serves, especially for treating a piece of tortoise shell which has become distorted. Put the piece in sufficient water to cover it, and bring the water to the boil. How long the piece should stay there it is difficult to say; the only guide is to examine it from time to time until it is comparatively supple. You will have provided yourself in advance with pieces of wood and weights or cramps to hold it in the desired shape, because tortoise shell quickly recovers its stiffness on being taken out of the water. The whole difficulty of repairing tortoise shell arises from the shape of the objects to be treated. It is quite a puzzle to keep them in the right position if they are curved throughout, or carved, or so slender as to be particularly vulnerable. Your ingenuity must supplement our advice. Meanwhile, here is the method for welding the material.

First of all, smooth the surfaces of the break which is to be welded together again. The best way to smooth them will depend entirely on the shape and cross-section of the broken part. You can scrape with something sharp and pointed in the case of a broken rib in an 18th-century fan, or gently and carefully file the spine of a comb, or scratch the lid of a sand-box with a scarifier or '*vaccinostyle*'.[1] In all cases the scraping must be as discreet as possible, except where the break has previously been mended with glue, in which event it is essential that every trace of glue be removed. The pieces to be welded are brought together and must of course fit each other perfectly. To keep them in place, under uniform pressure, you will use elastic bands, bits of wood and so on, prepared in advance. You then surround the article with a wet cloth to all of whose surfaces you proceed to apply hot irons which you have brought to a red heat. If the article is a small one you can use two irons, one on top and the other below. Leave them in contact with the cloth until they have cooled. Probably the cloth will burn as the water dries out of it, but this doesn't matter. Make sure the cloth is thick enough but not too thick; you want to get as much heat into the tortoise shell as possible. If the weld fails, don't hesitate, try again.

Excellent results can be attained with small articles by trimming the break with a razor blade and fixing the two parts together—small cramps are ideal for this.

You then place the whole thing in water and keep it on the boil long enough for the parts to fuse together. Cabinet makers, who still use tortoise shell, add a few handfuls of bay salt to the water; presumably in order to imbue the tortoise shell with its original element.

HOW TO POLISH TORTOISE SHELL

Professionals polish tortoise shell by a method called in French '*au gras*', that is, using a polish with a greasy base mixed with very fine abrasive particles. The abrasive can be the finely powdered pumice (*ponce soie*, 'silk pumice') which in Paris can be bought in the specialized shops in the Faubourg Saint-Antoine. The base can be ordinary Vaseline. The cabinet

---

1. A small lancet, something like a pen nib, which can in fact be mounted on a penholder. Used by doctors for vaccinating, it is also widely used in printing and in retouching.

makers' *popote* also yields excellent results. Rub the article with a chamois leather pad dipped in the mixture from time to time, and finish with a clean chamois leather. This method only applies to tortoise shell which has been scratched. To restore the brilliance of a piece whose surface has gone dull, the best results will be obtained by rubbing vigorously with a pad of chamois leather or cloth (not fluffy) coated with glycerine.

Cleaning tortoise shell has nothing difficult or special about it; soapy water, followed by thorough rinsing, is completely effective.

PART NINE

PEWTER

Gentle Brilliance: Tin and Pewter

TIN has at all times been, in a sense, a precious metal; perhaps the only one whose attractiveness was not reflected by its monetary value. Its price does not begin to compare with that of gold or silver. This may be regarded as a pointer to its intrinsic beauty, which was recognized from the infancy of the historical civilizations onward. Tin was loved for its own sake, not for its rarity. It has enabled mankind to achieve decisive stages in progress and to mark the history of art with its highest and most delicate successes.

For, if tin had not existed bronze would not have existed either, a deficiency whose consequences would have been incalculable. What witness would the civilizations of Egypt and Mesopotamia have left to posterity without the bronze tools of their sculptors? What would the earliest Chinese dynasties have bequeathed to us, those of the Yin period (14th–11th century B.C.), without the admirable bronzes brought to light by excavation? What would we know of Mesopotamia, Nineveh, Babylon or the Persians, without the delightful bronzes of Luristan and the figure-sculptures of Sumer?

Who can measure the cultural content of the trade to which tin gave rise, thousands of years before the Christian era? It is an attested fact that the ore utilized by the peoples of Mesopotamia was mined in Galicia (Spain), and doubtless also in Britain.

The earliest objects made of pure tin to have come down to us are a ring and a pot found in an Egyptian burial ground of the 18th dynasty (about 1450 B.C.). No deposits of tin were exploited in ancient Egypt and it is not yet known whether the ore was fetched from Syria, Spain or—as may have been the case—from northern Europe.

Europe was undoubtedly the true cradle of the art of tin and pewter. And to get to what concerns us here let us telescope time and jump forward to the Middle Ages, when pewter entered popular use.

In the reign of St Louis (Louis IX, 1226–1270), there were nineteen master pewterers exercising their craft in Paris.

In the 14th century, household vessels of wood and coarse pottery began to be replaced by pewter, which, in addition to its appearance, had the advantage that it could be periodically renewed by melting down. This is the main reason for the conspicuous rarity of really old pieces. The pewterers went round visiting households and melted down and remade worn-out vessels for a modest charge, calculated by weight. To stimulate trade and keep up with fashion they modified the shapes in use. This is why *no* tangible evidence has come down to us of the pewterware of the 13th, 14th and 15th centuries, and only a few isolated examples from the 16th and 17th centuries. Not until the 18th century are we confronted by a fairly large output, by which time the triumph of pottery and porcelain had initiated the decline of pewter. Relegated to the scrap-heap by 19th-century taste, these examples of a private, domestic art now gratify collectors and grace our houses or apartments with a deeply endearing decorative refinement.

FAKES

The incredible amount of fake pewter in circulation is not easy to study in the abstract, at second hand. Scarcity has always favoured counterfeiting; but these copies—of widely varying quality, be it said—are so numerous as to prompt the involuntary thought, which ought some day to be pointedly brought home, 'How is it that people who have chosen the honourable and beautiful trade of the antique dealer are capable of offering, to a reasonably informed public, a host of objects ordered from the nearest workshop?' If it is merely from financial necessity they should set up in some other line of business. They would do well out of souvenir articles—the folksy doll or the barometer surrounded by seashells, 'a souvenir from' any seaside resort you like to think of.

Some of these antique dealers say straight out, 'These are copies.' Their integrity does them honour; but does it affect the situation in any way? All it means is that their vocation is not for the souvenir trade but for selling furniture and decorative goods.

If the profitability of the antique dealer's profession depends on the combination swindler/dupe, it is to be feared that antique dealers will become extinct—with highly regrettable repercussions on our enjoyment, our way of life and art of living.

Nor are antique dealers the only culprits. What are we to think of the hacks who call themselves 'master pewterers' yet have never done anything but mechanical reproduction work, endlessly casting copies of forms created by others?

Pewter is a wonderful material; it has everything to attract a real artist, one of those who could leave a worthwhile memento of their presence on earth in our age. Such artists are few, and it must be admitted that they are denied the chief incentive possessed by the master-craftsmen of earlier days: utility. For, as we should remember, not a single pewter piece has come down to us that did not have an exact, daily, homely function. But how much does this drawback matter? Imagination has no frontiers.

RECOGNIZING FAKES

This needs much practice, and may prove a disappointing exercise at first, since a little knowledge is more dangerous than ignorance. The ignorant seeker can at least fall back on instinct.

First of all, educate your eye. Carefully study pewterware of known genuineness in museums or the shops of specialized antique dealers, whose standards would not permit them to trade in dubious pieces.

What should be your guidelines in such an examination? Bear it in mind that pewter is a highly malleable metal, not to say soft, and that long use may have made its marks on the most carefully preserved object: slight dents in the foot, neck or lid of a wine jug or the rim of a dish, traces of cuts on a plate or a bowl, faint or marked deformations in the belly of a pot or a tureen.

Imagine centuries of patient care, ranging from ordinary cleaning by a kitchen maid to the thorough polishing administered by a critical housewife. This is often the best touchstone. Old pewterware has been used and looked after—and don't tell us that many years of subsequent neglect will have wiped out the consequences. Once you remove the dirt and oxidation which can extinguish the lustre of the most brilliant pewter, the indescribable modelling peculiar to forms long caressed will reappear.

Fake pewter has sharp edges, even if care has been taken to disguise them. The care shows up and betrays the deception.

Even if the fake has been cast from an antique piece, the modelling will have acquired a flabby quality. This is one of the peculiarities which invariably distinguish a cast copy. It shows up glaringly in the marks. The master pewterers, or in certain cases the controllers of weights and measures (wine mugs, for example, had to conform to an official shape), possessed steel punches with which they marked the soft pewter, placing it over a 'stake' (a kind of miniature anvil) to give a bearing for the hammer-blow and to prevent the pewter from being dented or bent.

On genuine pieces these marks are clear and sharp—or at least part of them is; the hammer didn't always come down quite flat. On the inner surface, opposite the imprint, the 'stake' will have left its own impression, something like a hammer mark. On a copy these marks are soft and blurred. They are like what you would get by pouring molten lead or tin into the impression made by a coin in wet sand.

A more serious matter is that the forgers have acquired the habit of using their own punches. What should alert you to these is the opposite of the advice we have just given: the edges of the imprint are *too* sharp, the sunk parts are free of the metal polish and oxide which the polishing rag could not reach. In both cases it is a question of detail.

Forgers do not neglect to use acid baths to generate spectacular oxidations, various concoctions to produce a spurious patina and so on. Common sense and careful observation are your only guides; no fake in the world, however artful, can stand up against them.

It is worth pointing out that the presence of these punch marks proves nothing, anyway; countless genuine pieces are without them!

Finally, we can only urge the amateur to educate himself; there are excellent books which will open a fascinating field of research to him and teach him the language of punch marks. He will see that the forgers have been at pains to imitate the best known marks, such as the famous 'rose and crown' which, when genuine, has so many variants that even specialists get confused. It helps a little to know that certain master pewterers, such as the famous Bartholomé Leboucq of Lille, used five different punches which included versions of the rose and crown; so did his competitor, Lefebre. To confuse the matter nicely, we add that the celebrated rose and crown is also found on pewter from Brussels and Liège.

THE FOUR MARKS AND
WHAT THEY EXPRESS

Without trying to make oneself into a walking encyclopaedia of punch marks—which would be impossible, because there are still so many to be discovered and classified—it is a good thing to know the meaning of the most eloquent types of mark one is likely to encounter.

Master craftsmen's marks ('poinçons de maîtres potiers' or 'de fondeurs d'étain')

Guild organization in the Middle Ages is well known: it meant that every pewterer could put his own mark on his wares, provided he was accepted by a jury of guild masters. The craftsmen had to conform to certain standards, notably as regards the quality of his alloys. The corporation (guild) then considered itself responsible for the standard of what he produced.

According to law, every master pewterer was required to incorporate his initials in his personal mark. In some cases the whole name is given or is represented by a kind of visual pun. Several instances are known in which the name is depicted analogically. Tonnelier ('cooper'), a master pewterer of Paris, had as his mark a little picture of a cooper at work.

However, literal initials are by far the commonest form, accompanied by a hammer as emblem (a pewter-beater's hammer, with a peen at both ends). The famous rose and crown belongs to northern France; the equally famous 'angel weighing a soul' (if that is what it really is) or 'angel with the scales', to eastern France (and Lyon); name-pictures and similar graphic devices, chiefly to Paris (which itself is usually denoted by the letter P).

Where are these punch marks placed?

Usually on the outside of the bottom of dishes, miscellaneous utensils, and wine pots and wine jugs. In both of these latter, the marks may be on the lid.

In English, marks are often known as 'touches'.

Standard marks

As we mentioned, the guild *jurés* took responsibility for the alloys used by the members of the guild. Naturally they kept a check on standards. These standard marks are easily recognizable. They are never more than a centimetre across, and they embody either the letter F (often a double F, or sometimes two

F's back to back with the uprights coinciding), standing for 'fine' pewter, or a C (often double, sometimes back to back or interlaced) for common pewter. Of course there are variants: a coat of arms, a town's name, date, the quality of the pewter spelt out in full and so on.

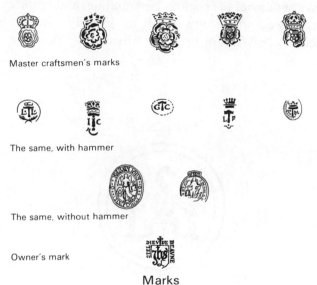

Master craftsmen's marks

The same, with hammer

The same, without hammer

Owner's mark

Marks

Measure marks

These concern us only when they occur on pewter vessels used as measures, notably wine pots, which were periodically checked by a visiting inspector of weights and measures. The marks are small signs placed on the lid or at the top of the neck. They are astonishingly varied; the systematic classification of them, though courageously undertaken by experts like Charles Boucau in Paris, is continually being augmented by newly discovered types.

Owner's marks

These are very rare, and should not be confused with the incised initials, symbols and blazons which are fairly common on pewter. Owner's marks are stamped; they are punch marks and can clearly be seen to be so. Presumably they were put on for the same reason as hotel keepers put 'Hôtel des Voyageurs' or 'Restaurant de la Plage' on their china and ashtrays. Known examples include the *Hospice de Beaune*, the *Hôtel royal des Invalides*, a number of religious communities and hospices, and certain others which are hard to identify but probably represent ecclesiastics or ordinary private owners.

Medallion type

Rose-window type

Countermarks

Countermarks

These are not punch marks in the usual sense but lozenges or other marks in relief; one finds them, especially in pots, on the inside—for which reason they usually go unnoticed. The signs they contain, such as initials, dates and decorative designs resembling rose-windows, are difficult to interpret. Their presence is due to a technical reason. Until the 18th century, pots were cast in two-piece moulds; the two parts, and any roughness in the join between them, were then smoothed on the lathe.

The pot was held in a mandrel and presumably by an opposing threaded part passing through a hole in the bottom.

The countermark was a stopper, soldered into place, closing and camouflaging the hole left by the mandrel.

So the importance of the countermark is obvious: it is a sure indication that the piece was made before the 18th century.

Tin and Its Alloys: Varieties of Pewter

AS we have seen, the qualities of tin and pewter used by the master pewterers were strictly controlled. The following were the three officially recognized grades:

Tin and fine pewter (*l'étain fin*)

This was probably pure tin with the addition of some substance (possibly bismuth) to facilitate casting; the amount of additive used defies definition. Pieces made of this material are extremely rare. They are mainly fine table vessels (tureens, ornamented soup bowls and the like), for which ordinary pewter, as we shall see, was also used; organ pipes, theoretically required to be of pure tin, were likewise made of either material; the distinction is evidently difficult to draw in many cases.

Common pewter

Here, too, any attempt to estimate the composition of the metal is risky, as it was common practice among the master pewterers to melt down old tin or pewter. It was even recommended not to use less than one-third of old metal when casting new pieces. Besides, each master had his own secret formula for the additives to be used: copper (*cuivre rosette*, as pure copper was called), bismuth, metallic oxides, antimony, tungsten and so on.

La claire étoffe

In this very inferior quality there was no check on the amount of lead. The pewterers, well aware of the poisonous properties of lead, were careful not to use *claire étoffe* for anything which might have to contain food or drink. It was used for clysters, cheap candlesticks, candle moulds and other prosaic purposes. It should be remembered that as well as the pewterers there were large numbers of tin and lead founders whose guild was not governed by regulations controlling quality.

Silver pewter

Pewter, if well enough polished, gleams rather similarly to silver, and this has given rise to a legend whose motivation is strictly commercial: the existence of silver and tin alloy. Technically at least, this is feasible despite the different melting points of the metals (tin, 232 °C., 450 °F., silver, 960 °C., 1760 °F.). Reasons of a different kind make the alloy improbable. A cause frequently adduced for the popularity of pewter is the sumptuary edicts issued in the closing years of Louis XIV's reign (there were others later), penalizing the 'outward signs of wealth' symbolized by the possession of silverware. But it would have afforded little satisfaction to the proud owner to bury part of his riches by alloying it with a metal of a baser kind. Moreover, in order to succeed in alloying silver and tin the pewterers would have needed more heat than was generated by the braziers illustrated in the technical treatises of the time. These were fired with charcoal and are unlikely to have produced temperatures above 600–700 °C. (1112–1292 °F.): this argument is not necessarily conclusive, of course; and the goldsmiths and silversmiths may well have resorted to working in less precious metals, including tin. Why, however, should they have used this particular alloy, which would have contributed very little to the characteristics of its principal ingredient, tin? The presence of silver in pewter is said to be proved by certain highly characteristic oxidations reminiscent of frost-patterns on window-panes in winter. But surely this is one of the typical oxidations of tin? However, to avoid discouraging the partisans of the 'silver pewter' theory we will concede that common pewters did contain a certain percentage of silver. Why common pewters rather than fine? Because common pewters contained lead—about 10–20 per cent of it; and galena, natural lead sulphide, the principal ore of lead, always includes a certain amount of silver.

HOW TO RECOGNIZE PEWTER

This is chiefly a matter for the eye and cannot be described in words. There are other tests, but these too depend on practice. Smell is one of them: pewter rubbed with a cloth, or even the palm of the hand, gives off a characteristic odour.

However, the objection will be raised that all metals do this more or less; or at least that silver does, or even lead. Another test is the sound, the peculiar note or 'cry' of the material—and to credit a metal with possessing a 'cry', and a specific 'cry' at that, is surely the sign of the passion of the true aesthete! The 'cry' of pewter is a cry of pain. The metal's markedly crystalline nature engenders a clearly perceptible effect: if pewter is slightly but forcibly twisted, an unmistakable creaking sound will be heard; a 'cry' produced only under torture. Consequently this test cannot often be used. How would an antique dealer react if he saw you twisting the rim of a 'Cardinal' dish or the lid of a wine tankard of the Parisian type?

PEWTER PATHOLOGY

Pewter has its own sicknesses; some grave, some even mortal. But before embarking on this distressing subject it is fitting to draw attention briefly to the health-giving properties of pewter. It is lethal to staphylococci. It can be plausibly argued that the pewter vessels used in hospitals from the Middle Ages to the French Revolution were responsible for largely suppressing the 'ward fever' which is still a scourge even today, in this age of organ transplants and pacemakers for the heart, and which is caused by an uncontrollable outbreak of the 'hospital staphylococcus', *Staphylococcus doreus*, against which modern asepsis is powerless. Tin, like silver, has bactericidal properties; in various forms it is an ingredient in ointments and other local applications, and is used in the treatment of boils, anthrax, influenza and even tuberculosis.

PEWTER'S 'CANCER'

We mentioned, in discussing 'silver pewter', an oxidation resembling hoar frost. It is sometimes referred to as '*le cancer de l'étain*'. This sinister title is highly exaggerated. Crystallizations of this kind are undoubtedly hard to get rid of but they do not eat away the body of the metal. A fine pewter vessel can always be restored to its proper brilliance, but it is prudent not to resort instantly to drastic methods. The sensible thing is to treat both the object and its material with respect, starting with gentle remedies and gradually adopting severer ones if necessary.

Simply use a commercial metal polish, rubbing hard and concentrating particularly on the oxidized patches. Wipe clean and shine up now and then, to check results. If these promise well, continue; the method is both right and safe.

A very dirty article, apparently oxidized in depth, can be immersed in paraffin (kerosene) and left there for several hours or even days.

Then dry it with newspaper (which is highly absorbent); probably all the accretions will come away easily. Finish by polishing with a cloth and any of the usual metal polishes.

Another method, which sounds even more home-made, is the 'hay bath'. Take a metal pan or pot, place a few handfuls of hay in it and put the object on top of the hay; fill the pot with enough water to cover the object. Heat the pot, bringing the water not quite to the boil; leave it to cool. After a few hours most of the dirt will have gone.

Potash, soda and ammonia all possess the property of precipitating the salts of tin. Any of these three will easily eliminate the most tenacious oxidations. But care is necessary. Rinse the pewter thoroughly as soon as you see that the action has gone far enough.

Dilute hydrochloric acid is sometimes recommended for cleaning pewter, but this is a serious mistake: tin is dissolved by hydrochloric acid. Of course, this treatment quickly gets down to the bare metal but, in our opinion, gravely compromises the appearance of the article by destroying the patina.

On this subject, it must be pointed out that the patina of pewter does not depend on preserving the blackish oxidation covering its surface. Specialists all agree that pewter should be clean and brightly polished. Motifs, mouldings, channellings and engraved details are bound to show differences of colour; and this is desirable, it brings out relief and modelling and thus shows up the line of the object as a whole.

PEWTER'S WORST 'DISEASE'

The most serious trouble that pewter can develop is a 'disease' (there is really nothing else to call it) which is essentially due to *cold*. Deep ulcerations or erosions appear on the surface and these miniature craters contain powdery salts of tin, showing that the metal has literally decomposed. These attacks may be local; unfortunately, they may on the other hand affect the whole surface. What is to be done? The question causes much argument, and more perplexity, among specialists.

In the case of a valuable, really old piece, especially if it is badly attacked, the currently favoured remedy is to let well alone, merely cleaning up any portions still intact with metal polish. The true amateur will cherish the article for its historical significance and be content to forgo its decorative qualities—but he will also be compelled to witness the further progress of the 'disease'!

This is hardly a solution. If action is not taken in time to arrest it, the deterioration will obviously become general. It is advisable first carefully to scrape out the 'craters', then to take chemical action against the salts produced by oxidation. As we mentioned, these can be eliminated with soda, potash or ammonia. Finally, after polishing as thoroughly as possible, apply a treatment which, in spite of its simplicity, is acknowledged the best by the most advanced metallurgical laboratories in the world. Make the article hot, within reason, and coat it with a substance produced by nature: beeswax. The wax melts on the hot metal and sinks into the minutest cavities of the surface, envelops the oxides and gets right down to the metal itself, isolating it from the oxygen of the air and rendering impossible any further spontaneous chemical or molecular reaction. Carefully wipe off any excess wax, and polish to brightness. This 'proofs' the article permanently.

But, as we need hardly point out, if your pewter is exposed all over again to the rigours of climate and atmosphere, no panacea will safeguard it from damage.

BEESWAX OR THE ATOM?

Anti-corrosion treatment with beeswax is a simple, common-sense remedy which the leading French specialist, Albert France Lanord, creator of the Laboratoire de Recherches Archéologiques and of the Musée Sidérurgique, Nancy, has successfully employed in preserving countless works of art and objects from excavations.

The discovery of the effectiveness of this method is based on an observation frequently made. Whenever excavation has yielded receptacles which once contained unguents or cosmetics—every civilization has bequeathed us items of this kind—these receptacles have been preserved intact, without serious deterioration, despite having lain underground in damp or acid conditions. Analysis of ancient beauty products regularly indicates the presence of beeswax. It even seems that beeswax has been recovered intact from fossil deposits dating from early periods in the earth's geological development.

The idea has occurred to some people that radio-activity could be used to arrest oxidation. The British Museum entrusted a fairly large collection of coins to the British Atomic Energy Commission.

After treatment, the coins were found to be emitting highly dangerous gamma-radiation and the collection was placed in lead containers, to be stored for centuries in a specially adapted cellar at the Museum; where, of course, it can be neither handled nor seen.

HEALTHY PEWTER

This review of the inferno and purgatory of our beloved pewter might lead one to suppose that it is fated always to be attacked by dreadful maladies. Far from it, there is also a paradise for pewter—the safety ensured by vigilant, regular care.

Talking of paradise, incidentally, it is worth recalling that the Catholic Church admits the use of pewter as a sacred metal; a venerable distinction to which we are indebted for various objects full of grace, such as ciboria and small vessels for the holy oils. A further advantage is that we can avail ourselves of the recipes for polishing pewter which an old maidservant in a curé's household will be able to supply, and which will be equally useful for all kinds of pewter, sacred or profane, fine or

common. Apparently, pumice powder is the material to which the care of pewter has been entrusted for hundreds of years. The traditional way of using it is to mix it with olive oil, put a dab of the mixture on a cloth and rub till the job is done. You can get pumice powder from specialized firms serving French polishers and cabinet makers. Ask for the finest grade. Spanish whiting mixed with ammonia is another stand-by, as generations of housewives could tell us; tripoli is likewise a very sound material for the care of pewter; so is the cabinet makers' *popote*. In France, excellent *popote* can be bought, whose ingredients are scientifically balanced. There are also many personal recipes; every antique dealer or cabinet maker has his own; but these are not to be trusted. Most polishing pastes include the ingredients mentioned above and are therefore the best general answer to your problems. Watch out for one thing: do not let whitish deposits of paste accumulate in the crannies and undercuts; take a hard brush, a paintbrush if need be, and lightly whisk them out.

Pewter, which is a soft metal, has anti-friction properties, like antimony or bronze. But whereas a pointed tool easily scratches it, the friction of cleaning does not wear it away as much as might be expected. How does one get a really good shine—given that all polishing is a process of controlled wear? The question particularly concerns owners of modern pewter pieces (not to say fakes). As already stated, genuine antique pewter has an inimitable patina. Various drastic methods have been recommended: pads of steel wool, soaked in paraffin or oil, or, more recently, the plastic saucepan scourers used by housewives. We regard such methods as brutal and unsuitable. They certainly make pewter shine but they work rather like glasspaper, that is to say by cutting miscroscopic glittering grooves in the bare metal. This is nothing like the matt, satiny gleam produced by gentle polishing.

Mechanical polishing is decidedly more attractive. A well-nigh perfect patina can be obtained by using a felt or fabric disc and smearing it from time to time with a cake of solid polishing paste. But this takes a long time, precisely because of pewter's low coefficient of friction. Fast running is essential: not less than 2500 r.p.m. The small discs supplied for the do-it-yourselfer's electric drill are inadequate: they have too small a diameter to be sufficiently flexible, and the metal mounting in the centre of the disc too easily comes into contact with the pewter, and may mark it. But if you possess a buffing wheel you can run it off a d.i.y. drill using 350 or 400 watts, and there is nothing to stop you from equipping it with a felt disc 15 or 20 cm. in diameter.

FOR THOSE WHO PREFER DARK PEWTER

Pewter can be left coated with a thin layer of oxide; it is a matter of personal preference. The metal can first be smoothed by light polishing, then hot-waxed. A good rub thereafter will produce a high gloss.

Paraffin (kerosene) or Vaseline can be used instead of beeswax. And there is a popular recipe which is very sound: rub the pewter with a cloth dipped in hot beer, and simply leave it to dry. Take care not to use too harsh a cloth when polishing it. A piece of soft knitted woollen material will polish up the film left by the beer but will not remove it.

REPAIRING PEWTER

This is undoubtedly a job for the specialist. It is a very difficult matter to solder two metals which have the same melting-point: in melting the solder one runs the risk of melting the metal under repair as well. Such a mishap would be merely tiresome when mending a dish, for example, but catastrophic in the case of a hollow vessel made over a former. The most the amateur can attempt is to stop a hole on the bottom of a plate or dish, using an electrician's soldering-iron. Never try to melt the metal of the article itself; simply put on solder, after cleansing the edges of the hole with hydrochloric acid. Excess solder can be removed by filing, followed by emery cloth, then gradually polished up with wet-and-dry and finally with metal polish.

FILLING A HOLE OR CRACK
WITHOUT SOLDERING

is always possible and requires no particular skill. A vase or a teapot may, after long use, show signs of weakness round the bottom, or at the base of the spout, or in the handle. Two-part epoxy resins will permanently repair these little defects. In such articles as a teapot or chocolate jug, the resin's resistance to heat, 300 °C. (572 °F.), is about 68 °C. (154 °F.) higher than the melting-point of pewter. The plastic pastes with a metal filler ('cold solder' or 'plastic metal') may be helpful in small repairs. Be prepared for its limitations, however: you may not be able to match the colour exactly, or to polish the finished join satisfactorily. Don't expect a high finish: the repair will always present a comparatively dull surface. So keep this method for places that cannot be seen.

Taking dents out of pewter

Here, a keen amateur can find a useful outlet for his skill. You will need a selection of the tools used by a panel beater or a tinsmith (they are much the same); namely: a round-headed hammer, a mallet of wood or hard rubber and a 'universal' former (a metal object whose faces have different curves). If you are not going to need this equipment often, you can improvise instead of buying it.

But the mallet is indispensable.

We suggest that you get your hand in first by working on an old tin, first bashing it up a bit, or on some white-metal article of small value. The principle is straightforward. You have probably watched panel beaters at work: they do not merely hit the inner side of the dent, because the impact which caused it also had the effect of stretching the metal so that knocking out the dent from one side would simply set it up again on the other. The knocking-out must be 'backed up' by holding a metal object against the face of the pewter exactly opposite the hammer or mallet striking the other side. This metal object is the former, mentioned above, and its shape must be the same as that which it is required to restore. If you need both hands for working with, you can fix the former in a vice. This, however, is not ideal; a certain amount of 'give', to take the impact of the hammer, is desirable.

Let us consider a few concrete examples. Anything *flat* should be laid on a perfectly flat surface, such as a table top or a bench top, and hammered into shape, with a piece of perfectly flat wood between itself and the hammer.

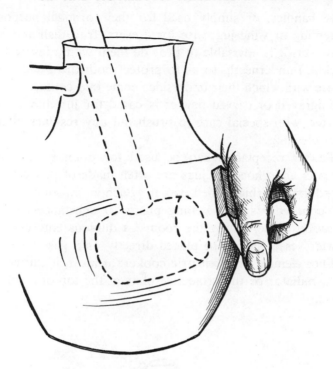

Anything *hollow*, such as a vase or a jug, should be beaten out from the inside, with a suitable former held against the outside. If you haven't got a former of the requisite shape you can make one yourself out of hardwood. The pewter should not be hammered with much force but with light blows accurately applied. To enable you to work effectively from the inside the hammer or mallet must be a small one.

The *foot* or *base* of any article should be treated in the same way: hit from inside, backing up with a wooden or metal former of exactly the right shape.

SOME FINAL HINTS

Pewter articles look well behind glass, or on a whatnot (*étagère*) or other piece of furniture, or hung on hooks if they

have handles, or simply used for their original purposes—
water jug or wine jug, vase for flowers, fruit dish and so on.
However, it is advisable to provide them with a felt pad (self-
sticking) underneath, so as to protect both them and the furniture with which their undersides come into contact.

Engraved or carved pewter is cared for just like all other
pewter, with special care to brush out any residues of polish
after cleaning.

Pewter receptacles can be used for holding hot liquids.
Teapots and chocolate jugs are often made of pewter; so are
potpourri jars (big-bellied pots in which an infusion was made
of supposedly sweet-smelling plants or substances, with the
intention of perfuming the room—a dubious enterprise). No
pewter vessel should be placed directly on a gas-flame or the
red-hot element of an electric cooker; at most, it can be stood
on a radiator or the protective plate at the top of a solid-fuel
stove.

PART TEN

POTTERY AND PORCELAIN

Pottery and Porcelain: You Can Repair Them

PARADOXICALLY, earthenware, faience and porcelain, rightly regarded as being some of the most fragile materials, pose only simple problems to the amateur restorer.

In saying this we are of course referring only to the ordinary repairs, those which make no call on the talent and knowledge of the specialist. Modern epoxy resin adhesives are better for sticking broken pottery or porcelain than all older types of glue, and render superfluous the rivets which china menders in the street—whose craft is among the minor ones now practically extinct—so liberally dispense to compensate for the precariousness of the old adhesives.

Nevertheless, technical progress is often surprisingly slow to impose its superiority. It clashes with professional tradition and only gradually takes the place of methods which, after all, did give satisfaction. One of the arguments most frequently put forward by professional restorers is precisely the great hardness of epoxy resins, a characteristic which (I quote) 'makes any subsequent restoration very difficult'. Can they really mean this seriously? If a restoration has been properly carried out, surely it will never need doing again? Anyway, from our own experience with these resins, which is already long, we can say that if an object already repaired by this means were to break for the second time the new break would not be in the same place as the old one.

Another advantage of epoxy resins, which nobody will dispute, is that an object so repaired 'rings' as it would have done if it had never been broken. As many people know, there is a test which shows whether pottery or porcelain has been repaired or has a hairline crack somewhere, a hidden weakness: you balance the piece on three fingers and, with the other hand, tap the rim smartly with a finger-nail. If the piece has no defect it gives a good, clean ring. A plate broken into several pieces will, after being repaired with an epoxy resin, ring like a new plate. We can testify to this from frequent experience.

Epoxy resins are sold in two parts—usually two tubes—the resin properly so-called and the hardener (see the chapter on Adhesives). To ensure adhesion and hardening they need a surrounding temperature of 15 °C. (59 °F.) or more. You can even heat them to make them act faster (up to 70° during polymerization, and up to 300° once hardening has occurred).

They are very simple to apply. After carefully mixing the two components in accordance with the manufacturer's directions, put a thin, very even coat of adhesive on each part to be stuck. If any traces of glue are present from an earlier repair, scrape them off with great care. The success of the whole operation depends on thorough preparation. The delicate question in repairing ceramics is how to hold the pieces together. You must solve this problem before sticking them. Use rubber bands and/or medical sticking plaster. There is a reason for preferring the medical variety: it is the only kind which is perforated to allow air to pass; and it is slightly elastic. When you have stuck it on one of the pieces to be held together you can stretch it before sticking it to the other piece, producing a tension which helps to cramp them together.

Clothes pegs, cramps, weights and so on, may all be useful. It is for you to decide what you need, according to the shape of whatever you are mending.

An important warning: if the shape of an article broken in several places is such that you have to repair it by stages instead of all at once, never leave any overflows of adhesive on a part you are going to stick later. If an overflow is left to harden you will be in trouble when you come to stick the next piece.

Another essential warning: there is NO satisfactory way of removing dribbles of epoxy resin once they have hardened. So it is vital to remove them while the adhesive is still soft. This is easily done with a wad of cottonwool dipped in alcohol.

Leave the repaired work under pressure, as described, without handling it at all, for about twelve hours.

A considerable advance in the repair of ceramics has recently appeared with the production of a one-part epoxy resin which is a contact adhesive. The two faces of a break, coated

thinly with this adhesive, are accurately brought together; adhesion is immediate and final, ingenious cramping arrangements are rendered unnecessary, and multiple breaks can be mended without intervening delays.

FOR THOSE WHO LIKE OLD TECHNIQUES

Here are a few well-tried, effective recipes which in the past— even the recent past—have been the basis of sound repairs.

Foremost of all we may place the remarkable '*mastic La Victoire*', which has been the salvation of generations of repairers. Sold in powder form, it is mixed with water to the consistency of thick honey. The resulting mortar is left to stand for a few minutes before it is ready for use as an adhesive. Its resistance to heat and water is very satisfactory. An interesting detail is that a chip or small hole can be effectively made good by building up with *mastic La Victoire* (whose composition is closely related to that of the cement used by dental surgeons).

Fish glue, mixed in equal quantities with acetic glue (which is not easy to find), undoubtedly holds well but is vulnerable to humidity. Moreover both surfaces must first be moistened with formalin (a 40 per cent solution of the gas formaldehyde), a disinfectant preventing attack by micro-organisms, which are often partial to fish glue.

If you like picturesque recipes here are two which, despite sounding home-spun, are still used. *White of egg*, well mixed with finely ground sieved lime, makes a mortar which sets fairly rapidly and is effective even on delicate porcelain.

Gruyère cheese, macerated in water for three days, is mixed with two or three snails (without their shells); the resulting paste (admittedly rather revolting) is then mixed with an equal quantity of quicklime, well pounded and free from lumps. This strange preparation will enable you to repair not only ceramics but, apparently, glass.

A variant of the same recipe (whose efficacy we are not in a position to judge): curdled milk, two or three *red* snails (slugs?) and quicklime.

The temptation to find a rational explanation for everything leads us to compare this formula with the well-known principle of casein glues (curdled milk) fixed with an alkali (lime). But the role of the slugs and snails must also be accounted for; a fertile field for conjecture! Possibly the idea was to make use of the slime secreted by these creatures, which is certainly sticky. Or perhaps we should be bold and push the reasoning further. Casein glues are sensitive to micro-organisms, like any other alimentary product. Industrially, they are stabilized by the addition of antiseptics. This might be the role played by the snail; which, as we know, has a place in the pharmacopoeia of popular medicine, notably in the treatment of infectious conditions of the respiratory tract.

This digression into empirical science is relevant here in so far as it may incline us to contemplate traditional recipes with an open mind. This is desirable for several reasons. Observation plays a large part in repairs to furniture and other antiques. Every material has a life of its own: some are *alive*— wood, ivory, bone and some textile fibres; others are *capricious*, such as metals, whose oxidation develops in accordance with the unpredictable interplay of atmospheric factors; *none is inert*, appearances notwithstanding: they are susceptible to heat, cold, light and humidity.

Why decline the teaching of the past—during which patient observation was always the basis of experimentation?

Finally, awareness of ancient solutions guides us in making an intelligent choice of new products and sometimes gives us a better appreciation of their advantages.

Building Up a Missing Fragment

STICKING broken parts together again, however effective, obviously works only when all the parts are there. A lost fragment reduces the most beautiful plate to the level of a humble potsherd. If the plate has a documentary or archaeological value the mutilation can perhaps be tolerated, but for anything of decorative value it is deplorable.

Building up a chip or other small fragment which has gone A.W.O.L. is by no means impossibly difficult, but it is useless attempting it without an adequate acquaintance with the materials described below.

Barbotine

This is very white, very finely powdered clay which regains its plasticity on being mixed with water. 'Barbola' is very similar.

Ceramic cold pastes

These are composite materials developed for use in schools. They are easy to model, and they set by exposure to the air, acquiring the hardness of ceramics. The resources of this new material for the restorer are immense. But they are not always fluid enough to make a satisfactory join with the object to be completed.

Plastic resins (coloured, quick-setting)

These should not be confused with epoxy resins, whose role is adhesive. Though comparable in nature with epoxy resins they differ from them in appearance and even more so in adhesive strength. Like them, they require a hardener.

They are sold in the form of a fairly thick paste, in different colours; the range is small but sufficiently varied for most ordinary repairs. Since they are frequently used for restoring marble you may find them classified not under colours but as

Potters (Diderot, *Encyclopédie*)

turquin, *orphite*, *comblanchien*, Carrara, etc. As you will colour them yourself this does not much matter, except (obviously) that you will not choose a dark shade to reproduce a pale one.

These resins are often our salvation; they are quick-setting and, after curing, acquire almost mineral hardness. They demand considerable deftness, as they cannot be modelled. They run, something like thick honey. This has both advantages and drawbacks. For filling in a missing chip in a flat place they are unrivalled, especially as they do not perceptibly shrink during polymerization. But when a complete missing fragment has to be replaced, ingenuity is required. It is impossible to envisage all the cases which may occur. The wall of a vase or cup, or the edge of a plate, can be easily mended by making a plaster mould of an intact part which has the same shape, and slipping this mould over the broken place. The resin is then put in (from the inside if the object is a vase or a cup, which is first laid on its side). For a small hole, a piece of card or sticky tape takes the place of a mould. If you have no plaster, children's modelling paste is ideal, especially since an exactly accurate mould is unnecessary, as you will find for yourself; imperfections are very easy to put right.

Polymerization takes place fairly rapidly, so you should use the resin immediately you have added the hardener, while it is still fluid. As soon as the chemical action gets under way the stuff goes tacky, and this is when bubbles may give trouble; when you polish the repair you may find an air-bubble or two, which will form holes. You will have to fill them in or else do the whole job again. For a few minutes the resin, though already fairly hard, will be of a consistency that can be worked with a flat chisel, a gouge or a razor blade. This makes it very easy to restore a moulding (e.g. at the edge of a plate or dish). But watch out: polymerization is going forward steadily, so do the rough finishing quickly, with edged tools; after that, you can carry on with a carpenter's rasp, followed by a file. Only the latter will make any impression on the resin once it has hardened. Final polishing will be effected with flower paper.

One can, at a pinch, use the same resin both for sticking and for rebuilding; the great advantage is that no cramping of any kind is needed, setting being fast enough for the pieces to be held in place by hand until perfect adhesion has occurred. In our opinion, these resins are not quite fluid enough to avoid leaving an excessively thick film along the line of the break.

For a small chip on the rim of a dish, plate or vase, *barbotine* offers a very satisfactory means of repair, and is easy to paint or enamel afterwards.

Cold ceramic pastes make it possible to reconstitute in their entirety such things as a handle, a spout or a foot. Your ability as a modeller is what will determine the success of the repair. Follow the manufacturer's directions carefully; they matter, especially as the composition of these pastes varies. Some of them behave rather like plastic resins. There are also special 'cold' glazes for these pastes; they are usually sold at the same shop; artists' colourmen, chiefly.

'Adhesives for pottery and porcelain' is a general title under which various products are sold; some are just conventional glues, others are epoxy resins. It may be difficult to tell which is what, even though the brand name is a reassuring one; in that case hold fast to the definitions given here. If you ask a supplier for an epoxy resin he will of necessity give you a branded product, but there will be no confusion.

'Enamel' *adhesives:* these are sold for repairing chipped enamel. They are generally used for kitchenware and the like, and they are very white. As it is impossible to alter their colour, they can hardly be recommended for repairing pottery. And their whiteness is too harsh and glaring for porcelain.

THE POTENTIALITIES OF
'COLD' ENAMEL

A repair well and beautifully executed with the help of the materials mentioned here deserves to be finished to the same standard. 'Cold' enamels (which are now easily obtained from firms specializing in artists' materials and equipment) are supplied in an excellent range of colours, making it possible to match either the ground-colour of a plate or its coloured motifs. Try out the required shades a few times before colouring your restorations. We know from our own experience that 'cold' enamel tends to be perceptibly more brilliant than the 'hot' (i.e. fired) enamels on pottery. Don't give up; let the new enamel dry completely and then reduce its brightness with wet-and-dry or a little pumice powder. Cracks can be imitated with a very fine watercolour brush, taking care to match them to those of the original.

If you fight shy of cold enamel, and especially if you have a complicated, many-coloured design to restore, gouache will be found completely satisfactory. When dry, it can be protected with a coat of clear varnish.

HOW TO LOOK AFTER POTTERY AND PORCELAIN

This is absolutely straightforward. To wash them just like ordinary dishes, with a suitable detergent, is the best way of looking after your collection; rinse carefully in very hot water, and dry with a good, absorbent tea towel. Then rub them with methylated spirit on a bit of cottonwool or rag. When the spirit has dried, polish them well.

For porcelain with raised or gilded decoration, use very little detergent, and no scourer.

Terracotta responds admirably to hot water and a few soda crystals. A stiff paintbrush will get into the details. Rinse in clean lukewarm water and leave to dry.

PART ELEVEN

WROUGHT IRONWORK

Wrought Iron: Simplicity and Splendour

TELL ME IF YOU LIKE WROUGHT IRON, AND I'LL TELL YOU WHO YOU ARE!

F EW things made from an ordinary, everyday material succeed in attaining such a pitch of visual and emotive power as wrought ironwork. Our observations in this realm can be summed up in a few words. No species of ironwork is useless. Almost no forged iron was originally intended as a 'work of art'. A fact which gives peculiar weight to our thesis is that everything starts from the tool; the tool is the source. . . . The most directly utilitarian object, its form determined by a highly selective function, has in the course of the ages succeeded in evolving into a 'work of art'. It is only recently that the lesson has been understood, with the result that the designer, the stylist, will be the man responsible for determining the forms of the tools of tomorrow.

Meanwhile, however, iron is pursuing a somewhat uncertain career. For every sincere craftsman there are dozens of hacks churning out 'artistic ironwork': standard lamps, wall-brackets for pots of flowers; 'horror on horror's head accumulating', encouraged by the owners of 'bijou country residences' who burden the simplest wooden shutter with 'rustic' hinges and bedeck their abodes with 'Venetian' lanterns painted with stove black, like so many poisonous fruits, the products of some little cheapjack workshop.

Genuine forgework is always easy to recognize; all that is needed is a little common sense. Down the ages, a block or bar of iron has always had to be shaped—drawn out, flattened or whatever else was required—with the hammer, so that the result always displays a certain slight irregularity, a perceptible modelling, even in the most carefully finished work. Differences in volume are almost always achieved by forging in one piece, i.e. from a single piece of metal, not by joining several pieces together. Joins in ornamental work are made by 'fire welding' or 'forge welding'. This technique demands a word of explanation. The pieces to be welded together are brought to a strong heat, only just short of melting point; they are then laid together and hammered to make them unite. The result is an assembly with a certain very recognizable character. This is not easy to describe in words; let us therefore content ourselves with a comparison and describe 'the others': the opposition, the betrayers.

Autogenous welding

If you have ever watched a welder at work you will have noticed that while with one hand he guides his welding torch, in the other he holds a metal rod. The function of the rod is to melt in the flame and deposit molten metal at the site of the intended weld. The method leaves easily discoverable traces: successive ripples, in a fairly regular pattern. Sometimes these

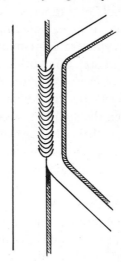

markings are eliminated by filing but they can never be entirely erased.

Electric welding

Most of the producers of cheap 'artistic' ironwork, referred to above, use this technique. On the joints they make you will see one or two round beads, usually rather regular in shape. This is the sign of electric welding, or rather of the particular kind called 'spot welding'.

Riveting

This is not in itself a modern technique. Very ancient ironwork sometimes contains rivets or at least relies on the riveting principle, which consists of joining two pieces of metal by means of a cylindrical rod passing through a hole in each. The head of the rod, on both sides of the join, is spread out with the hammer; this is done hot. An extension of the technique is possible: the rivet need not be a separate component but can be part (not necessarily round, it may be square or oblong in section) of one of the two members which are joined together. The stems of chandeliers or *landiers* are fixed into the feet or base in this way. [A *landier* was a special variety of fire-dog for kitchen use, the finial being forged into an openwork cup-like form to hold any small vessel that needed to be kept hot. *Trans.*]

Nevertheless, amateurs are recommended to observe rivets carefully. Modern, industrially-produced rivets have perfectly regular round or flat heads, and hammering never quite disguises their character.

Two points for special emphasis

To a connoisseur of antique wrought iron, riveting commands less interest than work that is forged in one piece or fire-welded. This should not be taken as a hard-and-fast rule but as a general guide.

The iron, or rather, mild steel, which is supplied by industry to the blacksmith of today is manufactured in shapes which make his work easier. For the genuinely creative worker this is all to the good. On the other hand, most of such craftsmen have

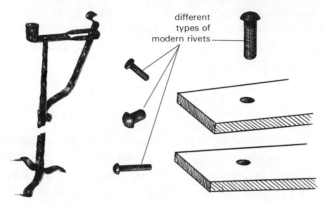

different types of modern rivets

Modern types of rivet

observed that the composition of the present-day metal is by no means so suitable for fire-welding. The old metal ('wrought iron', in the metallurgical sense of the term) was softer; probably also less homogeneous.

THE PATINA OF IRON AND
ITS LANGUAGE

Iron should not be masked by heavy layers of oxide, forming a nondescript blanket of patina, or, what is worst of all, smothered in stove black (Berlin black, matt black), as one has seen it only too often. Iron should display its own characteristic splendour; which implies that amateurs must use discrimination. For years, people have been polishing it up with grinding wheels; it is no longer possible to sell it with a natural surface—'*dans son jus*', 'in its own gravy', as French antique dealers say. It is handed over for polishing and stripped naked. This is wholly to be condemned, and we shudder at the thought of a genuine example of beautiful ironwork being subjected to such treatment. It is all very well doing it to quaintly romantic bedsteads (which are usually cast iron, anyway), or the hooks, bars and so on from a butcher's shop, or obsolete agricultural implements, promoted to the rank of art works; but the imprint of time on wrought iron should be respected. Can you imagine the hinges on the doors of Notre-Dame gleaming like a lawyer's brass plate, or the admirable curlicues on 13th-century chests and cupboards in the Musée des Arts décoratifs, or the Musée Carnavalet, polished up like silverware? Let us be loyal to the spirit of things. The blacksmiths who made the fittings for those chests, cupboards and doors attached them in their natural state, as they came from the anvil, with the roughness of the forge clinging about them. In many cases, wrought ironwork was polychromed and still shows traces of it: the so-called '*coffres de corsaire*' or Armada chests, shop signs, some candlesticks, and probably fittings on furniture, were enhanced in this way. To polish them all is to sacrifice to a passing fashion and to eliminate both the patina and any vestiges of polychroming, thereby destroying irreplaceable relics of the past.

An expert will tell you that the patina and appearance of iron vary according to period and provenance. It can be argued that they do, but the margin of error is so great that one cannot lay down any classification even of the most vague and general kind.

Some patinas are black (without any assistance from black paint), others are more of a dark chestnut colour (notably in some Spanish ironwork), and there is an infinite variety of shades caused mainly by the condition of the metal: in ironwork which has been looked after correctly the patina will be transparent in places, with the grey gleam of the metal showing through; the same piece, if neglected—oxidized, eroded by time—or even cleaned by over-zealous hands, is likely to retain the reddish glow of rust here and there.

An observation worth mentioning is that *genuinely antique ironwork is comparatively immune to rust.* This may be the result of the precise amount of carbon and phosphorus present in the iron produced in past centuries. Certainly the fact itself, whatever the cause, is undeniable. The gratings, balconies, rooftop ornaments, well-heads, signs and lamps which have resisted wind and weather for centuries have not been deeply affected by oxidation. Medieval locks on ancient chests *still work*, if one takes the trouble to have keys made for them (which is more than one can say for those of the last century, though admittedly these are more complicated).

Even more striking is the evidence provided by wrecked ships, still bristling with forged bolts, nails and ties which have remained almost intact, though the timbers have long since decayed.

The inference is that forged iron can stand up successfully to the passage of time provided it is not subjected to misguided interference.

HOW TO CLEAN WROUGHT IRONWORK

This depends entirely on the degree of oxidation and the size of the object. The ideal is prolonged immersion in paraffin (kerosene), but this is not always practicable. Paraffin is one of the best substances, in all cases, for loosening rust, scale or dirt. It sinks through, by capillary action, to the metal itself; brushing thereafter is rendered more effective.

Rusty iron can be heated and dipped in fuel oil or waste oil (e.g. from an oil-change in an automobile). With fuel oil there is of course the danger of its catching fire. Don't bring the iron to a red-heat, this is a mistake on two counts: it may ignite the oil, and it causes the iron to become mottled with unsightly marks.

'De-rusting' agents are inadvisable. They are powerful acids which do indeed strip the iron bare but also attack the metal itself. This is a problem which the chemists will eventually overcome but they still have some way to go, and at present it is not possible to recommend any of the products concerned for the purpose of cleaning antique ironwork.

Sand-blasting is also unacceptable. It wears down the surface all over, with aesthetically dubious results except for special effects. It should only be used on articles of little or no value.

Power-driven brushes: the wire brushes used for cleaning ironwork have now been produced in forms which can be electrically driven. This is a useful step forward. The brushes are of two kinds: those which spin in a plane at right angles to the axis of the motor, like a polishing disc, and those which work in line with the axis. They are much more effective than brushing by hand.

However, experience shows that they dull the surface of the iron to some extent. You can follow them up by using a soft polishing pad, also power-driven. This should be combined with a solid polish. Hold the polish against the pad and give the latter a spin, so that it automatically takes up an even, moderate coating of polish; then apply the pad to the iron. But remember the general caution given earlier: don't commit the blunder of polishing iron which was originally polychromed, or of destroying the character of forge-work by making it look like

Blacksmith in his forge

stainless steel kitchenware. The brushing and polishing described here are intended only to clean the iron and bring out its shape and character.

Emery cloth: this has always proved satisfactory for cleaning iron and it remains a standby. Obviously, being abrasive, it should be used in as fine a grade as possible, to avoid scoring the metal.

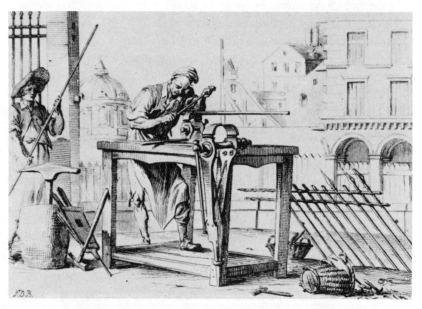

Locksmiths setting up the railings on the Terrasse des Tuileries in 1807

Steel wool: housewives are familiar with this in the form of scouring pads for cleaning saucepans. Antique dealers use it continually for one purpose or another, and in particular for cleaning *les armes blanches* (swords, bayonets, etc.) and firearms; indeed, it is known in France as '*paille d'armurier*', 'gunsmith's straw'. It can be used either dry or dipped in paraffin. While on the subject of weapons, it is worth mentioning that all the methods described here can be used with perfect safety.

Special care will be needed to remove all traces of rust. If there is any pitting, a de-rusting agent can be applied, in moderation, to ensure deep penetration. So as not to overdo this drastic treatment, limit the amount applied by trimming a match-stick to a point and dipping it in the liquid, or use a toothpick in the same way. After the fizzing which occurs instantly on contact with the dirty metal, rinse the liquid off and dry the work.

Protection with beeswax is excellent for swords, etc., but not so good for firearms, where it may cause the mechanism to clog. Use special gunsmiths' oil for these; Vaseline is not permanent enough. Linseed oil has the advantage of 'feeding' the wood of the stock as well as protecting the metal, but it dries too slowly and may collect dust.

THE PRESERVATION OF IRONWORK

There is only one way of preserving ironwork without altering the appearance of the metal, namely that mentioned in several previous chapters: *beeswax*. It is an advantage to heat the iron before waxing it, so that the wax melts on contact and gets right in everywhere. Wipe off any excess wax, let the iron cool, then polish with a soft cloth. No other treatment is worth mentioning; none yields such a satisfactory and lasting result.

RENEWING A PATINA

If you have a recently made piece which looks brand new, or one which has been mistakenly brought to a bright finish, there are various ways of darkening it to please your fancy.

Dip the article in waste oil, then heat it strongly until all the oil has disappeared. The result is a sombre patina of a dark grey, slightly bluish shade. Rub the object with a soft cloth and it will at once shine up beautifully. You can then wax it too if you wish.

An antique dealer's dodge which works very well: burn a pile of printed matter (old newspapers, magazines, posters, etc.) and hold the article to be 'patinated' in the flames. The vaporized ink combined with the lampblack deposits a film on the iron, which then merely requires waxing.

Shoe polish can be used instead of old oil; apply the polish, dry it out by heating the iron, and the colouring matter in the polish will be left behind (use black or dark brown polish).

Acid: on clean bare iron, acid vapours quickly cause the appearance of a delicate oxidation, almost powdery to the touch, which needs only to be waxed to become a brown patina.

To obtain this effect, place the pieces requiring treatment in a confined space, such as a trunk or a cupboard, with a little ordinary sulphuric or hydrochloric acid in an open glass vessel. Don't leave them too long: twenty-four or forty-eight hours will be quite enough to oxidize the articles evenly all over.

We would like to end this chapter with a recommendation whose value our readers will appreciate when they have tried it. Make up your mind to visit the Musée Le Secq des Tournelles at Rouen, the richest and most amazing specialized museum in the world, devoted exclusively to wrought ironwork from the early Middle Ages to the present day.

The exhibits are exceptionally well preserved and presented, and such a display of the blacksmith's craft will teach you something about the whole field of those material skills whose development is part and parcel of the life of mankind.

Among the funerary equipment discovered in Tutankhamen's tomb was a dagger. This weapon was an eye-opener to the experts: it is made of iron, whereas in the time of the Pharaoh in question the two most currently used metals were copper and bronze. The dagger was entirely free from rust; a phenomenon correctly attributed to the perfectly dry atmosphere inside the tomb.

PART TWELVE

ENGRAVINGS

Fig . 1 .

Fig . 2 .

Engravings: How to Restore Them to Their Pristine Whiteness

YOU have acquired some engravings—you glanced inside a portfolio in a junk shop or went treasure-hunting in a dusty attic, or perhaps a relation left them to you in his will. Some of them are infected with blotches of discoloration which mar the beauty of the design and blur the delicacy of the drawing.

What can be done?

The disfigurements may not all spring from the same cause. The commonest causes are age and damp. Occasionally, oil, grease or rust are responsible. And there is sometimes damage done by flies.

Provided you diagnose the origin of the blemishes it is easy to rejuvenate the engraving by means of the handful of recipes below.

GETTING RID OF OILY STAINS

Take a sheet of blotting paper or other absorbent paper and dust it evenly with Fuller's earth (if this is not available, use talc or finely ground plaster). Then very carefully irrigate the stain with turpentine, and lay the engraving face downward on the sheet covered with Fuller's earth.

On the back of the engraving, opposite the spot, spread more Fuller's earth. (Both in this and in the first operation, there is no need to put down a layer all over; it is enough to cover the area of the stain and a little more.) Then cover the whole with another sheet of blotting paper and place a suitable weight on top, such as a book or an ash-tray, and leave it for at least twenty-four hours.

If results at the end of that time are poor, proceed as follows:

Plug in your electric iron, setting it to 'silk' (if your iron has no thermostat, bring it to the heat suitable for the most delicate, vulnerable materials) and carefully iron the blotting paper (or other absorbent paper) until the stain vanishes. The same method can also be used on pencil drawings.

GETTING RID OF STAINS CAUSED BY MOULD

Fill a large bowl or a washbasin with a mixture composed of one part hydrogen peroxide 130 volumes (if unobtainable from a chemist or drugstore, you will be able to get it from a cabinet makers' supplies merchant) and two parts mineral water. Take care not to use tap water, it has too much lime in it. Add a few drops of ammonia.

Place the engraving in the mixture. Total immersion is necessary. Let it soak for about an hour.

The first immersion probably won't yield the desired result. Don't be discouraged by any persistent stains, repeat the immersion once or twice if necessary.

However, it is possible that your perseverance will be in vain and that a few particularly stubborn stains will still be there. In that case, make up a different mixture: one part bleach added to two parts mineral water (which should first be made very hot). Place the engraving in this and leave it, as before. Examine it at intervals to see whether the stains are gradually disappearing. As soon as they have gone take the engraving out and rinse it copiously in clean water (tap water is safe for this).

After rinsing, you may find that although the disfiguring stains have disappeared the whole paper now has a yellowish tinge. This slight defect is easily remedied. All you have to do is to put the engraving back into the first mixture (hydrogen peroxide, mineral water and ammonia): the appearance of premature ageing will disappear.

THERE IS NO ANSWER TO RUST

Of all the stains that spoil an engraving, those caused by rust are certainly the least responsive to the known remedies. They have all been tried but almost none has proved effective. However, here are two which, if the stains are a little obliging, may well succeed.

Plates being prepared for soft-ground etching

Start by washing the engraving several times in lukewarm water, concentrating (cautiously!) on the stains. Then dust the stains with potassium oxalate. Finally, rinse thoroughly.

One can also try using the anti-rust preparations sold for laundry purposes.

As we said, rust often defeats all attempts to remove it, so don't expect miracles. However, you will probably have the satisfaction of making the stains much dimmer, even if they don't totally disappear.

OTHER STAINS

Oily marks, mould and rust are not the only disfigurements to which engravings are subject. Stains resulting from damp, and others, make ugly inroads on them. Here are some ways of counterattacking, with more or less success as the case may be.

Lay the engraving flat on the bottom of your bath, and cover it to a substantial depth with coarse bay salt from the kitchen. Cut up two or three lemons and squeeze the juice on to the salt. Don't be too economical, the salt must get adequately soaked in lemon juice. Leave matters in this state for an hour or two, then rinse the engraving very thoroughly.

Another method employs a mixture made up thus:

To every litre of water, add two tablespoonsful of chloride of lime and two tablespoonsful of soda crystals. Soak the engraving in the mixture, take it out and wait for ten minutes. Rinse thoroughly, as usual, but add a little vinegar (*eau de vinaigre*) to the water first.

Both these mixtures can also be used for treating an engraving which has yellowed slightly with age. But don't be over-optimistic. Neither of them will dramatically restore the paper to its original whiteness. The yellowing will diminish but may not vanish completely, however hard you try.

HOW TO DRY ENGRAVINGS
DURING TREATMENT

To dry an engraving, the best way is to use new blotting paper spread out on a really flat surface (such as the glass top of a desk) and simply lay the engraving on it. But remember to proceed very carefully, avoiding creases or dog's ears (bent corners), which, once made, may be almost ineradicable.

A large engraving can be dealt with by removing it from the water in which it has been rinsed and sticking it to one of the inside walls of the bath. It will automatically come unstuck when it has dried out.

Important: never expose a drawing or engraving to sunlight. It should always be allowed to dry slowly, in the shade.

Also rigorously avoid hanging it on a line; the clips or pegs would mark the paper.

REPAIRING A SMALL TEAR

If, while treating an engraving, you make a clumsy movement and tear the paper slightly, don't curse yourself; the damage is not catastrophic and will soon be made good if you proceed as follows:

Turn the engraving over and lay it flat, face downward, on a smooth surface. Then coat the edges of the tear with flour paste and apply a strip of tissue paper 2 or 3 cm wide. Before putting the strip on, check carefully to make sure that the edges of the tear have met correctly. Leave the repair to dry for a few hours and then carefully tear off any spare tissue paper at either side of the join. If you are a perfectionist, very lightly smooth the repair with fine glasspaper; the damage will then be completely invisible.

In this kind of repair, never use ordinary sticky paper or plastic tape. In course of time it turns the paper yellow; it also shrinks and tears it.

STAINS ON A WATERCOLOUR

As a general rule, stains or spots of any sort on a watercolour are practically impossible to remove. But there is one simple procedure which sometimes works, within limits. We pass it on with reservations.

In a tinting saucer (the kind of little porcelain dishes used by watercolour painters and others) or, failing this, in a large spoon, mix 5 drops of ammonia with hydrogen peroxide 20 volumes.

Arm yourself with a fine brush which 'points' well; you can get this at an art shop. Dip it in the mixture and moisten the spot—and nothing else. Go very carefully. If you put on too much of the liquid, so that it overflows the frontiers of the spot, dry it quickly by dabbing very lightly with a bit of cottonwool.

You can apply the mixture three or four times in succession, but it is wise to let a few minutes elapse between applications.

FLIES

The dirt deposited by flies is hard to remove, especially from paper. The various methods explained here will make them less conspicuous and in many cases eliminate them, but we would advise that you first scratch them with a photographic retouching pen (or, as explained in an earlier passage, a *vaccinostyle*: the scarifier used by doctors for vaccinating). For good results, the paper must be perfectly dry. Don't overdo it on the most recalcitrant spots; just scratch the surface. The mixtures recommended here will then effectively complete the job.

PART THIRTEEN

CLOCKS

The Grandfather Clock Defies Time

PEOPLE used to say that a grandfather clock devoured time; that its pendulum of polished brass was an obsessive image of the hours, days and months in their remorseless flight.

You are perfectly entitled to prefer the urgent din of an alarm clock, '*Made in Germany*', but you will grow old just the same and its mechanical frenzy will doubtless accelerate the process. There was a certain nobility in the gait of our forefathers' clocks, whose two-beats-in-a-bar never outpaced the beating of the human heart. We contend that these lofty timepieces in their wooden cases were the allies of silence. The serenity of the night-time, measured out by the slow *tick-tock*, acquired a special quality. Every man to his taste, of course; but one does notice that the grandfather clock has slipped effortlessly back into the scheme of things by becoming the guardian of the weekend cottage. A point to be remembered is that it goes for eight days, so that at each weekend you are welcomed by a home that feels lived in. Most people's first action on arrival is to wind up the weights. By this symbolic action they resume possession of the place they love and mentally cast off their working uniform, simultaneously becoming aware that the clock treats time as the peasant treats his bread and cheese, chewing every mouthful thoroughly to extract the full flavour and showing therein an excellent sense of values. An attitude which at once defies time yet enables us to abide by it—which is no more and no less than what Einstein was expressing in his theory of relativity!

A SHORT COURSE IN HOROLOGY FOR
THE LOVER OF ANTIQUES

It would be beyond the scope of this book to study horology and its historical milestones in technical detail. Excellent specialized books exist for the purpose. However, in the limited field which is our concern, that of grandfather clocks (*horloges de grand-maman*; also known in French, but wrongly, as *comtoises* or *normandes*) there are distinctions which enable us to gauge, at least approximately, the age of the mechanism, to identify a given clock and hence also to look after it.

Clocks worked by weights have existed since the early Middle Ages. Examples have been preserved whose parts are made of forged iron, and whose design is very similar to that of the revolving spit (which also worked by means of weights). The pull exerted by a weight on a cable wound round an axle caused the axle to rotate. A gear-train at once made this rotation smoother and translated it into a slower speed. The earliest clocks had *one* hand only. The time, or an approximation to it, was read from the position of the hand on a graduated dial: the space between each number and the next was divided into halves and quarters; sometimes these divisions were indicated on a smaller, concentric dial.

This arrangement was accepted as adequate until the 16th century, when another hand was added to divide the hour into minutes and in some cases into seconds; and a third had made its appearance, indicating the days of the month; and an alarm mechanism with a bell was also included.

It was the 19th century which brought the grandfather clock, in its wooden case, to the apogee of its development.

But, as we have indicated, it had clearly existed for centuries before that period.

The style of the case (which French antique dealers, incidentally, call *la caisse*) is a valuable clue. If it has straight sides (without bulges) and is narrow, made of thick wood, carved, and designed to contain a comparatively small mechanism, it was probably made before the last century. It often exhibits the stylistic attributes of its period: panels with symmetrical divisions, each in the form of a curled, pointed arch, denote the age of Louis XIV; panels with asymmetrical divisions (but balancing each other symmetrically), with carved floral decorations—Louis XV; plain rectangular panels, surrounded by carved rustic decoration, 'pearl' borders and grooves—Louis XVI.

The straightness of the sides is of course related to the mechanism they enclose: the pendulum was only relatively important. Often the bob was just a very small lump of lead. In slightly more sophisticated designs it took the form of a sun or a face (in the reign of Louis XIV); sometimes it was a disc of polished brass; but it was only a few centimetres in diameter (4, or at the most 5).

The 'belly' which was soon evolved, giving the case a likeness to that of a double-bass, was called into being to accommodate the considerable increase in the diameter of the bob. Confining ourselves to the cabinet-making side before dragging the reader with us into the mysteries of the works, we note that the case was in step with *regional* stylistic development and was thus always in complete harmony with provincial furniture. Later there was a tendency towards uniformity: cases were made of lightweight woods such as pine or poplar and painted in several colours or 'grained', and ornamented with rustic décors, little flowers, flower-sprays and similar attributes. This was the terminus of development.

Although, as we have said, the shape of the case varied in tune with the style of its period, the chief factor determining it was the size of the mechanism and the pendulum. The latter is a valuable pointer to the age of any clock. Any pendulum consisting of a simple bar, flat or round in section, ending in a small weight (sometimes with a figurative design) or disc, indicates a period prior to the 19th century.

In that century, the polished brass disc developed rapidly; its surface was enlarged; originally resembling a small lens made of metal, it reached the size of a saucer and finally of a plate. An indication of age, but not one which denotes the period at all exactly, is the method of adjusting the pendulum: the earliest method was undoubtedly that of sliding the bob up or down on the rod. The decadence of the long-case or grandfather clock is marked by the appearance of the ornamented, coloured and animated bob. Clocks with this feature hardly go back farther than 1900. They represent a boy stealing apples and a farmer's wife chasing him with a broom, or even a donkey nodding its head at a carrot; sometimes a little girl on a swing. Such objects undeniably have charm; but the 'Westminster chimes' which drove out the grandfather clock are not far away, nor for that matter is the kitchen clock which really falls into the class of novelty goods, such as the model which imitates the grotesque clock appearing on French TV.

Let us return to the more peaceful age which is relevant here. The type of pendulum has further secrets to impart. The suspension of the bob from the mechanism has a hidden language of its own. Putting it simply, two types occur most frequently, those in which the bob hangs on a string or rod respectively. The first is thought to be the older.

Let us leave the pendulum and consider the face, which is often what most attracts the eyes and interest of the amateur. In the oldest clocks the dial is of brass or pewter; sometimes the numbers are painted with enamel on raised studs fixed to the dial. Later, we find dials enamelled all over, ceramic dials and, on some country clocks, wooden dials. Here again, local and period styles make themselves felt in the general character of the dial, its quality, and the character of the numbers. The latter may exemplify an ancient clockmaking tradition, a 'IIII' consisting of four upright strokes instead of the more logical Roman IV.

The surround of the face is another essential feature. If it is of heavy, moulded metal, with decoration embodying a cock or pierced arabesques for its pediment, you may be looking at a really antique clock (pre-19th-century). A surround of smooth wood or iron sometimes indicates the Empire period. After that, one finds brass backgrounds with highly luxuriant repoussé decoration, almost always rustic in character. When this decoration is polychromed it is a sign the ultimate incarnation of the long-case clock has been reached.

Let us now go into greater technical detail—reminding the reader that we are concerned solely with the long-case or grandfather clock. As will be obvious, our observations are not necessarily true of other types.

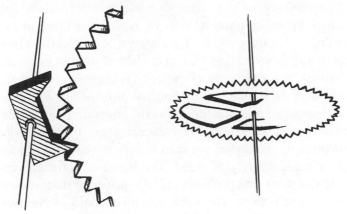

Let us look at the escapement. This indispensable component consists of a toothed wheel revolving step-fashion in time with the pendulum, and a rocker called the pallets (see sketch). When the axis of the escape-wheel is vertical, the movement is older than when it is horizontal.

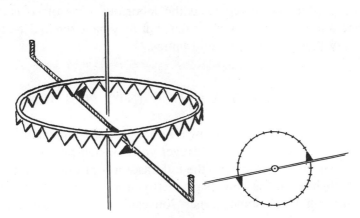

The pallets are called in French the 'anchor' (*ancre*), from their shape. At each swing of the pendulum, one pallet goes up and the other goes down, releasing one tooth of the escape-wheel in the process. This ingenious device is not present in all old clocks. In some, there is a 'verge escapement': a metal rod with a pallet at each end (see the sketch). This is obviously the ancestor of the first mechanism described. However, these indications are only a general guide and should be supplemented by other observations, of which the most important are those already given in this chapter. It is a well-known fact that rural clockmaking did not always march in step with technical improvements elsewhere. We must remember that there were villages in Savoy and the Jura which for centuries had virtually no contact with the outside world and no resources on which to draw except their own tradition of clockmaking. Examples are even known of reasonably accurate clocks made entirely of wood. These rudimentary movements really did work and probably still do, provided that woodworm hasn't ruined them. The same cannot be said of the wooden watch displayed in Magdeburg museum, whose face, pinions, hands and case are all of wood. The only exception is the driving wheel, which is of bone. The craftsmanship is astonishing but the contraption plainly doesn't go. This curio doesn't tell us much—exceptional things usually don't. Which is why we should think with fondness and respect of those country clocks which have regulated the laborious lives of so many generations. They are not rarities, but they have the undeniable beauty that attaches to useful things.

HOW TO PUT A CLOCK INTO POSITION

We are not trying to lay down the law concerning decoration. Your clock will look fine wherever you yourself prefer to stand it. Have you noticed how the tall case of a grandfather clock embellishes the narrow place between two windows, or an entrance-hall, or some corner you can't do much with? The advice given here is concerned only with enabling your clock to work properly.

You have set up the case as nearly plumb-true as you can, hooked on the weights and wound them up. *Remember that the big weight is hung from the escapement and the small one from the striking mechanism.* That is, when the weights are of different sizes, which they usually are. In this as in many other things, exceptions are common: the weights may be equal, in which case there is no problem.

Your sense of rhythm is about to be put to the test. You are going to put your clock 'in beat'. This is done not with an instrument of any kind, but *by ear*: you will listen carefully to the sound of your clock. The ideal is to have the same time-lapse between *tick* and *tock* as between *tock* and *tick*. Put like that, it sounds tricky, but in practice a little attention will enable you to detect the slightest irregularity. Correcting an uneven rhythm may require a little trial and error but will not take long. What you have to do is to level not the case but the mechanism. Provide yourself with some small pieces of cardboard and bristol, open the case, lift one corner of the mechanism, slip a sufficient number of pieces under it, and listen. Always put thin pieces first, replacing them with thick ones if necessary.

Check for accuracy—you will soon find out if your clock is gaining or losing. The error is easy to correct by altering the length of the pendulum. Raise the bob if the clock is losing, and vice versa. You will easily discover how to do this. Usually there is a small screw *below* the bob; sometimes the bob is so arranged as to stay in place by friction alone.

CLEANING A CLOCK

This may be made necessary by the dust and cobwebs which accumulate when a clock is neglected over a long period. You will have seen that the mechanism is reassuringly robust, so you needn't be shy of using vigorous methods.

In farms in the Landes, cleaning the clock was an operation carried out at regular intervals, necessitated by the use of resin candles whose oily smoke eventually made the mechanism dirty. Superstition also sometimes played a part. There was a tradition, colourfully embroidered with numerous supposed instances, that a clock infallibly stopped when its owner died. On such occasions it was never just set going again; it was felt the time had come for a thorough overhaul. The procedure, which we have actually witnessed, was as follows:

The movement was lifted out of the case and the cords suspending the weights were taken off; it was then placed in a copper filled with water to which lye had been added, and the copper was brought to the boil for an hour or two. The mechanism was well rinsed in clean hot water and put out in the open air, under the summer sun, until perfectly dry. The treatment was completed by a very special lubrication carried out with a slender feather dipped in goose fat.

As this description is intended to show, the process is as simple as can be. And, only slightly adapted, the method of the peasants of the Landes is perfectly valid. Surprising though it may sound, the most pernickety professional clockmakers are by no means averse to washing the mechanism in water.

If you can, relieve your clock of its hands, dial and the cords for the weights, dust it with a flat brush which you can dip in paraffin (kerosene) if you like, then put it in a boiling solution of washing soda (50 grammes to the litre). You will get excellent results by adding ammonia (one or two tablespoonsful) to the water, and potassium oxalate crystals (half a tablespoonful). Try to bring the water right up to the boil, because its ebullition then takes it into the smallest details of the works. Rinsing and drying are essential. Give it a good long rinse in running hot water and dry it with whatever means are available: a hair-drier, or in front of an open oven or on top of a radiator, etc.

Don't on any account lubricate the pinions, it would be the surest way of attracting dust and having to repeat the cleaning after a short while. Just use a little Vaseline on the bearings, without excess or mess.

A clock cleaned like this can go for twenty-five years without giving trouble, provided it is lubricated every couple of years. To complete the job, take some fine emery paper and remove any rust from the metal case which houses the movement. And a coat of anti-corrosion paint on this case will do no harm.

The cords should be changed if necessary. The hempen cords used by the old clockmakers can be advantageously replaced by woven nylon cords; these are easy to get from yacht chandlers.

When putting on new cords, take care to see that the turns lie *evenly*, *touching one another*, on the roller; they will then automatically return to the right position whenever they are wound up. Making them the right length is easy: the weights should just touch the bottom of the case (or in some instances the floor) when the cords are unrolled.

Your clock will now take on a long new lease of life.

PART FOURTEEN

IVORY

A Voice from the Age of the Mammoths

THE gentle, caressing touch of ivory has been familiar to man from the days when mammoths walked the earth. There is no doubt that this material has been fashioned by man ever since some very remote period. The Venuses of the Aurignacian period—figurines characterized by voluminous femininity—are a two-fold conundrum for specialists, because of the sculptural skill shown in the distribution of volumes undeniably denoting a conscious artistic doctrine, and also because it is hard to say just when these works, whose distribution ranges from south-western France to Siberia, were made.

It is also highly probable that ivory as an artistic medium was known from remote antiquity in China. However, it is not until a later period that tangible evidence appears of a more highly developed art, at once directed to more practical ends and endowed with more purely decorative qualities. In 1930, a dig carried out under two French archaeologists, MM. Schaeffer and Chenet, in the ruins of Ras Shamra in eastern Syria, opposite Cyprus, produced some very fine vases carved in ivory, which are thought to date from about 1400 B.C. Two years later, in 1932, excavations begun by an Anglo-American expedition and continued in 1934 by the Welcome Archaeological Research Expedition, at Tel Duweir, an ancient site in Palestine, 50 km. south of Jerusalem, brought to light numerous objects carved in ivory, notably a scent bottle in the likeness of a woman in a long tunic, and a portrait-miniature.

Many similar finds in Egypt make it plain that ivory-working was widespread under the Pharaohs. This noble material was used not only as a medium for ornament in temples and palaces but for making chairs and other articles of furniture, some of which have been recovered from Egyptian tombs.

The Phoenicians, those daring navigators and incomparable

traders, provided Greece with ivory. And to give themselves a yet more flourishing market there, they taught the Greeks the art of carving it.

Homer, in the *Odyssey*, makes it clear that his compatriots used ivory for ornamenting bridles, keys, chairs and beds. They also turned it into scabbards and combs.

Homer, again, has handed down the earliest recorded name of a craftsman in ivory, one Ismalios. By fixing small sheets of ivory, skilfully fitted together, to a wooden frame, Phidias made large statues, some as much as 10 or 12 metres high! Among them was the famous Zeus of Olympia, regarded as one of the 'seven wonders of the world'.

Rome used an unconscionable amount of ivory for statues of deities, sacrificial appurtenances and the interior decoration of temples. Senators were officially entitled to an ivory sceptre and seat, at their own expense. The tradition has acquired a niche in literature: Flaubert, in *Salammbô*, lyrically inventorizes sumptuous doors, magnificent beds, thrones and household furniture, all of ivory and gold. Victor Hugo, in *Les tables tournantes de Jersey*, treats us to an imaginative description of Carthage: '. . . It was a giant city. It was sixty leagues in circumference and possessed six thousand temples, three thousand of which were of marble, two thousand of porphyry, six hundred of alabaster, three hundred of jasper, fifty of stucco, forty-five of ivory,' and so on.

Byzantium, in becoming the capital of the Eastern Empire, also became the heir of Greco-Latin art. Intense activity in ivory working was one of the results, attested by priceless icons on ivory sheets.

Much later, towards the 11th century, ivory carving in the form of statues, seats and other furniture, and various articles of different sizes, tended to disappear; from then on, the ivory workers' energy was devoted rather to the production of things for everyday use. It was at this period that France began outstripping the other European countries, so that by the 13th century it can be said that *ivory was essentially a French art*; it had become an industrial art in the modern sense of the term.

Ivory 'lacework' fan

In the centuries following this development, the raw material gradually became more plentiful as a result of the great voyages and the new geographical discoveries achieved through them.

The Low Countries and Germany, strengthening their ties with the great traditions of Western art, manifested a certain brilliance during this period. The makers of small objects in ivory and kindred materials were not mainly concerned with fine art; most of their work went into a multitude of practical things, such as knife handles, snuffboxes, fans, shuttles, croziers, the heads of walking-sticks, rosaries, flasks, etc. Under Louis XIV, the billiard table made its appearance in the *salon*; the balls and the cues were of ivory. At the same period the clavichord and the spinet became hugely fashionable; in both, ivory inlays were common, and of course the keys were covered with ivory.

During the reign of Louis XV some very beautiful toilet sets appeared; the most celebrated were those of the Marquise de Pompadour and the Comtesse du Barry. Importation of the raw material turned Dieppe, one of the ports for the Near East and Africa, into a centre of an industry which rapidly attained prosperity.

There is a tradition that ivory was being carved at Dieppe as early as the 15th century. Villaut de Bellefond, whose book *La Relation des côtes d'Afrique appelées 'Guinée'* appeared in 1669, wrote that two ships equipped and manned from Dieppe brought back so much ivory that the citizens began carving it themselves. However, this account notwithstanding, it has to be said that no evidence exists that the craft was practised on any considerable scale at Dieppe at such an early date. In Rouen, on the other hand, ivory carvers are included in the list of artists named by the guild statutes of the 'imagers' (painters and sculptors) as early as 1507.

It was probably a hundred years later when a certain number of craftsmen in ivory set up shop in Dieppe. In 1694 the English author and diarist, John Evelyn, published a work in which he observed that the town was full of all sorts of curiosities fashioned in ivory. By that time the craftsmen of Dieppe had become pastmasters in ivory working. The delicacy of its carvings and other products was spoken of everywhere as being far in advance of anything that other towns could boast.

Much later, the Revolution was to deal a fearful blow to Dieppe's ivory industry, whose customers were mainly English tourists and a few other travellers. By 1794 there were only eight merchants, two ivory workers and six carvers.

During the First Empire the craft gradually picked up again; the fall of Napoleon caused a temporary crisis, but after that the output and sales of ivory articles in Dieppe completely regained their former prosperity.

It went on for some time; indeed, at the Exhibition of 1855 the comparison between ivory products from Dieppe and those made by the craftsmen of Paris, among others, favoured the former. The consequence was that many of the ivory sculptors and ivory craftsmen in Dieppe were invited to work in Paris. The terms offered must have been tempting, as many of these workers did move to the capital. In 1867, Barbien, in his *Esquisse historique sur l'ivoirerie*, observed that 'a veritable phalanx' of sculptors from Dieppe were to be found in the workshops of Paris. The ivory industry in Dieppe sank correspondingly into a decline. The shortage of artists closed one shop after another. There had been eighteen of these establishments in the Dieppe of 1854; in 1900 there were four.

Today, only Dieppe Museum bears witness to the fame and prosperity which ivory and the ivory craftsmen once conferred on the town.

Real or Imitation Ivory: Can You Tell the Difference?

THE dictionary informs us that ivory is a substance of a milky colour and of the same character, chemically speaking, as bone, but denser and more homogeneous in texture.

It occurs in the form of tusks: those of the elephant, rhinoceros and walrus, and the teeth of the hippopotamus.

However, the ivory most generally used, and the only one with a legal right to the name, is that produced by the elephant.

This falls into two classes: hard and soft.

Hard ivory is yielded by elephants whose lives have been spent in wooded, shady surroundings, in the proximity of rivers, streams and marshes, in the humid climate of Guinea, Gabon and the Congo.

It is heavier than soft ivory and has no grain, that is to say no vein-like markings. In colour it is a fine, roseate white which turns whiter still with age. It is used by sculptors, including sculptors of figurines; miniature painters, toymakers and similar craftsmen; and cutlers.

Soft ivory comes from open country with a dry climate. The animal's tusks gradually lose their 'sap' through continued exposure to hot sunshine. As a rule their points have splintered.

Soft ivory hails only from certain parts of Ethiopia, Egypt and the coast of Zanzibar.

Being tender and highly resilient, soft ivory is particularly sought after by the manufacturers of billiard balls and piano keys, because it enables uniform results to be achieved.

The African elephant is the species which provides practically all the ivory used by sculptors and craftsmen in both Europe and Asia.

THE GEOGRAPHY OF IVORY

The following are the principal ivory-producing regions of Africa and the characteristics of the ivory they yield:

Senegal: grey ivory, semi-soft, of inferior quality.
Sudan: grey ivory, semi-soft and soft.
Guinea: hard ivory of the best quality.
Ivory Coast: grey ivory, soft and semi-soft, deficient in quality.
Niger: hard and soft ivory.
Cameroon, Gabon, Angola: hard ivory, pink in colour.
Congo: green ivory, both hard and soft.
Cape: pink ivory.
Mozambique: grey ivory, hard and soft.
Zanzibar, Tanganyika, Kenya: hard and soft.

Africa's biggest supplier is the Congo. Congo ivory comes from the eastern part of the state, mostly from the districts of Stanleyville, the Bas-Véla and the Ituri.

Before World War II, the big ivory sales took place every three months. The most important were those held in Antwerp, London and Liverpool, in that order.

Today, these sales are virtually non-existent.

In fact, since 1920, when 300–400 tons of raw ivory were exported annually, the tonnage of ivory exported from Africa has fallen by over two-thirds. Legal restrictions on hunting, not demand in Europe, have diminished the amounts of ivory sold year by year. A review of the amounts sold, in relation to the respective countries contributing to the total, shows that the effects of legislation have differed as from one African country to another. Some of these countries had already almost disappeared from the world markets as early as 1940; particularly the French possessions, in which killing an elephant was a legal offence.

At the present time France uses 12–15 tons of raw ivory per annum. This is a very small quantity. The weight of a tusk varies according to length and diameter; a weight of 75–80

Ivory comb, 16th century

kilos, with a length of 2·30–2·50 metres, is by no means rare. The price of raw ivory is stable: 40–80 francs per kilo, according to quality.

LEGAL PROTECTION FOR THE BUYER OF IVORY

The advent of plastics dealt ivory a mortal blow, not only in the manufacture of useful accessories but also in the field of pure art. It also encouraged fraud. Fake statuettes, in both Eastern and Western styles, made entirely of plastic, have appeared in the market. Ivory has a much higher density than plastic; comparison between the weights of a genuine object and a fake shows up the difference. To mask it, some fakers have adroitly used ivory dust (an easily recoverable workshop by-product) as a filler to mix with synthetic resins, the resulting conglomerate being uncomfortably close in appearance to the real thing.

One large chemical firm has even succeeded in reproducing the grain and veining possessed by certain qualities of ivory.

In this case, and sometimes in the preceding one, the substance is sold honestly under the name '*ivoirine*' or '*ivorine*'.

An English industrialist, however, blithely attaches the name 'ivory parisiana' to a substance of his own composition!

Fortunately, such 'innovators' are blocked by a decree of the French Ministry of Agriculture dated October 17th, 1950, which lays down standards governing the sale of objects made of ivory.

Article 2 stipulates that the word '*ivoire*' shall apply only to the natural substance of which elephants' tusks are composed.

Article 5 forbids the sale under the name '*ivoire*', with or without any qualifying terms, of any substance containing a quantity, however small, of anything other than ivory.

Article 7 requires that when any of the products or objects covered by the decree are visibly labelled '*ivoire*' in a display or shop, accompanied by objects made of an imitation material, the latter must be clearly labelled with the name of the material or with the word 'imitation'.

Article 8 forbids the use, in any form, of any indication or mode of presentation, such as a drawing, illustration, sign or symbol of any kind, or of any verbal appellation capable of creating, even phonetically, any confusion in the mind of the purchaser concerning the nature, origin, characteristics or composition of the products or objects covered by the decree.

In addition to ivory, the decree covers tortoise shell, amber and meerschaum.

The decree is of the first importance for the customer's protection, being deliberately framed so as to preclude equivocal or alternative interpretations.

Repairing Ivory

IVORY is worked in the same ways as wood. It resembles wood in possessing a grain but is much more flexible, so that it hardly ever snaps under the craftsman's hand. Time and atmospheric factors, especially excessive dryness, are what makes ivory deteriorate and gives it a tendency to split; a knock or other clumsy move may then cause a break.

Fortunately, a break in a piece of ivory is nearly always clean, almost geometrically so. There is no difficulty in fitting the two parts together. They can be stuck with the same adhesives as wood. It is noticeable, however, that the adhesive does not always bond well; it should therefore be reinforced mechanically by the use of pegs, miniature dowels or the like. This requires extreme care. What is the best way of going about it?

On any projecting member, such as the arm of a statuette or a comparable part of an ornament, try putting in a metal pin (of copper or brass). But it must not show through in the light; thin ivory is translucent, almost transparent. If the thickness is insufficient you will have to make a delicate little dowel from a piece of scrap ivory. In either case, dowel or pin, you will have to bore a hole, taking care not to let it go right through from side to side; you want the repair to be invisible once the adhesive has set. Ivory is very easy to drill with ordinary wood bits; the drill must run rather slowly.

Ivory tolerates vinyl adhesives very well and is not stained by them. Moderate cramping is desirable. Ingenuity and the shape of the object will determine whether you use adhesive tape, elastic bands or suchlike.

A modern method: when dealing with a fragile object, avoid risky manipulations by using an epoxy adhesive alone, without pinning. Don't leave any dribbles of adhesive, clean them off with spirit, and allow the adhesive to harden in a warm atmo-sphere: 20 °C. (68 °F.) if possible, and in any case not lower than 15° or 16°. The repair will be permanent and invisible.

A heavier piece, with a broken projecting portion, can be treated in the same way but with a slight variation. Drill a hole in each surface of the break, as if to house a pin uniting the two pieces; fill both holes with epoxy resin and reinforce it with a few fibres taken from a bit of glass fibre cloth. The other end of the fibres, of course, goes into the other hole. You'll find it quite easy to lay the fibres together compactly so that they make a little pin, as it were, and do not catch on the sides of either hole. Cover the rest of the surfaces of the break with a thin film of adhesive. Put the two parts together and cramp them. Allow about twenty-four hours for hardening, in a warm place. One could not wish for a stronger repair than this.

Additional hints

A few fibres are enough; don't feel you must cram the hole with them. A characteristic of epoxy resins, which makes them so important, is that after drying they are of almost mineral hardness; if spread in a thin layer they are indestructible, but if used thick they may snap off clean, like glass; hence the neces-sity of reinforcement.

WARPED IVORY

Ivory sometimes warps if exposed to humidity over a long period, or if the object is a thin one such as a comb or hairbrush.

Before the shape can be corrected the ivory must be soft-ened. Place the object in water to which about one-fifth of nitric acid has been added, and leave it to soak for three or four days. This makes it fairly translucent and surprisingly pliable. Bend it into the required shape and leave it to dry. It will soon regain its normal stiffness and opacity. But avoid putting it for any length of time into hot water; this would soften it.

An advantage of this method is the help it gives in marquetry, or in covering an object with an overlay of ivory. An important point is to remember that, whenever you are sticking thin slips of ivory on a dark surface (wood or metal, as may be the case), a sheet of white paper should be stuck on first as a backing. Otherwise the support will show through the ivory; this would be unsightly.

THE PATINA OF IVORY

Specialists will tell you that ivory is white, and that a patina can be obtained only by some dubious external application. Various ivories age in different ways, depending on quality. Most kinds do not turn yellow with age, in fact they get whiter.

For those who simply must have a patina here are a few safe recipes.

Expose the ivory to woodsmoke (but not to heat).

A slight tarry deposit will settle in the recesses and after drying for a few hours will form a sturdy, durable patina. Rub it with a woollen duster.

Decoctions of tea and chicory also yield a brown or golden patina. Simply paint the liquid on, and leave it to dry.

'Natural' wood stains, such as walnut or Cassel extract, give excellent results. With time, they may even sink in to some depth.

Some exotic brownish-red ivories are tinted by the natives with betel nut or areca nut.

The Chinese are pastmasters at tinting ivory and use a wide variety of colours, blue, green, red and so on. Nowadays they either use ordinary chemical colouring agents, or dyes which are much the same as textile dyes.

To those for whom oddities hold a special appeal we present two recipes, the first of which gives ivory a bronze-green shade:

Put into some nitric acid as much bronze as it is capable of dissolving, then place the ivory in it overnight. The result is a very beautiful green. (But we must add that this is a dangerous thing to do with a valuable ivory piece.)

A truly Far Eastern method of giving ivory a golden yellow patina is to carry it next the skin. Bulky articles are not recommended!

HOW TO LOOK AFTER IVORY

Household recipes for cleaning ivory are plentiful and mostly quite harmless, especially those using lemon juice.

Just use soap and water. Alternatively, ivory will tolerate washing soda (15 grammes per litre of water).

Ivory can be polished by coating it with Spanish whiting mixed with lukewarm water. As soon as the whiting has dried, rub with a chamois leather.

Things that get used, such as brushes, combs, dressing-cases, knife handles and piano keys, can be kept in condition by regular cleaning with a mixture of Spanish whiting and methylated spirit.

When an elaborately carved ivory piece has become encrusted with dust or tenacious dirt, give it a bath for a few hours in fresh milk (not boiled or pasteurized). Then brush it with a stiff brush and rub it with a soft cloth until it is perfectly dry.

TO WHITEN IVORY

To give ivory a milky, matt appearance, coat it with turpentine and let it stand in the sun for a few hours.

Hydrogen peroxide 120 volumes is a safe means of making ivory white. The effect is immediate. You can either dip the ivory in the liquid or paint the liquid on. In the latter case, use a piece of cottonwool; a brush would be damaged. Rinse and dry.

There is an old recipe for whitening and cleaning ivory which is still applicable provided certain precautions are observed. Dissolve some rock alum in water, place the ivory in it, bring the solution to the boil and keep it on the boil for an hour. If any dirt still remains, brush it off. Wrap the ivory in several thicknesses of wet cloth and let the whole thing dry in the air.

The purpose of the wet wrapping is to slow down the drying process and avoid the little cracks which develop when ivory passes too abruptly from one state of humidity to another.

PRESERVING IVORY

Your pieces are like capital, the interest paid by which is chiefly the aesthetic pleasure you derive from them. Safeguard them against an insidious ailment: desiccation. Ivory always remains a living substance, and if kept in too dry an atmosphere it cracks and rapidly deteriorates. Equip your radiators with humidifiers, and never expose your ivory pieces to excessive warmth (such as that from a light-bulb); they will then remain in good condition for many years.

One of the most original collections of ivory we have seen is undoubtedly that of M. R. Brejoux, the President of the Chambre Syndicale de l'Ivoire. Every item in it was made by M. Brejoux himself. He produces replicas of old ships on a scale of 1/100; a unique achievement, without a parallel anywhere. M. Brejoux has invented a technique for producing ivory 'thread'; from a single 'vein' of elephant's tusk he can make threads of 0·3 mm. diameter for the rigging of his ships, the simplest of which has cost him 3500 hours of work!

His vocation sprang originally from a curious incident which deserves a place in 'mini-history', anecdotal history. In 1964, preparations were under way in France to receive President Kennedy on an official visit. To André Malraux, Minister of Cultural Affairs, occurred the idea of commissioning the craftsmen of the Musée de la Marine to make a model of the *Flore*, the first ship in the fleet of Louis XVI to salute an

American vessel; a *de facto* recognition by France of the United States, at that time not yet officially constituted. A very suitable present to offer John Kennedy, as a former naval officer; but though the idea was excellent in itself the Minister felt the gift was hardly adequate for a visiting Head of State. To match the result with the intention Malraux decided to have the *Flore* modelled in ivory, and the commission was handed to M. Brejoux—who was faced by unforeseen technical problems because everything, including sails and ropes, had to be made of ivory, unassisted by any other material.

The finished model, a wonderful achievement, was thrust into limbo by President Kennedy's death. The foundation item in M. Brejoux's collection was thus a doubly historical reject. But, so far from being disappointed, he had discovered his life's passion. The *Flore* was followed by a model of the *Astrolabe*, the ship of the great French navigator Dumont d'Urville. Next came four *chebecs* like those ordered by Colbert from ship-yards in the south of France (a *chebec* or *sciabecco* is a Mediterranean three-masted vessel, lateen-rigged). These were highly elegant but terribly difficult, the pieces being so tiny: 32 blunderbusses, 24 cannon, and sails of a special design—the latter alone kept M. Brejoux occupied for eleven months.

In May 1960 he finished a slave-ship, the *Ouragan*, and, using some very rare research information, began re-creating the *Paradis*, the ship that bore St Louis to the Holy Land.

A collection of this kind is not only invaluable in its own right; it is a testament of professional devotion and skill.

PART FIFTEEN

MARBLE

Broken Marble is no Headache

CERTAIN disasters, such as a commode with a shattered top, or a mutilated mantelpiece, should now be firmly dismissed from your mind. If you possess taste, a little knowledge and a sensitive pair of hands, you can mend the most jagged break almost invisibly.

Follow our advice: it will serve you well in these days when marble masons are scarce, marble expensive and bills high.

A smooth, straight break, like a cut, is always a disadvantage. Its very regularity makes it hard to camouflage. Moreover it may slip during cramping (a question we will explore in a moment).

Let's examine the commonest case: an irregular break— which in many instances has already been mended years ago.

1. With a file, a wire brush or coarse emery paper, clean up the surfaces of the break and carefully remove all traces of old glue.

2. Prepare your adhesive. We recommend a two-part epoxy resin adhesive. Nothing else, as yet, makes such a strong joint. The stuff comes in two tubes, the resin and the hardener. Mix the requisite quantity with great care.

3. Coat both surfaces. No blobs anywhere; use a small, flexible spatula; aim at producing a fine, even film of adhesive.

4. Bring the pieces together, having planned in advance how you are going to keep them there; with carpenter's cramps, elastic bands (cut from an old inner tube), pieces of wood and so on. A marble slab in a piece of furniture is unlikely to present any snags. A mantelpiece, and some other things, may not be so easy. On small objects, elastic bands come in handy in various ways; so does sticky tape. More detailed advice is really not possible; special cases abound and solutions vary infinitely.

When using your file or emery paper, collect the resulting marble dust in a dustpan or the like. If necessary you can supply yourself with extra marble dust—marble flour, as it is called—by gently scraping the back or underside of the marble. Mixed with a little adhesive this powdered marble makes a mortar for building up a small chip or smoothing the edges of the fracture. For white marble, talc gives good results.

Having glued the pieces together with absolute accuracy, take care to remove any dribbles of adhesive with alcohol and a bit of cottonwool.

Twenty-four hours later, when drying is complete, polish your work. Buy the finest flower paper obtainable and use it wet. By polishing the glue-line you will find you can make it practically invisible.

Sometimes, however careful you are, you won't be able to find all the fragments from the break. After gluing, splinters of considerable size will be missing. Don't worry. At a paint-shop you will find a range of assorted shellacs which can be poured hot into the cavities (always remember that shellac should be melted with a hot iron; never use a flame, which would char it). Having stopped the hole, polish as above.

MODERN TECHNIQUE TO THE RESCUE

Two-part adhesives, which attain mineral hardness, provide an extraordinarily strong joint. They are a remarkable advance on earlier methods. However, other two-part preparations have recently been developed which actually imitate marble. Their adhesive power is lower than that of the epoxy resins, but for building up a missing chip, even quite a large one, they are truly sensational.

When buying, match the shade carefully.

When using, mix up no more than you can use quickly, because with some makes the setting time is rather short. Follow the manufacturer's instructions about adding the hardener, and mix thoroughly.

Watch out for one thing: the mixture must be forced well down into the interstices; use a spatula, and press hard. The consistency, which is that of thick honey, makes this easy, but you must avoid letting bubbles form; subsequent polishing will turn them into holes.

Hardening occurs without delay. After a few minutes the adhesive becomes resistant to finger-pressure and gives off a strong smell. Make use of this intermediate period, while hardening is incomplete, to remove dribbles and to smooth your work with a wood chisel, a rasp or a file. When the work is completely hard you can still shape it a bit, but with much greater difficulty. The plastic can then be polished with flower paper, as already described.

We emphasize the advantages of the method. No cramping; simply bring the parts together and hold them in place by hand for the short time required for polymerization; and carry out the finishing process at once—no tedious wait for setting.

LEARN TO MAKE A MOULD

In order to reconstitute a missing corner or a moulding, or a motif on a mantelpiece, say, or a clock, you will have to take a mould from an intact portion. There are two methods, both very simple. *Plaster of Paris* is the first: the better, but if anything the trickier, of the two. The part to be reproduced must be coated, in moderation, with oil (use Vaseline, or salad oil on a rag). Fix up a 'fence', a miniature shuttering, of cardboard, to prevent the plaster from running. Plaster, unlike cement, is used pure, and is mixed not by adding water to it but by adding it to water (use about the same quantity of water as you require of wet plaster).

As soon as the plaster has 'worked' and has become a pourable slurry, pour it into the shuttering, meanwhile tapping the shuttering with a small tool of some sort so as to vibrate the plaster and cause it to enter the details.

After a few minutes your plaster will be hard. Take the

mould off; you will find the motif imprinted in reverse. All you have to do is to place the mould opposite the part to be reconstituted, and insert the plastic.

But watch it! Some motifs have undercuts. Check carefully before committing yourself; make sure the mould, once made, can be removed.

Modelling paste (e.g. Plasticine): the ideal method if the motif is a simple one. You take an impression by pressing the Plasticine on to the motif.

But take care not to distort your improvised mould while taking it off. Speed and simplicity are the advantages of this method. The disadvantage is the danger of distortion. This can be avoided by supporting the mould with bits of wood or cardboard.

The really up-to-date way: for coping with complicated

motifs, which would be very tricky to mould by either of the above methods, latex elastomers offer endless possibilities.

These elastomers consist of latex in a paste or liquid form; they vulcanize at ordinary atmospheric temperature and humidity. Their viscosity enables them to penetrate the smallest cranny. After vulcanization, the mould, which remains rubbery and flexible, is easily withdrawn without damage, and is unaffected by the plastic used for building up the missing part.

Care of Marble

MARBLE is cleaned with soft soap (rinse well afterwards). Failing this, a very weak solution of washing soda is quite suitable.

Virgin wax is the best protection for marble. The wax can be diluted with a drop of paraffin (kerosene).

HOW TO REMOVE SPOTS AND STAINS

Marble absorbs stains: they often mark it in depth. The most dangerous enemies of marble tops are wine (the foot of a glass or the bottom of a bottle) and vinegar and lemon juice (because they are acid).

Repolishing is the treatment for affected marble. This is a job for the professional, though one can get a fairly good result oneself with flower paper.

Ink stains are not necessarily permanent. Hydrogen peroxide may give you a happy surprise by removing the stain completely. If only partially successful, repeat. The hydrogen peroxide must have a chance of operating in depth if the ink has sunk some way into the marble, which is porous by nature. If necessary, add a few drops of ammonia to the hydrogen peroxide.

Rust often causes deep stains on white marble. Iron oxide penetrates insidiously and becomes very difficult to dislodge. Try hydrogen peroxide first. If this doesn't work, buy a little sodium bisulphite; only a few drops will be needed. Dust the stain with zinc filings and pour on the bisulphite. Wait for a few minutes; then wash the mixture off with water. If the result is still a failure there is another remedy: the rust-removers used by laundrymen. But be careful, these substances usually have an oxalic acid base and may attack the marble slightly. Make a quick trial: dust the stain with rust-remover, wet it with a dropper, wait for five or six minutes and rinse. If the marble has become rough at the spot treated, go no further; if it hasn't, try again, allowing more time for the treatment to work. Roughness, if only slight, can easily be rectified by polishing with flower paper.

HOW TO RECOGNIZE ANTIQUE MARBLE

There are several signs by which antique marble can be recognized:

General appearance. Its finely polished surfaces show signs of wear in places.

By placing a rule on it, you find the surface is *not perfectly flat* (the old marble masons didn't use machines).

The underneath, or the part against the wall, is roughly cut (examine it in a slanting light).

Grooves, mouldings and decorative carving are slightly irregular (hand-work again).

An interesting check: Whenever you have to remove a slab of marble for repair, you have a chance of making an interesting examination of the piece of furniture it covers. Usually, cabinet makers signed their work, but in concealed places. Commodes were generally signed *under the marble*, on the rails of the top drawer.

Your best procedure is to place a sheet of paper over the marks you find (they are often indistinct); rub with pencil lead or a graphite block; the signature, if such the marks really are, will then show up clearly.

If this quest is abortive, console yourself by remembering that the greatest painters often left their canvases unsigned; the sense of duty done was enough to satisfy their pride.

PART SIXTEEN

CHAIRS: STRAW SEATS AND RUSH SEATS

Learn to Re-seat Chairs

D ON'T waste time looking for that craftsman who, only a
few years ago, could be seen plying his trade in the open
air in town or countryside, and who figured in such engravings
as the series of *Cris de Paris*, 'Street-cries of Paris'. This
itinerant craft, popular and strange at once, of re-seating chairs
with straw, rush or cane, had vanished into limbo.

However, you possess some well-made cottage chairs whose
straw is in an advanced stage of disrepair and beginning to show
ominous, ugly gaps. What is to be done—short of discovering
a forgotten craftsman in a backyard or a rustic hovel? The
answer is simple: be your own craftsman.

The difficulty, despite your good intentions, is where to find
the straw. It must be the right kind, rye straw. But rye is hardly
ever grown today. The only thing is to scour the countryside,
asking farmers where to get this indispensable material. Without it, good results are impossible: oat straw is too short, wheat
straw too brittle. If your search proves in vain, try a manufacturer who specializes in cottage-type furniture; you can
probably find one who won't begrudge you a truss or so of rye
straw. Moreover, it will have the advantage of being already
dyed and treated against attack by mice. The usual amount to
allow is 250 grammes (a little over $\frac{1}{2}$ lb) per chair.

If you have bought your straw straight from the farm you
can either use it with its natural colour intact, or give it a
goldish hue by the following means:

Fill a preserving pan or similar vessel with water; cut the
straw at the knots and lay it in the water, all pointing the same
way. Bring the water to the boil and let it simmer a whole day.
Leave it to cool overnight. Then take out the straw and spread
it to dry thoroughly before use.

As well as the stout rye straw you will have taken care to

select, you may need the long, thin blades of various plants or grasses. This can be used for wrapping round each separate straw, so as to form the 'cords' which will give your work a smooth, regular appearance. The best advice we can give you is to examine the old, worn-out cords you have removed; this will teach you the secret of making them. You are, in fact, going to spin your own cords. Incidentally, there is a material which is easy to find and is extremely useful for cottage-type seating: the Great Reedmace, *Typha latifolia*, a semi-aquatic plant growing in marshes and on the edges of rivers, streams and ponds. Its seed-heads, dark chestnut in colour, look very well in a bouquet of dried plants. Its long, narrow leaves are thin and supple and, when twisted, make excellent cords for an out-and-out rustic style of seating. The leaves should be tied in bundles and left in a dry, well-ventilated place for some time, to prepare them for use.

To recapitulate the essential materials: 250 grammes of straw cut at the knots, and 500 grammes of long straw; this is enough for one chair.

Tools required are minimal and will have to be home-made; they cannot be bought.

Using holly or boxwood, both of which are hard and smooth, make an awl about 8 in. long and a spatula some 10 or 12 in. long. Add a good pair of scissors or a sharp knife, and your equipment is complete.

PREPARING THE STRAW AND THE CHAIR

The day before you intend to start, slightly damp both lots of straw: the long, uncut straw, and that which is cut at the knots. The object is to render it more pliable and easier to work with.

Take the nails out of the edging pieces (the thin wooden strips round the seat); remove the edging pieces and the old straw; clean up the rails. You are now ready to begin.

PATIENCE IS REQUIRED

You won't get the knack right away. But after a certain amount of experience you will find that re-seating a chair takes you only a few hours—about three. At first you may have to allow much longer; there is no blinking the fact that the work is of the slow, laborious kind and that you will often have to undo what you have done in order to make it as perfect as desired.

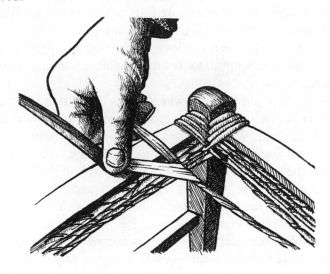

Don't let this fuss you; persevere patiently; you will learn to conquer all the little snags. You will have to sit on something fairly low in order to be at the right height in relation to the rails of the chair, with your straw on the ground beside you. Remember the posture of the craftsman in the street.

The first step is to take about twenty long straws and encase them (in a manner to be described) in a piece of short rye straw (the straw divided into pieces at the knots). To do this, slit the short piece of rye along its entire length with your thumb-nail. What you have to construct is a kind of string or cord with a spiral wrapping: the short straw, converted into a flat band, is to enclose the long straws so that only the wrapping is visible. We shall refer to the result as 'the cord'.

When you get near the end of the long straw, splice another one to it; carry on in the same way, producing what looks like an endless ribbon which, in unrolling, has remained twisted round an endless axis. The difficulty lies in the fact that the cord has to be of uniform thickness throughout its length.

To re-cap, for clarity: the split rye straw must surround the long straws, without gaps, the purpose of the long stems being simply to constitute the core or filler which is the foundation of the cord. When you have used up one piece of split straw, tuck the end in between the long stems and do the same with the next piece of split straw before you start winding it round the core.

We can now put the cord where it has to go. It is imperative to adhere faithfully to the path it is to describe in relation to the rails of the chair. Wind the cord twice round the right back leg of the chair (which is facing you to your left); stretch it tight towards the left back leg. Pass it once only round the frame and bring it towards the left front leg, then towards the right front leg, and lastly return it to the right back leg. You have now completed the first circuit.

Be careful: the back of the seat is narrower than the front, and you have to bring your work to a square shape. Therefore the next 7 or 9 circuits must be made as follows: 1 circuit on sides and front only; 1 circuit on all four sides, then 1 circuit on three sides; again 1 circuit on all four sides; 1 circuit on three sides; and so on, until you have achieved a perfect square. You then carry on, making circuits round all four sides and taking care to keep the cord tight between each leg and the next.

Generally, the whole seat will be covered by from 40 to 50 circuits. If the work is done well it will finish with the cord at the mid-point of the front or back. The cord is then slipped under the other cords with the help of the bodkin and its end is cut off under the seat. This is the correct way of 'stopping' the end and completing this part of the work.

FINISHING OFF

The next step is to turn the chair upside down and use odd pieces of the long straw for stuffing into the interstices between the cords. Use your spatula for this. Properly inserted, this stuffing makes all tight and firm.

Turn the chair the right way up again and work on it with the flat end of your bodkin. This is probably the trickiest part of the whole operation, on which success depends.

Slip the bodkin between each cord and its neighbour in such a way as to press the cords evenly together. Your movements should be firm, regular and forceful.

Your work will be first class provided all the cords are of equal thickness, packed close together, uniform in appearance and under strong tension.

The final step is to snip off any ends of long straw protruding under the seat.

You can also, if you like, give your work a pleasing 'patina' by means of one or two coats of a light golden-brown varnish, heavily diluted.

Re-upholster that Old Armchair

YOUR favourite old armchair makes you so comfortable, and you are so accustomed to its faithful presence, that you hardly notice it is there. Perhaps, though, the time comes when, returning from holiday, you see it needs to slough its old skin and acquire a new one.

But your local upholstery firm quotes you too high a price and asks you to wait too long. So you decide, wisely, to do it yourself. It's not particularly difficult, as you will see, and you will like the result so much better. So come on!

What you need is:

A good pair of tailor's scissors, a packing-bar (failing which, a good screw-driver will do), an upholsterer's hammer (the really sophisticated craftsman uses a magnetic hammer; the heads of the tacks stick to it and he doesn't give himself blisters by constantly handling them), a curved needle for difficult places, and a wooden mallet for hitting the packing-bar.

Don't rip off the old cover haphazard. Some of the nails would be left in, causing awkward bumps. Proceed in an orderly way. The vital thing is to strip the chair cleanly. Take the old cover off in one piece, so that you can use it as a pattern.

With the packing-bar (or the screw-driver) take out the brass-headed nails, using a turn of the wrist. You will sometimes find that this type of nail is not present. If tacks were used, the same tool will get them out but should be applied like a cold chisel and tapped sharply with the mallet. Pincers won't be necessary, except perhaps to extract a tack whose rusty head has come off when assaulted with the packing-bar.

Having removed the cover and nails (or tacks), inspect the

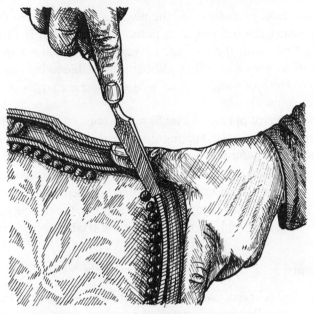

calico, webbing and stuffing. Obviously, to renew the stuffing
and the webbing, perhaps the springs as well, would demand a
professional standard of skill. Just bring the general condition
up to scratch by carefully refixing the pieces of calico which
confine the animal and vegetable fibres constituting the stuffing.
If need be, recondition the stuffing by breaking it up wherever
it has been felted together by long use, and add a handful of
new stuffing here and there if you think it necessary—
especially over the webbing and in the middle—fixing it with
the curved needle to the inside of the calico.

If your armchair is antique, a Louis XIV *bergère*, for
example, its stuffing will be in the old style, that is to say
without springs but embodying a down cushion on top. The
webbing will be fixed on the *upper* side of the rails, not the
bottom, as in sprung chairs. Hence you will find the webbing in
direct contact with the hair stuffing. Tighten the straps one by
one, if they need it. Sprung chairs are simple: the webbing is
easy to find (on the underneath, covered with a single thickness
of calico).

After these preliminaries, the next stage is to cut out the new cover, using the old one as a pattern. A good tip is to iron it lightly first; with the passage of years it will have acquired a shape of its own and will be almost impossible to lay out flat on the new piece of stuff. It is as well to leave a margin of 1 or 2 cm. all round.

The order of operations is: first, the back; then the sides and arms; finally the seat. Having cut out the new pieces with the old as a guide you will have no difficulties to get round. To be on the safe side you can tack on the new cover provisionally, using a larger size of tack and not driving them right in. If all is well, put in the full complement of smaller tacks and pull out the few big ones which you used for the trial fitting.

The arms:

These, like curved parts in general, are a little tricky. The amateur usually goes first for the convex side, because it is outside and immediately visible. This is wrong. *Start with the inner, concave side.* You will have no difficulty in accommodating the superfluous stuff and avoiding the necessity for making darts on the convex side. You simply make a series of tiny gathers, very close together; these are easily hidden by brass-headed nails, or braid.

Put in these nails as soon as you have finished covering the chair. If your aim is uncertain and you frequently hit the wood, protect it with a stout piece of cardboard, held in the other hand. Many armchairs, however, are not completed with nails but with braid, which gives an excellent finish, covering any imperfections at the edges and also the heads of the tacks. Don't cut the braid where it turns a corner; fold it over, making a tuck. Use one of the latex adhesives and spread it in lengths of 6–8 in. at a time (it dries very quickly); put it only on the braid, which will stick instantaneously. Adhesive braid of excellent quality has recently started making its appearance, but the colour range is still rather too restricted to be much use for restoring antiques.

SUNDRY TIPS AND WRINKLES

Your tools must be very clean. A slightly rusty hammer, or an awl which has been used for opening a tin of paint or has lain on a greasy bench, would mark your stuff.

With satins and other fabrics which crease easily, a flannel lining will be necessary. It need not be nailed but can be tacked to the calico with big stitches and, if you like, stuck at the edges with latex.

The edges of the stuff are likely to be frayed. This untidiness is often hard to conceal or trim off. Scissors won't do it; what you need is a razor-blade or a Stanley knife, extra sharp. A still easier way is to stick the frayed threads together with adhesive; they can then be trimmed without danger of their fraying again.

Tapestry is often difficult to work, to stretch, or to lay over a curved surface. Make it supple by damping the back. Stretch it in all directions to loosen the fibres. Leave it to dry on a board, first fixing it with pins to prevent it from shrinking.

To be surer of your positioning when putting on the stuff, use a stapler (stapling gun). Let the purists rage—they have no business to. Staples don't damage the wood and are easy to take out, and it is as if you had been given an extra hand with which to pull the stuff tight; otherwise, with a hammer and a nail to cope with, you must either neglect this essential aspect of the job or have someone to help you.

A recent innovation is a 'nail guide', made of plastic, which makes it easy to put in brass-headed nails at exactly equal distances.

PART SEVENTEEN

STATUES

Statues—The 'Obsessive Image'

STRANGENESS is the keynote here; statues are a world in which art is synonymous with emotion. What is it that so touches us—the spiritual radiance of a physical image, or echoes of religious practices, or a sense of the sacred or the supernatural? Every individual will seek whatever answer most satisfies his intelligence, but will not necessarily approach the truth. No statue leaves us indifferent; who has not felt the malefic power of an African or Polynesian idol, or responded to the serene ambiguity of a Buddha whose very pose constitutes a language; or the pathos of Christ on the Cross; or the elemental, pagan, prehistoric force of a Virgin and Child from Auvergne or Catalonia, combining the Oedipus myth of the mother with an idealized vision of fecundity?

Statues are not easy things to live with. Perhaps only the cool, admirable lines of an ancient sculpture in marble leave our intellectual comfort undisturbed, for then our aesthetic sense, with nothing extraneous to excite it, soon hardens into academicism.

Some people have a curious criterion for judging statues, claiming that while one statue has a tonic effect another is disturbing, and so on; individual sensibility being the only arbiter. Certainly the most powerful resonances are those emanating from the depths of one's own being. A statue is never *only* a work of art. If any form were divested of its cultural content, how much would be left? Time and experience bring conviction, and teach us that there is no art without doctrine; more precisely, without a spiritual doctrine.

We may see this reflected in the customary classification of Western religious art into three main epochs:

the *centuries of faith*, characterized by the hierarchical
serenity of Romanesque statues and the elegance and flexibility of the Gothic;

the *centuries of piety*, with the triumph of realism in the
Renaissance and of Puritanism in the 17th century;

finally, the *centuries of devotion*, full of swooning Virgins,
breathless bleeding Christs, gilded wooden clouds denoting
Paradise, and the bearded God the Father whose blessing
presides over the whole decadent pantheon—a decadence
reaching its consummation in the mass-produced plaster
casts typical of the most degenerate kind of religious art.

We cannot, in such a book as this, supply criticism for determining whether a statue is genuine or a fake. Such an analysis
of sacred art would demand several generations of specialists
and might even then defeat them.

Substantial works are available, especially on represen-
tations of Christ and the Virgin, which are crammed with
erudition yet have by no means exhausted the subject.

The common denominators of the statues that concern us
here are age and neglect. The reader will accompany us in
studying how to cancel or mitigate not only the ravages of
time but those perpetuated by dishonest or incompetent
restorers.

A STATUE ATTACKED BY WOODWORM

This should not unduly alarm you; the assault is not of recent
date and it may even be possible to assume that the insects can
find no more edible matter and have departed elsewhere. But if
you regularly find wood dust round the base of your statue, you
will have to apply treatment. Various commercial products,
which are insecticides and fungicides at once, are available for
you to choose from. Buy a sufficient quantity of a colourless one. Find a receptacle large enough to take your statue,
either standing up or lying on its side. Pour in enough of the

liquid (the product) partially to immerse the statue, and leave it until capillary attraction has drawn the liquid right into the wood.

Penetration may take several days; the colour of the wood will tell you how it is getting on.

Leave the statue to dry in a well-ventilated place before putting it back in its usual position. It will now be safe from further attack.

A WOODEN FIGURE CRUMBLING
INTO DUST

This is common enough with wood sculptures, especially with soft woods like lime (much used for sculpture) and even with walnut. The paint (polychroming) remains intact but the inside is like a sponge. This mainly happens with carvings which have been covered with a thin fabric as a basis for the polychroming; a fairly common technique which seems specially favourable to attack by woodworm. That is only a conjecture but it is founded on prolonged observation. The insect appears to have made its way in via the base; finding all other exits blocked by a thick armour of lime or plaster it proceeded to colonize the entire interior. An alternative hypothesis: a cloth covering was used only on softwoods, which are easy to carve—and whose tender grain is precisely what the woodworm, or wood beetle rather, prefers! In any case, the problem is an irritating one which usually evokes no better solution than a fatalistic shrug.

We have applied two methods to this type of case, with complete success.

1. A French-polishing mixture based on colourless shellac, heavily diluted: 1 litre of the mixture to 2 litres of spirit (alcohol). We put the wooden figure into a bowl or other receptacle and slowly inundate it with the liquid, giving the wood time to absorb it. (When absorption ceases don't throw the rest of the liquid away; on the contrary, keep it carefully and let the figure dry, which usually only takes a few hours;

then, and not before, start again and continue until the figure will absorb no more.)

2. We acquired a special liquid from a firm serving dressmakers and fashion houses. This liquid, whose composition varies from one manufacturer to another but usually has a cellulose base, is intended for stiffening fabrics and more especially the straw used by hat-makers and dressmakers. It costs little, and is more convenient than varnish because it requires no mixing or dilution and dries almost immediately. What is more, it sinks into spongy wood in spectacular fashion. As in the other method, don't be stingy; keep on pouring until the wood will accept no more. By this simple means you will have preserved a figure which the slightest knock or injudicious pressure could have destroyed.

A MUTILATED FIGURE

Many figures are in a mutilated condition; this is part of the price we pay for their being old. How much does it really trouble you? The reflex action of any specialist is to advise against restoration. There is a real danger of impairing the harmony of a figure-sculpture by inventing a missing limb or passage of drapery. The most one should do is to provide the piece with a base, if it really needs it. We are against any further addition.

However, cases do occur where slight restoration is not altogether unthinkable, when it is just a question of joining up; for example, when a fold in a garment is interrupted, or the tip of a passage in relief has been broken or has crumbled away.

Various makes of plastic wood are on the market; properly used, they can be satisfactory. They are composite materials, with the consistency of mastic, and can be modelled. After hardening, which is fairly quick, you can perfect the repair by sanding or shaping the plastic wood just as if it were real wood. In the shops you will find it supplied in various colours to match different kinds of wood.

In principle that is all that need be said, but in practice there are two things which may frustrate you. The first is that plastic wood, of whatever make, has poor adhesion and the repair may come off in your hand while you are giving it the finishing touches. Secondly, when the plastic wood has dried you may find it has shrunk, or especially that there is a good deal of cracking, if you have used too great a thickness of it. We will try to steer you round both these snags.

When buying your plastic wood, buy the appropriate solvent as well: alcohol or acetone, according to the make. Heavily dilute a suitable quantity of the plastic wood with the solvent until it is like liquid honey. It will penetrate the wood more efficiently and will stick perfectly. Don't put on too much; leave it to dry. On this foundation you can build up with plastic wood at its normal consistency; it will hold well. Cracking can be avoided by adding a layer at a time and letting it dry partially before adding the next. Or you can let cracking occur and simply fill it in with liquid plastic wood. If the repair is a big one you can reinforce it with tacks or small round-headed nails, which will fasten the plastic wood to the figure, or with pieces of wood, even quite sizeable ones, as fillers; this is preferable, as it does not affect the figure itself.

Note: Two-part plastic wood has recently appeared on the market; one part is epoxy resin mixed with sawdust, the other is the hardener. This is excellent for certain purposes but not for restoring wood sculptures. It is difficult to shape because it is so runny, and after polymerization it is a good deal harder than the surrounding wood, which makes it awkward to work down flush when finishing. Finally, we have found that stain and polychroming do not take well on it.

A more satisfactory answer is a home-made mixture of vinyl adhesive and fine sawdust (of the same kind of wood as the sculpture itself). The wood-dust produced by sanding is best, because it is so fine; you will be able to get it from a joiner's or cabinet maker's shop in which sanding-discs fixed to the benches are used. Incorporated in these machines is a device like a vacuum cleaner which collects the dust in a canvas bag.

The mixture sometimes takes rather long to dry, but it sticks perfectly and its consistency is ideal for final tooling. Cracking and shrinking may occur; to obviate them, put it on in successive layers.

HOW TO RESTORE POLYCHROMING

If you have restored a painted sculpture you will have to paint the restored part to harmonize it with the rest. If your taste is sound and your touch delicate you can manage this with complete success. Use gouache and watercolour. This will give you great flexibility in confecting different shades of colour; and if you go wrong you can wipe it all off with a sponge and try again.

If the original polychroming has cracked here and there and you have to match it for body and thickness as well as colour, gouache by itself will fill the gap; it, too, will crack a little as it dries, if you have put it on very thick. The cracks are easily eliminated by an extra coat, or on the other hand you may prefer to leave them because they harmonize with the rest.

If the gap is large and deep, don't hesitate to mix your gouache or watercolour with a little plaster of Paris or other suitable plaster; better still is the cement paint used by decorators; the missing material can be built up in successive layers. Put the final touch to your restoration with a coat of virgin wax; this will fix the watercolour and give it a shining patina.

LAYING BARE THE EARLIEST POLYCHROMING

This is undoubtedly the slowest, most delicate task you will be called upon to perform. As we know only too well, pious but misguided zeal caused religious sculptures to be periodically refreshed with a coat of paint, the colours being arbitrarily changed to suit the sartorial taste of the time. In addition, the long-suffering sculptures have often been done up a bit for other reasons; in many cases they have been scorched by a candle, or they have fallen over, or an attribute has been added—many figures of the Virgin, for instance, have been 'scalped' in order to accommodate a crown, an embellishment which was in fact just the opposite.

These successive polychromings frequently result in destroying the individuality of a sculpture; worse still, they blur its outlines and coarsen the facial character.

Only a practised eye, the result of long experience, can tell you whether or not to try to get down to the original polychroming. There may be as many as three or four layers; nor is there any certainty that the deepest layer was contemporaneous with the creation of the work—there is no guarantee that the paint was not stripped at one time or another. There is also the possibility that the decision to repaint was not dictated by the whim of fashion but by deterioration of the original colouring.

Which solution shall one choose? Is it better to risk finding only the merest vestiges of the artist's own treatment, or to preserve a later, apocryphal polychroming?

Every case is a special case, there is no general rule. A work still wrapped in its own intrinsic and genuine aura is doubtless more satisfying to possess than a dolled-up version, a travesty. On the other hand, a repainted figure is tolerable provided its essence has not been betrayed. The decision is for you alone.

You have the choice of two methods:

The first is mechanical, and indeed manual; the second, chemical.

Method 1 requires a long, thin blade such as a surgeon's

scalpel or an erasing-knife (as used on paper). Try to attach the paint at some spot where it has started flaking off; if possible, a spot which can't be seen; preferably towards the back, which in most cases was not painted. The *modus operandi* depends on the fact that, while each layer is stuck to the one underneath, it also retains its own consistency. With a sensitive touch, and above all with patience, use your tool to detach each layer in turn. You will progress only a few square millimetres at a time, perhaps even less, but the result is always excellent. *Warning:* don't try this method on figures on which fabric was stuck as a foundation for the paint; you will find yourself removing the first undercoat instead of saving the original top coat.

If you opt for this method, don't expect to finish in a few hours. It will keep you busy for days. You should therefore confine each bout of work to a single small area such as a hand, a foot or some detail of the carving.

Method 2 demands less patience but much greater finesse and perceptiveness.

Use fine washing soda (such as the French *lessive Saint-Marc*) in the proportion of 200 grammes (two handfuls) to every litre of water. The proportion can be adjusted after trying the liquid on the back of the figure, or the underside of a fold of drapery, or some other place that is not normally seen.

Use artists' paint brushes of sufficient stiffness to penetrate everywhere. Begin by reconnoitring the ground: discover how many layers there are and decide which one you want to preserve. Put some of the liquid in a saucer or a small cup and lay the figure *flat* before starting work, otherwise ugly runs will disfigure it.

As soon as the paint starts turning matt and the liquid starts picking up fragments of pigment, sponge the work clean before continuing. Work evenly; apply the soda solution only where necessary. The hollows, where it will collect, will of course be attacked more strongly than the protuberances and edges, where it will run off.

Rinsing at intervals, as required, carry on until you have reached the layer to be preserved. As soon as it starts to appear, reduce the strength of the solution to 15 grammes (about 3 teaspoonsful) to the litre; this will have the effect of freshening up the original colour. All that then remains is to rinse thoroughly, leave to dry, and finish off with a coat of virgin wax.

Commercial strippers are not to be recommended; most of them are too fierce for such selective, delicate work.

PART EIGHTEEN

PAINTINGS

Fig. 2.

Cleaning Pictures

OLD pictures get so obscured with the passage of time, and their richest harmonies and brightest colours so muted, that their decorative value is much reduced. Never believe that time ennobles all things. Patina is one thing, dirt is another. To restore a work of art to its original character is a mark of respect towards both the art and the artist.

The worst enemies of paintings are changes of temperature, variations in the humidity of the atmosphere (perdition seize all central heating!), and the assorted smoke with which the air of our cities is saturated (and which frequently deposits a film of greasy or acid matter). Flies, fortunately, have almost vanished from our dwellings, but have left their tenacious traces on many an aged canvas. Finally, man himself has something to answer for. The protective varnishes with which too many pictures are laden have cracked, and sometimes become almost opaque. In many cases, 'contemporary taste' has demanded the use of a coloured varnish, which has darkened with age. You will attempt to cleanse your own pictures of such outrages.

This will confront us with delicate problems in which, technical questions apart, your own intuition and instinctive touch will be your surest guide.

TAKING THE PICTURE OUT
OF ITS FRAME

In carrying out this essential preliminary, don't pull out the nails which hold the picture in the frame. Simply bend them upwards, and straighten them again when you put the picture back.

MINOR CLEANING—ANYONE
CAN DO THIS

This may sound like amateur stuff or an old wives' tale, but is in fact perfectly valid. Cut an onion in half and rub the picture with it. From time to time shave a thin slice off the onion so that you are always working with a clean piece. The combined chemical and mechanical effect of the juice and stratification of the onion will do the trick and make no stains on the paint.

Let us now pass to other, progressively more difficult, methods.

1. *Lukewarm water, ordinary household soap (not toilet soap) and a soft sponge* are a safe combination; they cannot possibly harm the picture. The sponge should be only just

Cleaning with a halved onion

damp, so as not to soak the canvas unnecessarily. Use the soap sparingly and rinse thoroughly as you go along. The method is undeniably effective and the effect is easy to gauge, were it only by the colour of the water which comes out of the sponge after rinsing!

2. *Washing soda* is used by the greatest experts; both the strength of the solution and its application demand great care. Dissolve a pinch of soda in a cup or saucer filled with luke-warm water; stir well, to make sure all the crystals are dissolved. Take a piece of cottonwool, dip it in the solution and wet one corner of the canvas by way of trial. After a few seconds you will gain an idea of the strength of the solution. If there is little or no effect, add another pinch of soda to the water, stirring as before. Holding the cottonwool delicately between thumb and forefinger, rub lightly with a circular movement. Rinse copiously with another piece of cottonwool dipped in pure water. Don't underdo the rinsing, otherwise the soda may leave white marks after drying. By following these directions you will achieve a cleaning-in-depth which will not damage the paint in any way; on the contrary, it will recover its lost youth to a surprising degree.

Note: This method is particularly recommended for ancient icons, which have usually been exposed to candle smoke and rough handling.

We must emphasize the limit beyond which an amateur should never venture. Do *not*, without long experience, attempt to remove varnish with soda. Indeed, only a varnish which had been applied comparatively recently would respond at all. We advise a different method, at once highly effective and easier to control.

REMOVING VARNISH WITH ALCOHOL

Set yourself up with all the requisites for completely removing the varnish, namely:

a bottle of ordinary *spirit* (alcohol), a bottle of *turpentine*, two large pads of *cottonwool* or, better, *cellulose wool* (which does not catch on the paint and leave threads behind it). Also have some dry cottonwool within reach.

The principle: De-varnishing, as you will have suspected, is at once delicate and easy (the speed of the operation is one of the risks). So, before explaining the method, a word about the principle.

Alcohol first softens the varnish, then dilutes it; turpentine, on the other hand, instantly inhibits both these reactions.

It is therefore appropriate to have a turpentine pad ready in one hand while de-varnishing with an alcohol pad in the other—because alcohol dilutes paint and its effect *must* be arrested in time.

However, turpentine also exerts a desiccating action on paint and this is specially harmful to old pictures, which have already become very dry in the course of years. Some restorers always counteract the effect by mixing linseed oil with the turpentine. This is an excellent precaution; you should follow it too. Another which deserves mention consists of 'feeding' an old picture with linseed oil before any cleaning or de-varnishing operation. For this purpose use the linseed oil which is sold expressly for artists; it is refined and will penetrate all the better. Coat the whole surface of the picture with it fairly generously, using a sable brush; lay the picture flat if possible (to avoid runs), protected against dust, and leave it for twenty-four or forty-eight hours.

You can then set about removing the varnish, confident that you have insured against risk as far as may be.

REMOVING VARNISH: THE JOB ITSELF

As when cleaning, begin in a corner. With your alcohol pad, rub with a circular motion. In the first few seconds, nothing will happen; then the pad will check very slightly, as if sticking, and the varnish will disappear. Keep the pad well wetted with alcohol so that it does not catch on the surface. You will see the picture becoming lighter and brighter with every pass you make. Don't be too severe; arrest the reaction with turpentine; if you find you have arrested it too soon you can start again with a clean pad, the alcohol will produce its effect as before. Carry on until, by gradually shifting from place to place, you have done the whole canvas. Do not try to treat the whole surface at once, you would not be able to keep a proper check on your work. When stripping large areas, such as skies or fields, step back from time to time to gauge the effect in relation to the rest and to make sure you are not overdoing it.

When you judge the varnish to have been adequately

stripped, swab thoroughly with turpentine and make sure that no part of the surface is still tacky.

Don't hesitate to impregnate the whole canvas with turps and linseed oil. Besides completely preventing further action by the alcohol, it will give new life to the paint and the fibres of the canvas or to the wood, if that was the support used by the painter.

RE-VARNISHING

After drying (which will take a few hours at most) comes re-varnishing.

This is essential both for preservation and for appearance. Choose a matt or a glossy varnish, whichever you prefer, but make sure it is a clear one (we are against brown varnishes, they darken a picture unnecessarily). A medium 'Rembrandt' varnish is excellent. Every good art shop sells varnishes put up in small bottles. Use a flat brush, starting at the top of the canvas and laying on the varnish criss-cross. Work in a good light, so as to avoid thin patches or runs. Don't load your brush too heavily, otherwise you will put on too much; and leave the picture to dry in a place free from dust.

A GENERAL CHECK

Your picture, once dry, can return to its usual place but will have first to go back into its frame. Take this chance to check that all is well with the cord, pins, rings, etc.; a worthwhile precaution.

If the canvas is slack (which it may be, though cleaning will not have made it so), it must be stretched taut. The stretcher (the wooden rectangle on which the canvas is braced) usually has small wooden wedges at its corners. A few careful taps with a hammer on these will restore tension.

But some stretchers have no wedges and demand a little ingenuity.

In such cases the canvas will have to be re-attached to the stretcher with upholstery tacks (use the smallest size) and drawn tight with the aid of small pliers with flat jaws.

The picture, re-hung, will reward you by shining with the lustre of youth regained. As it lights up the wall, you will be the first to be surprised by the transformation that simple cleaning can effect.

A FEW EXTRA HINTS

Before starting to clean a picture in depth, try to fix its values in your mind's eye. ('Values', pictorially speaking, are the relations of intensity between the colours.) This will be your guide in keeping your work uniform. The values, after cleaning, should be the same, but brighter.

Modern pigments and varnishes are much more sensitive to alcohol than those of past centuries. Watch out for this and be doubly careful.

Cracking is a valuable pointer to the age of a picture. Short cracks, forming rectangles: earlier than the 18th century. Irregular cracks: 18th and early 19th centuries. Concentric circles: 19th century. These simple, over-schematic distinctions form the foundation for a more expert appraisal.

HOW A FEW HOURS' WORK CAN MAKE A PICTURE LOOK CENTURIES OLD

Here are methods—tricks, if you like, but honest ones—for imparting the appearance of venerable antiquity to lithographs, engravings, reproductions or copies. We shall see how to provoke by artificial means everything we have previously sought to eliminate: cracking, patina, the yellowing wrought by age. An odd thing to do, perhaps; yet surely this deliberate doing and undoing is not far removed from creativeness itself? Well, that will serve as an excuse, anyway!

Certain substances are essential for success in any artificial ageing operation. They can be bought from specialist suppliers. They are:

size for lithographs;
ageing varnish for hangings;
gall for paint;
cracking varnish;
burnt umber or ivory black (paint).

MAKING PAPER LOOK LIKE PARCHMENT

This enables one to take advantage of the transparency of engravings, and is specially useful for making lampshades. All you have to do is to apply ageing varnish, criss-cross, with a flat brush, working the varnish well into the fibres of the paper. Allow plenty of time for drying (twenty-four hours at least), then repeat.

AGEING A LITHOGRAPH OR ENGRAVING

To avoid the transparent effect just described, and to age a lithograph or print without weakening or smudging the colours, put on size first and ageing varnish afterwards.

Use lithographers' size: one coat is usually enough, though a very porous or heavily grained paper will require two. Warm up the varnish in a pot with a water-jacket, and put it on when the size has dried out completely. Two coats of varnish, or three, will be necessary (with twenty-four hours' drying after each).

AGEING A PAINTING

Cracking, that wonderful signature inscribed by time, can be obtained artificially in a few hours. The technique is simple, all you have to do is to follow carefully the directions given here. First, treat the painting with ageing varnish; this is indispensable. 'De-grease' the varnish with gall, which should be diluted with two or three times its volume of water (all the supplies mentioned in this chapter can be bought from artists' colour men).

Rub the picture with a swab dipped in the diluted gall, and dry it with a clean swab. If you omitted the gall the cracking varnish which is applied next would not 'take' on the ageing varnish but would collect in isolated globules instead of spreading.

The remaining sequence of operations is as follows:

Brush on the cracking varnish. But note that, although the surface should already have been treated with ageing varnish, this should for preference *not* be allowed its customary twenty-four hours' drying time. From four to eight hours will be enough. The ideal moment for producing a sumptuous array of cracks is when the ageing varnish is no longer sticky to the touch but can still be marked by pressure with a finger-tip.

If you want a large number of small fine cracks, apply the cracking varnish in thin coats and dry it quickly at a moderately warm temperature (25–30 °C., 77–86 °F., in front of a central-heating radiator for example). If, on the other hand, a smaller number of large cracks is the effect you are after, apply the varnish in thick coats and let it dry slowly (the ageing varnish having also been put on in thick coats and covered as soon as it was almost dry).

In either case, the cracks do not take long to develop; anything from ten to thirty minutes.

THE ULTIMATE PATINA

To emphasize the tracery of cracks, dilute either umber or ivory black with turpentine and spread it over the whole picture surface with a swab. Rub it in with a circular motion so as to force it into the cracks. Give the whole surface a preliminary wipe-over; complete the wiping a few hours later with a soft, perfectly dry duster to remove the excess paint. The varnish will become completely transparent again, the paint being left only in the cracks.

The final touch consists of a coat of ageing varnish to fix and protect the whole. The nature of the cracking varnish makes this imperative.

MISTAKES CAN BE RECTIFIED

If the cracks don't turn out just as you want them, it is a simple matter to remove the cracking varnish with a sponge dipped in water; you can then have another try.

Reproductions on paper demand care: water may spoil or cockle them. Oil paintings have no such snags.

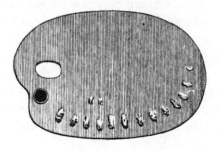

The Kiss of Life: Transferring a Painting to a New Canvas

IN a picture, the support is usually more vulnerable than the paint. Unfortunately, their fates are interdependent. Works of art of high quality demand the attentions of a specialist. We cannot sufficiently repeat that, without a regular apprenticeship, it is out of the question for you to attempt re-canvassing a picture, let alone to transfer the paint alone to a new canvas.

But there is nothing to stop you trying your hand on a torn canvas which is almost past praying for, some daub disinterred in an attic or picked up at a junk shop.

After this initial experience of re-backing a picture, followed by a few more, you can start thinking of rejuvenating that tired lot you inherited some time ago from a relation; pictures you might have thrown away if their aura of family associations had not stayed your hand.

We shall try to convey in clear terms the principles both of re-backing and of transferring; but please don't cast us in the role of sorcerer's apprentice.

Let us start with the simpler of the two: *re-backing*.

This consists of sticking a new piece of canvas on the back of an old one which is deteriorating or worn.

Before embarking on this operation, which requires care and delicacy, clean the picture (as described in the previous chapter); also get the back completely clean, so that its accumulated dust is not trapped by the glue, or paste rather, which you will be using.

Take your picture and expose it to steam. This has a very definite purpose: the excessive dryness of old canvas or paint may otherwise absorb too much of the water contained in the flour paste, and unsightly 'efflorescences' might result.

Very carefully detach the canvas from the stretcher and lay it on a smooth, flat surface, painted side uppermost. Give the paint a coat of flour paste. Take some very thin paper (tissue paper is ideal), stick it on the paint, apply several more coats of paste and add more paper. The thicker the protection the safer the picture will be; accidents can always happen. Don't hesitate to put on additional layers of ordinary paper, even newspaper.

This stage being completed, the next is to stick on a piece of new canvas slightly larger than the old one. First give a plentiful coat of fish glue to one side of the new piece, taking care to spread the glue evenly. Do the same to the back of the picture, then bring the two into contact and press them firmly together to make sure they stick all over. Take a warm iron and iron the new piece, pressing hard; this will make the glue still more liquid and help it to penetrate the smallest interstices of both canvases, until they become as one.

Let the reinforced picture dry thoroughly, then nail it to its stretcher, making sure of the tension as you do so. Proceed to remove the layers of paper from the paint surface with a sponge dipped in a solution of bicarbonate of soda in lukewarm water.

The layers will gradually loosen and become easy to take off. The paint itself will need to be well washed with water.

Before reinstating the picture in its frame you can give it a coat of much-diluted paint of the same colour as the dominant colour of the composition, all round the edges of the fabric, for better preservation.

TO TRANSFER OR NOT?

This is an extreme case. A picture may be in an even worse state, with its canvas so worn and frail that the paint is beginning to come off in little flakes. In some cases the canvas is actually crumbling into dust and is quite incapable of acting as a connection between the paint and a new piece of canvas; so the paint must be transferred.

This operation is definitely more delicate than re-backing; the task of removing the paint entire from the old canvas and transposing it to a new one demands relentless concentration.

If the paint is tending to flake off, begin by sticking to it a piece of gauze, slightly oversize. This will hold the paint together throughout the operation and will also act as a re-inforcement to the layers of tissue paper which are to be stuck on for protection in the way already described. Wait until all this is quite dry before very carefully removing the canvas from the stretcher. Remember that it is fragile and must be handled tenderly.

So much for Stage One. We now embark on Stage Two:

Put the canvas, face downwards, on a flat surface. The job now confronting you is to get rid of the old canvas. If it is extremely thin and tenuous, use very fine glasspaper; if stronger, a coarser grade of glasspaper. Some specialists prefer pumice stone. The aim is gradually to wear the canvas away until you reach the back of the paint. Concentrate very carefully when the abrasive comes into contact with the paint. Thoroughly wipe off the dust you have made, then stick the painting on to new canvas with a vinyl acrylic adhesive.

Every restorer has his own secret method for the sticking. Some of them manage to obtain natural adhesion by applying a hot iron to the back of the new canvas after laying it over the paint. But this, we feel, is not an example to emulate. Another method is to use fish glue, as in re-backing. In this case it is essential to give both the underside of the painting and the new canvas a thin coat of formaline before putting on the glue. The reason is that adhesives of organic origin (glues made from bones, hides, casein, fish, etc.) are always open to attack by moulds and micro-organisms. Formaline prevents these infections, which would destroy the adhesive film. The advantage of fish glue is its great flexibility. Other glues render the canvas excessively hard and rigid, eventually producing cracks which affect the preservation of the paint.

One of the 'secrets' known to restorers is the use of zinc white or white lead to join the paint and canvas together (white lead contains carbonate of lead, which is highly toxic; it must therefore be handled with care). This is supposed to give the paint a support having affinities with its own composition; which is true. But as white lead and zinc white are generally supplied in the form of a stiff paste, the usual practice is to dilute them with linseed oil. A fact not universally known is that linseed oil has a deleterious effect on the flax from whose fibres painters' canvases are woven (linseed, and the flax which is the raw material of linen, are closely related, botanically speaking). So that using linseed oil is 'one step forward, two steps back', and is bound to cause deterioration of the new canvas within a more or less foreseeable future.

Our own experience leads us to prefer a vinyl acrylic adhesive. A moderately thin coat should be given to the paint and to the new canvas. Avoid, at all costs, laying it on too thick. The adhesive must never soak through the canvas and exude from the surface.

After a few days' drying, the paper can be removed from the picture surface as described in the preceding section.

A painting on wood is also capable of being transferred but this is a task usually left to specialists; and even they are often unwilling to undertake an operation fraught with so many difficulties.

The process was discovered by Picault and Hacquin, two picture-restorers of the mid-18th century.

It consists of applying a protective shield of paper in the usual way, and then of making shallow saw-cuts in the back of the wood, generally in the form of small squares which can be removed with the help of a chisel. With further help from a rasp or a small plane the thickness of the wood is further diminished; from time to time it is wetted with a sponge to make it swell, so that it comes away more easily; and so the underside of the paint is eventually reached. It need hardly be stressed what a delicate technique this is.

There is, however, one peculiarity which makes the task easier. To prepare a wooden panel for painting it was usual to lay on a fairly thick ground, and this in most cases has proved to be less permanent than the paint.

This ground serves as a 'frontier' to your work; moreover it is bad at holding the fibres of the wood, which therefore come away nicely.

CAN YOU HANG A PICTURE?

Hanging a picture securely is often a nightmare for the amateur. Solid walls, cavity walls; soft, friable partition or impenetrable cement—every case is a law unto itself. Add to this the decorative problems involved, and the whole thing begins to look hopeless. However, without in any way limiting the imaginative possibilities, we can perhaps put forward ideas from which everyone can select those which satisfy his own tastes and requirements.

SOME PRINCIPLES OF DECORATION

Hanging a picture demands thought. Whether it be a painting, engraving, reproduction or photograph, its position will be determined by its character, shape and size (and weight). Let us look at a few examples.

Over furniture: the width of the picture should never be greater than that of the piece of furniture above which it is hung. Beware of frames which are too massive or otherwise obtrusive, overwhelming their surroundings. A picture so framed should be frankly isolated in the middle of a bare wall. If the piece of furniture is heavy or massive, the picture which bears it company should be of opposite format (if the piece of furniture is wide the picture should be tall, and vice versa; horizontal contrasting with vertical); and the picture should be hung fairly high.

A tall, narrow picture: this shape is not often used in painting; it is commoner in looking-glasses. The obvious place for it is between two windows or doors, or in an entrance hall or other small room.

A collection of pictures: many pictures, close together, are a combination to avoid unless the pictures are of fairly high artistic merit. A line of pictures side by side (or one above the other) is permissible in a passage. In any much-used room, hanging should be carefully planned not to disrupt the general harmony. You should determine an imaginary line to act as a basis; hanging should be such that the bottom edges of the frames, large and small alike, rigorously follow this line. But avoid symmetry. Two small pictures accompanying a large one should form a triad: the bottom of one of them should be level with that of the large picture; the top of the other, level with the top of the large one.

Height: it is always inadvisable to place pictures too high. They should be at eye level. This applies particularly to small pictures. If for some reason you do decide to hang a picture high up, tilt it forwards accordingly.

Frames: a serious problem! When choosing a frame for an old picture the style of the latter must be respected; but the character of the subject will assist you. A florid Louis Quinze frame, all volutes and arabesques, would be out of keeping with the ordered severity of an architectural prospect or a middle-class interior by a Flemish painter, but would be in perfect harmony with a battle scene or a *fête galante*, swarming with figures.

CONTEMPORARY WORKS ARE THE HARDEST

Hardly any general rules can be laid down; however, here are a few guide-lines. The frame should carry an echo of the dominant colour in the picture. For example, the paintings of Utrillo, so many of which are views in Montmartre—creamy white walls, the pure white of the Sacré-Coeur, and skies consisting of blue-white or grey-white clouds—demand light frames, shimmering like ivory, to suit the harmonies of the composition.

Very modern works can be classed with prints, in which the important thing is the structure or graphic quality of the subject; this should monopolize the attention; hence a frame is not always necessary. A very slim frame, of the natural colour of the wood, or painted black, gold or some very delicate shade, will be almost unnoticeable but will put a boundary between the picture and the space surrounding it.

PRACTICAL HINTS

'X' picturehangers have certain advantages, confirmed by long experience. Their steel pins penetrate well in most materials and do little harm to walls. The range of sizes from No. 0 to No. 4 is adequate to deal with most situations; it allows for light, normal, heavy (2 pins) and very heavy objects (3 pins). Note, however, that concrete may make the pins buckle or break. It is important to know how to avoid this by driving them in correctly. Accurate little taps, *in line with the pin*, are the answer.

'Swedish' hooks in moulded plastic are a new addition to the decorator's armoury; somewhat surprisingly, their three pins

are very short (about 5 mm.). But it must be admitted that they hold very well in extra-hard wall materials such as concrete, mortar, brick and stone. In plaster they are not always so satisfactory and the manufacturers therefore supply an extra steel pin, 25 mm. long, which goes in deep and reinforces the effect of the three little ones.

Expansion bolts: for hollow walls and soft materials, the manufacturers of expansion bolts have developed extra-strong hooks from which heavy weights can safely be suspended.

Mirror-hooks are essential for supporting decorative objects of great weight, such as engravings, whose weight is substantially increased by the glass (large engravings are often held between two sheets of glass, to keep them perfectly flat).

Forged mirror-hooks, which have to be bonded in, do not

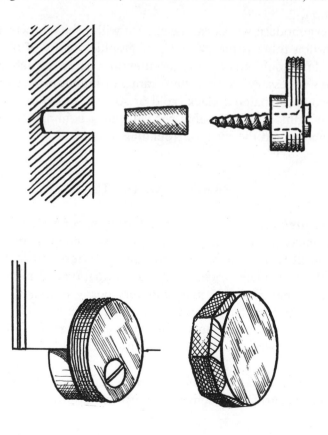

concern us: we always prefer the screw-in type. They work very simply: a sleeve is pushed into a hole drilled in the wall, and into this is screwed a metal component embodying a head with a groove to accommodate the mirror. The head is supplied drilled and tapped to receive a decorative cap which hides the screw.

To hang a very heavy engraving, three mirror-hooks can be put in at the bottom to support it, and another at the mid-point of the top edge to prevent it from tilting forward. Great care is necessary to ensure that the weight is taken up evenly by all three hooks, not just one or two. This is achieved by drawing a line on the wall, level with the lower edge of the engraving, and drilling the holes exactly on the line. Don't screw the hooks right home; put the engraving in first, then screw tight.

HINTS ON SPECIAL CASES

Concealing hooks: in all cases when the picture cord has to come up above the top edge of the picture to ensure that it hangs straight, the hook, of necessity, is visible. It can be concealed by adding a decorative motif in bronze in the form of a circular flower, a fleur-de-lis or a star; it is also possible to buy ready-made decorative hooks. An unframed print can be held in place by a little bronze hand, for example.

Clips: glazed prints or reproductions are often hung by means of clips. This goes marvellously with modern works and is also an excellent way of holding the sheet of glass at the back. The difficulty lies in fixing the picture to the wall. The usual method is to have a piece of steel wire connecting the hooks. But this is unsatisfactory; the tension on the wire tends to pull the hooks towards each other and in any case the attachment to the wall is visible. There is a very neat way out of the difficulty; it only requires a little care and accuracy. Right-angle cup-hooks are screwed into the wall and their heads left pointing horizontally instead of vertically, all in the same direction. Make sure of inserting them in the wall exactly in the positions where the clips will come. All you then have to do is to hold the picture up and slide it sideways, so that the head of each hook enters the tubular channel in the corresponding clip.

When buying hooks, make sure they are the right size to fit the clips.

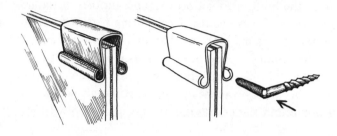

PART NINETEEN

CARPETS AND TAPESTRIES

Carpets and Tapestries: Nomad Arts for Sedentary Peoples

CARPETS and tapestries are made by different techniques, but in dealing with the two in a single chapter we are not perpetrating a confusion of *genres*. Briefly, the difference is that a carpet is composed of knots attached to a warp, whereas a tapestry is woven.

What we wish to emphasize is the obvious connection between them. There are excellent grounds for supposing they had a common origin. It cannot be seriously denied that the chief creators of both were the nomadic peoples whose seasonal migrations ranged between the Eastern Mediterranean lands and the steppes of the Far East.

As for the difference between carpets and tapestries, it is certainly not one of function. In a nomad's tent, a carpet is not used solely for covering the ground; it may also be mural decoration, partition or couch-cover. Equally, the celebrated French 'carpets' from the Savonnerie are, in many cases, woven.

The vogue for carpets and tapestries in the West, after the Crusades, was an art of living not unlike that of the steppes. Until the *Grand Siècle*, the age of Louis XIV (17th century), sovereigns and their courts were itinerant. Architecture, until the 16th century, was mainly military in conception and lacking in comfort. The ninety tapestries of the Château de Fontainebleau accompanied François I wherever he went; they were a necessity, not an unprecedented luxury or obsessional refinement. They made it possible to create smaller rooms within the damp great hall of a fortified castle, and to mask the cold, unsightly roughness of the walls. The emperor Charles V had his collection always with him, whether at Aix-la-Chapelle, Ghent or Madrid, for the same reason. The tapestries of

Charles the Bold were found lying on the battlefield from which his dead body was recovered; they now adorn Berne Cathedral. He had previously left others scattered on the fields of his defeats, at Granson, Morat and Nancy; clearly he never travelled far without them.

Renaissance architecture, though more appealing than that of the feudal period, was equally remote from the human scale, and the Château of Chambord, on a tributary of the Loire, may have been even chillier than Château-Gaillard, towering above the Seine; carpets and tapestries were necessary as well as ornamental.

A sign of the directly utilitarian aspect of tapestry in the Middle Ages, and even after the Renaissance, is its almost unchanging technique. From its 13th-century beginnings until the 16th century, only about fifty colours were used.

Apart from the introduction of gold and silver thread there were no innovations before the late 17th century, by which time 10,000 different shades of colour had come into use.

Carpets, on the other hand, were something special and apart. They were not made in the West but came from distant countries and, being expensive, were precious. They were rarely used as floor-coverings, coarse mats were good enough for that; historians tell us that the flagstones in castle interiors were often covered with straw. Doubtless it was only in a few of the least primitive, rustic rooms that carpets were used for their original purpose.

Nevertheless in paintings of interior scenes, prior to the 17th century, carpets are in evidence mainly as tablecloths and sometimes on ceremonial daïses. Such details are common in pictures signed by Holbein, Le Nain, Vermeer, Pieter de Hooch, Gabriel Metzu and Abraham Bosse.

Henri IV tried to render carpets after the fashion of Turkey and the Levant available to his people by setting up workshops. The industry had since prospered and been mechanized, but the machine-made carpet, though within reach of most pockets, remains only a substitute devoid of charm. Those who know and love the genuine knotted carpet and hand-woven tapestry are aware that there *is* no substitute.

In 1844 the novelist George Sand, during a visit to the Château de Boussac in the valley of the River Creuse, discovered the sumptuous six-piece series representing *The Lady and the Unicorn*.

Her enthusiasm was such that she converted her contemporaries to a taste for medieval tapestries which saved many masterpieces from oblivion.

Buying a Carpet

SUPPOSE you have picked out a carpet which suits your taste, the use for which you intend it, and your pocket. You have made sure it is a genuine knotted carpet, not a machine-made one (see below). What else should you look for?

Hold it up against the light from a window, and look at it from the back. Weak places, holes and repairs will show up at once.

A carpet of high quality should be soft and supple. This can be checked first by the feel of it in your hand, then by letting it fall on to itself in a crumpled heap. There should be no stiffness anywhere.

Also examine it carefully for rot in the fibres. This insidious form of deterioration may not be detectable by eye; you can sometimes spot it by the colour having altered or faded, but not always. It is a serious fault, caused by prolonged exposure to damp, whether in a warehouse, the hold of a ship or an empty house. All you have to do is to examine the warp for soundness by pulling it firmly in various directions and at different places. Rub the carpet between your hands like a washerwoman, then stretch it boldly. A faint but characteristic rending sound will inform you of its condition.

KNOTS, *ABRACHS*, DATES

Knots

It is a difficult task for an amateur to identify the type of knot from a superficial examination. However, the sketches given here are a valuable guide and may save you from serious errors. The vital thing is to be able to tell at a glance whether a carpet was made by hand or machine, as this considerably affects its value.

There are *two* main types of knot: the Ghiordes or Turkish, and the Senne (Sehna, Senneh) or Persian.

The *Ghiordes knot* encircles two strands of the warp; its ends come out between them and constitute the pile.

The *Senne knot* goes round only one strand of the warp; one end comes out next to that strand, the other passes under the adjacent strand and comes out without having gone round it.

If the Senne knot goes round both strands it is a sign that the carpet is incorrectly made, possibly even a fake, although produced by hand.

The *'double'* knot (*tête d'alouette*, 'lark's head') is a sign of Western handicraft, in which the warp is in reality a canvas (like an embroidery canvas).

Industrially manufactured carpets are easy to identify: there are no knots. The 'pile' is not really a pile at all, but a velvet whose fibres are held in place only by the tension of the weaving. A simple little test is enough to demonstrate this: isolate a single fibre, and pull. It will come away easily.

Ghiordes knot

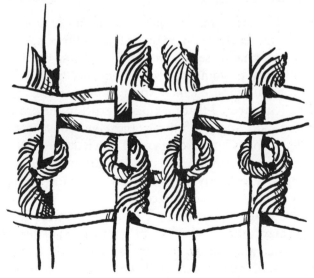

Senne knot

Abrachs: defect or merit?

A really old carpet may display variations in colour, particularly in the background. You will sometimes see different
shades of red, blue or some other colour. These details, which
stand out most prominently when they occur in prominent
parts of the pattern, are called *abrachs*. As for their origin, it
should be remembered that making a carpet in the craft way is
a long-term job and that, under the conditions of nomadic
tribal life, wool is prepared as and when it is wanted. The
colours are usually natural vegetable or mineral dyes. They are
fast to light, excellently so, but vary in shade because the
ingredients may have been mixed in varying proportions, and
because the water available in one place, as the tribe seasonally
migrates, may differ from that in another. The *abrachs* are
irregular contrasts which give an indispensable liveliness to
the whole. No doubt the careful work produced in factories

established by royal decree is almost always devoid of *abrachs*, which are essentially defects; but we must point out that the presence of these has never detracted from the value of a fine carpet. On the contrary, they may be part of its charm.

Dates

Determining when a carpet was made is a matter for specialists. Apart from a few exceptional pieces which can safely be said to be several centuries old, most antique carpets are a hundred years old at the outside. We must remember that in most cases we are dealing with a folk art, in which the relevant criterion is not so much age as spontaneity. Dating a carpet therefore does not matter much, except for information and interest. But, with this reservation in mind, it is worth knowing the system of the Islamic calendar. It begins at the Hegira, the day on which Mahomet fled from Mecca; in our terms, July 16th, A.D. 622.

The Islamic year is several days shorter than ours; 32 of our years correspond to 33 of theirs. By means of some simple arithmetic any Islamic date can be expressed in our own chronology. Divide the date on the carpet by 33; subtract the quotient from the dividend and add the 622 years from the start of the Hegira.

For example:

$$\text{Islamic date:}\quad 1221$$
$$\text{divided by } 33:\quad 37$$

$1221 - 37 = 1184$
$1184 + 622 = 1806$, the date according to the Gregorian calendar.

The date of manufacture is sometimes on the edge of the carpet, close to a corner; sometimes close to the central motif. In more recent pieces it is written on a piece of cloth sewn on to the back of the carpet, and the place of manufacture is also given.

Our numerical symbols, though known as 'Arabic figures',

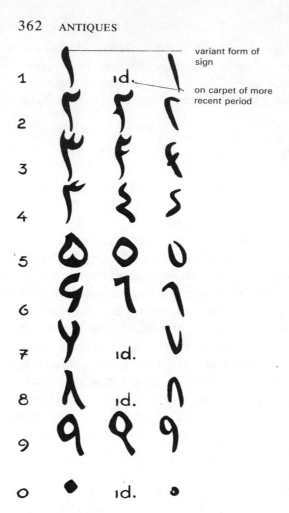

variant form of
sign

on carpet of more
recent period

Oriental numbers indicating date of manufacture of carpet. The
first two columns give the old forms of the numbers; the third
column, those found on carpets of recent manufacture

have lost almost all resemblance to their distant ancestors. The
present-day Eastern forms, moreover, display local variations.

DISTORTIONS

The fact that a carpet was made by hand, on a warp stretched
on a fairly primitive loom, and also the fact that some of its

fibres will since have shrunk, will have caused it to have been pulled out of shape to some degree. Like *abrachs*, these distortions are often a sign of genuineness but they sometimes make the carpet wear in an uneven, unsightly way. They must be dealt with; a badly distorted carpet must be given a flexible backing which will prevent the members of the warp from shifting this way or that. Thick flannel or felt, or plastic foam sheet, is the answer.

Borders: always keep a sharp eye on the state of a carpet's edges. Neglect of these often allows damage to begin developing. The sides of a carpet are reinforced simply by closely set whipstitching. You don't need to be an expert with the needle to repair and maintain the edges of a carpet; there is nothing difficult about it. (See diagram of whipstitching.)

Fringes: these get worn out and may even disappear completely. This is very serious; a fringe is composed of the ends of the warp, and when it wears away the whole carpet may begin coming to pieces. Action is urgently required. As a general rule it is better to go to a professional and get him to reconstitute the threatened part. If you think your carpet is not worth the expense of professional repair you can try carrying out the rescue operation yourself.

All the strands of the warp must be caught and 'stopped' with chainstitch, possibly with several parallel rows of chainstitch. But take care to avoid extremes: the stitches must neither be drawn too tight, which would crimp the edge of the

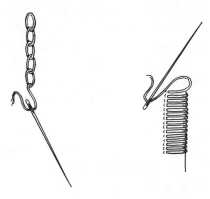

carpet, nor left too loose, which would serve no purpose, giving too little support to the warp.

Afterwards you can buy some worsted or cotton fringe, which is sold by the yard in shops specializing in such things, and sew it on in place of the original fringe.

The importance of this artificial fringe is obviously not only aesthetic, it prevents wear.

CLEANING

Nothing in a house or flat is so much exposed to dust and dirt as a carpet. Its pile has the further unfortunate privilege of attracting its own deadliest enemies: clothes-moths and their eggs and larvae. Careful maintenance can contribute directly to the preservation of a carpet, but it must also be remembered that violent or incompetent cleaning can do more harm than the worst depredations by parasites.

The vacuum cleaner is perfect for daily use; but *don't*, please, use the head which has a hard brush, it would inflict an excessive amount of wear. And don't shake the carpet out of the window; it is obviously harmful. The carpet's whole weight is borne by the small portion of the warp gripped by your hands, and every shake, whether violent or gentle, adds to the strain.

Slinging the carpet over a line and beating it is also a treatment to be avoided, or at any rate, to use only in moderation. Don't give great hefty blows but light, quick taps; and don't do it more than twice a year. Mechanical carpet-beaters with brushes mounted on rollers are not advisable either.

The vacuum cleaner, of course, only keeps the surface of the carpet clean; the dust goes much deeper, becoming encrusted in the pile and warp. Only large, specialized firms, with the necessary equipment, can deep-clean your carpet.

In the long run, despite your care, your carpet will lose its brilliance; the light colours will be dim, the dark ones dusty. It will have to be washed.

If you judge that only superficial cleaning is required you can buy one of the carpet shampoos which are available. They work well and do not necessarily involve moving the carpet first, as they can be used almost dry. A damp sponge after shampooing is all that is required; no messy rinsing. The result will be good as far as it goes, but will be no more than a visual effect; the deep-lying dirt will not be affected. A similar effect can be obtained with a soft brush dipped into a mixture of ammonia and water (2 parts water, 1 part ammonia); follow this by brushing with water to which a little vinegar has been added.

DISASTERS GREAT AND SMALL

There is no end to these, alas! Cigarette burns in the pile are the worst. Fortunately wool is not highly combustible and the damage never spreads far. Repair consists of surrounding the hole with one or more rings of stitching on the back of the carpet so as to strengthen the warp, and then, if necessary, rebuilding the warp by stitching criss-cross—darning, in fact. Finally, to show your dexterity by building up the missing bit of pattern, knot pieces of wool round the warp you have renewed, and cut them off exactly flush with embroidery scissors.

Chewing gum, which sticks the pile together, gets trodden flat and looks hideous, is luckily not as hard to remove as it might seem. Never try to prise it off with a knife or any other tool. Take a clean rag, wet it with acetone and rub gently. The gum will soon dissolve.

Grease-spots: talc or Fuller's earth will help you get grease out of a carpet. Dust it on the affected part of the pile, leave it for twenty-four hours, and brush it off thoroughly. If the spot is still there, wet it with benzene, first placing an absorbent rag under the carpet. On a very light-coloured carpet (this applies specially to Chinese carpets) use ether instead of benzene; it cuts the grease without leaving a halo. But you will do well to

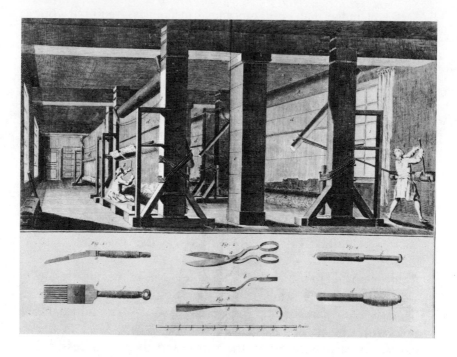

proceed cautiously, with little dabs, not letting the solvent run far.

Ink is dreadful! If you get there in time, boldly swab the spot with a wet sponge, taking care not to spread the stain further; then hold it under a cold tap to dilute the remaining ink as much as possible; if necessary, turn the tap off at intervals, swab off the water, then repeat. This will avert the worst damage.

If the stain has already dried, consult a specialist. All treatments powerful enough to deal with an inkstain are harmful to carpets; only a specialist has the necessary remedies and precautions at his command.

Urine: carpets are liable to being wetted with urine, which is usually corrosive to some degree, by pets and small children. Never regard this lightly; swab the place at once, otherwise the colours, and perhaps the warp and the knots, will suffer.

Proceed as for ink. Make sure the affected place has dried out completely before putting the carpet back.

Last but not least, *insects*.

Even the best-kept houses are not immune from predators which sometimes are tiny or even invisible. Those which are specifically dangerous to carpets include clothes-moths, carpet beetles (fortunately rare in our temperate climate) and mites. Insecticides which deal with these have long been known, notably the familiar naphthalene, and others based on benzene and chlorine; but their smell makes them unacceptable in a drawing-room, living-room or bedroom. Aerosols and D.D.T. powder work well, except that they do not affect the insects' eggs. No doubt it can be argued that the young larvae will be killed; not necessarily, however, without having had time to attack a few essential fibres before ingesting the poison. However, there is a simple means of ensuring that any living eggs in a carpet get killed off: refrigeration. If you have a large enough refrigerator, treat your carpet to as long a stay in it as possible (not less than forty-eight hours), and let the carpet be close to the freezer. But if your fridge is too small send the carpet to a specialized firm which has large refrigerating chambers.

Exposing the carpet to frost in winter, provided the air is dry, will do no harm—and no good, because it is in the spring and summer that moths, etc., are most active.

WHERE AND HOW TO LAY A CARPET

A few precautions—elementary, no doubt, yet requiring mention. Anyone can see that the feet of chairs and other furniture, stiletto heels, or much going to and fro, can subject a carpet to abnormal wear. When laying a carpet, avoid the 'main road' through a room; don't put the carpet under furniture; and do put felt pads on the feet of chairs. An uneven floor is the worst enemy of the warp of a carpet—loose parquet blocks, rough or badly laid tiles. Always protect a carpet with an under-felt or a thin sheet of flexible foam plastic.

DO YOUR CARPET JUSTICE

You will, of course, have noticed that every carpet has a direction, a 'grain' as it were. The pattern itself usually makes this clear; in any case the shimmer of the colours will do so. The pile, in fact, always points in the direction of the weaving and absorbs or reflects the light accordingly. When laying it, take care to choose the position most favourable to its beauty. Similarly, when buying a carpet examine it from various angles to make sure how it really looks.

Hanging a Tapestry

THE way in which a tapestry is hung determines whether it remains in a good state of preservation or not. There are two schools of thought about this.

One school maintains that a tapestry must be kept supple and that it was always intended to be allowed a certain amount of movement—to 'live', as the expression is in French. The other school argues that a tapestry should hang against a wall as it did on the loom, i.e. stretched tight, with every detail of the design plain to see.

There is an elegant, logical solution which reconciles the two; namely to hang the tapestry so that it is taut along the top, while the sides, bottom and surface in general are left loose.

An important point is that a tapestry should never be in contact with a wall, however sound. Old tapestries, regrettably, display marks left by damp. One of the most striking examples of this is the famous *Lady with the Unicorn*, now in the Musée de Cluny. Right across the bottom of the panels a straight band of discoloration is clearly visible. In the Château de Boussac, where they were discovered, the panels were in contact with the base of a damp wall exuding saltpetre. Since then not all the skill and care of the specialists employed by the Fine Arts Administration have been able to diminish the damage more than a little.

ORIENTATION

Textiles in general, particularly if coloured, are endangered by sunlight. It is claimed for the old natural dyes, both vegetable and mineral, that they are fast to light. This is true but not absolutely so; if it were, how could we account for the softness, the melting gradations which add such charm to ancient tapestries? On the other hand, it is noticeable that certain colours have resisted the ravages of time and ill-treatment. The set of tapestries of the Apocalypse, which are now the favourite child of the National Fine Arts Administration in France and have been given a remarkable museum all to themselves in the castle of King René at Angers, were once used as horse-blankets and

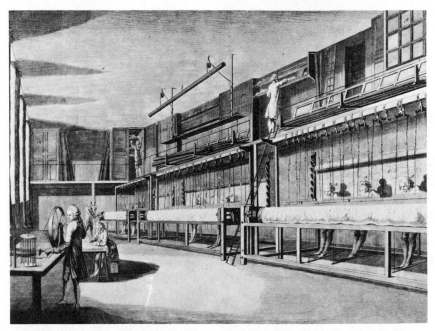

Basse-Lisse tapestry workshop, Les Gobelins, with various operations of *basse-lisse* tapestry weaving in progress. (*Basse-lisse* and *haute-lisse* are the two types of tapestry loom employed in Europe)

coverings for vegetable frames on the episcopal estate in that locality! Though undoubtedly no longer as fresh as when completed, five centuries ago, they are still admirable.

Tapestries, then, should not be hung opposite sunny windows. Even oblique sunlight is to be avoided. Hang a tapestry on a section of wall between two windows, out of reach of the sun. Give it suitable lighting, artificial if need be, but do not let the bulbs be too near it; their heat would dehydrate the fibres excessively and cause local fading.

SECURE SUSPENSION

To keep the tapestry away from the wall, fix to the wall a square-section wooden batten which can be anything from $1\frac{1}{4}$ to 2 in. thick; this will provide the necessary separation and an adequate surface for suspension. A tapestry can't be just pinned up like a poster. The damage done by that method can easily be seen in old tapestries, which are stretched out of shape and disfigured by holes, indelible rust-stains, etc. Various other methods are available to you which are not only kinder to the tapestry than using nails but have the additional advantage of making it easily removable.

RINGS

A simple solution is to sew curtain-rings on to the back of the tapestry and to hang it on a curtain-rod or hooks. To keep these arrangements out of sight, sew the rings on 2 or 3 in. below the edge. The edges of the tapestry should always be strengthened with stout braid, which should be as wide as possible.

'FLEMISH' CURTAIN-HOOKS

This type of curtain-hook is designed for double curtains. Sew them to the braid at intervals of about 10 in. The advantage of 'Flemish' hooks is that they cannot be seen and that they make it easier to conceal the rod.

THE BEST SOLUTION OF ALL

—is an unashamedly modern one. Border the back of the tapestry with 'Velcro' right across the top (and down the sides too, if you like). The corresponding strip of 'Velcro' is fastened, either with hooks or an adhesive, to the wooden strip. This is the solution we regard as the best in every way. We have found by experience that 'Velcro' is quite strong enough and holds securely, in addition to enabling one to stretch the tapestry evenly.

LOOKING AFTER TAPESTRIES

In writing of carpets and how to clean them, we looked in detail at various products and the ways in which they could be used in special cases. Most of them are also perfectly suitable for tapestries.

But there are also special problems posed by tapestries, demanding specific answers.

Beware of insects! Moths and silver-fish are even deadlier enemies of tapestries than of carpets. A tapestry hung on a wall is easy to treat with an insecticide in powder form. Or you can sew little bags on to the back and fill them with paradichlorben-zene.

If you see any silver-fish on the tapestry you should realize at once that it is threatened by a more insidious enemy than these insects themselves, which can be killed immediately with a good insecticide. Silver-fish need a high degree of humidity in order to live, and their presence is a warning sign that your tapestry is suffering from damp. Either move it elsewhere or damp-proof the wall.

Cleaning is based on the application of ox-gall, a natural substance which not only removes dirt but brightens the colours. Dry shampoos containing ox-gall, for carpets and tapestries, are easy to buy. Diluted with water, they produce abundant froth, which is what you use. Pick it up on a very soft brush and apply a moderate amount all over the surface; assist its action by brushing, preferably parallel to the weave. Make a pad of a clean white rag which doesn't fray, and remove the froth with it; whenever the pad gets dirty, re-fold it so as always to work with a clean part. Continue wiping until the pad ceases to pick up dirt.

You can finish off by lightly wiping with a rag dipped in water with a little vinegar in it; squeeze the rag out well after each dip.

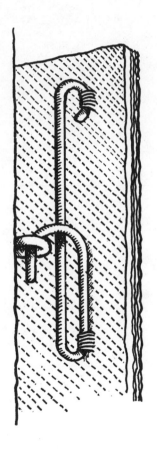

1800

Gonzalo Torrente Ballester
SANTIAGO DE ROSALÍA CASTRO

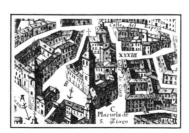

Ciudades en la Historia

Ésta es una colección de retratos de ciudades en sus momentos más brillantes, curiosos y significativos. Su ambiente, su vida cotidiana, sus personajes, sus mitos y anécdotas, la configuración urbana y sus características, el arte y la literatura, los restos más importantes de la época que aún se conservan y que pueden ser objeto de una especie de itinerario turístico, cultural o nostálgico, todo lo que contribuyó a hacer la leyenda y la historia de una ciudad en el período de mayor fama, se recoge en estas páginas de evocación del pasado.

Grandes escritores que se sienten particularmente identificados con la atmósfera y el hechizo de estas ciudades de ayer y de hoy resumen para el lector contemporáneo lo que fue la vida, la belleza y a menudo el drama de cada uno de estos momentos estelares de la historia que se encarnan en un nombre de infinitas resonancias. Una copiosísima ilustración de planos y mapas, grabados antiguos, reproducciones de obras de arte, fotografías y caricaturas completan admirablemente los textos de los autores.

Siendo mucho más que una simple guía turística y algo muy diferente de un libro de historia en su acepción usual, «Ciudades en la Historia» presenta un panorama ameno y muy bien documentado de lo más profundo, interesante y vistoso que cada ciudad, en su momento de máximo esplendor o de mayor singularidad histórica, puede ofrecernos.

Gonzalo Torrente Ballester
SANTIAGO
de Rosalía Castro

Apuntes sobre la vida en Compostela
en tiempos de Rosalía Castro

Planeta

CIUDADES EN LA HISTORIA
Dirección: Rafael Borràs Betriu

Consejo de Redacción: María Teresa Arbó, Antonio
Padilla, Marcel Plans y Carlos Pujol

Índice

PLANO DE SANTIAGO

1 Catedral
2 Hospital Real (s. XV Hostal de los Reyes Católicos)
3 Palacio de Rajoy (s. XVIII Concello)
4 Colegio de Fonseca (ss. XVI-XVII)
5 Casa do Dean (s. XVIII)
6 Casa do Cabido (s. XVIII)
7 Convento de San Martiño Pinario (ss. XVI a XVIII)
8 Palacio de Gelmírez (s. XII-XIII)
9 Facultad de Medicina
10 S. Martiño Pinario (s. XVII-XVIII)
11 Universidad (ss. XVII-XVIII, reformada XIX-XX)
Facultad de Geografía e Historia)
12 Convento de San Francisco (ss. XVI-XVIII)

Introducción

A Compostela se llega por bastantes caminos, pero el más conocido, al mismo tiempo el más antiguo, es el que se llamó siempre de Santiago, y también Francés, denominación un poco exagerada, pero no injusta, pues si bien es cierto que a Compostela llegó gente de todas partes, el grueso de los peregrinos de a pie vino de Francia, centuria tras centuria, y en Francia más que en otros lugares (aunque no exclusivamente) se encuentra repetido el nombre de Saint Jacques, desde el corazón mismo de París. Casualmente, los que hoy llegan por vía aérea recorren la última parte de este camino, y es afortunado azar que el aeropuerto compostelano se llame de Labacolla, topónimo que designa el lugar donde los peregrinos se sometían a las prácticas lustrales de que salían más compuestos y, sobre todo, mejor olientes. Se pasa por el barrio de San Lázaro, se atraviesan unas calles de casas modestas, aunque características, y después del susto breve de unas cuantas edificaciones modernas, horrorosas, se entra en las Casas Reales, que es como llegar a lo que la ciudad tiene de propio e inalterable: el noble granito sometido al rigor de la forma, la elegancia de la cal enmarcada en el granito. Es lo que vamos a ver en la ciudad si no salimos del perímetro sagrado,

Es afortunado azar que el aeropuerto compostelano se llame de Labacolla, topónimo que designa el lugar donde los peregrinos se sometían a las prácticas lustrales de que salían más compuestos y, sobre todo, mejor olientes.

La maravilla de la colegiata del Sar, que, vista desde arriba una mañana sin niebla, se asemeja a un barco hundido, con las cuadernas visibles, con el casco volcado.
(Vista exterior e interior de la colegiata del Sar.)

si resistimos a la siniestra ocurrencia de saltar a la ciudad moderna. Pero a nadie, en Compostela, se le ocurre enseñarla, ni nadie que busca la esencia de Compostela cuenta entre sus propósitos la visita a esa parte de la ciudad. La delimitación de la vieja Compostela ayuda. Fuera de su perímetro queda poco que ver: un par de monasterios de monjas y la maravilla de la colegiata del Sar, que, vista desde arriba una mañana sin niebla, se asemeja a un barco hundido, con las cuadernas visibles, con el casco volcado. El recorrido de Compostela no es lo mismo de noche que de día. Hasta bien entrada la mañana no se puede evitar el tropiezo con automóviles y camionetas de reparto. Después, la ciudad vieja queda vacía de artefactos ruidosos, sin más que la piedra de las rúas y la luz de los faroles, o de la luna, si corresponde. No es lo mismo Compostela de día que de noche. El que busca información y arquitectura, que haga de día el recorrido. El que aspire a emociones menos precisas, pero más hondas, que escoja la noche. Las formas son las mismas, los mismos los materiales, pero la colaboración de las luces y de las sombras modifica la visión. El uso de la palabra fantasmal queda descartado, porque ni de día ni de noche es Compostela fantástica, sino recia y pesada, además de bella: con la reciedumbre y la pesantez del granito. Esto no excluye el hecho indiscutible de que muchos lugares

y rincones compostelanos sugieran el recuerdo de decoraciones teatra-
les, aunque de un teatro cuyas dimensiones sobrepasen lo usual y
tenga los cielos por límite. Todo visitante de ciudades históricas busca,
aunque no lo sepa, esto de teatral, y si posee un adarme de fanta-
sía, llena el espacio de figuras, acordes con la decoración. En Vene-
cia, de noche, los canales se pueblan de góndolas en que viajan aman-
tes, que, a veces, se asesinan. En Siena es inevitable imaginar el
tropel de caballeros corriendo por su plaza. En Florencia se recuer-
dan escenas pintadas y hermosos petimetres en persecución de dami-
selas. Y en Roma... ¿qué imagina uno de Roma? ¿El fasto papal?
Compostela, con ser tan antigua, no sugiere ni caballeros ni pere-
grinos, ni siquiera ilustrados de peluca y espadín, sino conspirado-
res románticos, parejas de muchachas que se disimulan en las som-
bras, canónigos bien envueltos en sus manteos, y, todo lo más, todo lo
más, una procesión del Corpus. Compostela no está anclada en el si-
glo XVII ni en el XVIII, a pesar de la abundancia de piedras barro-
cas, sino en el XIX. Fue durante ese siglo cuando adquirió la fisono-
mía que hoy podemos contemplar, y el sombrero de copa y el polisón
van a sus rúas mejor que el chambergo o la peluca o la francesa.

Compostela siempre tuvo conciencia de ciudad sacra, lo
cual no impidió jamás el desarrollo paralelo de una conciencia secu-
lar muy acusada, singularmente en los ámbitos del poder y del ne-
gocio. La conciencia de ciudad bella es un fenómeno posterior, del

Compostela no está anclada
en el siglo XVII ni en el
XVIII, a pesar de la
abundancia de piedras
barrocas, sino en el XIX.
Fue durante ese siglo cuando
adquirió la fisonomía que
hoy podemos contemplar.

11

Los canónigos ordenan completar la plaza de Platerías con una fachada a todas luces inútil, pero estéticamente justificada.

siglo XIX. *La afirmación parece paradójica a la vista de tantas piedras hermosas trabajadas en siglos anteriores, incluso remotos; pero estas piedras lo que revelan es una conciencia parcial, aunque continuada, y no limpiamente estética, sino, como es sólito, muy mezclada a la necesidad de expresar el poder. Pero, dejando a un lado estas cuestiones, los sucesivos cambios de fisonomía de la catedral y sus entornos no obedecen a la necesidad de componer o crear una unidad estética que abarque la ciudad, sino sólo alguna de sus partes. Los canónigos ordenan completar la plaza de Platerías con una fachada a todas luces inútil, pero estéticamente justificada. La situación de las grandes construcciones, los grandes monasterios, por ejemplo, obedece a otras causas o a otras necesidades que lo que hoy llamaríamos urbanismo. Todo va surgiendo, a lo largo del tiempo, por razones parciales o locales en el sentido menos amplio de la palabra, y, un día, inexplicablemente, la ciudad está completa y es perfecta: perfecta con la perfección de lo orgánico y de lo espontáneo, no de lo racional y meditado. Y sólo entonces se puede hablar de una conciencia colectiva de belleza, semejante a la que tienen los habitantes de otras ciudades históricas. El influjo del romanticismo es indudable. Las primeras descripciones entusiastas de la ciudad pertenecen al siglo XIX. Con anterioridad a este siglo, los documentos gráficos y literarios son escasos, aunque existan. El siglo XIX los produce en abundancia, porque esa conciencia de ciudad bella no sólo la tienen los compostelanos, sino, ante todo, los gallegos, y, después, cualquier visitante, hasta que la fama de la ciudad se equipara a la de otras europeas. Se establecen parangones, innecesarios por cuanto las ciudades comparadas, por únicas, son incomparables. No deja, además, de ser posible que al compostelano le importe más la condición histórica y religiosa que la estética. Existe incluso un momento en que esta última desaparece, y en que hay muchos compostelanos dispuestos a sacrificar la belleza de una calle o de un rincón a la comodidad de una casa moderna. Por fortuna, ese impulso constructivo, al mismo tiempo que destructor, fue frenado, y aun anulado, por la ley, y al recinto sacro se le puede hoy llamar el recinto intocable. Los valores teatrales quedan incólumes. El viajero puede hoy recorrer los mismos lugares (con escasas diferencias) en que se acantonaban las patrullas de un regimiento pronunciado, las mismas rúas, bajo los soportales sombríos, por los que pasaba, con su cuerpo doliente apoyado en el paraguas, la Rosalía madura, aquella de cuyo pasado recio no quedaban más que los ojos vivos, la que no tenía para su dolor otra salida que los versos.*

Las líneas generales
de un mundo distante

La gran transformación de la ciudad se opera hacia finales del siglo XVII y principios del XVIII. Todavía cuando un príncipe de la casa de Médicis la describe, por los ochenta, y su dibujante la reproduce, las grandes moles de piedra contrastan con las casas habitadas, de madera y yeso. Un buen día, retirados los andamios y ya en silencio los picapedreros, los compostelanos pueden contemplar (¿con asombro?, ¿con indiferencia?) la maravilla barroca de las torres. ¡Hay que ver lo que la piedra da de sí! La experiencia que los compostelanos tienen del arte gótico es escasa, y las labras románicas les son tan familiares que se fijan poco en ellas: no falta quien las tache de vejestorios, quien desee para la catedral estructuras más modernas. ¡Pues ya las tienen, ahí están! Y lo que prueban, una vez más, es que el granito, trabajado por manos hábiles, es tan plástico como el barro. Por otra parte, muchos

La gran transformación de la ciudad se opera hacia finales del siglo XVII y principios del XVIII. Todavía cuando un príncipe de la casa de Médicis la describe, por los ochenta, y su dibujante la reproduce, las grandes moles de piedra contrastan con las casas habitadas, de madera y yeso.

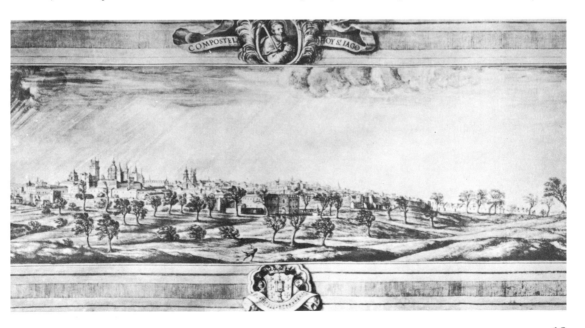

Muchos de aquellos compostelanos han levantado en piedra sus residencias campesinas, que llaman, en gallego, «pazos», que vale tanto como palacios, y que a veces lo son, mezclados de fortalezas: ¡es tan insegura la campiña!
(Pazo de Oca, La Coruña.)

A quién se le ocurrió labrar también en piedra su casa ciudadana, no se sabe, pero el ejemplo lo dio el cabildo, con la casa del Deán y con ese maravilloso disparate que cierra por uno de sus lados la plaza de Platerías.
(Casa del Deán.)

de aquellos compostelanos han levantado en piedra sus residencias campesinas, que llaman, en gallego, *pazos*, que vale tanto como palacios, y que a veces lo son, mezclados de fortalezas: ¡es tan insegura la campiña! Enormes construcciones de granito, de piedras escuadradas si tiran hacia el Sur; de piedras irregulares, pero bien enmarcadas y tomadas de cal, si hacia el Norte. A quién se le ocurrió labrar también en piedra su casa ciudadana, no se sabe, pero el ejemplo lo dio el cabildo, con la casa del Deán y con ese maravilloso disparate que cierra por uno de sus lados la plaza de Platerías. Así, poco a poco, han ido surgiendo, a lo largo de las viejas rúas, fachadas pétreas y arquerías viarias, los soportales, que en una ciudad de tanta lluvia son especialmente útiles. También en este siglo se construyeron o reformaron iglesias, y el obispo Rajoy mandó a un ingeniero militar construir el palacio de su nombre, de traza clásica, todo lo contrario de la frontera fachada del Obradoiro, pero que, no se sabe por qué (quizá sea el milagro de la lluvia, que lo unifica todo), completa armoniosamente la plaza inmensa; cuatro edificios distintos que ya en este siglo quedan constituidos como uno de los grandes conjuntos europeos.

Al lado de estas casas ricas, con soportales y notables fachadas, van surgiendo algunas más modestas, también de piedra, regulares en la disposición de sus vanos, colaboradoras sin saberlo en una fisonomía común. No deja de ser curioso que, a lo largo de dos siglos, con distintos propósitos y distintas voluntades, se haya logrado esa unidad, que quizá pudiéramos llamar atmosférica, que caracteriza a la vieja Compostela. Porque las casas que van sustituyendo a las viejas edificaciones de madera (de las que aún se conservan hoy, como reliquias, hasta media docena) se labran en granito de noble apariencia; porque durante el siglo XIX se sigue construyen-

En el siglo XVIII se construyeron o reformaron iglesias, y el obispo Rajoy mandó a un ingeniero militar construir el palacio de su nombre, de traza clásica, todo lo contrario de la frontera fachada del Obradoiro, pero que, no se sabe por qué (quizá sea el milagro de la lluvia, que lo unifica todo), completa armoniosamente la plaza inmensa.
(*A la izquierda,* el palacio de Rajoy; *arriba,* la fachada del Obradoiro.)

*Las casas que van
sustituyendo a las viejas
edificaciones de madera (de
las que aún se conservan
hoy, como reliquias, hasta
media docena) se labran en
granito de noble apariencia.*

*Aparecen los miradores, que
son la característica gallega
de la arquitectura del
siglo XIX. Los miradores
gallegos, más que otros
aditamentos arquitectónicos,
hacen pensar, o soñar, en la
intimidad de los habitantes.*

do, ya no palacios o casas blasonadas, sino edificaciones burguesas, cuya fisonomía, siempre armónica, depende un poco del lugar donde las edifiquen: si en alguna de las dos viejas rúas principales (la Nueva, la del Villar), se acomodan al imperativo, o a la necesidad, de los soportales; pero prescinden de ellos y ostentan nuevas trazas si el emplazamiento es en lugares de menos exigencias. Se puede seguir el rastro de estas nuevas construcciones, que terminan con algún asomo de modernismo; las dos esquinas de la calle del cardenal Payá son buena muestra de lo que dio de sí la arquitectura del siglo XIX, así como otras casas desperdigadas por la ciudad. De piedra, claro, pero en muchas de ellas colabora la cal, y aparecen los miradores, que son la característica gallega de la arquitectura de este siglo. Fuera ya del recinto casi sagrado, en la calle de la Serna, en el Hórreo, quedan todavía algunas muestras espléndidas de este modo de construir. También es corriente

que encima de una casa del dieciocho se construya un piso nuevo, con galería. Las galerías están pintadas de blanco y son de madera. Las ventanas, de las llamadas de guillotina. El sol, cuando sale, suele formar en ellas fiestas de luz. Los miradores gallegos, más que otros aditamentos arquitectónicos, hacen pensar, o soñar, en la intimidad de los habitantes. Solían completarse con cortinas de arriba abajo: con sólo moverlas un poco, se podía mirar sin ser visto. Durante el siglo XIX la gente dio en la costumbre de pasear, además de pasar. Los soportales de las rúas resultaban pintiparados para esa expansión, aunque con el inconveniente de que se hacía difícil examinar a los paseantes, llevarles la cuenta, escrutar sus atuendos. Alguien, tampoco se sabe quién, inventó una especie de observatorios de los que todavía quedan restos. Consistían en un agujero cuadrangular perforado en el suelo de la primera planta y tapado con una especie de trampilla. Se levantaba, con la fami-

Alguien, tampoco se sabe quién, inventó una especie de observatorios de los que todavía quedan restos. Consistían en un agujero cuadrangular perforado en el suelo de la primera planta y tapado con una especie de trampilla.
(Soportales en la rúa del Villar, foto de 1919.)

lia sentada alrededor, y se podía ver al paseante sin ser visto, aunque sí sospechado. Pero las costumbres tienen las ventajas de ser efímeras, y, cuando ya han pasado, difícilmente se comprenden. Cuando algún forastero pregunta por la función de aquella especie de tragaluces que aún subsisten en el techo de los soportales y se les explica, no suelen creerlo. No hay mucha gente, hoy, capaz de imaginar la vida de una ciudad como Compostela durante el siglo XIX. Lo cual, por otra parte, es comprensible. La literatura de la época no dejó testimonios, los llamados «costumbristas» prestaron escasa atención a aquella sociedad provinciana y, encima de provinciana, pueblerina, a causa no se sabe bien si de su lejanía o de su escaso pintoresquismo. ¿Y no sería por su excesiva, extraña originalidad? Se habían aceptado unos patrones de la vida española, y la de Compostela, como en general la de las ciudades del Norte, no encajaba en ellos. Compostela careció de la fortuna de contar, entre los profesores de su universidad, con un Leopoldo Alas; contó, en cambio, con un Pérez Lugín, que vio de Compostela lo más superficial y efímero, si bien gracias a su novela se sabía en España que en Compostela había una universidad. Pero, a lo que se deduce de semejante narración, ¿se le puede llamar universidad sin incurrir en error? El señor Pérez Lugín no se distinguió por su perspicacia. Había una universidad mucho más atenta a lo que pasaba por el mundo de lo que pudiera suponerse o esperarse de su relato. Mas, para el gusto de aquel autor, no era tema novelable. Sin embargo, a lo largo del siglo XIX, se desarrolla, si no un drama, al menos una batalla dialéctica entre la tradición enquistada y el progreso no muy bien orientado, ésta es la verdad. No faltan atisbos de genialidad, resplandores inesperados, pero Compostela, antiguamente comunicada con Europa por un camino propio, quedaba ahora, no ya lejos de París, de Berlín o de Roma, sino del mismo Madrid. El examen minucioso de los periódicos y revistas publicados en la ciudad a lo largo del siglo XIX nos permite averiguar qué sabían los compostelanos de cuanto sucedía en el mundo, si no eran algunos extravagantes que viajaban a él a conocerlo, y que regresaban de él encandilados. Un poeta gallego de aquel tiempo, Manuel Curros Enríquez, escribió un poema memorable, en lengua vernácula, a la primera locomotora que apareció en Orense; pero, cuando el poema fue escrito, cientos de locomotoras recorrían los espa-

Don Gaspar Núñez de Arce veía con temor y repugnancia aparecer la cabeza de un simio «tras la noble cabeza de Palas», mientras en Santiago de Compostela se habló de Darwin y del darwinismo mucho antes que en Madrid y que en la mayor parte de las universidades españolas.
(*Arriba*, G. Núñez de Arce, por I. Suárez Llanos; *a la izquierda*, Ch. Darwin, por J. Collier.)

cios europeos sin que nadie se asombrase ya de su fuerza y de su rapidez. Aunque llamarlas «rápidas» a las locomotoras no fuese lo usual, sino «raudas». Don Gaspar Núñez de Arce, poeta algo anterior a Curros, había escrito un peregrino verso:

... a lo lejos silba y pasa la rauda locomotora

con el que termina su historia versificada de los líos más o menos melodramáticos de Felipe II con Escobedo y la hermo-

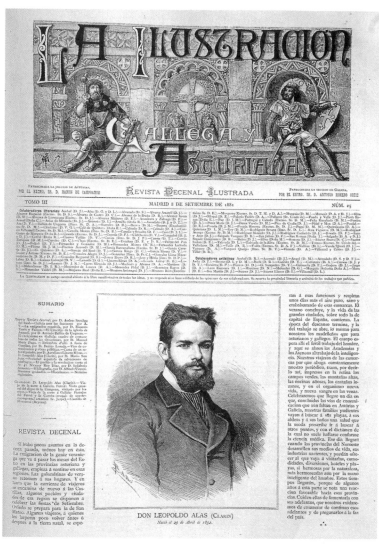

Compostela careció de la fortuna de contar, entre los profesores de su universidad, con un Leopoldo Alas; contó, en cambio, con un Pérez Lugín, que vio de Compostela lo más superficial y efímero, si bien gracias a su novela se sabía en España que en Compostela había una universidad.

(A la derecha, L. Alas; abajo, A. Pérez Lugín; arriba, la Casa de la Troya.)

sísima y terrible doña Ana de Mendoza. Sin embargo, generalizar es arriesgado: don Gaspar Núñez de Arce veía con temor y repugnancia aparecer la cabeza de un simio «tras la noble cabeza de Palas», mientras en Santiago de Compostela se habló de Darwin y del darwinismo mucho antes que en Madrid y que en la mayor parte de las universidades españolas.

Durante la Edad Media, como se dijo ya y todo el mundo sabe, Compostela se comunicaba con el mundo por su camino propio, pero este camino se había olvidado, casi borrado, y llegar a Galicia por tierra, hasta la construcción del primer ferrocarril, era tarea ardua y peligrosa. George Borrow, en su famoso libro, describe este viaje, y es para espeluznarse. Pero esto no quiere decir que Galicia estuviese enteramente aislada del mundo. Le quedaba la mar, y por la mar llegaba la mayor parte de lo que no venía de Madrid en forma de reales decretos y malas noticias de guerras civiles. Los gallegos empezaron a emigrar durante el siglo XIX, como única solución a su precario modo de vivir. La lectura de los diarios compostelanos, aquellas modestas hojitas de que antes se ha hablado, insertan de vez en cuando anuncios de barcos que, desde La Coruña, viajaban a ultramar; pero muy pronto aparecen los de viajes de mayor entidad, compañías extranjeras que hacen escala, no sólo en La Coruña, sino en Carril, primero; después, en Villagarcía; más tarde, en Vigo. Nombres extraños, como *La Mala Real Inglesa* o *La Mala Real Belga*, se hacen familiares. Estos barcos van al Caribe, al Río de la Plata e in-

Un poeta gallego de aquel tiempo, Manuel Curros Enríquez, escribió un poema memorable, en lengua vernácula, a la primera locomotora que apareció en Orense; pero, cuando el poema fue escrito, cientos de locomotoras recorrían los espacios europeos.
(*A la derecha,* Manuel Curros Enríquez; *a la izquierda,* grabado publicado en «La Ilustración Gallega y Asturiana», en abril de 1881, con motivo de la llegada a Orense de la primera locomotora.)

Los gallegos empezaron a emigrar durante el siglo XIX, como única solución a su precario modo de vivir.
(Grabado publicado en «La Ilustración Gallega y Asturiana», 1880.)

cluso al Pacífico. Los precios del pasaje vienen anunciados en reales de vellón, y a los viajeros de tercera clase se les ofrece literas con colchoneta, vino en las comidas y asistencia médica gratuita. Es corriente creer que estos barcos sólo llevaban emigrantes, pero lo cierto es que también desembarcaban mercancías, y, entre ellas, libros. ¿Fue por la mar por donde llegaban, durante el siglo XVIII, los productos más cotizados y perseguidos de la cultura francesa, con preferencia a otras europeas? No se conoce, que se sepa, un estudio exhaustivo de los fondos de las grandes bibliotecas gallegas, las de los monasterios, las de los pazos, las de algunos particulares. El citado George Borrow se asombra de la que posee, y le muestra, un caballero pontevedrés. En la de los monjes de San Martín Pinario, de Compostela, que se conserva, abundan los libros franceses del dieciocho, incluidas deliciosas ediciones de los poetas eróticos latinos, y un número bastante crecido de autores entonces prohibidos, algunos en excelentes ediciones, como la segunda de las *Obras completas de Descartes,* maravillosamente encuadernadas e ilustradas. Un poco más abajo de Compostela, en Santa Cruz de Rivadulla, la biblioteca del pazo asombra por su riqueza y por la libertad de espíritu de quienes la fundaron. El marqués de ese título recibió y acogió, en su pazo, a don Gaspar Melchor de Jovellanos cuando salió de su prisión y su destierro. Y existen barruntos de que los mismos canónigos de la catedral, o al menos algunos de ellos, recibían de Francia, con marbete de piadosos, los libros de la Ilustración y los repartían por las bibliotecas privadas. La provincia de La Coruña, o lo que hoy se llama así, fue uno de los centros más activos de la obra ilustrada, que el recuerdo de Cornide preside todavía. Así se explica que esta ciudad, y sus contornos hasta más allá de Compostela, hayan sido el foco más candente del liberalismo en España, después de Cádiz, y no con menor actividad. Paralela y lógicamente, es también un centro de la reacción. La sede compostelana, y algunos de los canónigos que la sirven, refuerzan ideológicamente, alrededor de los años veinte, al despotismo centralista. ¡Cuántas afirmaciones del *Syllabus* no están previstas y casi formuladas en esta campaña de apoyo al absolutismo! Así no es de extrañar que los núcleos de ideologías contendientes, tras de las cuales se esconden, o a veces se muestran claramente, intereses de los que entonces llamaban materiales y ahora lla-

mamos económicos y de poder, se equilibren en número y fuerza en estas tierras, en estas ciudades. Existen, sin embargo,
algunas diferencias, que explican ciertas singularidades. La Coruña es una ciudad donde se ha constituido una burguesía
próspera y antigua, de tendencia claramente liberal; los núcleos
resistentes son menores. Por el contrario, Santiago, ciudad archiepiscopal cuya economía se asienta, en buena parte y desde
antiguo, en el campesinado, es, desde muy pronto, el centro
de la resistencia absolutista, tanto en sus manifestaciones intelectuales como en las más activas de la política diaria. Para
los liberales, Santiago es una ciudad de conquista; para los
absolutistas, La Coruña es una ciudad de misión. Para los historiadores modernos de este largo período, los militares parti-
cipantes en los numerosos pronunciamientos, triunfantes o fa-
llidos, no son más que instrumentos triunfantes de la burguesía coruñesa. Quizá no vayan descaminados. En La Coruña,
los comerciantes exceden, en sus actividades, los ámbitos loca-

*En la biblioteca de los
monjes de San Martín
Pinario, de Compostela, que
se conserva, abundan los
libros franceses del dieciocho,
incluidas deliciosas ediciones
de los poetas eróticos latinos,
y un número bastante
crecido de autores entonces
prohibidos.*
(Escalera y claustro de San
Martín Pinario.)

23

El marqués de Santa Cruz de Rivadulla recibió y acogió, en su pazo, a don Gaspar Melchor de Jovellanos cuando salió de su prisión y su destierro.
(G. M. de Jovellanos, por Goya.)

les: muchos de ellos mantienen relaciones con ultramar y con algunos puertos europeos. La economía de Santiago se nutre de la clientela que acude a los mercados semanales. Es curioso encontrar todavía en los diarios de los años treinta la palabra *alhóndiga*, que, repentinamente, desaparece. No existe un mercado de valores, pero sí informes diarios de sus cotizaciones, lo cual hace suponer cierta actividad bancaria y un asomo de mentalidad moderna. Pero la base económica de las clases dominantes y de la mitra son los tributos de origen medieval, los *foros* y otras rentas. Las rentas feudales, su mantenimiento o desaparición, serán uno de los caballos de batalla de la vida económica y política gallega hasta bien entrado el siglo XX. Don Ramón del Valle-Inclán, en alguna de sus narraciones cortas, se refiere a los arcaces, situados en los zaguanes, donde las familias beneficiadas guardaban estos tributos campesinos, generalmente en especie. Los diarios, a lo largo del siglo XIX, anuncian compras y ventas de foros. Es un mercado como otro cualquiera, pero de mercancía anticuada. A pesar de su permanencia, su cuantía es insuficiente para sostener económicamente la vida de los pazos. Sin embargo, los burgueses recién acomodados y los aldeanos ricos los adquieren, y se sienten por ello políticamente afines a quienes todavía los mantienen y los defienden. El fin de la cuestión foral queda muy lejos del período que nos ocupa. Pero como también la Iglesia percibe foros, lo mismo las episcopales que las meras parroquias, no tarda en aparecer toda una doctrina sancionada por los eclesiásticos y, por supuesto, elaborada por ellos.

La economía gallega, pues, a pesar de los intentos de los ilustrados y de otros esfuerzos renovadores, se mantiene en una etapa estrictamente agraria. Existen, o existieron, algunas fábricas. En Sargadelos, la producción de loza aparece y desaparece según las circunstancias. No se observa que los gallegos, en general, se preocupen gran cosa por mejorar las producciones, por innovar. Son grupos de inmigrantes los que impulsan los cambios, no sin conflictos. Grupos de catalanes, a finales del siglo XVIII, se asientan en la costa, preferentemente en la ría de Arosa, y transforman, no sin conflictos, a veces graves, las artes de la pesca. Estas inmigraciones catalanas se repiten, entre los años veinte y treinta (zonas de Ferrol y Mugardos) y hacia los años setenta (ría de Vigo). A ellas se debe el desarrollo de las industrias pesqueras. Otras inmigra-

ciones, de maragatos e incluso de riojanos procedentes de la zona de Cameros, impulsan ciertas clases de comercio, el que entonces se llama de coloniales, el de tejidos, y una incipiente banca. Las leyes de desamortización traen consigo disputas ideológicas y cambios económicos. Al desaparecer la figura del *vinculeiro* (*hereu* en Cataluña; mayorazgo en otras tierras), la unidad económica del pazo se rompe, y, poco a poco, la propiedad de la tierra se fragmenta hasta formas inimaginables. La clase dominante gallega no se muestra muy apta para hacer frente a la situación económica. Los hijos de las familias nobles se hacen abogados, militares, eclesiásticos, profesiones improductivas. Y los que permanecen en el pazo, empobrecidos, inician un proceso de decadencia moral y social cuyas manifestaciones han descrito, en épocas distintas, doña Emilia Pardo Bazán y don Ramón del Valle-Inclán. Don Juan Manuel de Montenegro, a pesar de sus defectos, es todavía una figura noble; no así sus hijos, si se exceptúa a Cara de Plata, que

Un poco más abajo de Compostela, en Santa Cruz de Rivadulla, la biblioteca del pazo asombra por su riqueza y por la libertad de espíritu de quienes la fundaron.
(Fachada principal del pazo de Rivadulla.)

25

52. CORUÑA. OBELISCO Y PARQUE DE MÉNDEZ NUÑEZ

La Coruña es una ciudad donde se ha constituido una burguesía próspera y antigua, de tendencia claramente liberal; los núcleos resistentes son menores.
(Foto de archivo.)

tampoco llega a nada. Las grandes construcciones de granito, pazos o monasterios, comienzan a desmoronarse. Es cierto que la burguesía liberal adquiere los bienes de la Iglesia, así como las antiguas tierras comunales de los municipios, pero esto no cambia las cosas en gran medida, ya que no surgen, ni nadie las imagina, empresas modernas de explotación agraria, por mucho que la modernización del campo se predique en las ciudades, las prediquen los políticos y los ideólogos. La única novedad, al margen de los cultivos tradicionales, es la del maíz, que salvó más de un hambre colectiva. También aparecen los pinos, que cantó el poeta Pondal: árboles rumorosos y de elegante fuste, pero de escaso valor económico. Es cierto que su crecimiento es más rápido que los parsimoniosos robles, que los frondosos castaños, que las hayas, que los graciosos *vidueiros*, cuya madera sólo sirve para elaborar el calzado de los campesinos. Sin embargo, la desamortización da origen a fuertes capitales, cuyos beneficios no revierten al campo, sino a las ciudades. La situación de los compradores de bienes desamortizados no difiere, en Galicia, de la de otras regiones españolas. El comprador de bienes eclesiásticos es *vitando* por de-

cisión de la Iglesia, mal visto por las clases aristocráticas: liberal en política, comerciante o pequeño industrial de aires modernos. Como en España no se llega a instituir una república democrática viable; como subsisten, más o menos baqueteados, los antiguos estamentos, el liberal enriquecido por la adquisición de bienes desamortizados no se encuentra cómodo en la sociedad establecida. Su suerte hubiera sido distinta de haber triunfado «su» política. Los varones son más resistentes: en todas las ciudades gallegas, Santiago entre ellas, se puede rastrear la existencia de grupos progresistas, señores muy serios de respetables barbas que, a su modo, colaboran en el triunfo de la sociedad burguesa, que en ciudades como La Coruña llega a tener verdadera importancia política y económica, pero que, en general, se limita a dar señales de su existencia por medio de instituciones de escaso alcance social y cultural, aunque a ellos se deban ciertas mejoras urbanísticas, como la creación de paseos públicos —en Santiago, la Herradura y la Alameda, con su palco de la Música, su escalinata de acceso (de cuya construcción quedan noticias de prensa)—, diarios o periódicos de vida efímera y actitudes muy

Por el contrario, Santiago, ciudad archiepiscopal cuya economía se asienta, en buena parte y desde antiguo, en el campesinado, es, desde muy pronto, el centro de la resistencia absolutista, tanto en sus manifestaciones intelectuales como en las más activas de la política diaria.
(Grabado de D. Roberts.)

La economía de Santiago se nutre de la clientela que acude a los mercados semanales.
(Día de mercado en Santiago, según una foto de archivo.)

definidas en el orden político y en el religioso. Aparecen como republicanos y anticlericales, pero esta generalidad, como todas las generalidades, es falsa. Hay algunos, quizá muchos, republicanos entre ellos; hay algunos, quizá muchos, anticlericales, pero sus esposas y sus hijas van a la iglesia, se confiesan con curas reaccionarios y se sienten molestas de ocupar un lugar secundario en la sociedad. Son bastantes los nietos de estos enriquecidos con los bienes desamortizados (no sólo de la Iglesia; también de bienes comunales) que, tras un donativo a la Iglesia que se parece mucho a un precio, adquieren un título pontificio. Los títulos pontificios no son transmisibles: hay que conseguir que el estado monárquico los catalogue como títulos de Castilla. Es una historia que se repite en toda España, también en Galicia. El noble de origen pontificio, más rico que los nobles tradicionales, adquiere también, muchas veces, los palacios que los antiguos propietarios, seriamente afectados por la desamortización, ya no pueden sostener.

Don Juan Manuel de Montenegro grita una vez, desde lejos, al marqués de Bradomín: «Voy a apalear a un secretario de ayuntamiento.» El secretario del ayuntamiento y el maestro son los representantes, en el mundo rural, del poder central, frente al cura y al señor del pazo. Esta realidad del poder central, del Estado moderno, no se entiende muy bien, no se acepta, por los viejos estamentos. En todas partes, en la aldea más remota, existe una tensión, más o menos fuerte, entre lo viejo y lo nuevo, o, dicho con otras palabras, entre lo ortodoxo y lo pecaminoso. No perdamos de vista que, en todo este proceso, anda metida la Iglesia (o, más exactamente, andan metidos los eclesiásticos, que se creen «la Iglesia»), y que, en consecuencia, las cosas se presentan bastante confusas. Si nos reducimos al ámbito compostelano, donde la modernidad, la progresía, está representada, más que por los burgueses enriquecidos, por los universitarios, frente a ellos hallamos al clero, intelectualmente bien pertrechado de armas, no sólo espirituales, sino también intelectuales, así como a la nobleza, cuyo único refugio es el carlismo. Es cierto que no todos los clérigos son reaccionarios ni todos los nobles carlistas, pero las excepciones no llegan a constituir, al menos durante los años centrales del siglo, núcleos de actividad suficiente. La lucha ideológica entre la universidad y el cabildo cambia ligeramente cuando, instituido el seminario diocesano, éste alcanza una importancia local suficiente. La lucha ideológica transcurre entre las dos universidades, la civil y la religiosa, entre la teología tradicional y la ciencia moderna. El seminario tiende a apoderarse espiritualmente de la universidad, que, en otros tiempos, fue patrimonio eclesiástico. El forcejeo entre ambas instituciones se prolonga más allá del siglo XIX, halla en el XX momentos de grave dramatismo. Las relaciones entre ambas instituciones después de la guerra civil del año treinta y seis son otra historia.

La economía gallega se mantiene en una etapa estrictamente agraria. Existen, o existieron, algunas fábricas. En Sargadelos, la producción de loza aparece y desaparece según las circunstancias.

29

Grupos de catalanes, a finales del siglo XVIII, se asientan en la costa, preferentemente en la ría de Arosa, y transforman, no sin conflictos, a veces graves, las artes de la pesca.
(Dibujo de J. Pérez Villaamil, 1849.)

La única novedad, al margen de los cultivos tradicionales, es la del maíz, que salvó más de un hambre colectiva.

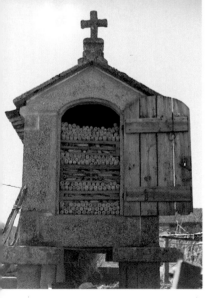

Compostela es, durante más de un siglo, una ciudad dividida, enfrentada, en la que repercuten, de manera muchas veces dramática, los grandes acontecimientos de la vida nacional. Todavía, cuando se constituye el Batallón Literario que pelea con gloria en la guerra de la Independencia, los disidentes de la unidad son escasos, apenas forman grupos, y no influyen en la vida local, menos aún en la regional. Las cosas comienzan a partirse, a presentarse escindidas, después de 1820, aunque antes hayan aparecido manifestaciones hostiles a la Constitución del doce. Por oponerse a la política triunfante, dos arzobispos, al menos, conocen el destierro. La fecha de 1820 es decisiva, y la de 1836, especialmente interesante. Compostela, sin embargo, no es el centro del liberalismo gallego, sino La Coruña, donde existe una burguesía comerciante de gran peso: como que a ella hay que atribuir el impulso de los movimientos militares de matiz liberal. Después de Cádiz, La Coruña es la ciudad más avanzada, ideológicamente, de toda la Península, como ya se dijo, y Santiago queda lo suficientemente próxima como para que las ideas y los movimientos coruñeses repercutan con gravedad. La Coruña se va perfilando como la ciudad más importante del reino de Galicia, y no es cosa de olvidar aquí el hecho curioso de que un diputado a Cortes, mente utópica si las hubo, haya propuesto en el parlamento central una reforma del clero que incluía el traslado a La Coruña, no sólo del arzobispado compostelano, sino el de las discutidas reliquias del Apóstol. El tal parlamentario, cuyo nombre es preferible olvidar, carecía, el hombre, del más elemental sentido histórico, lo cual no le impedía representar, en un tiempo y con no muy clara conciencia, el pensamiento gibelino de que el Estado puede intervenir en las cosas específicas de la Iglesia.

¡Cuántas novelas modernas pudieron tener en Santiago su asiento y su desarrollo! No carecía de ninguno de los

Es cierto que el crecimiento de los pinos es más rápido que los parsimoniosos robles, que los frondosos castaños, que las hayas, que los graciosos «vidueiros», cuya madera sólo sirve para elaborar el calzado de los campesinos.

También aparecen los pinos, que cantó el poeta Pondal: árboles rumorosos y de elegante fuste, pero de escaso valor económico.

31

*Ni doña Emilia Pardo
Bazán, ni don Ramón del
Valle-Inclán se valieron de
la materia compostelana
más que para pequeñeces,
aunque alguna sea tan
perfecta como «Mi prima
Antonia», del segundo.*

ingredientes requeridos, pero los novelistas del siglo prefirieron otros ámbitos. Ni doña Emilia Pardo Bazán, ni don Ramón del Valle-Inclán se valieron de la materia compostelana más que para pequeñeces, aunque alguna sea tan perfecta como *Mi prima Antonia,* del segundo. Sin embargo, en *Mi prima Antonia* los motivos son de otra índole: pertenecen a una Compostela más profunda, menos transitoria; por lo tanto, menos histórica, menos novelesca. ¡Ah, la gran epopeya de la lucha entre tirios y troyanos, entre clericales y anticlericales, entre liberales y reaccionarios, entre nobles y burgueses, la gran historia del siglo XIX vista como un microscopio en un ámbito reducido, si bien en uno de los escenarios más hermosos de España!

Comercios, tenderetes, tiendas y algunas novedades sociales

Todavía, como ya se dijo, en los anuncios de prensa de los años treinta aparece la palabra *alhóndiga*, rápidamente desaparecida de los periódicos y del vocabulario vivo. La sustituyen los anuncios de comercios y de tiendas. Por estos años, el comercio compostelano parece sufrir un cambio importante, la aparición de sus formas más modernas, aunque en años anteriores se hubieran amasado buenas fortunas. En la historia de la economía gallega y, por tanto, en la compostelana influyen decisivamente ciertas emigraciones, de catalanes y maragatos, sobre todo. De que Compostela fue una ciudad comercial y burguesa ante todo no cabe duda, pues una economía muy regular y muy definida aparece muy pronto al-

De que Compostela fue una ciudad comercial y burguesa ante todo no cabe duda, pues una economía muy regular y muy definida aparece muy pronto alrededor del sepulcro del Apóstol, la que con palabras modernas llamaríamos de «souvenirs» y de hostelería.

La economía de «souvenirs» engendra industrias importantes y delicadas, como las de la plata y del azabache, subsistentes hasta nuestros días, aunque en formas ya muy evolucionadas y distantes de los modos originales, si bien ciertos prototipos se sigan fabricando sin apenas cambios en las formas.

rededor del sepulcro del Apóstol, la que con palabras modernas llamaríamos de *souvenirs* y de hostelería. La primera engendra industrias importantes y delicadas, como las de la plata y del azabache, subsistentes hasta nuestros días, aunque en formas ya muy evolucionadas y distantes de los modos originales, si bien ciertos prototipos se sigan fabricando sin apenas cambios en las formas. Pero una ciudad necesita algo más que conchas de peregrino y rosarios de azabache. Las novedades específicamente decimonónicas son las tiendas de comestibles, que se llaman de ultramarinos, y las de tejidos. La venta de tejidos la hacían profesionales ambulantes que instalaban en las ferias sus tenderetes, cuando no vendían a domicilio (todavía en el primer tercio de nuestro siglo quedaban restos de

esta clase de comercio). Pero comienzan a fundarse establecimientos de venta permanente, tiendas si se las llama al modo
antiguo, comercios si al moderno. La diferencia entre tiendas
y comercios se establece muy pronto: serán tiendas las de comestibles, serán comercios los de tejidos y, más tarde, los de
otros productos de consumo más lento, de duración más larga.
Unas y otras las regentan gentes venidas de fuera de Galicia,
y lo que venden tampoco es de origen local, ni siquiera regional. En Compostela, las nuevas formas coexisten con las antiguas, no las destruyen. Por ejemplo, el mercado semanal sufre
variaciones, lo instalan aquí y allá, pero lo que se compra en
él es siempre lo mismo: ganado y productos agrícolas de procedencia regional, bien de aldeas próximas, bien de lugares más
alejados, pero siempre de los límites de Galicia. Es cierto que
abundan los tenderetes en que se expenden productos de más
lejos, pero son el aditamento, no la sustancia de la feria. El
mercado semanal congrega en Compostela abundancia de aldeanos, que traen y venden sus productos, que compran en
las tiendas y en los comercios lo que necesitan y no producen. El comercio compostelano es un negocio permanente y
fructífero. Sólo en tres generaciones, un maragato, llegado os-
cura, humildemente, se convierte en una potencia económica, se

*El mercado semanal
congrega en Compostela
abundancia de aldeanos, que
traen y venden sus
productos, que compran en
las tiendas y en los
comercios lo que necesitan y
no producen.*

35

Con su habitual inocencia, don José María de Pereda dio forma novelesca a este fenómeno (la sustitución de la clase aristocrática por la burguesía enriquecida) en «Blasones y talegas», pero allí no se trata de comerciantes, sino de inmigrantes enriquecidos.

enriquece en la medida suficiente como para impulsar nuevas formas de comercio, las expansivas, que llevan el mismo nombre, la misma firma, a las otras ciudades gallegas, donde los tejidos, la ferretería, se venden bajo el mismo rótulo. Ni doña Emilia Pardo Bazán, ni don Ramón del Valle-Inclán, los novelistas regionales, concedieron la debida importancia literaria a un acontecimiento, no original, ya que situaciones semejantes se dieron, con parecidas circunstancias, en muchos lugares de Europa: la sustitución, en el poder social, de la clase aristocrática por la burguesía enriquecida, y la compra por esta clase advenediza de títulos y honores; modos de adquisición que tienen más relación con la literatura que con la economía visible, pero que tampoco constituyen un fenómeno nuevo. Con su habitual inocencia, don José María de Pereda dio forma novelesca a este fenómeno en *Blasones y talegas,* pero allí no se trata de comerciantes, sino de inmigrantes enriquecidos, los homólogos de aquellos que aparecen en la literatura del siglo XVII, los peruleros. No es que éstos no existan también en Galicia, y que el fenómeno no sea semejante, y que en muchas ocasiones, históricas y no novelescas, no contribuya a la prolongación de la vida del pazo, mediante matrimonios desiguales que, si no los registran los novelistas, quedan en la memoria familiar y en la unión de apellidos vulgares con estirpes ilustres. Pero, en Galicia y, más concretamente, en Compostela, los que llaman la atención, los que transforman el orden social y establecen uno nuevo, no son los de peruleros, sino los de maragatos y catalanes. El matriarcado gallego impone a estas nuevas familias ciertas condiciones, las somete a los viejos sistemas de valores, y así vemos cómo los descendientes de esta burguesía dejan de ser liberales para pasarse a los bandos carlistas o, por lo menos, conservadores. El fenómeno social del pazo, aún sin estudiar suficientemente, que sepamos, sí se ha registrado en la literatura. Doña Emilia Pardo Bazán lo describe en el momento de mayor decadencia, la que sigue a las leyes de desamortización. Don Ramón del Valle-Inclán prefiere años algo anteriores. Otero Pedraio se remonta, en sus historias, al siglo XVIII. Elena Quiroga prefiere etapas más modernas. Todavía, en nuestros días, el pazo conserva valor y significación. Por lo general, las viejas estirpes, aun las ya mezcladas, se van alejando de él, y son sustituidas por gente nueva sin el menor respeto por las formas tradicionales. La restaura-

ción de las viejas fábricas graníticas y blasonadas con criterios modernos todavía no ha sido tratada por la literatura, porque el tema ha pasado de moda, pero podrá serlo.

      Esta transformación de la vida económica no altera sustancialmente la fisonomía compostelana. Como en la mayor parte de las pequeñas ciudades de provincias, el comercio se agrupa, o se alinea, en determinadas calles céntricas, que conservan sus viejos nombres (la Calderería, el Preguntoiro). Parece como si prefirieran las vías más transitadas, fuera de las cuales los establecimientos son menos abundantes, casi

Si un concejo decide la construcción de un gran edificio en que se cobije el mercado urbano de servicio diario, no le busca remoto emplazamiento, sino que utiliza aquella parte de la ciudad donde se había asentado el mercado espontáneo de antaño, en cuyos alrededores es fácil hallar tiendas centenarias.

esporádicos, y son bastantes las calles, las rúas, donde las plantas bajas sirven todavía de habitación, no para el negocio. Esta distribución del comercio guarda mucha relación con las partes de la ciudad afectadas por el tráfico tradicional de los mercados semanales. Todavía hoy, el comercio compostelano, bastante estable en relación, por ejemplo, con las industrias, menos sometido a los vaivenes económicos que aquéllas, se mantiene en las calles y lugares de hace ciento cincuenta años. Si un concejo decide la construcción de un gran edificio en que se cobije el mercado urbano de servicio diario, no le busca remoto emplazamiento, sino que utiliza aquella parte de la ciudad donde se había asentado el mercado espontáneo de antaño, en cuyos alrededores es fácil hallar tiendas centenarias. Acaso la novedad, si se recuerdan los años centrales del siglo XIX, e incluso las décadas posteriores, sea la desaparición del comercio

ambulante, del producto que se pregona en voz alta y con fórmulas verbales estables, cada cual con su música. El «afilador y paragüero» de hace un siglo, hoy dispone de un local estable. En cambio, se mantiene la venta de productos regionales en puestos irregulares a cargo de los propios productores aldeanos, que, como hace mil años, acuden al mercado con sus vituallas.

La posición central de Compostela, en el área geográfica de Galicia, la convierte muy pronto en centro de comunicaciones. El ferrocarril de Santiago a Carril es toda una historia de proyectos, esperanzas, realidades e incluso festejos. Pero ese único ferrocarril coexiste con los transportes por carretera en vehículos de tracción animal, compañías familiares, o de capitalismo familiar, que explotan las diligencias que parten de Santiago hacia las ciudades más importantes y de ellas regresan. Santiago no es sólo el centro universitario de Galicia, sino el centro médico más importante. En Santiago, en torno a la Facultad de Medicina, muy acreditada, y del hospital General, se organiza muy pronto el negocio de la salud. El enfermo gallego que no halla curación ni esperanzas de ella en el lugar donde vive, aspira a «ir a Santiago». Esto, no sólo sostiene el negocio de las comunicaciones, sino también el de la hostelería. Los estudiantes, desaparecidos hace ya mucho

Santiago no es sólo el centro universitario de Galicia, sino el centro médico más importante. En Santiago, en torno a la Facultad de Medicina, muy acreditada, y del hospital General, se organiza muy pronto el negocio de la salud.
(*A la izquierda,* foto actual de la Facultad de Medicina; *arriba,* portada del hospital, según un grabado publicado en «El Museo Universal», 1860.)

39

tiempo los antiguos colegios mayores (San Clemente, Fonseca, etc.), viven en pensiones, generalmente modestas y bastante elementales, de las que la Hacienda pública no tiene constancia: son pequeños negocios familiares, accesibles al peculio de un país medianamente pobre. Ya más tarde van apareciendo establecimientos con el nombre de «hoteles», algunos de ellos de cierto empaque, al menos arquitectónico, como el Suizo, en la calle del cardenal Payá, donde se alojó el rey Alfonso XII. En realidad, no es más que una casa de pensión, algo más grande y algo más cara. La aparición de hoteles en el sentido moderno es bastante más reciente, y obedece a situaciones económicas y sociales distintas.

La presencia, durante ocho meses, de la clase estudiantil origina la permanencia de un tipo de establecimiento tradicional, la taberna (y casa de comidas), y la aparición de un tipo nuevo, inventado en el siglo XVIII fuera de España, propagado en el siglo XIX, de enorme importancia sociológica y, en menor grado, económica. En Compostela hubo cafés que duraron cien años. Acaso no hayan alcanzado en Compostela la importancia política que se reconoce a los de Madrid (recuérdese La Fontana de Oro), pero sí social y económica. En una ciudad húmeda y fría, donde las casas carecen de cualquier clase de confort, por mínimo que sea, el café es un lugar caliente y relativamente cómodo, sin las exigencias del casino: abierto a todos con tal de que paguen, y, a veces, aunque no paguen. Tampoco está escrita, que sepamos, la historia de los cafés compostelanos, y es difícil que se escriba, por falta de documentación y muerte de los testigos. Las formas de vida que allí se fueron creando no coinciden en absoluto con las que se engendran en los cafés modernos, o establecimientos similares, cuya función, si bien sustitutiva, no es equivalente. El mundo del café de estudiantes, formado a lo largo del siglo XIX, desapareció con el primer tercio del siglo XX. Fue un mundo abigarrado, intrascendente, pintoresco. No es de creer que haya influido en medida respetable en la cultura local, ni que haya actuado como sustituto, o, al menos, como sucedáneo, de la universidad. El café de estudiantes compostelano, a nuestro juicio, careció de la importancia cultural que alcanzaron otras instituciones, liceos o ateneos de vida efímera, pero a veces brillante. Uno de los actos político-culturales más importantes de la historia de la ciudad, el *banquete de Conjo,* tuvo la fortuna de ser cantado por uno de los poetas más brillantes (hoy bastante oscurecido, aunque sea el autor del *Himno gallego*) de aquel tiempo, que es asimismo el del Renacimiento regional. El banquete de Conjo resulta de la existencia, activa, de unos cuantos jóvenes de los que el propio Pondal llamó *osbos e xenerosos*: gente tocada del romanticismo moribundo, entusiastas de las nuevas ideas, sobre todo cuando coinciden con la abundancia de su corazón. El banquete de Conjo figura hoy en primera fila de la mitología política gallega, por lo que tiene de regional y por lo que tuvo de democrático, no se sabe si de doctrina suficientemente esclarecida, pero sí de ánimo generoso y un tanto utópico (lo cual es una de sus virtudes, entendámonos). A él concurren, y en él se sientan, estudiantes y obreros, no en mezcla tumultuosa, sino ordenada: cada estudiante, entre dos obreros; cada obrero, entre dos estudiantes. Se pronunciaron en él discursos que hoy son historia, y, para que no faltase nada, el poeta mencionado, Eduardo Pondal, recita, casi canta, un brindis entusiasmado, aunque hoy, al leerlo, no nos conmueva tan profundamente, y no por sus sentimientos, sino por su imperfecta forma poética:

El «afilador y paragüero» de hace un siglo, hoy dispone de un local estable.
(Dibujo de F. de Guisasola.)

> *Brindo por quien, señores, la victoria,*
> *muerto, mas no vencido, dio al tirano*
> *el ilustre varón de alta memoria*
> *el célebre Catón republicano:*
> *de nuestra idea a la futura gloria*
> *y brindo por el pueblo soberano,*
> *y a quien acate, libre como el viento,*
> *el vuelo del humano pensamiento.*
>
> *Oye, ¡oh, pueblo!, sectario de una idea,*
> *bendecida por Dios; oíd, hermanos,*
> *no abandonéis el campo de pelea,*
> *todos sois en la tierra soberanos.*
> *Ya rompe nuestra aurora y centellea,*
> *ya ha quemado la frente a los tiranos,*
> *que, cobardes, los ciega y les asusta*
> *el resplandor de la verdad augusta.*

Esto acontecía el dos de marzo de 1856. Se puede considerar, ¿por qué no?, el punto de arranque de un proceso

Ya más tarde van aparaciendo establecimientos con el nombre de «hoteles», algunos de ellos de cierto empaque, al menos arquitectónico, como el Suizo, en la calle del cardenal Payá, donde se alojó el rey Alfonso XII.
(Foto actual de la calle del cardenal Payá.)

político no clausurado. Hoy, como tantas cosas de aquel tiempo, nos parece bastante ingenuo, tanto como entusiasta y generoso. En su tiempo, la noticia de aquel banquete en que estudiantes (burgueses) y obreros se mezclaron ordenadamente y confraternizaron bajo la palabra altisonante del bardo y el acicate de discursos encendidos, como el de Aurelio Aguirre, sobre todo, tan colmados de esperanzas como de promesas, pareció al mismo tiempo peligroso y escandaloso. Todo el mundo, en aquel tiempo, veía el diablo detrás de la cruz y la revolución detrás de las palabras generosas. Lo menos que dijeron de los organizadores del acto fue que estaban locos, pero esto lo habían dicho antes. ¿Adónde vamos a parar? ¿Y ese Pondal, que sueña con la restauración de los celtas, que aspira a sustituir Santiago por Breogán? Lo que se cuaja en actos como éste, en poemas como tantos que van pululando, aunque no se entiendan bien, por lo confuso, no presagia nada bueno. La gente bien pensante de Compostela no sintió el menor entusiasmo al enterarse de que, en Conjo, como quien dice en la misma ciudad, estudiantes y obreros habían confraternizado bajo la protección de la Oratoria y de la Poesía.

Calles, plazas, estatuas: burguesía y urbanismo

      ¿Cuándo están hechas las ciudades? La pregunta puede parecer impertinente, e incluso serlo; pero, séalo o no, la verdad es que no resulta fácil responderla. Todo depende de los puntos de vista, y, entre otros, del cómo y del cuándo. Pero también de cuál sea la ciudad. Las hay que culminan en su perfección, tras lo cual comienzan a desmoronarse; así Venecia. Otras existen, lo mismo de notables, menos sensibles a la destrucción del tiempo, cuya perfección aguanta y permanece, y podemos decir que ya están, y que no conviene tocarlas, sino, todo lo más, retocarlas; esos retoques que requiere todo lo que se va haciendo viejo. Los retoques son de distinta naturaleza: reponer una piedra gastada, reforzar unos muros vacilantes, completar por medio de un pastiche un conjunto incompleto (¿los pastiches de Oxford?), destruir lo caduco y miserable para que resalte lo permanente y valioso, aplicar a lo viejo admirable los criterios modernos de conservación y de resalte... ¡La de expedientes a que se ha recurrido ante el problema de las ciudades que valen por sí mismas y conviene conservar! Tales ciudades son patrimonio de la humanidad, se las declara así, forman parte de la cultura de un pueblo o de todos los pueblos. Pero todo esto tiene como último referente ciertas ideas modernas, aunque no demasiado: ideas vigentes hace más de un siglo, sin llegar a dos. La conciencia de conservación de las ciudades es relativamente moderna, y tiene su origen en los románticos. Todavía el filósofo Kant, en el siglo XVIII, hallaba monstruoso el estilo que llamamos gótico, y muchos más con él, pues para Kant, como para los más de sus contemporáneos cultos, la perfección de la arquitectura se había alcanzado en la antigüedad clásica, y sólo tenía valor lo que la imitaba o lo que la repetía; pero no mucho tiempo después de su muerte, el poeta Heine llamaba a Munich «Atenas de cartón piedra». En tan poco tiempo, la sensibilidad había cambiado. Y de ese cambio fue surgiendo la nueva conciencia, el amor a las viejas piedras de mírame y no me toques, con las que los pueblos se identifican, que incorporan a sus señas de

Todavía el filósofo Kant, en el siglo XVIII, hallaba monstruoso el estilo que llamamos gótico, y muchos más con él, pues para Kant, como para los más de sus contemporáneos cultos, la perfección de la arquitectura se había alcanzado en la antigüedad clásica.

identidad. Pero surge también como conflicto lo que antes había sido un proceso de evolución natural. ¿Qué hacer de la cochambre? Si por una parte carecía de valor real, por la otra engendraba, con su mera existencia, otra cochambre, ésta no urbanística, sino humana. ¿Cómo era París antes de las reformas de Napoleón III? ¿Fueron maravillas lo que cayó bajo la piqueta implacable, o sólo callejas y casuchas? Es otra pregunta a la que no se puede responder, pero, a la vista de ciertos cuadros, incluso de ciertos rincones todavía existentes, se piensa que aquel París estuvo bien derribado. La lástima es que no lo hubieran pintado antes algunos buenos pintores que pintaron, años más tarde, el París subsistente. ¡Qué hermoso cuadro, ese del japonés Fujita, en que aparecen casuchas y callejas de las que rodeaban a Notre Dame! Pintadas, eternizadas así en lo que tenían de atractivo, su carácter miserable, sus formas nacidas del azar y no de la previsión de un arquitecto, su color envejecida y cochambrosa, no se perdió gran cosa si las han derribado. En tales ámbitos, sólo pueden vivir aquellas gentes de *Los misterios de París,* vida inhumana, que hoy juzgamos intolerable. La reforma de Napoleón III se realizó en un tiempo en que la noción de la gran arquitectura no se había perdido, en que el saber urbanístico era una importante novedad que despertaba entusiasmos. El siglo XIX es el que asiste al triunfo social de la burguesía, no sin dificultades, no sin oposiciones. La burguesía, desde los tiempos románticos, goza de mala prensa entre los artistas, pero éste es un fenómeno un tanto oscuro que debe ser revisado, que en parte lo ha sido ya. Por lo pronto, el romanticismo es un fenómeno burgués, como lo será más tarde el marxismo: hijos de la burguesía, nacidos a su pesar, que la maltratan (el marxismo, no tanto como se cree). La burguesía, al instalarse en el poder, toma a su cargo la dirección de la cultura e intenta establecer sus puntos de vista, su criterio propio. Al gusto estético que manifiesta se lo moteja con voces peyorativas, las más de ellas engendradas y puestas en circulación en París, *pompier, filisteo.* Buena parte de la mejor literatura, del mejor arte del diecinueve, se proclaman antiburgueses, lo cual los lleva a instalarse inevitablemente en los extremos que confinan la burguesía, la aristocracia por arriba, el pueblo (plebe) ciudadano por abajo. La burguesía toma más de los de arriba que de los de abajo; no en vano ha padecido siempre la tentación del esno-

¡Qué hermoso cuadro, ese del japonés Fujita, en que aparecen casuchas y callejas de las que rodeaban a Notre Dame! Pintadas, eternizadas así en lo que tenían de atractivo, su carácter miserable, sus formas nacidas del azar y no de la previsión de un arquitecto, su color envejecida y cochambrosa, no se perdió gran cosa si las han derribado.

bismo, pero, cuando actúa con espontaneidad y consigue expresarse, obtiene logros tan respetables como la Barcelona nueva, y otros muchos barrios de otras ciudades. En Galicia, durante este período, la frágil burguesía instalada en sus pueblos y ciudades más importantes, grupos generalmente minoritarios, imponen unos tipos de viviendas urbanas de gran elegancia y comodidad, para lo que entonces se usa. Si uno se acerca, provisto de una cinta métrica, a una de esas fachadas de seis huecos tan abundantes y toma las medidas, comprobará que, de lejos y sin saberlo, los maestros de obras (jamás los arquitectos) que las construyeron permanecieron fieles desde lejos al número de oro. El espíritu burgués llega a Galicia más temprano que a otros lugares de la Península, y es responsable de todas las alamedas, de todos los paseos urbanos, de todos los templetes de música, de todos los monumentos a los grandes hombres, algunos de los cuales, no demasiados, no fueron burgueses. Políticos, poetas, héroes militares, reproducidos en bronce y encaramados a pedestales de piedra, surgen en las plazas urbanas, desde Vivero hasta Vigo. Bastantes

45

Políticos, poetas, héroes
militares, reproducidos en
bronce y encaramados a
pedestales de piedra, surgen
en las plazas urbanas, desde
Vivero hasta Vigo. En
Santiago, don Casto
Méndez Núñez fue más
afortunado que Rosalía
Castro, aunque el
monumento a ésta intente
ser más grandioso.

El monumento que
Compostela dedicó al más
ilustre de los políticos
nacidos en su recinto,
Montero Ríos, si respetable
en el bronce, no lo es en la
piedra: el que firmó el
Tratado de París de 1900
merecía un soporte menos
achaparrado.

46

de estos monumentos fueron erigidos en el siglo XX, pero conforme al espíritu del XIX. Pero ¿dónde termina uno y dónde comienza el otro? Hacia 1930, todos los grandes gallegos, y algunos que no lo eran, como Porlier, ya estaban suficientemente conmemorados, en estilos diferentes, a veces en estilos exagerados o simplemente equivocados. En Santiago, don Casto Méndez Núñez fue más afortunado que Rosalía Castro,

A la izquierda, monumento a Méndez Núñez; *a la derecha,* monumento a Montero Ríos.

47

aunque el monumento a ésta intente ser más grandioso. En Ferrol, el almirante Sánchez Barcaiztegui supera en gallardía al almirante Jorge Juan, cuya grandeza se encierra en un bronce minúsculo. Nicomedes Pastor Díaz no puede quejarse de la estatua que se le erigió en su pueblo. Hay medallones, bustos... Los que se dedicaron a Concepción Arenal fueron poco afortunados. Pero no hay alameda o paseo urbano sin algún bronce o piedra conmemorativa. La pequeña burguesía de estas villas y ciudades no escatimó recuerdos a los hombres de mérito, lo cual demuestra cierta generosidad de espíritu, toda la que encierra la palabra liberal. Que, cosa curiosa, no es una palabra burguesa, al menos en su origen. El monumento que Compostela dedicó al más ilustre de los políticos nacidos en su recinto, Montero Ríos, si respetable en el bronce, no lo es en la piedra: el que firmó el Tratado de París de 1900 merecía un soporte menos achaparrado. Y no deja de ser curioso que esta ciudad, que fue la capital del carlismo gallego, no haya levantado un monumento a ningún héroe carlista. Se debe, seguramente, a que los concejos, durante el siglo XIX, fueron, con preferencia, liberales, o al menos moderados. Los nombres de los eclesiásticos ilustres hay que buscarlos en las calles y en las piedras funerarias.

Fiestas

Contaba cierta vez un político salmantino que, cuando entraron los franceses en Salamanca, se celebró su llegada con un Te Deum en la catedral, y que cuando, años después, entraron los ingleses victoriosos, se cantó el mismo cántico en el mismo lugar y, por supuesto, con la misma intención. En Compostela no sólo entraron los ingleses y los

Se hizo una corona de ilustres momias alrededor de los huesos del Apóstol, y todas ellas son festejadas por lo menos una vez al año: regocijos populares, que, antaño como ahora, congregaban bailarines con música de charanga y de gaita, alternadas.
(Urna con los restos del Apóstol Santiago.)

49

La aparición de la portada mudéjar, que todavía hoy se quema frente a la catedral la víspera del Apóstol, es posterior: en los anuncios publicados en los diarios de la mitad del siglo, todavía no figura.
(Foto actual.)

Funcionaba, por supuesto, el botafumeiro, el mismo que vuela ahora en las fiestas de respeto y ante los turistas, bólido de metal barato en sustitución del de plata que se llevaron los franceses.

franceses, aunque fuera de paso (que en ocasiones no lo fue), sino varias clases de tropas pronunciadas, y otras tantas de tropas represoras. El ritual difería un poco del salmantino, ya que, además de gorigoris, había colgaduras en los balcones y fuegos de cohetería. Los compostelanos eran especialmente aficionados al buscapié, cohete rastrero con cierta tendencia inmoral a estallar debajo de las faldas de las mujeres, lo cual lo hacía especialmente interesante para los varones de todas las edades que, en su fuero interno, se identificaban en medidas variadas con el cohete. La aparición de la portada mudéjar, que todavía hoy se quema frente a la catedral la víspera del Apóstol, es posterior: en los anuncios publicados en los diarios de la mitad del siglo, todavía no figura, aunque sí los buscapiés. A la fiesta nocturna en la plaza del Obradoiro tampoco se la llamaba verbena. Lo más importante de la celebra-

La Alameda fue muy pronto lugar de reunión general, pero el instinto clasista aprovechó pronto sus estructuras para evitar la confusión. En los andenes laterales paseaban «las artesanas»; en los centrales, «las señoritas».

En la Alameda se conservan unos bancos de piedra con respaldo de hierro forjados nada menos que en los talleres de Sargadelos.

ción era, sin embargo, el ceremonial interno, misas de pontifical, procesiones mitradas, coros y chirimías. Funcionaba, por supuesto, el botafumeiro, el mismo que vuela ahora en las fiestas de respeto y ante los turistas, bólido de metal barato en sustitución del de plata que se llevaron los franceses, a pesar del Te Deum, pero igualmente impresionante en su vuelo ígneo a través de las naves.

Compostela es ciudad rica en huesos santos, como consecuencia del expolio llevado a cabo por Gelmírez en la ciudad de Braga, lo que se conoce en la historia como *el pío latrocinio,* del que fue víctima el santo obispo bracarense. Se hizo una corona de ilustres momias alrededor de los huesos del Apóstol, y todas ellas son festejadas por lo menos una vez al año: regocijos populares, que, antaño como ahora, congregaban bailarines con música de charanga y de gaita, alternadas. La costumbre era el vender rosquillas de varias clases, figurillas de caramelo y copia regular de chucherías. No faltaban tampoco los buscapiés. Y en las escasas fiestas civiles sucedía lo mismo, aunque también en ellas se sacasen colgaduras, y, casi siempre, los inevitables gigantes y cabezudos. Así, cuando vino la reina Isabel II, llegada con algunos días de retraso a ganar el jubileo, o cuando estuvieron en la ciudad los duques de Montpensier, acontecimiento extraordinario que mereció los honores de una crónica especial, lujosamente editada, con una portada un tanto fuera de lo común. La visita de Alfonso XII fue posterior y no tan celebrada. Paró en un hotel de la ciudad, no en palacio privado o eclesiástico. Los concejos ilustrados, y otras gentes de bien, promovieron la construcción de una alameda para que los compostelanos dispusieran de un lugar de esparcimiento público digno de la ciudad. Existe todavía, bien situado, y se conservan unos bancos de piedra con respaldo de hierro forjados nada menos que en los talleres de Sargadelos. Repasando los diarios, se hallan noticias, por ejemplo, de que el ayuntamiento destinó varios miles de reales a la construcción de una escalinata. La Alameda fue muy pronto lugar de reunión general, pero el instinto clasista aprovechó pronto sus estructuras para evitar la confusión. En los andenes laterales paseaban *las artesanas;* en los centrales, *las señoritas.* Los estudiantes tenían bula para ir de un sitio a otro, y a acompañar a quienes les apeteciera. La separación se llevaba con rigor: se llevó hasta bien entrado el siglo XX. Cuan-

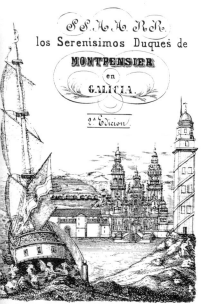

Cuando estuvieron en la ciudad los duques de Montpensier, fue éste un acontecimiento extraordinario que mereció los honores de una crónica especial, lujosamente editada, con una portada un tanto fuera de lo común.

do se instalaron las farolas de gas, en la Alameda se podía pasear de noche, pero no solían acudir las mujeres. En un diario aparece, publicada varios días seguidos, una invitación a que lo hagan. Se dirige especialmente a las «pollas» (muchachas solteras): por aquellas calendas, esta palabra carecía aún de connotaciones vitandas, y se limitaba a designar a las mujeres sin compromiso y a las gallinas jóvenes. Cierto es que a los muchachos se los llamaba «pollos», se sabe el desde cuándo y el cómo, y tanto el masculino como el femenino coexistieron durante el primer tercio de nuestro siglo. En los diarios de la época no se dice si las «pollas» acudieron o no a la invitación, pero es de esperar que sí: primero, las más osadas; después, poco a poco, unas y otras, hasta la totalidad, si no fue alguna recalcitrante cuyo nombre no conserva la historia. La música municipal tocaba también de noche, y las ocasiones festivas de gran iluminación y abundante concurrencia, llegaron a recibir el nombre importado de «foliones»: «Gran folión en la Alameda.» Este ceremonial urbano se practicaba cuando no llovía. En caso de tiempo inclemente, los paseos eran en la rúa del Villar, bajo los soportales y las miradas inquisitivas de las fisgonas, en las trampillas del techo practicadas a tal efecto, como se dijo en alguna parte de estas notas. Los paseos nocturnos con iluminación extraordinaria de farolillos a la veneciana, cada uno con su cabo de vela, se incluían en el programa de las fiestas patronales, y concurrían muchos forasteros y, sobre todo, forasteras.

Después de la fundación del casino, la fiesta central del año, quiere decirse la civil, era el baile del Apóstol, al que se concurría de frac los caballeros y de tiros largos las damas. Fue, naturalmente, un baile de clase, y ni siquiera cierta burguesía podía acudir a él. Se celebraba en varios salones, del que el más famoso fue el amarillo. Era un baile refinado y distinguido, donde el mayor fracaso era el «pavear», es decir, pasarse el baile entero sin dar una mala vuelta de vals. Las costumbres internacionales habían llegado, naturalmente, a Compostela, no sólo en las modas, sino también en los usos: cada señorita concurrente al baile llevaba colgado del cinturón un carné en el que los aspirantes a abrazarla por la cintura y a embriagarse en las vueltas del baile inscribían sus nombres. La orquesta era, en un principio, de cuerda. Cinco o seis profesores que también tocaban en la orquesta de la catedral, y

Arco de triunfo levantado en la puerta Fajera con motivo de la visita de Isabel II a Santiago en 1858.

Después de la fundación del casino, la fiesta central del año, quiere decirse la civil, era el baile del Apóstol, al que se concurría de frac los caballeros y de tiros largos las damas. Fue, naturalmente, un baile de clase, y ni siquiera cierta burguesía podía acudir a él.
(Vista actual de la sala de baile del casino.)

en la del teatro, si había zarzuela u ópera: cuando intervinieron los clarinetes, el ruido de la música rebasaba con mucho las ventanas y balcones abiertos a la noche de julio y llenaban la rúa del Villar, colmada hasta muy tarde de papanatas: hasta que la gente iba desfilando, a pie o en coche, y el casino cerraba sus puertas. De estos bailes salieron matrimonios, rupturas, muchos cotilleos y dos o tres desafíos. Uno de ellos tuvo como protagonistas a un caballero maduro y a un joven teniente de artillería. El conflicto comenzó por la acusación que hizo el caballero al teniente de haber desairado a su hija (del caballero). Hubo disputa, actitudes solemnes, palabras trágicas, y el guantazo final del teniente al caballero, guante blanco sobre bigotes puntiagudos. Los padrinos concertaron el duelo, a pistola, en el bosque de la Condesa, al rayar el alba. La noticia se expandió. Hubo revuelos y patatuses. Casi todo el mundo estuvo de acuerdo en que aquello no podía ser, aunque unos cuantos se frotasen las manos de gusto. Empezaron a funcionar las gestiones urgentes para evitar el duelo. Sonó la palabra excomunión. Se llegó al arzobispo, el arzobispo llamó al jefe de la artillería, que era un teniente coronel, y éste envió al teniente arrestado al cuartel. No pudo comparecer, a la alborada, en el bosque de la Condesa. Se levantaron actas, y el caballero consideró su honor restaurado. Un año después, al ascender a capitán e ir destinado a Ferrol, el joven militar contrajo matrimonio con la hija del caballero, la supuesta desairada, que no se sintió tal. El caso fue muy comentado: todavía se relataba, en el casino, como acontecimiento ejemplar de los buenos tiempos pasados, en que los hombres, además de bigotes, tenían redaños: en los tiempos de Primo de Rivera, acaso porque abundasen los desaires a las señoritas y nadie cruzase con el guante blanco una cara bigotuda.

Las fiestas en Compostela comenzaban, y comienzan, con repiques de campanas. Es también frecuente la presencia, en las calles y plazas, de los gigantes y los cabezudos. Los precedía una banda de gaitas y tambores. El pueblo llano hablaba la lengua regional y los empingorotados el español, dicho entonces castellano. Las coplas de los ciegos se escribían en lengua mixta. Los romances de crímenes, cantados por foráneos del oficio al amparo de cualquier pared, los días festivos y los domingos por la mañana, venían impresos en un castellano bastante raro. Se vendían en papeles de colores, a perra chica la historia. Había también barracas y, muy adelantado el siglo, empezaron a aparecer los tiovivos mecánicos, las barracas de tiro al blanco y las tómbolas: solían situarse en la Alameda, a un lado y otro del paseo, que con tanto tenderete quedaba angosto, y la gente protestaba de aquel robo de espacio por lo que no pasaba de baratijas y engañabobos. En los diarios de la época aparecen censuras al municipio, protestas de los vecinos por el ruido, pero también alguna opinión progresista que defendía las diversiones del pueblo. Las cuales culminaban en el carnaval. Por mucha pesadumbre que el poder de los curas impusiese a la sociedad, el carnaval, como esparcimiento popular, fue siempre incontenible. Lo fomenta-

Las fiestas en Compostela comenzaban, y comienzan, con repiques de campanas.

55

Programa de las fiestas del Apóstol, 1891.

ban, naturalmente, quienes hacían en él su agosto, pero, sin esos aprovechados, hubiera sido lo mismo, una fiesta tumultuosa, un estallido de libertad. Lo anunciaban las caretas grotescas expuestas en las ventanas de las tiendas, antecedentes del presuntuoso escaparate actual. Eran caretas de cartón, grotescas, de preferencia sensuales o ridículas, pintadas de chafarrinones, con unos agujeros circulares para los ojos y una abertura alargada para la boca. Los que las usaban vestían preferentemente de aldeanos, una versión convencional del traje campesino, que ya había desaparecido: polainas, calzones blancos, chaleco oscuro con algún animalejo recortado en fieltro y cosido en la espalda. Llevaban una montera negra y, por lo general, una *aguijada* en la mano. Salían en grupos o en parejas, raramente solos, y su modo más frecuente de expresión era el grito. Algunas veces, los que se ordenaban en comparsas elegían este disfraz, pero de estos carnavaleros en pandilla musical podía esperarse cualquier disfraz, doctores con gola y toga o caballeros medievales. De estas comparsas, había de dos clases, principalmente: las populares, que cantaban musiquillas con letras satíricas de la actualidad local, y las de más refinamiento, trajes de aparente seda y gorros emplumados, con músicas en que figuraban un danzón y un vals, y letras sentimentales dedicadas a las señoritas que no descendían al ruedo y veían el carnaval desde la ventana. Estas comparsas, o algunas de ellas, solían ser viajeras, como las tunas, y se acercaban a alguna ciudad vecina, Betanzos o Puentedeume, si acaso a Padrón, nunca más allá. Las hubo con espada al cinto y capa corta, sueños de dependientes de comercio que aprovechaban para metamorfosearse la permisividad del carnaval. Las comparsas populares eran broncas, irreverentes en sus maneras, y no temían, sino que cultivaban, el aspecto grotesco. Las otras tiraban a cursis, generalmente con éxito.

No he rastreado, en la memoria popular, recuerdo alguno de aventura o escándalo carnavalescos. Se decía, acaso con razón, que muchas señoritas aprovechaban el carnaval para mezclarse al populacho y ser tratadas como cualesquieras, es decir, traídas y llevadas por la riada, ser tocadas e incluso hurgadas en sus lugares más íntimos, pero no sólo para esto, sino para dar rienda suelta a los deseos contenidos de gritar, de soltarse el pelo, de responder con desparpajo a la insinuación o a la oferta insinuada. Bajo el techo multicolor de la iluminación a la veneciana, pisando polvo de confeti y de la harina que llenaba las cáscaras de huevo destinadas a la agresión incruenta, estas tardes bulliciosas del martes de carnaval transcurrieron muchas aventuras de escapadas, acogidas al disfraz de viudas o de criadas, máscaras del polvo, las llamaban, quizá por la socorrida escoba que enarbolaban y les

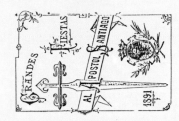

Es también frecuente la presencia, en las calles de los gigantes y los cabezudos. (Foto de 1922.)

Por mucha pesadumbre que el poder de los curas impusiese a la sociedad, el carnaval, como esparcimiento popular, fue siempre incontenible.

servía de arma defensiva. Todos los martes de carnaval, en todas partes de Galicia, tuvieron algo de goyesco.

Los bailes de carnaval fueron tardíos. No los acogieron las sociedades refinadas hasta finales de siglo, cuando ya en la corte (depravada, ¡ay, Dios!, y escasamente ejemplar) eran corrientes y aceptados, por muchos como mal menor. En Compostela comenzaron con carácter popular, un espabilado que alquila un local suficiente y consigue el permiso de la autoridad, con el compromiso de que se guardará el orden y no se ofenderá a la moral. Se entraba en ellos por una cantidad módica, y, en un principio, la gente se portaba con comedimiento, como si la policía estuviese presente y disimulada bajo un antifaz barato. Después, las cosas cambiaron, pero era la sociedad entera la que había cambiado. La de Compostela, en sus estamentos altos, siguió fiel a las tradiciones y se resistió cuanto pudo a los tiempos nuevos, como otras muchas sociedades provinciales. El siglo XIX se prolongó hasta bien entrado el XX. Tuvo que encabritarse la historia para que todo este mundo al que nos referimos desapareciera, o cambiase hasta no reconocerlo. Pero éste es ya otro cantar.

Una niña de ésas...

Un diario compostelano, en los primeros días del mes de julio de 1872, inserta en sus páginas los siguientes datos demográficos:

NACIDOS ENTRE EL 1 DE ENERO Y EL 30 DE JUNIO

Nacidos legítimos

Varones	175
Hembras	171

Nacidos ilegítimos

Varones	75
Hembras	80

Estas cifras pueden originar toda clase de comentarios, los más contradictorios: desde quienes juzguen que la vida compostelana de ese tiempo alcanzaba un grado intolerable de inmoralidad, hasta los que estimen que, en materia de libertad sexual, Galicia se había adelantado en varios lustros a las demás regiones españolas. Los responsables de los comentarios son quienes los hacen: allá ellos. Las cifras aducidas correspondientes al año 1872 pueden servir de indicativo para años anteriores y posteriores, sin necesidad de hurgar en archivos parroquiales y judiciales. ¿Serán la mitad, más o menos, en 1837? Pero, en el fondo, ¿qué más da? De los nacidos ilegítimos de ese año, interesa solamente uno, la niña que vino al mundo el 2 de febrero, en la casa de los señores de Romero Ortiz, no muy céntrica, y que fue bautizada, un atardecer lluvioso y frío, en la capilla del hospital Real con el nombre de Rosalía, sin más. Hija del aire o del milagro, sin padre ni madre que la abonen. Otras como ella, nacidas fuera de matrimonio, llevan al menos el apellido de la madre, que es, en este caso, el único que no puede, que no debe aparecer en el acta de bautismo, porque sería escandaloso. También lo es así, aunque de otra manera. Hay el escándalo que se apoya en documentos, y el que se nutre de la conjetura, de la comidilla, incluso de la seguridad sin pruebas. Lo que se sabe en Compostela, al día siguiente, es que una señorita de la buena

De los nacidos ilegítimos de 1837, interesa solamente uno, la niña que vino al mundo el 2 de febrero, en la casa de los señores de Romero Ortiz, no muy céntrica, y que fue bautizada, un atardecer lluvioso y frío, en la capilla del hospital Real con el nombre de Rosalía, sin más.
(*Arriba,* casa donde nació Rosalía, en Santiago de Compostela, hoy derrumbada; *a la derecha,* capilla del hospital Real, donde fue bautizada.)

sociedad, miembro de una familia linajuda, ha parido una hija de soltera, acerca de cuyo padre las fantasías se echan a volar, y aunque todas coincidían en su condición de eclesiástico, la atribución de títulos y de jerarquías va desde el prelado al simple seminarista. A esta niña nacida en día tan escasamente apacible, la incertidumbre del padre la perseguirá siempre como una *negra sombra,* que algunos identifican con «... *unha cousa que vive e que non se ve»,* verdadero fantasma del que no logrará librarse a lo largo de una vida rica en dolores, que hace de su voz poética una de las más auténticas y profundas de su siglo. Pero ¿quién de los que aquel atardecer de febrero, lluvioso y frío, que la acompañaron a la iglesia donde iba a bautizarse, después de atravesar bajo el paraguas la plaza del Obradoiro, podía imaginarlo?

A la niña la llevaron en seguida a la aldea, donde las hermanas de su padre la tomaron a su cargo. Aquella gente ponía la humanidad por encima de las conveniencias, y aunque un cura sea un cura, es también un hombre. A esta criatura, que sólo se reconoce en el mundo de las burocracias como Rosalía, y en el de los comadreos como «esa niña», no le falta cobijo, pero no el de su madre, al menos de momento, porque en el ámbito a que esta madre pertenece, una hija de soltera es cosa bastante mal vista, y su reconocimiento obligaría a la repetición, acaso a la caricatura de un drama calderoniano. El mundo de su padre, un clérigo de origen popular, quizá aldeano, es mucho más comprensivo, y acoger una niña sin nombre no altera de modo grave lo establecido. La niña llamada Rosalía crecerá y conocerá la realidad lejos del hogar en que nació, lejos del mundo a que su madre pertenece. Hablará otra lengua, y sus primeras experiencias no serán de calles ciudadanas, de grandes edificios de piedra labrada, de espléndidos monumentos a cuya grandeza nadie presta atención porque se ven todos los días. Su mundo será el de ríos y fuentes, el de los regatos pequeños, el de las leyendas campesinas, en el que la hazaña de Vidal, el del veral cargado de morcillas, ofrece una grandeza heroica, al menos una extrañeza. Esta niña, no muy guapa, aunque de grandes ojos inquietos, conoce y vive la sociedad popular, la gente que emigra a las Américas en busca de fortuna o viaja a la Castilla ardiente y rica en busca de unos cuantos jornales, cobrados en plata, que se traen atados en el nudo de un pañuelo: monedas de plata que sirven para el pago de los foros, o para la adquisición de un ferrado de tierra; en muchos casos, para el pago de los tres mil reales que cobran en La Coruña o en Carril los barcos que van a América. «Cando van, van como rosas; cando vên, vên negros.» El sol de la Galicia aldeana no tuesta la color; el de la Castilla triguera, sí. La pequeña Rosalía, lo que ve, es el cambio de la tez, y no le gusta.

Ella ignora, por supuesto, no puede imaginar, esas cosas aún no le caben en la cabeza, que desconoce, que ni siquiera imagina, que la situación de su madre no es nada cómoda. ¿Quién le puede decir, a la señorita de Castro, que ha parido una hija ilegítima, más aún, una hija sacrílega? Las pruebas, lo que se dice las pruebas, el haberla ayudado a parir, el haber tenido en brazos a la niña, el haberla bañado y vestido con el mínimo decoro para llevarla a la iglesia, las tienen unos amigos de fiar, de los que no abren la boca, de los que responden con evasivas resbaladizas y laberínticas, de esas que conducen al mismo tiempo al sí que al no: al no por el camino del sí, y viceversa. Estos compostelanos han recibido por tradición el arte de no mentir sin decir la verdad, y para eso está el canónigo penitencial, que enseña el arte de las respuestas. Sin embargo, las mujeres murmuran en los sobrados, los caballeros en las tertulias. Las murmuraciones de unos y de otros son, sin embargo, muy distintas. En general, las damas empingorotadas, de apellidos ilustres, a cuyo círculo pertene-

*A la niña la llevaron en
seguida a la aldea, donde
las hermanas de su padre la
tomaron a su cargo.*
(Casa de la familia paterna, en
Castro de Ortoño, donde vivió
Rosalía.)

*El mundo de Rosalía será el
de ríos y fuentes, el de los
regatos pequeños, el de las
leyendas campesinas.*

ce (o pertenecía) la señorita de Castro, suspecta de materni-
dad clandestina, sienten la ofensa como propia, pues a esas
alturas de la sociedad todos son primos, y las consecuencias
del desliz de una recaen en todas. De una, y no de uno, pues
los deslices de los hombres se miden por otro rasero, y pocas

serán, entre las murmuradoras, las que no tengan un padre o un hermano que no hayan sembrado de bastardos los alrededores del pazo original. No olvidemos la propensión de la nobleza gallega a multiplicar el número de bastardos. Un dato, o acaso una leyenda, dice que don Felipe II, cuando embarcó en La Coruña para casarse con María Tudor, antes de hacerlo, legitimó tres mil quinientos bastardos de la nobleza gallega. Y Pedro Madruga, nombre de canción y de romance, fue un bastardo de la casa de Soutomaior. ¿Y no montó doña Emilia Pardo Bazán, sobre uno de estos bastardos, la trama de la más conocida de sus novelas? Pero los hombres son los hombres. La sociedad gallega, en general, fue más permisiva que la castellana, pero no tanto que no castigase con la murmuración a la transgresora. Conviene sin embargo recordar que la señorita de Castro ni fue agredida ni expulsada de su casa. Hacía ya mucho tiempo que en Galicia no se entendería, menos aún se aprobaría, *La casa de Bernarda Alba*.

      Una cosa es lo que se dice, otra lo que se piensa. Esta afirmación, si es válida en todas partes, lo es en Galicia con mayor razón, porque hace muchos siglos que los gallegos desconfían de todo, incluida la verdad. Murmurar de una señorita de la mejor sociedad que ha tenido una hija de soltera puede ser una obligación impuesta por las conveniencias; reprobarla en lo íntimo de la conciencia es más dudoso. Son muchas las mujeres que, al mirarse a sí mismas, tienen que reconocer que, en cierta ocasión, hubieran hecho lo mismo, o que lo harían si la ocasión se presentase. También es cierto que la misma sociedad establece un sistema de cautelas, de precauciones y de trabas para que la ocasión no se presente. Pero las trabas, las precauciones y las cautelas no mandan en las conciencias. ¿Qué pensarían, a solas con la almohada, esas damas y damiselas que criticaban, sin dar nombres, el acontecimiento del día, esa niña (todas sabían que era niña, ¿y cómo?), el tema de todas las conversaciones? En una ciudad pequeña de provincias, y más si es una sociedad clerical, los temas de que se puede hablar son escasos, y muy pocos llegan a apasionar a la gente. La verdad es que las señoras de la buena sociedad local, y en sus círculos, las señoritas, están hartas de las disputas políticas, de que si el rey o la reina, de que si este general o aquel otro, de que si las partidas de los facciosos (que el diario local llama, con insistencia, latrofaccio-

Un dato, o acaso una leyenda, dice que don Felipe II, cuando embarcó en La Coruña para casarse con María Tudor, antes de hacerlo, legitimó tres mil quinientos bastardos de la nobleza gallega.
(«Felipe II» por Sánchez Coello.)

*La verdad es que las
señoras de la buena sociedad
local, y en sus círculos, las
señoritas, están hartas de las
disputas políticas, de que
si el rey o la reina, de que si
este general o aquel otro, de
que si las partidas de los
facciosos (que el diario local
llama, con insistencia,
latrofacciosos) han asaltado
este o aquel pazo sólo por
las dudas que existen de que
el señor sea o deje de ser
partidario de don Carlos...*
(Carlos María Isidro, por V.
López.)

sos) han asaltado este o aquel pazo sólo por las dudas que existen de que el señor sea o deje de ser partidario de don Carlos... Lo que interesa a las mujeres es lo que cuentan los folletines, las novelas traídas de Francia por algún viajero (pasan de mano en mano, se leen a hurtadillas, las que no saben francés lamentan su ignorancia), es decir, las cosas de hombres y mujeres prohibidas por la moral y las buenas costumbres, que, sin embargo, son reales, y se sospecha que existan en el seno de la misma sociedad: adulterios, hijos de contrabando, hombres seductores y malvados, mujeres víctimas del amor, y, también, ¿por qué no?, esa otra clase de mujeres por las que los hombres se arruinan o se suicidan, o se matan entre sí en nombre del honor y de sus leyes... ¿Qué sería de estas sociedades tranquilas, aburridas, irreprochables, sin semejantes escapes imaginativos, sin la sospecha de que lo que cuentan las novelas es o fue real, de que incluso en el interior de ese grupo restringido donde todos se conocen y se tratan como iguales, gentes honradas y honorables todas, han existido o existen, o pueden existir, personajes semejantes? Madrid es una realidad, y París... ¡París! Si un marido va a Madrid, la esposa se echa a temblar, pero si va a París... Y hay algunos que van a París, o, al menos, a Francia, por aquello de la política y de don Carlos, que nunca se sabe si está aquí o allá. Cuando, medio siglo más tarde, un escritor joven y talentudo busca materiales para su primera salida al campo de las letras, una imitación de *Les diaboliques*, escoge sus personajes femeninos de esta sociedad, o al menos los sitúa en ella. ¡La condesa de Cela! ¿Y la pobre Concha, que muere en brazos de su amante, un personaje sacado de este mundo, feo, católico y sentimental? Nadie sabe las historias secretas de este pueblo envuelto en lluvia o en niebla, pero la historia existe, y el caso de la señorita de Castro, que tuvo una hija de soltera, es uno de sus capítulos más breves e insignificantes. Las señoras y las señoritas evitan a la de Castro; si pueden, no la saludan; si no hay más remedio que hacerlo, lo hacen fríamente. Más de una, al hurtarle el saludo con una mera inclinación del paraguas, vuelve después la cabeza y la mira con envidia, porque para ella, para la señorita de Castro, el misterio ha dejado de serlo.

Las cosas, en el mundo de los hombres, pasan de otra manera. Ninguno de ellos habla francamente del caso pero sí cuchichean, en un rincón del liceo, o en pareja, paseando.

La señorita de Castro no es tan hermosa que puedan envidiar al mozo que la sedujo. (¿Un mozo o un hombre hecho y derecho? ¿Un monje exclaustrado o un seminarista? Porque hay versiones para todos los gustos.) A ellos los preocupa ante todo la situación del señor de Castro, todo un caballero, linajudo y honorable, si bien los más eruditos recuerden que en su familia se cuenta que hubo mujeres casquivanas. ¿No lo fue aquella doña Inés, que reinó en Portugal después de muerta? Y algunas otras, menos notables. Sin embargo, y aquí para entre nosotros, ¿en qué familia no sucedió lo mismo? Por mucho que los varones hayan procurado tener a las mujeres de las riendas, nunca falta una jaca que las rompa y galope por su cuenta. Lo que sucede es que esas historias se entierran y después se olvidan, aunque quede la conciencia de que han sucedido, y esta conciencia, si inclina a algunos a la intransigencia, aconseja a otros la comprensión, y si no el perdón público (sería como aprobar el mal ejemplo, dejarlo sin sanción), al menos sí el disimulo y echar encima toda la tierra posible. Pero el caso del señor de Castro está ahí, y hay que resolverlo. El señor de Castro se retrae, no acude a tertulias ni a reuniones, rehúye sus amistades, va a misa del alba, anda como escondido. El señor de Castro se cree deshonrado, pero no falta quien se pregunte que qué es eso de la deshonra. Es una pregunta arriesgada, detrás de la cual se esconden ideas liberales que,

El señor de Castro, en su pazo de La Retén, cultiva hermosas camelias: blancas, rojas y amarillas. Camelias de exquisita forma, igual que dibujadas y pintadas a mano; camelias bellas y frías.

65

con otro motivo cualquiera, pueden también aflorar: preguntas que ponen o pueden poner en tela de juicio realidades bastante más importantes que la aventura de una muchacha soltera. ¿Tiene el rey o no tiene derecho? ¿Hay que hacer caso a los curas en todo lo que dicen, o sólo en lo que conviene? ¿Y esa cuestión de los foros? Y, sobre todo, ¿somos o no iguales todos los hombres? Si fuéramos iguales, a nadie se le ocurriría plantear si el señor de Castro quedaba deshonrado o no por la conducta de una hija casquivana. En los medios artesanos no es infrecuente que una hija quede preñada. El padre se limita a darle más o menos bofetadas, pero cuando nace la criatura, el mismo abuelo la lleva de paseo si sale el sol, o si hace tiempo tibio, aunque sea nublado. Las clases se distinguen por muchas cosas, entre otras por ésas. Nadie imagina al señor de Castro dándole de bofetadas a su hija, aunque bien pudiera matarla: no han faltado casos, y el mundo no tembló por ello. Pero sacar a la niña de paseo a que tome el sol... No. Eso no puede hacerlo ni lo hará jamás el señor de Castro. Se dice que su hija, aunque vive en casa, no come a la mesa.

En el liceo hay un contertulio que tiene, sobre el caso, su opinión particular. Es un hombre rico, de buena familia, aunque con algún matrimonio desigual en su prosapia. Inquieto en su juventud, no le bastó andar en conspiraciones, sino que le dio por gastar su fortuna en recorrer el mundo. Se dice, o al menos lo dice él, que estuvo en Alemania, en Francia, en Inglaterra; se sospecha que anduvo a tiros en alguna revolución, o en alguna de esas guerras que se arman cuando los países sometidos aspiran a ser independientes, Grecia o Polonia. Se murmura que en su dormitorio guarda miniaturas de mujeres hermosas, de las que no se ven por aquí (aquí también hay mujeres hermosas, pero con menos escote). Y también hay libros en idiomas desconocidos. Los canónigos lo miran con desconfianza, y el penitenciario asegura que, si no está excomulgado, debe al menos de ser vitando. Hubo un tiempo en que quisieron hacerlo catedrático de la universidad, y costó Dios y ayuda evitarlo; pues se metió en la cuestión nada menos que el capitán general de La Coruña, un liberal redomado que intentó nada menos que imponerse al claustro... Pues este hombre, que tiene ideas, pero que nunca las da como suyas, dispone de una explicación, sacada de algún libro alemán, sobre las razones por las que las sociedades, desde la más remota antigüedad, excluyeron de la familia los hijos de soltera... «No, no. No es que yo piense así. Son ideas del profesor Tal, un alemán de Baviera que vive desterrado en París.» Frente y contra las ideas del profesor de Baviera, se traen a colación las de santo Tomás de Aquino. «Oiga, santo Tomás no es un cualquiera, es el ángel de las escuelas, el filósofo más importante que se recuerda, un hombre que no dijo más que verdades...» El contertulio del liceo, a quien los canónigos declaran vitando, pero en secreto, no sea el diablo, ante la cita de santo Tomás, sonríe.

Al señor de Taboada se le encomendó hacerse el encontradizo con el señor de Castro y darle a entender que,

Pazo en Padrón, donde vivió y murió Rosalía; hoy museo.

sus amigos, como si no hubiese pasado nada. El señor de Taboada carece de ideas, pero no de sentimientos; y de ciencia, pero no de experiencia. Aprendió a perdonar los devaneos comentiéndolos él mismo, y aunque ignora la historia, nadie conoce más historias; él fue quien dijo una vez en el corrillo: «Y qué, caballeros, ¿qué pasaría si contásemos los hijos de puta y los maridos cabrones que ha habido en nuestras familias?» De esto hace ya mucho tiempo cuando se hablaba de una casada y de un oficial francés: todo el mundo quedó en silencio; después habló de la sequía pertinaz, que los iba a dejar a todos sin el vino de sus viñas.

El señor de Taboada reintegró al redil al señor de Castro. Se le recibió como si no hubiese pasado nada. «¿Y qué tal por el pazo, esta temporada que estuvo fuera? ¿Se le dan bien las camelias este año?» Porque el señor de Castro, en su pazo de La Retén, cultiva hermosas camelias: blancas, rojas y amarillas. Camelias de exquisita forma, igual que dibujadas y pintadas a mano; camelias bellas y frías.

Hubo un clérigo que también trató el caso, pero pasándose de listo. Se le atribuye origen campesino. Fue durante una novena muy popular, a la que acudían muchas señoras y señoritas de la clase escogida. Dijo que las clases elevadas cometían los mismos pecados que las populares, y que todos éramos iguales delante de la ley de Dios. Nunca tanta gente se sintió solidaria de la señorita de Castro como aquella tarde (también fría, también de lluvia).

Dos que a lo mejor se cruzaron

Al niño le llaman Pablito Martín. Para algunas personas de su intimidad o de su contorno, *O Pabliño*. Le ven pasar todos los días, espigado y melenudo, hacia la casa del primer violinista de la catedral, de quien recibe lecciones. Antes las recibió en Pontevedra, y más tarde las recibirá en La Coruña. Pablito Martín no es de estos lares, sino de bastante lejos, pamplonica. Si transcurre entre nosotros, tan pequeño, tan precoz, se debe a que su padre, músico militar, fue destinado a esta banda, a esa otra. A alguna persona se le ocurrió compararlo a Mozart, pero no serán muchos los que incurran en el tópico, porque Mozart no es de los músicos más conocidos por estos aledaños: todo lo más, entre profesionales, aficionados y eruditos. Su primera apoteosis, la de Pablito, no será, sin embargo, aquí, sino en La Coruña, en una sociedad recreativa y cultural, de tinte liberal, Reunión Recreativa e Instructiva de Artesanos, en una exhibición promovida por la condesa de Mina, doña Juana de Vega, la cabeza pensante, directora y promotora del liberalismo coruñés y quizá gallego. El niño, que se sigue llamando Pablito Martín, provoca aplausos inacabables y enternecidos con unas variaciones sobre temas de *La gazza ladra,* de Goldoni. Las variaciones son de su incumbencia, aunque no es imposible que su padre le haya ayudado. La condesa de Mina le asigna una pensión de dos mil reales para que siga estudiando. También el regimiento en que trabaja su padre se preocupa de su porvenir. Y no deja de ser curioso que, corriendo el tiempo, aunque no demasiado, otro Pablito, éste Ruiz, se haya ensayado, aquí, en La Coruña, en el dibujo. Es una coincidencia de la que no se deben sacar conclusiones aceleradas. Pero las coincidencias no se acaban aquí. Al uno no se le conocerá como Pablo Martín, sino como Sarasate; al otro, no como Pablo Ruiz, sino como Picasso. La diferencia, sin embargo, estriba en que Martín era nombre, y Ruiz, apellido. Picasso nunca estuvo en Compostela, y sólo por los pelos se le puede traer a este texto. Sarasate, en cambio, aunque marchó de Galicia a Madrid, donde la reina doña Isabel le regaló un stradivarius y le ayudó económicamente, volvió a Galicia, y a Santiago, dos o tres veces más; ya conocido

Pablo Martín Sarasate, aunque marchó de Galicia a Madrid, donde la reina Isabel le regaló un stradivarius y le ayudó económicamente, volvió a Galicia, y a Santiago, dos o tres veces más.

y aclamado en toda Europa, dio conciertos en Vigo, en La Coruña, en Ferrol. Entre sus obras menos conocidas figura una *muiñeira*, baile cuyo ritmo rápido y complejo se presta a las filigranas del violín. Cuando muere, en Biarritz, en 1915, ya el otro Pablo, el Picasso, ha comenzado su tarea de destruir la pintura. Por aquel tiempo, está también en Francia. No hay datos que permitan suponer que se hayan conocido, que se hayan tratado, que hayan hablado de la Galicia que ambos conocieron en su infancia. De Picasso nadie puede asegurar que la haya recordado mucho. ¿Y Sarasate? Su paso por Compostela fue breve, aunque, como se vio, rico en consecuencias. Si a los siete años tocaba el violín a las mil maravillas, se debió probablemente a que sus maestros de Pontevedra y Santiago no fueron malos. El primero, cosa que no deja de ser curiosa, fue sastre, y se llamó, de apellido, Casasvellas; el segundo, José Courtier, y tuvo un hijo compositor, del mismo nombre. Todo lo más que se puede imaginar es al pequeño Pablo Martín, con su violincito bajo el brazo, atravesando las rúas lluviosas, en demanda de la catedral, en uno de cuyos recovecos el maestro le enseñaría los secretos del arco. Es demasiado joven para poder pensar que la ciudad lo haya influido estéticamente, o de alguna otra manera. No. No hay que exagerar ni salir-

No deja de ser curioso que otro Pablito, éste Ruiz, se haya ensayado, aquí, en La Coruña, en el dibujo.
(«Escena campesina» de Picasso, La Coruña, 1895.)

No es imposible que, ante los ojos atónitos de Rosalía, haya pasado una partida carlista: hombres armados, a caballo, bajo la lluvia, a los que hay que alimentar y cobijar; hombres que vienen de la muerte y van hacia la muerte.

se por peteneras imaginativas: la estancia de Sarasate en Compostela, alrededor de los cinco, de los seis años de edad, es sólo un accidente. De no haber hallado a Courtier, se hubiera tropezado con un maestro igualmente eficaz. Lo de La Coruña parece haber sido más importante: quinientas pesetas, en aquel tiempo, y para un niño de siete años, quizá fuese dinero. Además, la condesa de Mina tenía cierta vara alta en Madrid, en palacio: la reina había sido su discípula. No es imposible que haya mediado alguna carta de recomendación, o de presentación. Las relaciones de Sarasate con la reina, el regalo del stradivarius, son más tardías, pero pueden ser una consecuencia retrasada, aunque lógica.

La otra criatura que, por estos mismos años, anda ya por Compostela, nos toca más de cerca y, sobre todo, su relación con la ciudad es más prolongada y honda. La hemos visto bautizar en una tarde fría y lluviosa, en la capilla del hospital Real, y sabemos que se la llevó a la aldea la familia de su padre. Del tiempo pasado fuera de la ciudad se tienen pocas noticias y, las que se tienen, poco seguras. Dicen que ya entonces hacía versos. ¿Quién lo sabe? Lo que es lícito conjeturar es que, durante estos once o doce años, la niña Rosalía habrá asimilado la cultura aldeana en que se desenvuelve. Ha escuchado relatos de leyendas, ha aprendido canciones, habla la lengua aldeana, y no es imposible que, ante sus ojos atónitos, haya pasado una partida carlista: hombres armados, a caballo, bajo la lluvia, a los que hay que alimentar y cobijar; hombres que vienen de la muerte y van hacia la muerte. Son ellos los que alteran la vida aldeana, monótona, sin otros acontecimientos que el vendaval que zoa, la lluvia que inunda, la vaca que pare, el raposo que se lleva las gallinas. Y cosas así, nada más. Pero las mismas cosas engendran almas distintas, porque las almas ya lo son antes de que las cosas sucedan. De las niñas que jugaron con Rosalía, allá en la aldea, durante estos tantos años, ninguna padecerá los dolores de que *Follas novas* dan constancia.

El primer acto debidamente documentado de la vida de Rosalía en Compostela, su intervención en una función teatral de aficionados en que se representa *Rosamunda,* de Gil y Zárate, es posterior en bastantes años a su regreso a la ciudad donde nació y de donde la llevaron por razones de conveniencia social. Este regreso no deja de plantear dificultades al que quiera averiguar, más bien imaginar, sus razones. Doce años es un tiempo lo bastante largo como para que un suceso escandaloso, aunque lo haya sido en voz baja, se haya olvidado, pero no del todo. Que poco a poco la señorita de Castro se haya reintegrado a la normalidad social se puede explicar y entender, sobre todo porque su conducta fue recatada, porque jamás se supo que hubiera vuelto a las andadas de sus amores con un eclesiástico rural, porque pertenece a una familia ilustre, y eso siempre pesa. Pero, de pronto, la hija del pecado viene a la casa que le pertenece por la sangre. ¿Cuáles fueron los trámites que condujeron a esta decisión? ¿Cómo volvió Rosalía, quién la trajo, en calidad de qué se instaló en la casa de su madre y llevó su apellido? Estas cosas suelen saberse por comadreos, por cartas, por memorias, pero de todo carecemos. En la vida de Rosalía, desde su venida a Compostela hasta los primeros rastros que deja en ella su presencia, permanecen en secreto, salvo, quizá, la noticia, bastante vaga, de sus estudios, y no son años cualesquiera, sino los de la adolescencia, los de la formación de la personalidad, los años en que, humanamente, se cuaja la mujer que ya se llama Rosalía Castro. ¿Receptáculo, ya, de dolores?

Hay conjeturas lícitas. A veces, las toma a su cargo un novelista, y, si acierta, cobran valor de realidades indiscutibles. Tienen la ventaja, sobre las del investigador minucioso, que, aunque carezcan de apoyos documentales, suelen llegar más allá en la descripción de una biografía. Tienen la desventaja de que, dos novelistas de igual capacidad imaginativa, pueden describir dos procesos distintos e igualmente convincentes. Todo consiste en el enfoque, si se admite que el enfoque es la manera de ver las cosas una persona concreta, el lugar donde se instala para ver e inventar. Pero también depende de a cuál de los puntos conocidos de la vida de la biografiada se le da más importancia. Si estimamos que lo más auténtico de la futura poeta es esa media docena de poemas que podemos llamar sociales, en que el tema son los dolores de su pueblo, entonces hay que imaginar una niña que viene de un paraíso y que, en la ciudad, descubre la injusticia, la miseria, el dolor. Pero el mundo de Rosalía abarca mucho más que esos poemas sociales. Su tema no es la redención de su pueblo, sino quizá la redención de ella misma, que forma parte de ese pueblo, que en muchos momentos es su voz, pero que no coincide exactamente. En todo caso, es lícito preguntarse por la respuesta personal de la niña al pasar del campo a la ciudad; al dejar una vivienda aldeana para ocupar un espacio, el que haya sido, en una vivienda ciudadana; al tener que cambiar de idioma o, más exactamente, al verse obligada a aprender el que hablan los que ahora la rodean, que no es el romance aldeano en que ha venido expresándose. Tampoco es indispensable imaginar que todo esto le haya causado traumas irreparables, aunque sí dificultades y perplejidades. El que amase los ríos, las fuentes, los regatos pequeños, no autoriza a pensar que la piedra de la ciudad le haya disgustado. No la han llevado a un mundo de cemento y de asfalto, sino a una ciudad hermosa en la que muchas veces se ha sentido feliz y cuyas piedras ha cantado. Cómo las haya ido descubriendo y aficionándose a ellas no se sabe, pero el proceso no tiene por qué haber sido anormal, menos aún doloroso, sino satisfactorio. Puede que alguna vez la contemplación de las piedras la haya consolado de sus penas. Puede, pero nunca lo dijo, ni en prosa ni en verso.

Toda muchacha de su edad, si no ha sido previamente advertida, se asusta una mañana, al levantarse y hallarse húmeda de sangre. ¿Quién, cómo se lo explicó? ¿Y qué le hizo pensar de sí misma la explicación? Este acontecimiento produce en las muchachas efectos semejantes: esto es lo que

Rosalía Castro ha superado su adolescencia, tiene una personalidad distinta y no sabe lo que quiere, o, al menos, lo que quiere no coincide con lo que quieren las demás señoritas de su edad y de su clase. Se marcha a Madrid. ¿Qué se le habrá perdido allá?

se admite. Pero la indagación en cada caso concreto conduce al descubrimiento de diferencias muy notables. Y estamos autorizados a pensar que Rosalía, en la sociedad en que empieza a moverse después de su traslado a Compostela, muy pronto se revela distinta de las demás de su edad. En estas sociedades pequeñas hay que andarse con ojo con las diferencias, sobre todo si se es mujer. El margen que se concede al despliegue de la personalidad es más bien escaso, y los límites los componen los prejuicios, los principios, las normas que rigen esta misma sociedad, en las que se halla su defensa y su fortaleza. Por lo pronto, es muy joven cuando la vemos interpretar un papel protagonista en una representación teatral de aficionados. No, indudablemente, ni la primera ni la única, e incluso existe la costumbre de que las señoritas de la buena sociedad actúen como actrices aficionadas. En las reseñas de las representaciones realizadas en un lugar semejante, por los tiempos en que ella nació, y también unos años antes, aparecen como actrices aficionadas un par de señoritas de Castro. ¿Eran de su parentela? No consta, pero es de pensar que sí, más o menos próximas. Pero no se mantienen en el candelero, a pesar de sus excelentes cualidades. Lo más probable es que se hayan casado. Estas representaciones teatrales en estas pequeñas sociedades cerradas y bastante estrictas (al menos en apariencia), las funciones de aficionados sirven, entre otras cosas, para que las actrices se den a conocer de un modo distinto al habitual, que normalmente termina en boda. Si cosas así sucedían en el primer tercio del siglo XX, no hay razones para pensar que, cien años antes, no sucediera lo mismo, o parecido. La diferencia, en nuestro caso, está en que la protagonista de *Rosamunda* abandona su sociedad provinciana y se marcha a Madrid. Aquí empieza la diferencia más visible. Las otras se casaron; ésta se va a Madrid, acción que requiere audacia y decisión firme, y que nos permite imaginar un proceso familiar previo y doloroso. Por estos años mediados del siglo XIX, aunque la sociedad compostelana no sea un remanso de paz, sino un conjunto humano muy agitado por las ideas políticas, religiosas y científicas, por las graves situaciones sociales, por la lucha entre lo tradicional y lo nuevo, son muchos los prejuicios que mantienen su vigencia. ¿Qué va a hacer a Madrid una señorita veinteañera, de origen no muy claro, que quizá sea más inteligente que lo acostumbrado, pero en

Puede que alguna vez la contemplación de las piedras haya consolado a Rosalía de sus penas. Puede, pero nunca lo dijo, ni en prosa ni en verso.
(Pórtico de la Gloria, catedral de Santiago.)

Eduardo Pondal.

una sociedad donde la inteligencia de las mujeres no sólo no se estima, sino que se teme? Rosalía Castro ha superado su adolescencia, tiene una personalidad distinta y no sabe lo que quiere, o, al menos, lo que quiere no coincide con lo que quieren las demás señoritas de su edad y de su clase. Se marcha a Madrid. ¿Qué se le habrá perdido allá?

Hay un poema de Eduardo Pondal, no escrito, seguramente, para esta ocasión, pero que le viene pintiparado:

ROSALÍA CASTRO

*Pobre hoja del seco estío ardida
deja que te arrebate el huracán...
Nuevas playas tal vez y nueva vida
en otros nuevos mundos hallarás.
Cuando la voz gigante diga: ¡Marcha!,
emprende resignada el vuelo audaz.
Algún destino cumples en el vértigo...
Marcha sin murmurar.*

Romanticismo

España fue un país romántico: por su historia, por sus costumbres, por sus ciudades, por su paisaje. Galicia también lo fue, aunque muy distinta a la vista y al conocimiento. Como el resto de España, Galicia fue un país romántico con escaso romanticismo cultural. Fue, en el mejor de los casos, un estilo importado; en el peor, una moda. Compostela apenas si mereció la atención de los viajeros, si se exceptúa a don Jorgito el inglés, que no fue precisamente un viajero romántico. Fuera de las rutas literarias (Granada, por su exotismo, resultaba más atractiva), hubieran hallado en Compostela pintoresquismo, aunque no demasiado, y no una ciudad en decadencia, donde el polvo vuelve al polvo, sino la inalterabilidad del granito gallego, así como escasas formas góticas, mucho barroco y bastante renacentismo y estilos intermedios. La sociedad compostelana fue romántica en la misma medida en que lo fue la del resto de España, en usos y costumbres. Los caballeros compostelanos usaban levita y sombrero de copa, y los novios se hablaban en el lenguaje sentimental a la moda, pero esto no basta más que para una estampa superficial. El marqués de Bradomín fue un romántico, pero difícilmente hallable en las rúas o en los salones de Compostela. Tenemos que abandonar la literatura y atender a la historia: entonces sí que podemos hallar unas cuantas personalidades que responden con mayor o menor precisión al arquetipo admitido. No son poetas ni hombres de mundo, aunque hayan ejercido la poesía y formado parte de la sociedad. La originalidad del romanticismo compostelano, tardío por lo demás, es de orden ideológico y biográfico. Podemos elegir, entre un buen puñado de nombres, los de Antolín Faraldo y Aurelio Aguirre. Son nombres que figuran en la historia política gallega más que en su literatura. Yo los incluiría en el grupo de los que Pondal llamó *os bos e xenerosos*. Gentes con la conciencia de la situación social y económica de Galicia, partícipes en mayor o menor grado de las ideas vigentes de libertad y nacionalismo, o de libertad nacional, si se prefiere. La situación de Galicia es lamentable: diríamos que clama al cielo. Estos nombres, y algunos más, hacen de Galicia el objeto de su pensamiento

La originalidad del romanticismo compostelano, tardío por lo demás, es de orden ideológico y biográfico. Podemos elegir, entre un buen puñado de nombres, los de Antolín Faraldo y Aurelio Aguirre. Son nombres que figuran en la historia política gallega más que en su literatura.
(Retrato al óleo de Aurelio Aguirre.)

y de su acción, pero, en ninguno de estos dos casos, de manera exclusiva, sino sólo amplia. El repaso de sus textos, el examen de los contenidos ideológicos de las publicaciones dirigidas por Faraldo, el famoso discurso pronunciado por Aguirre en el banquete de Conjo, revelan una amplitud de miras que no deja de sorprender. No incurramos en el error de atribuirles la creación de un pensamiento propio, sino de haberse apoderado de las generalidades ideológicas de aquel tiempo y de haberlas desarrollado, por escrito o activamente. En cierto modo, fueron dos revolucionarios platónicos. En situación más

Otro representante del romanticismo gallego fue don Manuel Murguía, el marido de Rosalía Castro.
(Manuel Murguía, caricatura de Castelao.)

favorable, hubieran llevado a buen término las reformas económicas y sociales de que Galicia estaba necesitada. Esto les
hizo participar en actos extraordinarios, como lo de Aguirre
en el citado banquete o la relación de Faraldo con movimientos y aun pronunciamientos liberales. Pero nada de eso modi-
ficó la fisonomía de la región. Y, por supuesto, no afectó en
nada a la vida compostelana. Aquella sociedad ante todo in-
movilista, pero fuerte todavía, pudo permitirse el lujo de tole-
rar a personajes como Faraldo y Aguirre, de quienes se decía,
o se podía decir, que la fuerza se les iba por la boca. Las peri-

*De su papel como marido de
Rosalía se ocupan
escasamente los historiadores:
existen zonas oscuras en
estas relaciones que nadie
parece interesado en
dilucidar. Hay cartas que
permiten atribuirle
infidelidades, y corre la
leyenda de su inusitada
potencia sexual,
constantemente ejercitada.*
(Fotografía de 1884 en la que
aparecen Rosalía con su marido
y sus hijos.)

79

HISTORIA
DE
GALICIA

POR

MANUEL MURGUIA

2. edicion:
impresa á costa de " El Centro Gallego" de la Habana

TOMO PRIMERO

CORUÑA
LIBRERIA DE DON EUGENIO CARRÉ
MCMI

Murguía es el historiador, el que intenta y consigue a su modo ver a Galicia como unidad a lo largo de los siglos. Carecía de la formación científica y de la especialización indispensables para ser un verdadero historiador positivista.

pecias vitales de estos dos gallegos a los que la conciencia de la región debió tanto fueron muy distintas: Faraldo, enamorado de una mujer, fue a morir a Andalucía; Aguirre, jovencísimo, se ahogó en las playas coruñesas. ¿Se ahogó? No faltó quien dijera que lo ahogaron, pero esto no se ha dilucidado nunca, ni nadie puso empeño en dilucidarlo.

Otro representante del romanticismo gallego fue don Manuel Murguía, el marido de Rosalía Castro. Como Aguirre, era de origen vasco. Vivió lo bastante no sólo para ver morir a sus compañeros de generación («Los precursores») y a su propia mujer, sino para que las ideas románticas murieran dentro de él. Murguía es el historiador, el que intenta y consigue a su modo ver a Galicia como unidad a lo largo de los siglos. Carecía de la formación científica y de la especialización indispensables para ser un verdadero historiador positivista. Su historia es entusiasta, pero poco de fiar. Más seguro, al menos en lo que a datos se refiere, es lo que escribe acerca de sus contemporáneos, esos «precursores» citados, o el *Diccionario de escritores gallegos*. Su labor periodística fue amplia y nada desdeñable. De su papel como marido de Rosalía se ocupan escasamente los historiadores: existen zonas oscuras en estas relaciones que nadie parece interesado en dilucidar. Hay cartas que permiten atribuirle infidelidades, y corre la leyenda de su inusitada potencia sexual, constantemente ejercitada. A la estampa tópica de un escritor romántico le van mejor historias de amores imposibles, que nadie atribuye a Murguía. Es muy posible que, con estas infidelidades, intentase, y quizá lograse, curarse del complejo de inferioridad engendrado por su desmedrada estatura: para ciertas operaciones no basta encasquetarse un sombrero de copa de gran tamaño. Se habla también de otra clase de infidelidades, como publicar versos de Rosalía a espaldas de su mujer y contra la voluntad de ésta. Posiblemente haya sido así. En todo caso, un matrimonio entre intelectuales, cuando el genio de uno de ellos sobrepasa con mucho al del otro, es difícil que no sea conflictivo. Pero de estas complejidades se trata pocas veces al hablar de don Manuel Murguía.

La gran cuestión del siglo

La alianza entre el altar y el trono fue realidad durante siglos, una realidad varia, y aun contradictoria, en sus episodios, que atraviesa la historia de Europa y, en cierto modo, la define; pero esta frase, Alianza entre el Altar y el Trono, no aparece hasta el momento de la crisis, como fórmula de respuesta a las nuevas concepciones del Estado, de la sociedad y del Hombre, engendradas en los siglos XVII y XVIII y hechas realidad a partir de la Revolución francesa. La ideología en que se resumen las nuevas maneras de concebir la relación entre los hombres se llama, por fin, liberalismo, ante el cual tanto el Altar como el Trono se mostraron, primero, descon-

En 1864, el papa Pío IX publica la encíclica «Quanta cura», acompañada del «Syllabus»: a partir de este momento, a los católicos liberales se les niega legitimidad, se les amenaza con expulsarlos del seno de la Iglesia; de hecho, algunos son excomulgados.
(El papa Pío IX con los peregrinos, según un dibujo de Pradilla publicado en «La Ilustración Española y Americana», 1876.)

La llegada a la mitra de Compostela del arzobispo Miguel García Cuesta coincidió casi exactamente con una de las épocas más penosas de la ciudad y de su contorno, las hambres de los años cincuenta, que volcaron en Santiago miles de campesinos afectados por las malas cosechas y abrumados por los impuestos de todas clases.

En página siguiente:
Fue un momento difícil —años cincuenta—, que la inteligencia de un alcalde remedió dando trabajo a los campesinos en una obra que aún subsiste en Compostela y de cuyo promotor, don Nicolás García Vázquez, no se acuerda nadie. Se trata del paseo de la Herradura, llamado entonces de la «Buena Vista».
(Foto actual.)

fiados y, después, hostiles. El desarrollo de la contienda no es el mismo en los países protestantes que en los católicos. En los primeros, salvo en Inglaterra y acaso en Holanda, siendo los jefes del Estado los de la Iglesia, la contienda, si llega a plantearse, se resuelve en sumisión eclesiástica; por otra parte, esos países, principalmente Alemania y Rusia, rechazan el liberalismo y mantienen la realidad del Estado autoritario e imperialista, un imperialismo, por cierto, muy distinto del de Inglaterra, que basa el suyo precisamente en ideas liberales, en el liberalismo económico, con altibajos proteccionistas. Pero la fórmula inglesa no es transportable a los países católicos, cuya Iglesia no sólo reclama la libertad, sino que forma parte de un cuerpo internacional, o supranacional, cuyo centro de acción y dirección reside en Roma. El anticlericalismo virulento es un fenómeno propio de los países católicos, Francia, España, Italia y Portugal. Durante una temporada, se cree en la compatibilidad de las nuevas ideas con las antiguas creencias, pero este liberalismo católico acepta (o postula también) un cambio del estatus de la Iglesia en la sociedad, una acomodación al

nuevo derecho y a las nuevas concepciones económicas. Ahora bien: en estos países católicos, la Iglesia mantiene, o intenta mantener, unas preeminencias que el liberalismo no admite. El conflicto surge aquí y allá y se manifiesta en diversos acontecimientos nacionales. El más importante de los sucedidos en España fue la Ley de Desamortización, contra la que la Iglesia se defendió con armas espirituales a troche y moche. Por otra parte, y paralelamente, los Estados Pontificios se oponían al movimiento de unidad italiana, dirigido por la casa de Saboya y realizado, en planos distintos, por Cavour y Garibaldi. En 1864, el papa Pío IX publica la encíclica *Quanta cura,* acompañada del *Syllabus*: a partir de este momento, a los católicos liberales se les niega legitimidad, se les amenaza con expulsarlos del seno de la Iglesia; de hecho, algunos son excomulgados. Estos documentos van, en sus alcances, más allá de la política: repudian en bloque el mundo moderno en cuanto tiende a independizarse de la Iglesia, a desarrollarse con autono-

mía. *Quanta cura* y el *Syllabus* pretenden nada menos que detener la historia. No lo logran, por supuesto, pero engendran en las sociedades católicas situaciones conflictivas que se desarrollan de distintas maneras, según la idiosincrasia de los países respectivos. En Francia existe una burguesía poderosa que, en parte, no es católica, y que acabará por darse un régimen de república laica. En Italia, el deseo de alcanzar la unidad nacional se relaciona profundamente con el liberalismo y pone a los católicos en un aprieto grave, ya que, como se insinuó, la unidad supone la desaparición de los Estados Pontificios. España y Portugal resuelven la situación cada una a su manera, pero coinciden en que, en ambos países, las fuerzas contendientes se asemejan, y alternan en la dirección política de los países. El reinado de Isabel II, en España, se ve constantemente sacudido por la contienda, que excede en mucho lo espiritual y que manifiesta implicaciones, no sólo políticas, sino económicas y sociales. Un grupo muy nutrido defiende la inmovi-

lidad, el Antiguo Régimen, pero no es compacto: se divide en carlistas e isabelinos; en el bando contrario, las fuerzas progresistas se subdividen a su vez en muchos grupos cuyas ideologías apenas si manifiestan sus coincidencias básicas: incluyen ya los partidarios de la república como forma de gobierno; los anarquistas y, muy pronto, los socialistas. La confusión ideológica es mayor en España que en el resto de Europa.

Este estado de cosas transcurre, en Compostela, durante el pontificado del arzobispo don Miguel García Cuesta, varón virtuoso y de buenas letras pero fundamentalmente ultramontano. Su llegada a la mitra coincidió casi exactamente con una de las épocas más penosas de la ciudad y de su contorno, las hambres de los años cincuenta, que volcaron en Santiago miles de campesinos afectados por las malas cosechas y abrumados por los impuestos de todas clases. Fue un

Otro colega del arzobispo García Cuesta, y sucesor en la mitra, el arzobispo Payá, se destacó en la asamblea con un discurso en defensa de la infalibilidad del papa: fue también gratificado con el capelo, además de con la sucesión de García Cuesta.

momento difícil, que la inteligencia de un alcalde remedió dándoles trabajo en una obra que aún subsiste en la ciudad y de cuyo promotor, don Nicolás García Vázquez, no se acuerda nadie. Se trata del paseo de la Herradura, llamado entonces de la «Buena Vista», obra urbanística cuya permanencia y posible conocimiento directo hace inútiles los elogios. Pues bien: el arzobispo García Cuesta, más tarde cardenal, ante la situación de miseria colectiva en que se hallaba su diócesis, repartió sus bienes entre los necesitados y colaboró, en la medida de lo posible, a paliar su situación.

Su pontificado fue largo: duró más de veinte años. En su tiempo, pues, se proclamó el dogma de la Inmaculada, se publicaron los documentos pontificios arriba nombrados, y se convocó y realizó el concilio Vaticano I. La proclamación dogmática no trajo novedades, sino celebraciones litúrgicas y algún que otro escrito laudatorio. El dogma de la Inmaculada, de antigua tradición española, defendido principalmente por los franciscanos, no tuvo en España oponentes de relieve, ninguno en Santiago. El repaso de los diarios de la época no aporta datos de interés.

No así los documentos pontificios de 1864: su contenido doctrinal venía a reforzar las posturas, no sólo del clero y de los clericales, sino también de muchas personas interesadas en la conservación de las cosas, no como estaban por aquellas fechas, momentos más bien confusos, sino de cómo habían estado. Por mucha que fuera la fuerza de los estamentos conservadores, no parecía posible, sin embargo, corregir medio siglo de historia y remediar los efectos de la desamortización, que era lo que más dolía a unos y a otros. El propio arzobispo aceptó de hecho la situación al tratar con las autoridades civiles el trueque del antiguo colegio de San Clemente, propiedad de la mitra, situado frente a la puerta Fajera, por el desierto y medio derruido monasterio de San Martín Pinario, en el que proyectaba instalar el seminario diocesano fundado por el arzobispo anterior, monseñor Vélez. El trueque se hizo, a pesar de las circunstancias poco favorables (coincidió con la caída de Isabel II). El seminario, y otras instituciones episcopales, se instalaron en el viejo y recuperado edificio, salvado de esta manera de la ruina.

Don Miguel García Cuesta se granjeó, además, una buena reputación de intelectual y hábil polemista, a causa de ciertas cartas que publicó en un diario madrileño en defensa del derecho del pontífice a mantener sus Estados en libertad. La cuestión se planteó cuando el Estado español se vio en el trance de reconocer el nuevo reino italiano, redondeado a costa de los territorios papales. Hubo un movimiento, entre los católicos españoles, para que tal reconocimiento no se llevase a cabo. Surgió la polémica y saltó a la prensa. El arzobispo de Santiago se mostró paladín de los derechos pontificios, y esas cartas publicadas en Madrid por un diario de ideología adversa muestran su buena pluma al par que la naturaleza de su pensamiento: que no fue original, aunque sí bien informado; que consistía principalmente en los contenidos de *Quanta cura* y del *Syllabus*; que mostraba la incomprensión y la repulsa de la modernidad en su conjunto y en sus diversos aspectos y que mantenía con argumentos jurídicos tradicionales, emanados del seno mismo de la Iglesia, el derecho del papa a su jurisdicción histórica. Era demasiado pedir, probablemente, que un prelado decimonónico comprendiera que, al despojar a la Iglesia de su condición de Estado (el país peor gobernado del mundo), se beneficiaría a la larga a la propia Iglesia. El arzobispo García Cuesta fue creado cardenal con tiempo suficiente para que acudiese a Roma a recibir el capelo, después de haber tomado parte en el concilio Vaticano. Otro colega suyo, y sucesor en la mitra, el arzobispo Payá, se destacó en la asamblea con un discurso en defensa de la infalibilidad del papa: fue también gratificado con el capelo, además de con la sucesión de García Cuesta. El cardenal Payá, durante cuyo pontificado se redescubrieron los huesos del Apóstol y de sus discípulos, enterrados en lugar secreto durante el siglo XVII, por miedo a los corsarios ingleses, tiene una calle en Santiago.

Los pontífices sucesores de Pío IX tuvieron el trabajo de rectificar su política y su pensamiento sin que su antecesor quedase malparado. ¿Qué se hizo de las invectivas y excomuniones contra quienes defendieran el liberalismo, la libertad de cultos, la libertad de investigación científica y otras realidades condenadas por Pío IX? Su recepción por la Iglesia compostelana se alarga durante más de medio siglo, durante un siglo entero. Sin embargo, algunos párrafos de las *Cartas* del arzobispo García Cuesta parecen pensadas y escritas hoy. No todos los contenidos negativos de los documentos de Pío IX han sido superados.

Varios intelectuales

Los hombres de ciencia son, en principio, sospechosos, y, para algunas mentes, diabólicos. La reputación popular de los hombres de ciencia abarca, desde el aura algo siniestra del brujo, hasta la no menos temible del enemigo solapado de la Iglesia. No parece que ni el brujo ni el hombre de ciencia hayan sido los creadores de esa aura, que hoy podríamos definir como mito, sino que es la consecuencia de su modo especialísimo de insertarse en la sociedad, de actuar en ella. Sin embargo, estos hombres de ciencia, aunque cuenten a los brujos entre sus antepasados, ya no lo son, ni es ya su pretensión actuar sobre las potencias oscuras o misteriosas. Estos hombres de ciencia, cuyos perfiles en Compostela se dibujan hacia los años treinta, comienzan por no creer en nada oscuro ni misterioso, sino en la naturaleza, que sólo es secreta en cuanto está sin descubrir. Pero, precisamente por su modo de entenderla, chocan con los representantes locales del saber eclesiástico: el cual está anclado en un pasado inmóvil, en virtud de un principio que dice que si la Verdad es una, y ya se posee, no hay por qué hurgar más. Feijoo y Sarmiento, eclesiásticos gallegos, no pensaban lo mismo, pero en Compostela no se los tiene en cuenta. A poco que se hurgue en la pequeña historia, se descubre que estos magnates modernos (decimonónicos) de la oratoria sagrada no comparten la actitud de sus antecesores en las mismas prebendas que, durante el siglo XVIII, importaban, so capa de piadosos, los libros franceses más impíos, y los repartían, como ya se dijo, por los pazos donde los señores estaban tocados de la Ilustración. La Revolución francesa interrumpió aquellas alegrías intelectuales, aquellos conatos de racionalismo más o menos secretos. Que en esta época haya habido canónigos sin fe se puede sospechar, mas no probar. La realidad política e intelectual del tiempo ya no permite aquellas escapatorias de antaño. Lo que está en juego ahora, lo que trae consigo la modernidad, son reformas que afectan al bolsillo, al prestigio, al mandarinato intelectual y social. Es muy sospechosa, y hay que defenderse contra ella, la coincidencia, por no decir el concubinato, entre el liberalismo y la ciencia. ¿No basta con que un capitán general de La Co-

El saber eclesiástico está anclado en un pasado inmóvil, en virtud de un principio que dice que si la Verdad es una, y ya se posee, no hay por qué hurgar más. Feijoo y Sarmiento, eclesiásticos gallegos, no pensaban lo mismo, pero en Compostela no se los tiene en cuenta.

89

Don Ramón de la Sagra no fue precisamente un compostelano, ya que nació en La Coruña y su actividad intelectual se desarrolló fuera de España en su mayor parte; pero pasó por estas aulas, y de ellas, y del ambiente de aquel tiempo, recibió ideas y orientaciones.

No es un clásico, pero su libro es un documento excelente. A don Ramón de la Sagra lo que más le preocupa, más aún que la situación de su ciencia de botánico, es la organización carcelaria.

CINCO MESES

EN LOS

ESTADOS-UNIDOS

DE LA AMÉRICA DEL NORTE

DESDE EL 20 DE ABRIL AL 23 DE SETIEMBRE DE 1835.

DIARIO DE VIAJE

DE D. RAMON DE LA SAGRA

DIRECTOR DEL JARDIN BOTANICO DE LA HABANA Y MIEMBRO DE VARIAS
SOCIEDADES SABIAS NACIONALES Y EXTRANGERAS.

PARIS,

EN LA IMPRENTA DE PABLO RENOUARD,
CALLE GARANCIÈRE, N. 5.

1836.

ruña haya pretendido imponer, casi *manu militari,* un catedrático a la universidad? Sin embargo, estos hombres de ciencia, ni por su aspecto, ni por sus pretensiones, aspiran, al menos aparentemente, a desplazar a los eclesiásticos del lugar que ocupan. Ni siquiera hablan de ellos. El hecho de que uno de estos catedráticos, antes que en ningún otro lugar de España (de él se ha hablado o se hablará), se haya referido, haya expuesto lo que es la teoría de la evolución, en principio, no va contra nadie. Este hombre que lee unos papeles en una inauguración de curso lo único que pretende es informar a la gente de que existe ese modo de pensar. También es posible que, al mismo tiempo, intente enterar a los demás de que es un hombre informado, de que está al tanto de lo que pasa por el mundo, pero de esto tampoco hay constancia documental. Sin embargo, si aceptamos la teoría, aunque sólo sea provisionalmente, ¿qué vamos a hacer del *Génesis,* donde se dice claramente que Dios creó el universo de la nada y al hombre lo modeló de un puñado de barro? Esta cuestión, que se plantea en Compostela anticipadamente, llega a constituir una de las fuerzas que mueven, secreta o públicamente, la ciudad durante más de un siglo. Al cabildo se le escapa el gobierno (hoy diríamos el control) de la universidad. En ocasiones, consigue dominarla. En otras, se le escapa de la mano. En esta lucha, el cabildo no está solo. La clase dominante, por un procedimiento o por otro, ha monopolizado la propiedad de las cátedras, al menos en su mayor parte, sobre todo las de aquellas cuya materia puede originar divergencias ideológicas. Los nuevos procedimientos de provisión, surgidos de diversas situaciones políticas, traen a la universidad gente nueva, gente desconocida. A veces, consiguen atraérselos e incorporárselos mediante matrimonios (he aquí otras novelas compostelanas que nadie ha escrito: la del catedrático forastero, de mentalidad sospechosa, que se recupera para el redil mediante una historia de amor). Pero los hay que ya vienen casados, y otros que se manifiestan insensibles al señuelo. ¡Son tan raros, estos intelectuales! ¿Qué más pueden querer que una muchacha bonita, o, por lo menos, bien dotada, y un puesto distinguido en la jerarquía local? La sociedad compostelana ha sido especialmente hábil para mantener en el purgatorio, o en las márgenes de menos relieve, a los recalcitrantes.

Don Ramón de la Sagra no fue precisamente un compostelano, ya que nació en La Coruña y su actividad intelectual se desarrolló fuera de España en su mayor parte; pero

Don Ramón de la Sagra, en Bélgica, entra en relación con los discípulos de Krause y es el primer español que habla de este filósofo, antes que Sanz del Río.
(*A la izquierda*, Sanz del Río.)

Tampoco nació en Compostela don José Rodríguez González, aunque haya muerto aquí. Era un ilustrado típico, lejos del especialismo, atento y preocupado por las ciencias de la naturaleza.
(*A la derecha*, J. Rodríguez González.)

91

pasó por estas aulas, y de ellas, y del ambiente de aquel tiempo, recibió ideas y orientaciones. A don Ramón de la Sagra, para quitárselo de encima, el gobierno central lo envió a La Habana, a que se encargase de la botánica de aquel país. Desde La Habana hizo un viaje a los Estados Unidos, donde permaneció cinco meses, y, como resultado de este viaje, publicó un curioso libro, un diario de viaje (ésta es su forma literaria). Se llama *Cinco meses en los Estados Unidos de América del Norte, desde el 20 de abril al 23 de setiembre de 1835...*, publicado en París al año siguiente. Entre don Ramón de la Sagra y Alexis de Tocqueville existen bastantes diferencias: de personalidad, de formación, de clase social. Pero coinciden en la visión de algunos aspectos del país norteamericano, más penetrante y mejor expresada la mirada del francés que

La fama de José Rodríguez González es tan grande que recibe la invitación del zar Alejandro II para dirigir el Observatorio Astronómico de San Petersburgo. No aceptó la oferta. ¡Qué lástima!
(Alejandro II de Rusia.)

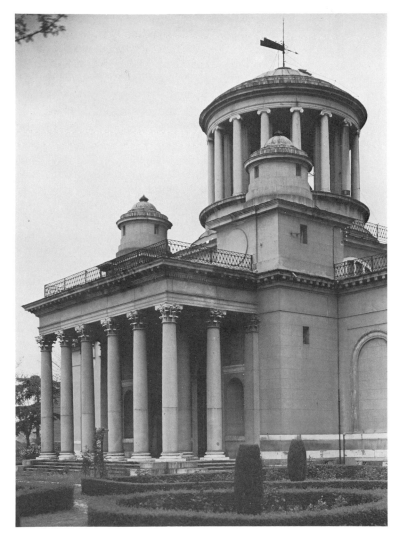

la del gallego, pero nada despreciable, sin embargo, la de este
último. No es un clásico, pero su libro es un documento excelente. A don Ramón de la Sagra lo que más le preocupa, más
aún que la situación de su ciencia de botánico, es la organización carcelaria. En este sentido, se anticipa a Concepción Arenal, también gallega. Sus descripciones de las cárceles nortea-
mericanas son minuciosas y, a veces, pintorescas. Visto que

los penados norteamericanos trabajan, calcula lo que se gana y lo que se pierde con aquel trabajo, si es negocio rentable o no. En sus descripciones, en sus evaluaciones, el último término de referencia es la correspondiente realidad española, a la que ofrece su experiencia como modelo. Cuando los países recorridos y estudiados no son Norteamérica, sino Bélgica y Alemania *(Relación de los viajes hechos en Europa...),* busca lo mismo y lo publica con el mismo fin. Don Ramón de la Sagra, en Bélgica, entra en relación con los discípulos de Krause y es el primer español que habla de este filósofo, antes que Sanz del Río. También, en alguno de sus trabajos, habla de Kant. Estas anticipaciones, sin embargo, por prematuras, son estériles. Don Ramón de la Sagra, que comenzó como radical y avanzado en su pensamiento, en los últimos años de su vida, viviendo en París, se contagió del integrismo francés: fue un liberal que acabó en ultramontano, uno de tantos asustados por los avances de la ciencia y de la sociedad.

Tampoco nació en Compostela don José Rodríguez González, aunque haya muerto aquí. Se le llamó «el matemático de Bermés» por haber nacido en esa aldea pontevedresa, próxima a Lalín. (Poca gente, fuera de Galicia, habrá oído hablar de esta villa y de las aldeas de su contorno. ¿Existirá alguna razón por la que esta comarca haya criado hom-

Don José Varela de Montes los primeros estudios, hasta el bachillerato, los hizo en Compostela. La carrera de Medicina, en Madrid, pero volvió a Compostela, de cuya universidad fue figura eminente. Se le puede considerar el fundador de la moderna escuela de medicina de Santiago.

Don Antonio López Ferreiro fue el gran historiador gallego, además de escritor no demasiado notable.

ANT. LOPEZ FERREIRO
HUJUS ALMÆ ECCLESIÆ CANONI-
CUS, SAPIENS REI HISTORICÆ PERS-
CRUTATOR, QUI ANTIQUITATIS MO-
NUMENTA PATIENTER VOLVENS MAG-

bres distinguidos en la ciencia y en el arte? De Lalín era, en
Lalín trabajó, el presbítero Aller, importante astrónomo, cuya
labor se desarrolló ya dentro del siglo XX; cerca de Lalín nació,
vivió y sigue viviendo el pintor Colmeiro...) A don José Rodríguez se le destinaba al sacerdocio, y, como tal aspirante, fue
colegial de San Jerónimo, de Santiago. Esto era por los últimos años del XVIII. No llegó a cura, aunque sí a catedrático de
Matemáticas de la universidad. Era un ilustrado típico, lejos del
especialismo, atento y preocupado por las ciencias de la naturaleza. Vivió en París en un buen momento de la historia eu-

Antonio López Ferreiro fue nombrado canónigo de Santiago, y el cabildo al que pertenecía le encargó la redacción de una «Historia de la Iglesia compostelana», libro que, cualesquiera que sean sus defectos y limitaciones, no ha sido superado, y a él hay que acudir si se quiere saber algo sólido de Compostela y de su historia.

ropea, de 1803 a 1806. Trabajó después en la triangulación de la costa mediterránea española. La junta central le tuvo a su servicio. Reintegrado a su cátedra compostelana en 1812, dos años después viaja a Alemania para enterarse de cómo funcionan los centros científicos de aquel país. Vuelto a París, su fama es tan grande que recibe la invitación del zar Alejandro II para dirigir el Observatorio Astronómico de San Petersburgo. No aceptó la oferta. ¡Qué lástima! Probablemente hubiera hecho más en Rusia que en España. Se dedicó a la mineralogía, y de Francia se trajo para la Universidad de Compostela una colección de modelos cristalográficos regalados por el abate Haüy, el fundador de la cristalografía. Organizó, por encargo regio, el Observatorio de Madrid. Fue diputado liberal. Sólo tenía cincuenta y cuatro años cuando murió.

De su talante fue don José Varela de Montes, éste sí compostelano (1796), a quien cupo la tarea de traer al mundo a Rosalía Castro, puesto que parteó a su madre aquella tarde fría de febrero, y él mismo llevó a bautizar a la recién nacida. No es de creer que este acontecimiento haya constado en su hoja de servicios. Los primeros estudios, hasta el bachillerato, los hizo en Compostela. La carrera de Medicina, en Madrid, pero volvió a Compostela, de cuya universidad fue figura eminente. Se le puede considerar el fundador de la moderna escuela de medicina de Santiago. Fue uno de estos sabios para los que la medicina era más que un arte, aunque el de curar y el de prevenir la enfermedad hayan sido objeto de su preocupación y estudio. Hizo incursiones a la antropología y a la sociología, y con ideas hoy incomprensibles, intentó oponerse al socialismo entonces vigente, el que hoy llamamos utópico. Fue miembro de todas las sociedades científicas habidas y por haber, y porque no faltase nada de su biografía, representó a La Coruña en las Cortes en dos ocasiones. No parece que le haya tentado el materialismo de su tiempo, circunstancia que hace bastante difícil de interpretar la calidad de su ciencia y de su actitud ante ella. Murió en 1868. Por aquellas calendas, ya Rosalía Castro era conocida como escritora. ¿Qué pensaría, don José Varela de Montes, de aquella muchacha que había ayudado a traer al mundo? (Pero ¿es discreto hacerse esta pregunta?)

Don Antonio López Ferreiro fue de la generación de Rosalía, además de su paisano, si bien haya venido al mundo hijo de un matrimonio que le destinó al sacerdocio. Lo radical de sus ideas tradicionalistas e integristas hace suponer que las mamó en su primera infancia y que, más tarde, no hizo más que reforzarlas con el estudio y la acción. Fue el gran historiador gallego, además de escritor no demasiado notable. Tenía una buena preparación teológica (para lo que se estudiaba de teología en su tiempo) y se perfeccionó en las técnicas de investigación histórica, entonces marcadamente positivistas. Después de un corto espacio de ejercicio del sacerdocio en medios rurales, que no le impidió continuar sus investigaciones, fue nombrado canónigo de Santiago, y el cabildo al que pertenecía le encargó de la redacción de una *Historia de la Iglesia compostelana,* libro que, cualesquiera que sean sus defectos y limitaciones, no ha sido superado, y a él hay que acudir si se quiere saber algo sólido de Compostela y de su historia. Es una obra en once volúmenes ingentes y un buen número de apéndices. Toda la documentación seria referente a Compostela se encuentra en ella. Don Antonio López Ferreiro conocía, además, el origen de cada piedra compostelana, y lo más probable es que, después de él, nadie haya alcanzado parecida extensión de conocimiento. Le tenía amor a la ciudad, aunque las razones por las que la amaba acaso no sean hoy compartidas por muchos. Fue una de las figuras destacadas del carlismo gallego, su mentor teológico en cierto modo, y llevó su pasión a extremos tales que fue castigado por la Santa Sede. ¡Cualquiera lo diría! Murió ya entrado el siglo XX. Cuando se le estudia y se le juzga, se suele olvidar, bien olvidado, que profesó de reaccionario, que sostuvo doctrinas hoy inadmisibles. Resulta difícil explicárselo.

El canónigo López Ferreiro es uno de los primeros cultivadores de la novela en lengua gallega. Con muchos años de retraso, permanece en la estela de Walter Scott, y trata de temas históricos o pseudohistóricos. No podemos decir que haya aportado grandes cosas al arte narrativo, aunque desde el punto de vista lingüístico sus novelas no carezcan de interés. Pero son ingenuas, de buenos y malos; usan de procedimientos trasnochados. Podían interesar, en su tiempo, a una sociedad restringida y bastante arcaica para la que la Edad Media seguía siendo un espejo y un ideal. No parece, sin embargo, haber tenido muchos lectores. Y uno se pregunta cómo pudo ser posible que su coetánea Rosalía, por sí sola y sin gran información de lo que pasa en el mundo, haya alcanzado, por los mismos años, una cota de modernidad en la que todavía permanece. Es evidente que la literatura no fue el terreno en que el canónigo López Ferreiro se movió con más desenvoltura. Lo suyo fue la investigación histórica, una investigación apasionada, regida desde el centro mismo de su cerebro por un manojo de ideas (entonces dirían ideales) que este gran historiador, o este gran trabajador de la historia, no se tomó el trabajo de someter a crítica.

Don Antonio polemizó con su paisano Montero Ríos acerca del matrimonio. Aún no era canónigo compostelano, sino sólo cura rural. Montero Ríos defendió en las Cortes un proyecto de ley que introducía en la legislación española el matrimonio civil. López Ferreiro le respondió con un opúsculo, que le valió la canonjía. Rezuma, ese texto, sabiduría jurídica y teológica, pero, cosa curiosa, no tanto sabiduría histórica, porque don Antonio, en sus argumentaciones, se olvida (acaso porque lo ignore) que la intervención eclesiástica en el matrimonio es un hecho tardío, y que, antes, los cristianos se casaban de otra manera. Posiblemente tampoco lo supiese Montero Ríos. La polémica es una consecuencia distante de la lucha de las investiduras, de la rivalidad entre los dos poderes nunca zanjada mientras la Iglesia aspire a mantener su poderío social. Don Antonio López Ferreiro, por su ideología, podía haber figurado, varios siglos atrás, entre los güelfos más ilustres.

«El Iris del Bello Sexo»

Anverso

¡Dios mío! ¿Quiénes habrán sido Enarda y Galatea? Es casi seguro que entre los eruditos locales y regionales, alguno habrá que lo sepa; pero, al redactar este capítulo sobre *El Iris del Bello Sexo* es de mejor gusto ignorarlo, puesto que ellas, quienes fuesen, con sus nombres convencionales se presentaron al público, o, más exactamente, se enmascararon para disimularse en el acto de la presentación.

Camino viejo de Santiago.

La cosa aconteció exactamente el domingo, 2 de mayo, de 1841, y consistió en la asombrosa aparición de un semanario, del título que arriba figura en mayúsculas, redactado íntegramente por dos señoritas de la localidad que escogen, para disimularse, los nombres literarios de Enarda y Galatea. El primer número de la revista comienza con un largo artículo titulado «¿Quiénes son las redactoras?», y su comienzo no deja lugar a dudas: «Pasmada estoy del mundo. ¿Quién podía figurarse que el anuncio de un periódico redactado por dos damas levantase tanta polvareda? Esto, sin embargo, será tolerable y, si se quiere, natural; pero ¿quién creyera que una cosa tan inocente y sencilla excitase la indignación de las gentes? ¿Cómo persuadirse una (de) que las mismas de nuestro sexo sean las que más cruelmente nos atacan? (...) ¡Qué vanas!, ¡qué orgullosas!, ¡qué desenvueltas!, ¡qué poco respeto al mundo!, ¡qué falta de pudor!, ¡qué indecentes!...» Es Enarda la que escribe ese artículo y recoge esos dicterios. Se describe a sí misma como de temperamento sanguíneo, corpulenta y adusta, la más vieja de las dos. La otra, Galatea, es delicada, dulce, sentimental... La malicia contemporánea (la nuestra) se verá tentada inmediatamente a imaginar entre ambas una relación amorosa, con o sin prácticas tribádicas. ¿Quién lo sabe? A falta de testimonios fidedignos, hay que decir que no, hay que sostenerlo. Dos mujeres que se complementan la una a la otra no tienen por qué estar unidas por relaciones complejas, de las llamadas exquisitas. Lo más probable es que el lesbianismo (no ya sus prácticas) fuera desconocido en la Compostela de aquel tiempo, salvo por los doctores en moral, que ésos lo sabían todo, pero se lo callaban.

Lo interesante, lo novelesco, es el suceso en sí. Se anuncia (¿cómo?, ¿por quién?) que dos señoritas desconocidas van a publicar una revista semanal escrita íntegramente por ellas, y el solo anuncio arma la marimorena. ¿Y mucho mayor se habrá armado cuando, al leer las páginas de un número y de otro, aparecen en sus textos afirmaciones que hoy podríamos llamar como de un feminismo que ignora su propio nombre, pero que consiste nada menos que en la pretensión de que las mujeres abandonen su estado de sumisión y adquieran por lo menos la posibilidad de expresarse. Cuando se publicó *El Iris del Bello Sexo* (que más tarde fue *El Iris de Galicia*) Rosalía Castro era una niña y vivía en la aldea; pero

En la revista que dirigió Antolín Faraldo, «El Progreso», las ideas feministas se proponen y defienden con vigor y claridad.

no es imposible que, pocos años después, incorporada a la vida compostelana, haya oído alguna vez recordar la aventura, la audacia, de dos muchachas que se atrevieron a decir lo que pensaban escribiendo una revista de colaboración exclusivamente femenina, una revista en algún aspecto reivindicativa. Fue demasiado el escándalo que se armó, y que continuó a la aparición de cada número, para que se olvidase rápidamente. Un novelista termina una novela cuando cree que debe terminarla, pero, en la realidad, los hechos novelescos ofrecen otro desarrollo y otra estructura. Lo razonable, lo imaginable, fue que, a la salida de cada número, en reuniones dominicales y vespertinas de chocolate, bizcochos y murmuración, se repitiese lo dicho la semana anterior, se repitiese como nuevo, sin otras sorpresas que las nuevas conjeturas acerca de la identidad de Galatea y Enarda. Ellas mismas se definen de tal manera que la identificación es difícil: ni aristócratas ni artesanas; ni ricas ni pobres, ni guapas ni feas, sino gente del montón, o del término medio. Habitantes, sí, de una de las rúas principales. Pero ¡vive tanta gente en ellas! A juzgar por lo que ellas mismas dicen, podemos imaginar a media ciudad inquiriendo, averiguando, conjeturando, si éstas, si las otras... ¿Cuánto tiempo habrá durado el anonimato? De los números conservados de *El Iris del Bello Sexo* nada se puede decidir. Únicamente que a estas muchachas tan arriscadas las dirigía un varón, hombre viejo y desengañado, que en alguna ocasión colabora también en la revista: un hombre de ideas generosas y experiencia triste que, a pesar de sus años, todavía cree en la justicia.

Porque *El Iris del Bello Sexo* no sólo se anticipa, si bien tímidamente, al feminismo, sino que desde su primer número presenta un carácter social y reivindicativo. «La canción del inválido», que firma Carmen, y que puede verse en los apéndices, es un documento de intenciones bien claras. «Cuando joven, por la patria / en mil lides combatí, / y la sangre más preciosa / en su defensa vertí: / Mas creía hallar descanso / en la vejez, ¡infeliz! / Esa patria abandonóme, / ingrata fue para mí.» No es precisamente un poema inspirado, ni siquiera perfecto en su forma, pero como muestra de la poesía social de aquel tiempo no está mal. Que lo firme «Carmen» nos hace pensar en una mujer, piadosa y escandalizada de la justicia, que hace suyas las quejas del inválido abandonado. Hay muchas otras muestras de sátira social, de protesta política... No es disparatado suponer que, en Santiago de Compostela, existe un núcleo de gente sensible al desorden social, a los problemas sin solución, a lo mal que andan las cosas. Sería absurdo imaginar la vida de esta ciudad, hacia mediados del XIX, en función solamente de su significación religiosa, de su magnificencia estética. En otro lugar de este libro se dice que el hábito de contemplar lo bello también puede engendrar indiferencia, y reducir el entusiasmo a un lugar común. La lectura de los periódicos de la época autoriza a pensarlo. El nom-

En el sentido del humor compostelano hay bastantes ingredientes satíricos. La suave sonrisa del san Daniel, en el pórtico de la Gloria, tiene pocos secuaces: la gente prefiere tomar como modelo a los monstruos de la base.

bre de la ciudad aparece acompañado siempre de los mismos adjetivos, que ya no quieren decir nada. Sin embargo, la ciudad sigue siendo bella, más bella cada día. El siglo XIX le da el toque final.

¿Y estas audaces señoritas, Enarda, la sanguínea, y Galatea, la soñadora? ¿Cuánto tiempo se tardó en descubrir su identidad, en señalarlas, por la calle, con el dedo? «¡Ésas son las transgresoras!» Es indudable que, durante cierto tiempo, la sociedad compostelana se entregó de todas las maneras imaginables a investigar. Los textos dan pie a la suposición. Otra novela compostelana, ésta del género policíaco. Sin detective infalible, por supuesto, pero con abundancia de ejercitantes de la observación y de la deducción: mujeres y hombres, clérigos y laicos. La estructura de la narración no se acomodaría, por supuesto, a lo usual. La pasión de los curiosos, sin embargo, pudo haber sido más cálida que la de los interesados en descubrir un crimen. Porque un crimen, con misterio o sin él, es, al fin y al cabo, algo que sucede con frecuencia. Pero, en 1841 y en Compostela, que dos señoritas se lancen a la literatura con periodicidad semanal y tan en contra de lo convenido...

Reverso

En el *Diccionario bio-bibliográfico de escritores gallegos,* de Couceiro Freijomil, se dice, al tratar de Alberto Camino, que, siendo estudiante en Santiago, colaboró en *El Iris del Bello Sexo* con el seudónimo de Galatea. Nuestro gozo en un pozo. Todos los entusiasmos que puede haber provocado el descubrimiento de una revista feminista escrita y publicada en Santiago de Compostela en 1841, se desmoronan, quedan en nada. Las cosas, ahora, hay que verlas de otra manera. Hay que pensar, ante todo, en una broma de estudiantes, bien realizada, en la que, al repartirse los papeles, no han olvidado el detalle estético de atribuir a cada uno un carácter. «Enarda» era la adusta, la seria; «Galatea», la tierna. Y ahora resulta que era un hombre.

Este Alberto Camino dicen que nació en Ferrol, hacia 1821, aunque no falta quien afirme que el lugar de su nacimiento fue Santiago. En todo caso, en esta ciudad se crió y estudió. Se licenció en Derecho, y ejerció de abogado por tierras de Xallas durante poco tiempo. Dicen que allí aprendió la lengua gallega y que conoció la vida aldeana. Dicen también que fue el primero en escribir en gallego poemas líricos. Sus poemas se publicaron en revistas locales de la más varia índole. Los recogieron, más tarde, en un volumen, *Poesías gallegas,* editado en La Coruña en 1896, cuando ya el autor había fallecido. Sus prosas en *El Iris...* (si son suyas todas las firmadas por «Galatea») revelan un pensamiento social e inconformista, aunque no estridente. Todo se queda en firme, aunque suave, feminismo. Si intervino en la dirección de la revista, como es de suponer, cabe atribuirle la amplitud de criterio necesario para dar cabida a colaboraciones de espíritu e intención más radicales.

Alberto Camino fue un romántico tardío, aunque no de los bien formados. Como en todos los casos de románticos españoles, es mayor el impulso que la doctrina. Acaso suceda también que Camino no fue un gran poeta, sino sólo lo suficientemente inspirado para que sus poemas en lengua gallega, muy celebrados por cierto, le den derecho a figurar en la nómina de los precursores. Su impulso, o su pasión, sin embargo, no alcanzó el calor ni el temple de Faraldo o Aguirre. Cuando un profesor de la universidad, el doctor Amigo, escribió y publicó un folleto denunciando airadamente la ficción de *El Iris...*, su respuesta fue práctica pero no brillante: cambió el título de la revista en *El Iris de Galicia,* donde no publicó la respuesta que el doctor Amigo merecía. El doctor Amigo tuvo que ser uno de esos hombres serios que sólo conciben la conducta humana como realización de normas invariables y, sobre todo, respetables. No puede aprobar la superchería, aunque aparezca como una superstición tan inocente como la de *El Iris...* A lo mejor era un liberal, pero de los dogmáticos. Si fue un verdadero hombre de ciencia, que eso se ignora, perteneció a la clase de los que no admiten la relatividad de nada. En cualquier caso, careció de sentido del humor. Su folleto rezuma indignación y respetabilidad. Merecía una respuesta burlona, acerada y piadosa. Ni Camino ni ninguno de sus compañeros de redacción supo o quiso escribirla. Llega a ser posible que la gente, sabedora ya del fraude, estuviera de su lado; pero ¿cuántas veces, a lo largo de la pasada centuria, la gente compostelana estuvo del lado de los bien pensantes? Casi siempre. El sentido colectivo del humor, que no faltó, que existió con exceso, o se manifestó privadamente, en motes, chismes y bromas pesadas, o se empleó en menudencias. Ante los prostíbulos cerrados del Pombal, a altas horas de la madrugada, un grupo de estudiantes pregunta a gritos: «¿Hay coro o hay claustro?», y esto se cuenta medio siglo después. En el sentido del humor compostelano hay bastantes ingredientes satíricos. La suave sonrisa del san Daniel, en el pórtico de la Gloria, tiene pocos secuaces: la gente prefiere tomar como modelo a los monstruos de la base.

El Iris del Bello Sexo, transformado en El Iris de Galicia, conservó su carácter, pero duró poco. No es de creer que haya influido en las conciencias femeninas más allá de lo anecdótico. Sin embargo, en la revista que dirigió Antolín Faraldo, El Progreso, las ideas feministas se proponen y defienden con vigor y claridad. La revista abre sus páginas a colaboraciones femeninas. Pero el hábito, el temor, la rutina, pueden más.

La liberación de las mujeres y Rosalía

¡Qué lástima que los redactores de *El Iris del Bello Sexo* no fuesen de verdad mujeres compostelanas! Hubieran dado una respuesta interesante y valerosa a una de las ideas que bullían en los caletres y corazones de aquella gente generosa, dispuesta a transformar el mundo en nombre de la justicia y de otras entidades abstractas igualmente irrealizables. La liberación de las mujeres figuraba con más o menos precisión en los idearios más ampliamente compartidos, y fue formulada alguna vez de manera precisa, aunque general: como una ley a la que falta el reglamento que la hace viable. Dijérase, a primera vista, que se trataba de una cuestión teórica, inexplicable para la sociedad a la que se dirigía, una de tantas cuestiones irreales, allegadizas, más propias de otras sociedades, distintas o más avanzadas: uno de los muchos globos vacíos que las ideologías mal digeridas producían. Pero existe una realidad viva que desmiente esta hipótesis, la de la propia Rosalía Castro, que no sólo sufrió en su carne las dificultades que cualquier mujer, y más si era escritora, tenía para desenvolverse, sino que les dio forma literaria, que las expresó con palabras claras y sin lugar a dudas: las mismas dificultades que ella padecía.

Rosalía Castro.

La situación de las mujeres en una ciudad provinciana del siglo XIX fue lo bastante duradera como para entrar en el siglo XX, y adquirir carácter de experiencia lo que de otro modo se hubiera limitado a una mera hipótesis. Existe, sin embargo, abundante documentación literaria que permite afirmar que la diferencia entre lo experimentado y lo desconocido no es muy grande. Es cierto que la igualdad real entre los dos sexos no se ha alcanzado en ninguna parte, aunque se proclame la igualdad legal, pero resulta indudable que, en la práctica, la situación social de las mujeres ha cambiado, y, en muchos aspectos, se ha equiparado a la del varón. Esto era inimaginable a mediados del siglo XIX, aunque algunos y algunas lo desearan e incluso lo defendiesen como justo. Las mujeres, en nuestro tiempo, reciben la misma educación que los hom-

Hacia mediados del siglo XIX, se defendía una educación típicamente femenina, basada en la doble condición de que las mujeres eran ornato del hogar y sus primeras servidoras.
(Foto de 1919.)

bres, tienen acceso al trabajo y derecho a la libertad personal. Hacia mediados del siglo XIX, se defendía una educación típicamente femenina, basada en la doble condición de que las mujeres eran ornato del hogar y sus primeras servidoras. Según los informes que han llegado a nosotros, Rosalía Castro, en el tiempo en que fue alumna de la Sociedad Económica de Amigos del País, de Santiago, aprendió música y francés, dos disciplinas de las llamadas «de adorno», que hacían bien en una mujer, que le daban realce, sin que su alcance fuese más allá. Todo lo más, el conocimiento del francés les servía para leer en lengua original novelas sentimentales, fabricadas especialmente para ellas, un elemento más de ese conjunto educativo y coactivo que buscaba mantener a las mujeres de ciertas clases en un aislamiento que convenía a determinados intereses.

Las libertades intelectuales y sociales alcanzadas por las mujeres en el siglo XVIII habían naufragado ante el temor a la Revolución francesa y sus excesos, las había tragado la enorme y universal reacción de la primera mitad del siglo XIX. La instalación en la sociedad de la burguesía capitalista, con su carga de moral puritana, refuerza la actitud protectora de las mujeres y limitadora de su libertad. La afirmación, sin embargo, como todas las generalidades, queda desmentida por algunos

Según los informes que han llegado a nosotros, Rosalía Castro, en el tiempo en que fue alumna de la Sociedad Económica de Amigos del País, de Santiago, aprendió música y francés, dos disciplinas de las llamadas «de adorno», que hacían bien en una mujer, que le daban realce, sin que su alcance fuese más allá.
(Antiguo colegio de San Clemente donde tuvo su sede la Sociedad Económica de Amigos del País.)

109

Sin salir del ámbito gallego, el caso de Emilia Pardo Bazán es bastante elocuente. Recibió una educación esmerada, pero parcial, y el francés que aprendió le facilitó el conocimiento de Zola y de otros escritores vitandos.

(*A la izquierda*, E. Pardo Bazán; *a la derecha*, É. Zola, por E. Manet.)

hechos concretos: hubo muchas burguesas ilustradas, como hubo muchas burguesas libertinas. Sin salir del ámbito gallego, el caso de Emilia Pardo Bazán es bastante elocuente. Recibió una educación esmerada, pero parcial, y el francés que aprendió le facilitó el conocimiento de Zola y de otros escritores vitandos. Pero recordemos al mismo tiempo que, con otra sociedad y en otros términos, la Pardo Bazán libró en su tiempo una batalla semejante a la de Rosalía en el suyo: con graves diferencias, por supuesto. Fueron distintas las situaciones matrimoniales, las económicas, al alcance de las obras literarias respectivas. Doña Emilia contendió con los grandes genios españoles de su tiempo; Rosalía, con los seminaristas de Lugo. Doña Emilia, no sólo defendió la libertad, sino que la puso en práctica; Rosalía, no. Sin embargo, el pensamiento profundo de Rosalía fue mucho más avanzado que el de su paisana. Fue una mujer de vanguardia. No imitó, en la conducta, a George Sand, de quien habla alguna vez, y no dedicó su poesía a la defensa de ideales redentores, salvo en aquellos escasos y brillantes poemas en que plantea y denuncia situaciones sociales y personales específicamente gallegas. Podemos deducir de sus escritos (sobre todo de los prólogos puestos en castellano a sus narraciones) que lo que preocupaba a Rosalía era la dificultad de las mujeres escritoras para ser aceptadas, de las mujeres cultas para ser toleradas en sociedad, y de la necesidad del matrimonio para alcanzar una situación social estable y una seguridad económica.

Las quejas de Rosalía denuncian un entorno de cortas luces, de escasa comprensión, de mínima tolerancia. No debemos olvidar que Rosalía fue contemporánea de Carolina Coronado y de Gertrudis Gómez de Avellaneda, y también de la condesa de Mina, la coruñesa Juana de Vega. Al lado de estas mujeres brillantes, la vida de Rosalía es la de alguien que pasa inadvertido, a quien no se tiene en cuenta, al menos a escala nacional. Lo mismo Carolina que Gertrudis fueron mujeres de biografía tumultuosa, ricas en amores, adulterios e hijos del amor, como quizá lo haya sido Rosalía. Pero la sociedad

No debemos olvidar que Rosalía fue contemporánea de Carolina Coronado y de Gertrudis Gómez de Avellaneda. Al lado de estas mujeres brillantes, la vida de Rosalía es la de alguien que pasa inadvertido, a quien no se tiene en cuenta, al menos a escala nacional.
(*A la izquierda*, C. Coronado; *a la derecha*, G. Gómez de Avellaneda, ambas pinturas de F. de Madrazo.)

en que vivieron, en parte la misma que conoció nuestra poetisa y de la que obtuvo tan amargas satisfacciones, no sólo las toleró sino que les aplaudió. Es cierto que no se movieron, como Rosalía, en estrechos medios pequeñoburgueses, pero, la sociedad de Sevilla, ¿era más tolerante que la de Santiago? También es cierto que tanto Carolina como Gertrudis fueron elogiadas por los críticos más exigentes de su tiempo y encumbradas a la cima de la poesía, en tanto que Rosalía ni siquiera figura en el *Florilegio* de Valera, al menos en su edición de 1903, que fue la consultada: un centón en que se recogen, al lado de los escasos poemas líricos del XIX y del XX que valen la pena, incontables muestras de aburrimiento rimado, de tópicos retóricos. Don Juan Valera acreditó su buen gusto muchas veces, aunque también sus limitaciones críticas y estimativas. Hay que pensar, no que desconociera la lírica de Rosalía, ampliamente difundida ya en la fecha del *Florilegio,* sino sencillamente que no le gustaba, como no le gustaron las novelas rusas de su tiempo. Reconocer los muchos talentos de Valera no impide dar cuenta de sus traspiés.

Hay razones para pensar que las quejas de Rosalía no se limitan a su sociedad provinciana, sino que algo o mucho de ellas le toca a la madrileña en que se desenvolvió durante sus años de estancia en la corte. Es cierto que los poemas castellanos de *La flor* no eran gran cosa, y que tampoco lo fueron sus novelas, ni las primeras, madrileñas, ni las que escribió después, salvo, acaso, *El caballero de las botas azules.* Pero una personalidad como la suya, aunque esté en formación, tiene que sorprender. Hay datos que nos permiten asegurar que no fue una chica corriente. ¿Quiénes la tuvieron por marisabidilla, por una *femme savante,* entre los que la rodeaban? No gente, por supuesto, de calidad espiritual ni siquiera mediana. La mujer culta tuvo siempre la cualidad de sacar de quicio a los varones mediocres, a los que se saben observados y juzgados, y cuanto más en silencio, peor. Tampoco las mujeres corrientes perdonan a estas que llaman «bachilleras», a las que por el saber o por cualquier cualidad intelectual muestran su diferencia. El código de cualidades femeninas elaborado por los varones fue aceptado por las mujeres corrientes, que veían en él su mejor instrumento de defensa, y, a veces, de dominio. Para las mujeres como Carolina o Gertrudis solían usar un sustantivo que las confinaba en una mar-

Hay que pensar, no que Valera desconociera la lírica de Rosalía, ampliamente difundida ya en la fecha del «Florilegio», sino sencillamente que no le gustaba, como no le gustaron las novelas rusas de su tiempo. Reconocer los muchos talentos de Valera no impide dar cuenta de sus traspiés.

(Retrato de J. Valera, por R. Casas.)

ginación menos real que deseada. Rosalía, como se dijo, cita una vez a George Sand. La cita debe tenerse por significativa. En aquella sociedad de mediados del XIX, incluso en la española, George Sand tuvo mucho de arquetipo, y fue quien fue, no por haber conquistado para sí misma el ejercicio de la libertad, sino por haberlo mostrado. Hubo muchas mujeres cuya vida privada se pareció a la suya, pero ninguna vistió de hombre. En España lo hizo Concepción Arenal, pero no como expresión de libertad, sino para hacer posible su asistencia como oyente a cursos universitarios. Otras mujeres que usaron las ropas viriles, como lady Stanhope, tampoco alcanzaron categoría arquetípica, por menos conocidas y porque su atuendo

obedecía a otras razones. Hay que quedarse con el ejemplo de George Sand, que en la sociedad española debía de parecer diabólica. Existía una vieja conseja según la cual el anuncio del fin del mundo sería el uso de pantalones por las mujeres: esto daba a George Sand un matiz apocalíptico, o, en cualquier caso, terrible. Seguramente los que rodeaban a Carolina y a Gertrudis no pensaban así, pero el entorno social de Rosalía sin duda fue muy diferente, incluso el entorno intelectual. Es más fácil defender los principios de la Revolución francesa, tal y como se hallaban ya codificados por el liberalismo, que renunciar a los prejuicios de la sociedad burguesa sobre la conducta de las mujeres. Y estos prejuicios, en España, venían a reforzar sentimientos muy antiguos, también codificados. La mujer, la pierna quebrada y en casa.

Si por su nacimiento Rosalía era una desclasada, su matrimonio con un intelectual pequeñoburgués como Murguía no contribuyó a elevarla de categoría.
(Retrato de M. Murguía, por su hijo Ovidio.)

En aquella sociedad de mediados del XIX, incluso en la española, George Sand tuvo mucho de arquetipo, y fue quien fue, no por haber conquistado para sí misma el ejercicio de la libertad, sino por haberlo mostrado.
(Retrato de G. Sand, por C. Blaize.)

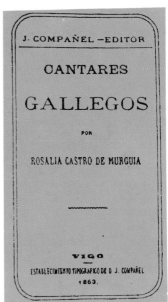

J. COMPAÑEL —EDITOR

CANTARES

GALLEGOS

POR

ROSALIA CASTRO DE MURGUIA

————

VIGO

ESTABLECIMIENTO TIPOGRAFICO DE D J. COMPAÑEL

1863.

Se dice que, en Santiago, en los primeros años de su matrimonio, Rosalía participó en fiestas literarias y en espectáculos teatrales.

Después de la publicación de «Cantares gallegos», la vida de Rosalía transcurrió entre el amor o al menos el respeto de sus paisanos.

Cuando Rosalía, ya cuarentona y poetisa afamada, arrastraba por las rúas compostelanas su humanidad doliente, la llamaban «A Tola» (la Loca).
(Último dibujo de Rosalía, realizado por J. Peña.)

Rosalía viajó por España. Después de su matrimonio, vivió en Castilla y en varias ciudades gallegas. No sabemos lo que se pensaría de ella en Vigo o en La Coruña. En Santiago, la gente se acostumbró a ella. Después de la publicación de *Cantares gallegos,* su vida transcurrió entre el amor o al menos el respeto de sus paisanos. Se dice que, en Santiago, en los primeros años de su matrimonio, participó en fiestas literarias y en espectáculos teatrales. Las actrices aficionadas eran una figura social aceptada, y en las representaciones del Liceo actuó, antes de Rosalía, alguna señorita que llevaba su apellido. Estas actividades pudieron distinguirla, pero no marginarla. Sin embargo, no se sabe de que ocupase, en su ciudad natal, un puesto social importante, menos aún destacado. Si por su nacimiento era una desclasada, su matrimonio con un intelectual pequeñoburgués como Murguía no contribuyó a elevarla de categoría. La sociedad española miró siempre con desconfianza a los intelectuales, y, en aquella sociedad gallega del XIX, el grupo al que pertenecían Rosalía y su marido nunca fue bien mirado: eran gentes que querían cambiar el estado de las cosas en una dirección que no convenía a las clases dominantes, sobre todo en lo referente a la transformación de la vida del campesino de cuyo trabajo vivía mucha gente, aunque tampoco demasiado bien. Les dejaban hablar, escribir, vociferar a veces, pero sin tomarlos demasiado en serio. Cuando Rosalía, ya cuarentona y poetisa afamada, arrastraba por las rúas compostelanas su humanidad doliente, la llamaban *A Tola* (la Loca). Ni siquiera le quedó el consuelo de vivir holgadamente: aquel matrimonio de un historiador utopista y de una poetisa más profunda que brillante nunca conoció la holgura económica. Sus actividades no eran rentables.

Figuras menores

No han dejado rastros documentales por los que se pueda reconstruir su biografía, sino sólo el recuerdo de sus personas, transmitido por tradición oral, a veces bastante remota: «Le oí contar a mi abuelo...»; «Decía mi abuela, cuando estaba en vena...» Es de suponer que, personajes de éstos, abundarían en aquella sociedad estabilizada, de escaso radio, un mundo breve en que todos se conocían y en el que cualquiera podía vivir a su aire, siempre que respetase un mínimo de reglas, alguna de las cuales permitía expresamente la extravagancia. En cualquier ciudad provinciana sucedía otro tanto, antes de que la moda igualitaria borrase del recuerdo a las excepciones. Y en Compostela las hubo en todos los estratos, en todos los barrios, en todas las esquinas. Se advierte, cuando se contempla el conjunto de esas figuras recordadas todavía hoy hace medio siglo, hoy olvidadas, que las reglas no eran las mismas para unos que para otros: los de abajo, peor tratados por la vida, disponían en cambio de más libertad, y la usaban haciendo lo que les daba la gana, fuese o no conveniente, fuese o no pecado. Entre las clases altas existía la convicción, nunca expresada documentalmente, pero viva hasta hace no mucho tiempo, de que de los de abajo no había que preocuparse, que estaban todos condenados, y que sólo en algunos casos se podía intervenir, por si acaso. La discusión, sorda, pero real, consistía en averiguar si sólo se salvaban los ricos, o si eran los nobles los que se salvaban. Había quienes opinaban que el pecado capital era el sexo, mientras que otros (los caballeros nobles, sobre todo) consideraban la liviandad con benevolencia e insistían en que el pecado capital era el liberalismo. Sé adicto a la Iglesia y haz lo que quieras, era su principio de conducta, y, al mismo tiempo, la base de sus juicios. ¿Se salvaría el marqués de Bradomín? ¿Se salvaría don Juan Manuel? Por eso, como entre los ricos los había liberales, algunos públicamente confesos, se creía en el estamento privilegiado que la posesión de un establecimiento próspero no garantizaba nada, ni en esta vida ni en la futura. Las esposas de los tenderos, puritanas por conveniencia, sin que se recuerde que en todo el siglo hayan dado un escándalo por adulterio o

Hubo chismorreos que duraron generaciones, y que se siguieron contando alrededor de la camilla vespertina. El cuento, de generación en generación, se enriquecía o empobrecía en detalles según la fantasía de la narradora. Muchos de ellos los escuchó Valle-Inclán y los aprovechó para escribir «Femeninas».

RAMÓN DEL VALLE-INCLÁN

Femeninas

(SEIS HISTORIAS AMOROSAS)

CON UN PRÓLOGO DE

MANUEL MURGUÍA

PONTEVEDRA
IMPRENTA Y COMERCIO DE A. LANDIN
1895

El zapatero del Franco tenía un sotabanco un poco más abajo de Fonseca, hacia la puerta Fajera, al lado de una taberna en que vendían, además de vinos regionales y de Castilla, pulpo «a feira» y calamares a la romana.
(*En página siguiente*, foto actual de la calle del Franco.)

Allí el zapatero del Franco jugaba una partida de brisca con unos correligionarios, republicanos como él, de Pi y Margall: republicanos federales de la mejor cepa, anticlericales y ateos profesos, todos de conducta honrada, si se exceptúa lo del vino.
(Retrato de F. Pi y Margall, por J. Sánchez y Pescador.)

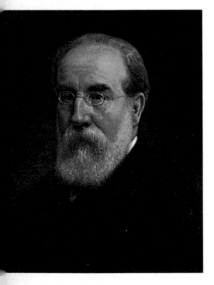

relaciones ilícitas de cualquier clase, echaban mano, en su defensa (que era al mismo tiempo un ataque) de los devaneos de ciertos señorones, y de lo que se atribuía a ciertas damas que viajaban a Madrid, ciudad de perdición por las facilidades que dan tamaño y demografía. Hubo chismorreos que duraron generaciones, y que se siguieron contando alrededor de la camilla vespertina sin otra modificación que el modo gramatical de señalar al sujeto: «Doña Fulana hizo...»; «La madre de Fulanita hizo...»; «Se cuenta de la abuela de Zutanita...» El cuento, de generación en generación, se enriquecía o empobrecía en detalles según la fantasía de la narradora. Muchos de ellos los escuchó Valle-Inclán y los aprovechó para escribir *Femeninas*.

El zapatero del Franco

Tenía un sotabanco un poco más abajo de Fonseca, hacia la puerta Fajera, al lado de una taberna en que vendían, además de vinos regionales y de Castilla, pulpo *a feira* y calamares a la romana; a veces, también, sardinas fritas, de las grandes de su tiempo, o de las pequeñas llamadas *xoubas,* y, en algunos lugares de la costa, parrochas. El zapatero del Franco se llamaba José, y mantenía buenas relaciones con el tabernero, que se llamaba Víctor. Sin necesidad de pedírselo, a ciertas horas de la jornada, Víctor le enviaba a José medio cuartillo de vino en una jarra popular, de colorines, bastante decorativa. José la ponía a un lado, y la cataba rítmicamente, cada tantos martillazos en la suela, conforme iba sacando los clavos de la boca. Se decía que soplaba de la jarra sin que un solo clavo se le fuera con el líquido al estómago, y no por habilidad bucal que poseyera, sino porque el vino rechazaba la compañía de aquel metal amarillento. Al caer de la tarde, José cerraba el sotabanco, encendía un cabo de vela, y, a su luz, contaba los ingresos del día, que solían ser bastantes, porque José era un excelente zapatero y tenía buena clientela entre las clases pudientes. Rechazaba, sin embargo, los encargos de los estudiantes, por malos pagadores. Cuando había

hecho la cuenta, separaba unas monedas para los gastos de su casa, y el resto se lo embolsaba. Entonces, encendía un cigarrillo y esperaba a que Rosario, su mujer, golpease a la puerta. Le abría, le daba sus dineros, le decía si iría a cenar o no, y volvía a quedarse solo. El cigarrillo, que era de los que se liaban en papel amarillento y amplio, tenía que encenderlo varias veces, porque, pegado como lo llevaba a la comisura del labio, se le apagaba después de cada chupada: en realidad, se le apagaba por falta de atención, ya que, entre chupada y chupada, se incluía un turno de meditaciones o de añoranzas. En el fondo, José, el zapatero de la calle del Franco, era un sentimental, y no podía olvidar una novia habida allá en Logroño, ciudad donde había servido al rey (o, mejor, a la reina): una baturra rolliza y misericordiosa, que no se dejaba palpar, pero que le traía sobras de comida, a veces bistés enteros, de lo que sobraba en la casa donde prestaba sus servicios para todo. No se había casado con ella por haber dejado, aquí en Santiago, a su padre impedido. Y el deber filial había podido, en aquella ocasión, más que las promesas de felicidad que se desprendían de aquel cuerpo como el perfume de una flor. De estas cosas hablaba José cuando ya estaba borracho, aunque sin perder el sentido. Era un borracho elocuente, aunque monotemático, porque de aquellos recuerdos (una ciudad, una mujer) no le sacaba nadie, ni tenía otro motivo sino nostalgia.

Se levantaba tras arrojar el resto del pitillo, una colilla apurada hasta lo inverosímil, amarillenta y de acre color. Cerraba la puerta con una enorme llave de hierro, que dejaba en la taberna de Víctor, al tiempo que le pagaba el gasto. Y después se iba por las callejas mojadas hacia la Algalia de Arriba, donde tenía Braulio la taberna. Allí el zapatero del Franco jugaba una partida de brisca con unos correligionarios, republicanos como él, de Pi y Margall: republicanos federales de la mejor cepa, anticlericales y ateos profesos, todos de conducta honrada, si se exceptúa lo del vino. Solían tener, los cuatro jugadores, altercados diarios con un presbítero entrado en años y escaso de dineros, vecino de aquellas calles, que por las noches hacía su colación de jureles y pan pringado en un rincón de la taberna: un hombre silencioso hasta que le sacaban de quicio las pullas y alusiones de los jugadores: que si el papa, que si el arzobispo, que si el clero en su conjunto, y uno a uno cura por cura, sin exceptuar a nadie. El presbítero se llamaba don Casto, y era hombre en declive, más bien tosco, la cabeza blanca mal cortada, si no era la corona, que se percibía claramente por su color encendido con manchas de púrpura. El nombre les servía de pretexto, a aquellos descreídos, para determinada clase de insolencias referentes al pasado de don Casto, y uno de ellos sostenía a grandes voces y con repetición diaria que los curas debían casarse, y no andar a lo que cae, con especial interés por las hijas de familia, a tantas como habían desgraciado. Y solía ser entonces cuando don Casto dejaba a un lado la indiferencia, verdadera o fingida, y le preguntaba al vociferante si creía que con aquellos pocos reales que sacaba de su misa diaria, y de algún que otro funeral, se podía sostener una familia. Y la disputa corría por esos cauces de economía deficitaria y más bien miserable, dejando a un lado las demás razones, las razones elevadas, por las que un sacerdote no podía casarse. Braulio, el tabernero, a cuya hija un seminarista había dejado encinta, decía desde su puesto detrás del mostrador: «Ahí, ahí», con diversas modulaciones, y en estas dos palabras resumía, al mismo tiempo que proclamaba, su coincidencia de opinión con el republicano gritón: no obstante lo cual solía tratar bien a don Casto, que era una buena persona y que pagaba el gasto puntualmente. Al final se llegaba al acuerdo de que el cabildo debería repartir con los presbíteros pobres la incalculable cuantía de sus rentas, llegadas de todas partes de España.

Una de aquellas tardes, José tenía entre las monedas de cobre habituales, más o menos, dos monedas de plata; alguien le había pagado un trabajo de lo fino. Había cobrado tres, para decir verdad, pero una se la había llevado Rosario, apretándola en la mano como se puede apretar la carne de un ser querido. A José le parecía justa aquella participación de su mujer en las ganancias profesionales, aunque sobre la proporción tuviera ideas propias, pues no se paga lo mismo el martilleo sobre la suela que el ajetreo en la cocina: de tres monedas, una, y va que arde. Y, en efecto; Rosario sale contenta, y calcula la capacidad adquisitiva de aquel redondel de plata en orden a sus necesidades más acuciantes: el cálculo le permite separar una parte para unas medias.

Por lo pronto, José anunció que, aquella tarde, todo el mundo estaba convidado, y mostró al tabernero las dos monedas de plata, relucientes en medio de la calderilla.

Era una pandilla de cinco o seis estudiantes con guitarras y bandurrias que cantaban una habanera de las últimas llegadas de la Perla del Caribe.

121

La plaza de las Platerías con la casa del Cabildo al fondo.

Luego jugó su brisca con bastante fortuna, y cuando alguien intentó iniciar la habitual cantinela anticlerical, enderezada contra el paciente, contra el resignado don Casto, que comía con los dedos unas sardinas asadas de buen olor, dijo que aquella noche no, que alguna vez había que descansar, y fue entonces cuando se dirigió al preste y le dijo que también él entraba en el convite, y que por muy cura que fuese era un cristiano como los demás, y también tenía derecho a un día de fiesta; con lo cual le animó a que pidiera otro vaso de vino, y a que rematase la cena con un par de melindres de los que el tabernero recibía directamente de Puentedeume y que eran bocado de cardenal. Don Casto remató la cena y se marchó, después de haber dado las gracias y de añadir que, en el fondo, todos eran iguales y, por supuesto, hermanos. A los federales de Pi y Margall también les llegó la hora, y con su marcha, quedaron en la taberna el patrón y el zapatero. «Un día es un día, Braulio. Vamos a emborracharnos.» Pero el patrón lo rechazó, alegando cierto flato, que le aquejaba desde hacía unos días, y que le atormentaba sobre todo de noche. De modo que quedó solo Pepe: solo, junto al mostrador de pino manchado de vino tinto, en aquella habitación de suelo de tierra, de paredes sucias contra las que se amontonaban los pellejos de vino. José señaló uno: «Dame de aquél.» Le fue servida una taza de tinto espumeante, y la bebió. «Ahora, de aquel otro», y lo mismo. Cuando iba por el cuarto, le preguntó a Braulio si el dinero que llevaba en el bolsillo le alcanzaría para pagar, y el tabernero le tranquilizó. «Entre plata y calderilla llevas por lo menos cinco pesetas.» «¡Dios mío, en la vida me vi con tanto dinero junto!» Sacó del bolsillo del pantalón casi tres puñados de monedas. «Cobra lo que te debo, y lo que tú calcules que necesito beber para coger la poderosa.» El tabernero hizo un cálculo, cogió las monedas de plata y unas cuantas de cobre y le devolvió el resto. «Por mucho que aguantes, ya me he cobrado.» Y le siguió sirviendo tazas de diversos pellejos. Pepe, en un principio, bebía de frente al mostrador, y todo lo que tenía que decir se lo comunicaba al tabernero con miradas. Después dio la vuelta y bebió cara a la puerta, mientras apoyaba en el mostrador su cuerpo a la altura del talle. Así aguantó un par de tazas más. De pronto, cerró los ojos y empezó a deslizarse suavemente. Primero, quedó sentado, las piernas espatarradas, el cuerpo apoyado en la pared del mostrador; después, cayó también el cuerpo y quedó, doblado en ángulo, con los brazos abiertos, y empezó a dar ronquidos. Braulio salió de su lugar habitual e intentó enderezarlo, inútilmente. «Tendría que mandar recado a Rosario, pero, ¿por quién?» Abrió la puerta de la calle, una cristalera sucia. La Algalia, hacia abajo y hacia arriba, estaba desierta, y caía un fino orballo. Dejó abierto, por si el frescor de la noche espabilaba al zapatero: llegó entonces un rumor lejano de músicas que se acercaban. Volvió a asomarse: era una pandilla de cinco o seis estudiantes con guitarras y bandurrias que cantaban una habanera de las últimas llegadas de la Perla del Caribe. Al ver la taberna abier-

Cuando el lego portero abrió el portón (aún no rayaba el alba), el cuerpo de José, el zapatero, cayó rodando sobre las losas del zaguán, que está, en aquel convento, por debajo del nivel del atrio, y las escaleras de entrada, dos o tres, en vez de ascender, descienden.
(Fachada de la iglesia de San Francisco.)

123

ta, entraron en ella. «Oigan, si me sacan de aquí a ese tío y me lo llevan a su casa, no les cobro la ronda.» «¿Vive muy lejos?» «No, por ahí abajo, detrás de las Casas Reales.» Uno de los estudiantes lo sacudió. «¡Cómo pesa el condenado!» Quedó cerrado el trato. Cogieron entre cuatro al zapatero, por los brazos y las piernas, y lo sacaron al orballo: al recibir el agua en la cara, Pepe masculló una protesta que lo mismo podía ser una queja o una declaración de amor. Pasaron frente a un portal abierto donde se metieron a descansar; Pepe quedó en el suelo, sobre las losas frías. Los estudiantes sacaron cigarrillos y se pusieron a fumar. «Me da pena —dijo uno— llevar a este tío a su casa.» «¿Qué se te ocurre? ¿Arrojarlo a la fuente de los Caballos? Se ahogaría.» «No. Eso sería una brutalidad aburrida. Algo más ingenioso...» Apretaron el corro, cada uno expuso su proyecto. Tardaron su buena media hora en ponerse de acuerdo y establecer un plan. Al cabo, uno salió calle abajo, mientras los otros esperaban y Pepe el zapatero dormía. Regresó, pasados veinte minutos, con un hábito de franciscano, hecho un lío debajo del brazo, y bastante húmedo. «Sí, pero he venido pensando que con el hábito no basta, que hay que hacerle la corona.» Acordaron llevarlo a la posada donde vivían dos de ellos, en la calle de San Francisco, a un paso del convento. Bajaron luz al portal, y uno de ellos fue a buscar a Melquiades, el peluquero, que se acostaba tarde: lo hallaron en la taberna, y no fue más que ir a casa por los utensilios. Pepe el zapatero estaba quieto como un madero, y fue fácil afeitarle la cabeza y dejarle una corona bien visible, una corona humilde de mendicante giróvago. «Pero ¿qué diablura queréis hacerle al pobre zapatero, que sois unos demonios?» «Tú ya verás. Si quieres, vienes también.» Pepe el zapatero parecía talmente un fraile franciscano, si no eran los zapatos, que habían olvidado el detalle de las sandalias; pero los zapatos, en el caso de un fraile descarriado, no quedaban del todo mal. Entre todos, escoltados por el barbero, que no hacía más que amilagrarse, lo llevaron hasta la puerta del convento, y lo dejaron allí, bien arrimadito, lo más lejos posible de la lluvia, feliz en su inconsciencia.

No se quedaron, y el final de la aventura se lo habrán supuesto en líneas generales más o menos aproximadas. La verdad completa se supo por los frailes, que eran muchos, entonces, en aquel convento, y que no tenían por qué guardar el secreto. Cuando el lego portero abrió el portón (aún no rayaba el alba), el cuerpo de José, el zapatero, cayó rodando sobre las losas del zaguán, que está, en aquel convento, por debajo del nivel del atrio, y las escaleras de entrada, dos o tres, en vez de ascender, descienden. El fraile quedó perplejo, tocó el cuerpo, examinó el rostro, lo dejó como estaba, y le fue con el cuento al prior, que se preparaba para la primera misa. Fueron juntos, el prior se amilagró, en algún lugar remoto sonó una campana de alarma, y acudieron varios frailes, unos detrás de otros, calmosos o despavoridos, temiendo a fuego o a otra calamidad. Hicieron corro alrededor de aquel fraile desconocido que despedía olor a vino. El prior dispuso, lo cogieron y metieron en una celda, en cuya cama lo acostaron, sin desnudarlo, y allí quedó el cuerpo del zapatero, vigilado por dos frailes que se turnaban cada media hora. Hasta que a media mañana dio señales de despertar. Entonces vino el prior con algunos más y rodearon la cama. José, el zapatero, cuando se espabiló, se vio rodeado de unas figuras encapuchadas, presididas por un varón severo sin capucha; un varón que, cuando se halló José sentado en la cama e intentando entender lo que pasaba, le dirigió la palabra, una palabra seria, reconvenciones y preguntas. ¿Quién era? ¿De dónde venía? ¿Por qué se hallaba en tal estado de ebriedad, impropio de un tonsurado? Por la mente de José habrán pasado, se supone, suposiciones y temores. Pero escuchó al fraile sin pestañear, y, cuando acabó la perorata, le dijo.

—Mire, señor: mande a la calle del Franco, a la zapatería de José Méndez, que está al lado de la taberna de Víctor, un poco más allá de Fonseca, y pregunten por él. Si está en casa, que me lleve el diablo si sé quién soy.

Don Juan el de las locas

Alguien dijo de él, en el casino, que era un hombre de medio pelo, pero la definición no sólo era injusta, sino inexacta. Lo que probablemente se quiso decir fue que don Juan era, a todas luces, un hombre mixto, hijo de señorito y de artesana rica; el padre, liberal; la madre, beata mientras pudo serlo. A don Juan le habían sugerido que testase a favor de la Iglesia, pero él se hacía el remolón, con el pretexto de su madre y de su hermana, que estaban locas, y que tenía que cuidarse de ellas, vivo y muerto. Jamás se le había oído una opinión política, pero, si por una parte iba a misa los domingos, a la de doce en la catedral, la más visible y ostentosa, era un lector de periódicos de todas clases, y solía mostrar interés por las noticias referentes a la monarquía de don Amadeo. El que dijo de él una vez: «Ése es de la cáscara amarga, pero lo disimula por miedo», se acercó en cierto modo a la verdad, pero sólo en cierto modo. Se puede conjeturar que don Juan fuese un liberal prudente, pero nada más. Lo de prudente era lo único indiscutible: había que ver el silencio con que había asistido, en su tiempo, a las disputas, a veces estrepitosas, acerca de los derechos del nuevo Estado italiano frente a los vulnerados del papa. Fueron muchos los años en que la cuestión se discutió en todos los corrillos; jamás nadie escuchó una opinión de labios de don Juan. Diríase que la cuestión no le importaba.

Se había licenciado en Medicina, muchos años atrás, y no había sido mal alumno, pero tampoco de los que destacan por su sabiduría o por su interés. Se dijo también de él que sabía más de lo que mostraba, y no de curar enfermos, menos aún de meter el bisturí en un cuerpo vivo y anestesiado, sino de la ciencia en general, de aquella ciencia moderna de que se hablaba en revistas casi clandestinas, traídas y distribuidas bajo cuerda, a pesar de que el tiempo era de libertades. Le sucedía lo que a muchos otros, que no estaba seguro de que aquella situación durase, y la que vendría a sustituirla lo mismo podía ser de un color que de otro. Manifestarse partidario del progreso científico era como rechazar la Biblia, y semejante osadía traía inevitables represalias. Decían que don Juan estaba muy informado de la física y de la biología, y que había leído los libros de cierto doctor francés dedicado a la curación de locos. Si esto se justificaba por el hecho de tener él dos en casa, se pensaba que bien podía acudir a maestros más de fiar que el señor Charcot, de quien hablaban en la Facultad de Medicina los catedráticos más señalados por su liberalismo. El nombre de Charcot era vitando, como el de Kant o como el de ese otro filósofo de quien hablaban tanto en

Si por una parte don Juan iba a misa los domingos, a las doce en la catedral, la más visible y ostentosa, era un lector de periódicos de todas clases, y solía mostrar interés por las noticias referentes a la monarquía de don Amadeo.
(*En página siguiente,* retrato anónimo de Amadeo de Saboya.)

127

Manifestarse partidario del progreso científico era como rechazar la Biblia, y semejante osadía traía inevitables represalias. Decían que don Juan estaba muy informado de la física y de la biología, y que había leído los libros de cierto doctor francés —Charcot— dedicado a la curación de locos. El nombre de Charcot era vitando, como el de Kant.

(Lección clínica del profesor Charcot, según una pintura de P. A. Brouillat.)

Madrid, resumen de todas las aberraciones intelectuales, del que también se venía hablando en Compostela, aunque en voz baja y con cierto escepticismo: a los señorones del casino no les cabía en la cabeza el que un señor nacido en el centro de Europa, por inteligente que fuera, por sólo escribir un libro, pudiera destruir el orden. Sin embargo, a veces alguien preguntaba, refiriéndose a don Juan, «si no será de esos krausistas». Pero como nada era seguro, don Juan transitaba por el mundo sin marbete ideológico. Era un cuarentón de buen ver, de los mejor vestidos de Compostela, aunque poco llamativo, como que por su discreción no figuraba ni había figurado nunca en la lista de los elegantes, aquella media docena de «pollos» con reputación de tales, que se vestían en sastres de La Coruña y que habían estado en París, o pensaban ir allá antes del viaje de novios. Don Juan había viajado poco, siempre sujeto por sus locas, y todo lo que sabía del mundo lo había leído, o lo había escuchado en el casino de boca de los más viajeros, a los que, sin embargo, no solía hacer caso, porque sus versiones de otros países no coincidían con lo que don Juan leía o había leído. Él tenía sus ideas y sus informaciones, y desde aquellas seguridades podía escuchar con atención irónica a los narradores de acontecimientos extraordinarios, por exagerados o por falsos, y a los que describían la vida más allá de las fronteras como una acumulación de desgracias y de pecados, aquellos que terminaban sus relatos con frases consabidas: «España es el mejor país del mundo», «Como en España, en ninguna parte», y los más atrevidos: «El único país verdaderamente católico es España. Ni Francia ni la misma Italia... Dicen que Irlanda, dicen también que Polonia, pero tan lejos no estuve.» Sin embargo, cuando aparecía algún peregrino que había hecho a pie, o a caballo, el camino de Santiago, solía ser francés. «Es que los franceses se creen dueños de lo nuestro, se creen que Santiago lo hicieron ellos.»

Don Juan aparecía en el casino, puntual, a las diez, y se incorporaba a la tertulia mayor del mentidero, generalmente algo alejado de los que más hablaban, generalmente silencioso. Fumaba mucho, eso sí. Y a veces hacía preguntas obvias o inocentes, preguntas a las cuales, sin embargo, se atribuía intenciones sospechosas. «Ya está don Juan con sus preguntas.» Por ejemplo: «¿Es cierto que en París bailan las mujeres desnudas en los cabaretes, como dijo don Fulano? ¿Usted las vio, don Perengano?» Y don Perengano, que acababa de llegar de una visita al rey, con desviación a París para satisfacer la curiosidad de su cónyuge, decía que él no las había visto, pero que lo había oído lo mismo que don Juan. Aquella noche se discutía si en París las mujeres bailaban desnudas o dejaban de bailar en los famosos cabaretes, y no faltaba entre los presentes quien había estado en París unos años atrás, cuando todavía había emperador, y no república, como ahora:

Y no faltaba entre los presentes quien había estado en París unos años atrás, cuando todavía había emperador, y no república, como ahora: un emperador no tan despreciable como decían, al fin y al cabo era un Bonaparte, y tampoco de la cáscara amarga, como decían los curas.
(Napoleón III.)

un emperador no tan despreciable como decían, al fin y al cabo era un Bonaparte, y tampoco de la cáscara amarga, como decían los curas, aunque era lo cierto que, en su tiempo, podían verse en el teatro las piezas desvergonzadas de un tal Offenbach, judío tenía que ser, donde las mujeres no salían desnudas, aunque sí vestidas de manera inconveniente; y lo peor no era cómo vestían, sino cómo bailaban. Y esto daba pie para describir una sesión de can-can, con su revuelo de faldas y de culos. «Podía ser usted más correcto, don Pancho, y decir de traseros.» «Como usted quiera, don Carlos. A mí me da lo mismo de traseros que de culos.»

A partir de las doce, o de las doce y media, los sábados, comenzaba a deshacerse la reunión. Si llovía, los había que habían llevado zuecos y paraguas, y comenzaba el rito de buscar unos y otros en el portal. Don Juan no solía moverse. Hacia la una, quedaban cuatro o cinco. «¿Le acompaño, don Carlos?» «¡Como usted quiera, don Juan!» Don Carlos vivía cerca, casi a la vuelta de la esquina, y el tiempo de la compañía no bastaba para cuajar una conversación que exigiera detenerse ante el portal, con los paraguas abiertos, y darle a la lengua; pero si alguna vez acontecía, don Juan no mostraba prisa o impaciencia. Una vez cerrado el portal de don Carlos, volvía a la tertulia: aún quedaban, como rescoldos en una hoguera, don Felipe y don Federico. «Le estábamos esperando, Juan, para marcharnos juntos.» El camino era más largo. Don Felipe hablaba mal de todo el mundo, pero, aun siendo mucha la distancia de su casa, no daba espacio para hacer un repaso de todos los contertulios. «En fin, mañana seguiremos.» Desde la casa de don Felipe a la de don Federico había un par de manzanas, una calleja y una plazoleta, lo suficiente para que don Federico pusiera verde a don Felipe, que por muy señorito que fuera se había casado con la hija de un tendero, y que si bien era cierto que había recorrido buena parte del mundo, no se había enterado de nada. El portal de don Federico relucía de bien pintado, aun en la noche, y ostentaba un llamador de bronce, mano enjoyada agarrando una bola, por el que resbalaban las gotas de la lluvia sin que ninguna quedase en la superficie bruñida del bronce: tan pulida, que espejeaba la luz remota de una lamparilla de hornacina. Todas las noches, don Juan imaginaba el estruendo de aquel llamador cuando lo golpeasen, como que, en la noche, seguramente se oiría

desde la plaza del Obradoiro; pero don Federico no llamaba jamás: sacaba el llavín, abría la puerta. «¡Hasta mañana, don Juan!», y se colaba en el portal oscuro. Pero no subía, sino que esperaba el tiempo que tardaría don Juan en salir de la plazoleta, y unos segundos más. Entonces, abría la puerta, y recatándose en las paredes marchaba a casa de su querida. Don Juan jugaba todas las noches a esconderse y ver cómo salía y tomaba el camino del pecado. Después, miraba el reloj, y según lo que pasase de la una y media, iba más lento o más de prisa hacia su casa, que estaba en la curva que hace

Claustro del hospital General.

la rúa del Villar cuando cae hacia la puerta Fajera, una casa de piedra de dos pisos, con un escudo religioso grabado encima de la puerta: bienes desamortizados que había sido adquirida por el abuelo artesano de don Juan, y habitada por su padre, clerical, sin el menor escrúpulo; seguramente tenía bula o permiso especial de Roma. En el bajo había una tienda de quesos y otros comestibles regionales. Don Juan buscaba a tientas la linterna de aceite dejada en el portal, la encendía con una yesca y subía por la escalera temblorosa de puro vieja, pero bien tenida en cuanto a cera y alfombrilla, con un paragüero y un espejo en el descansillo. Se libraba de la capa, abría la puerta del piso, y, en una lamparilla de aceite, de las llamadas mariposas, que alumbraba levemente, encendía los quinqués, el del pasillo, el del comedor y el de la cocina; más tarde serían los del salón y el del despacho. En mangas de camisa, aunque con chaleco, se metía en la cocina, encendía el fogón y ponía a cocinar las tarteras que Eduvigis, la criada, le había dejado listas, y la misma Eduvigis solía aparecer a la mitad de la faena, en camisón, cubierta con un chal y la palmatoria en la mano, a ver si necesitaba algo. «Vete a dormir, que yo me arreglo solo», era la respuesta que don Juan daba cada noche al ofrecimiento de la fámula. Y cuando las viandas estaban ya calientes, preparaba dos bandejas, servía lo cocinado en dos platos. Si eran de carne, la cortaba en pedacitos; si eran de pescado, los limpiaba de espinas y troceaba. De cubiertos, dos cucharas. El agua, en dos vasos metálicos, hierro con porcelana, a la última. Generalmente, cuando había terminado, o estaba a punto de terminar, llegaba hasta la cocina algo así como el rumor de un escándalo remoto, voces furiosas de mujeres amortiguadas por paredes y puertas, pero perfectamente perceptibles. Cargado de una de las bandejas, subía las escaleras, hasta la segunda planta, abría la puerta y dejaba la bandeja encima de un arcón. El furor de las voces femeninas quedaba al lado, colmaba aquel espacio de groserías y de rezos. Eran dos voces de mujer, una más joven que la otra. Con las voces llegaba también un tufo desagradable. Don Juan regresaba a la cocina, traía la segunda bandeja, la colocaba asimismo encima del arcón, y sólo entonces entraba en una habitación iluminada, al cabo del pasillo. Era un espacio cuadrado, no demasiado grande, al que abrían dos puertas con recias rejas de hierro, y unos candados descomunales al cierre. A una de ellas solía asomarse, desmelenada, medio desnuda (cuando no en pelota viva), una mujer cuarentona, de no mal ver, de garganta ronca y palabra procaz. Sus insultos se dirigían a la otra mujer, la que no se veía, la que rezaba en el fondo oscuro de la otra habitación. Rezaba a grandes voces, rosarios inacabables, queriendo tapar los insultos de su hija y al mismo tiempo compensar, ante el cielo, sus blasfemias. Cuando entraba don Juan, su hermana callaba, de momento; callaba y se retiraba con temor a la penumbra inmediata a la reja. Desde allí, le increpaba, le gastaba bromas picantes, llegaba a veces a insultarle; pero cuando don Juan la amenazaba con dejarla sin chocolate, se retiraba, compungida, a lo más oscuro de su celda, y desde allí musitaba: «Soy buena, soy buena. La mala es mamá.» Don Juan traía una tinaja con agua caliente, preparada también por Eduvigis, abría el candado y la reja, metía la tinaja en la celda de su hermana. «Vamos, a lavarse.» Unas noches, la loca lo hacía de buen grado; otras, lloriqueaba y pataleaba, pero siempre acababa remojándose. Don Juan la dejaba envuelta en una toalla, mientras sacaba de una cómoda ropa limpia y la dejaba encima de una silla. «Ahí tienes, vístete, y después haz la cama. Si no, no hay cena.» La loca le obedecía, aunque alguna vez llegase a rebelarse y llegase excepcionalmente a arrojar la ropa seca a la tinaja de las abluciones. Pero esto sucedía mientras su hermano acudía a su madre con el mismo trajín. La madre era más dócil: no había que amenazarla casi nunca, sino sólo escuchar sus quejas, referidas cada noche con las mismas palabras, acerca de la maldad de su hija, que la insultaba, que le atribuía amores con eclesiásticos y con frailes, que le anunciaba su entrada en el infierno. «Bueno, mamá, no te quejes, ya sabes que está loca.» Les llevaba la cena, añadía a la de su hermana, como postre, una pastilla de chocolate, que le negaba si se había portado mal; las dejaba acostadas y a oscuras, y, entonces, volvía a la cocina, se preparaba un refrigerio, lo llevaba al salón o a su despacho; hasta las seis o las siete de la mañana, sentado en un sillón y las piernas abrigadas con una manta de viaje, leía los libros que le enviaban de Francia, por mar, vía Villagarcía: los libros de los que sacaba paciencia y sabiduría para seguir viviendo.

Plaza de la Quintana.

Vista exterior del palacio
Gelmírez.

La señorita Adelina

La señorita Adelina nació en Compostela hacia
1865, hija de padres modestos, aunque ambiciosos y trabaja-
dores. Como las cosas en Compostela no les iban bien, ven-
dieron la casa en que vivían y emigraron al Nuevo Mundo, sin
que se supiera bien adónde: que si a La Habana, que si a Río
de Janeiro. Tampoco se sabe bien lo que hicieron durante el
tiempo que permanecieron allá, salvo que se enriquecieron.
¿Negocios lícitos o sucios? ¿Qué más da? A esas alturas de
siglo, se estimaba el dinero sin que importase la procedencia,
pero el caso es que el matrimonio regresó muy rico. Eso no
fue, sin embargo, lo importante, porque gente que iba pobre y
volvía rica, aunque no abundase, existía. Lo que llamó la atención fue la persona de Adelina, a la que todo el mundo trató
de señorita. Los recalcitrantes decían que no lo era, sino hija
de artesanos, y artesana también, por eso, pero después del
ochenta el modo de considerar las cosas y las situaciones
había cambiado, al menos para ciertos casos. La señorita Adelina fue uno de ellos. Pues no sólo era guapa y gallarda, sino
que hablaba tres idiomas, montaba a caballo y sabía preparar
una mesa atractiva como si en su vida no hubiera hecho otra
cosa. Los padres de Adelina compraron una casa de mucha
prestancia, que había sido de gente de pazo, arruinada por las
barrabasadas de los varones. Del antiguo hogar humilde, ni
acordarse. También ellos se habían refinado, y el dinero los
había hecho orgullosos, aunque supiesen disimularlo. Era evidente que esperaban para su hija un gran matrimonio, un en-
lace que la alzase en la consideración social por encima de
suspicacias y disputas. Llegó a decirse que querían para su
hija un marqués, y que no les importaría comprarlo. Y no es
que hubiese tantos marqueses en venta, pero, en fin, nunca se
sabe lo que traerá la suerte. Otros casos hubo, que se conta-
ban, que se recordaban...

Mientras tanto, en torno a la señorita Adelina se
había formado una leyenda, que podía resumirse en la afirmación, hecha de buena tinta, de que se había educado en los
Estados Unidos, en un colegio caro, de monjas francesas, cerca
de Nueva York. La leyenda de la señorita Adelina no la favo-
recía, en el sentido de que una educación tan perfecta alejaba

de ella a los hombres, por mucho que los atrajesen su belleza, su gracia y habilidad al bailar, su donaire, que tampoco le faltaba. Mentarla en los mentideros del casino y echarse a temblar los casaderos era la misma cosa. Estaban acostumbrados a mujeres dóciles, sumisas, tolerantes. Y pensaban, o temían, que la señorita Adelina no sería ninguna de aquellas cosas. Se corrió la fama de su independencia, de que era voluntariosa. Los caballeros en situación de desposarla, los más audaces, habían sufrido ruidosas derrotas verbales por parte de Adelina, cuando no mohínes despectivos, a veces francos plantones. Cundió la pregunta: ¿pero quién se cree que es? A pesar de lo cual, no hubo baile ni sarao en que Adelina estuviera sola. Siempre le sobraban moscones.

Es posible que las mujeres la odiasen, es seguro que la temían. De ellas salió la interrogación humillante: ¿quién se cree que es? Y las madres a sus hijos, las hermanas a los hermanos, los zaherían por andar detrás de ella: «Nadie piensa casarse. Nos limitamos a tontear.» Pero esas respuestas defensivas no tranquilizaban a las mujeres. «Fijaos, llegó a decirse que no sólo sabe de dónde vienen los niños, sino cómo se hacen.» Aquellos varones, pagados de la inocencia femenina, esperanzados por ella, temblaban al escucharlo. «Ya será menos.» «Las mujeres americanas son muy distintas de las de aquí, y ella es una mujer americana.» Lo de siempre. Sin embargo, a pesar del carácter de Adelina, a pesar también de sus supuestos saberes, incluso a pesar de la personal cobardía, eran muchos los que, en silencio y casi sin confesárselo, esperaban declararle su amor, pedirla en matrimonio. ¡Habría que ver los remiendos, los puntales que la fortuna de Adelina, heredera única, podía echar a fortunas desvencijadas! El argumento contra todas las insidias era pesado y convincente: «¡Es tan rica!»

Y sucedió que un día Adelina desapareció de casa. Sus padres estaban estupefactos, y no sabían ni llorar. Todo el mundo pensó en una fuga amorosa, pero, de los varones conocidos, no faltaba ninguno, ni soltero ni casado. Abundaron las conjeturas, pero ninguna resultó cierta. Y durante una semana no se habló de otra cosa en Compostela, lo mismo en los hogares que en los círculos sociales. Alguien acertó con la frase que corrió y definió la situación: «Siempre creí que esa muchacha no era trigo limpio.» Adelina no era trigo limpio. La especie llegó a sus padres, que la rechazaron, pero

Salón sinodal del palacio Gelmírez.

Grabado publicado por F. de Guisasola en «La Ilustración Gallega y Asturiana», 1881.

que quedaron dudosos. Ellos, sin embargo, preferían la hipótesis del rapto. Que hubieran robado a Adelina para pedir rescate, no se les había ocurrido, pero sí que la obligasen a un matrimonio que, después de consumado, no tendría remedio. La mente de aquella pareja era bastante folletinesca, más o menos como la de todo el mundo. Adelina se había convertido en heroína de varios folletines, de las historias más inverosímiles, de las suposiciones más irracionales. Y esto duró poco más de diez días. Un grupo de caballeretes se había juramentado para rescatarla en cuanto se supiera dónde estaba. Pero, cuando se supo, todo el mundo quedó paralizado, nadie se atrevió a opinar. Las malas lenguas callaron: Adelina se había metido en un convento. Se supo porque un clérigo de los de más prestigio en la ciudad había visitado a sus padres portador de una carta de Adelina, una carta cuyo texto se conoció y comentó a pesar de su sencillez. Pedía perdón a sus padres por el disgusto que les había dado y aseguraba la firmeza de su decisión. No había nada que hacer, más que resignarse.

Lo que sucedió inmediatamente aún hoy resulta confuso. Aparecieron, anónimas y difundidas, las diversas explicaciones de aquella retirada a sagrado de aquella mujer de la que cualquier cosa podía esperarse, menos una crisis mística. Predominaron dos hipótesis: que si estaba enamorada de un hombre casado, que el hombre a quien quería era un clérigo. Hubo más candidatos al coprotagonismo entre los clérigos que entre los casados, y se eligieron varios prestes, así del clero regular como del otro, distinguidos por su apostura, por su elocuencia o por su sabiduría, pero nadie pudo aportar pruebas. La familia prefirió una hipótesis menos espectacular, aunque muy socorrida durante el siglo XIX: a la señorita Adelina la había convencido un confesor, o un clérigo cualquiera, pero de los doctos y convincentes, de que su destino, si quería salvar su alma, era el claustro, con la Iglesia en tercer plano como futura receptora de la herencia. La permanencia en América había influido en el concepto que de la Iglesia tenía aquel matrimonio, por lo demás cristiano y cumplidor. Como esta última versión era la preferida por el mundo liberal compostelano, no les faltó a los padres de Adelina quien los aconsejase. Presentaron una denuncia. La denuncia se hizo pública. Surgieron los partidarios del sí y del no. Se escribieron artículos de prensa, se suscitaron polémicas, las polémicas excedieron el ámbito compostelano y se reprodujeron en otras ciudades de Galicia. Partidarios de la Iglesia. Enemigos de la Iglesia. A través de la polémica, el país sintonizaba con Europa, donde se habían organizado rifirrafes semejantes, no por la profesión de una monja, sino por la confesión, *in articulo mortis,* de un conocido ateo. Como el juzgado siguió sus trámites, llegó el día en que el juez se personó en el convento y exigió entrevistarse con Adelina. Lo llevaron al locutorio, pero él extremó la exigencia hasta requerir la presencia ante él de Adelina sin testigos. Esto último no lo consiguió, porque la entrevista fue escuchada y presenciada por representantes de las dos partes. Adelina compareció, aún vestida de ropas civiles. No apareció triste, ni preocupada, ni temerosa, sino alegre y tan desenfadada como era su costumbre. Respondió a las preguntas del juez con tranquilidad y reposo. Declaró que había entrado en el convento por su voluntad, y que podía hacerlo porque era ya mayor de edad y dueña de sus destinos. El juez se limitó a tomarle declaración y a pedir a los testigos que la firmasen. A partir de este momento, el asunto cambió de cariz. Los padres de Adelina prepararon su regreso a América, llevándose su fortuna. Si los liberales quedaron perplejos, los cavernícolas no lo quedaron menos. Las hipótesis explicativas cambiaron de signo. Hubo una señora que dijo, y sus palabras fueron como la verdad de Dios: «Lo que le pasó a esa niña es que le dio miedo el matrimonio. Un día u otro tenía que casarse, fuese con el marido que fuese. Y aguantar a un hombre, parir hijos, llevar una casa, le pareció difícil y probablemente insoportable. Las mujeres nos casamos ignorándolo todo, pero ella sabía más que cualquier muchacha. El miedo es explicable. De monja, no tiene que parir ni que limpiar los mocos a los niños. Eso es lo que le pasó y no otra cosa.»

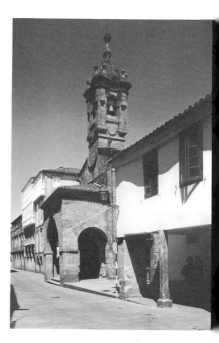

Rúa Nueva.

Los padres se marcharon, despidiéndose por medio de una carta seca y tajante. Adelina no hizo ninguna reclamación económica. Se supo cuando tomó el hábito de novicia, y que la habían destinado a un convento fuera de Compostela. El asunto fue olvidándose, aunque de vez en cuando el caso se trajese a colación como ejemplo de esto o de aquello. Un día alguien contó que Adelina había profesado: se consideró natural, no se le dio demasiada importancia. La orden en que había ingresado era de las dedicadas a la enseñanza de señoritas. Adelina, con su nuevo nombre de sor Verónica, se reveló como una excelente maestra, aunque como monja fuese bastante extraordinaria, pues, según alguien contó, era frecuente que, al enseñar a las alumnas a montar a caballo, lo hiciera ella misma, sin quitarse los hábitos y a horcajadas. También enseñaba el francés, y corregía los modales de las muchachas. Las primeras alumnas salidas de sus manos se presentaron como modelo de educación. Las madres hablaban de sor Verónica, no de la señorita Adelina, olvidada como si hubiera muerto. Pues resulta que aquellas monjas en cuyo colegio ella enseñaba, daban una educación más conforme con los tiempos. El convento en que enseñaba Adelina estaba fuera de Compostela y admitía alumnas internas. Muchas hijas de las señoras que la habían denostado fueron enviadas allá, con el ruego de que fuese sor Verónica quien las tuviese a su cargo. A los treinta años, Adelina, como tal sor Verónica, dirigía el internado, y de ella salían las líneas generales de la educación discernida en aquel centro. ¡Pues resultaba que las niñas salían hablando francés! Lo de que montasen o no a caballo les preocupaba menos, sobre todo a las que no poseían casa de campo donde las muchachas pudieran ejercitarse y, llegado el caso, exhibirse. A los cuarenta años la eligieron por primera vez como madre superiora, y le duró, en sucesivas elecciones, hasta bien entrado el siglo XX. La sustituyeron cuando, por la edad, iba perdiendo energías, pero, retirada y todo, podía ayudar con su consejo. Parece que, al final de su vida, se había hecho irónica, y, algunas veces, sarcástica. Murió de vieja, sencillamente. De sus padres no había vuelto a saberse, ni ella misma. Cuando alguna vez se hablaba de ella, era lo único que se le censuraba, el no haber pensado más en sus padres.

Doña Ernestina nació, vivió y murió en la casa más bonita de la rúa Nueva: soportal de tres arcos, cuatro luces, una fachada en piedra labrada que es un primor. En la fachada, además, cuatro escudos imponentes, que ya fueron puestos allí en el siglo XVIII, cuando se levantó la casa.

(*En página siguiente,* casa de la rúa del Villar, parecida a la de doña Ernestina.)

Doña Ernestina la mandona

Doña Ernestina nació, vivió y murió en la casa más bonita de la rúa Nueva: soportal de tres arcos, cuatro luces, una fachada en piedra labrada que es un primor, y, para subir a los pisos, una escalera a la que todo el mundo concede mucho mérito. En la fachada, además, cuatro escudos im-

ponentes, que ya fueron puestos allí en el siglo XVIII, cuando se levantó la casa, y a los que, en el siglo largo transcurrido, se hubieran podido añadir muchos más. Doña Ernestina resumía en su sangre toda la nobleza gallega, las rivalidades feudales, los odios heredados, las altiveces, intransigencias, incomprensiones de setecientos años de historia, que se juntaron y resolvieron al casarse sus padres, dicen que para hacer las paces de un pleito secular. La sangre le hervía a doña Ernestina desde niña. De haber nacido hombre, hubiera alcanzado victorias militares o grandes puestos en la corte carlista; siendo como era mujer, se contentó con figurar como dama de la princesa de Beira y armar a su alrededor líos morrocotudos. Se casó con un coronel lisiado que le duró poco, pero que la dejó madre de una hija que no tenía nada de su madre: espiritada, enfermiza, melancólica y con tendencia a la mística: se le metió monja en el convento de Belvís y murió joven de una tisis galopante. Doña Ernestina la lloró lo indispensable, para que no dijeran, porque lo que ella necesitaba no era una familia a quien amar, sino gente en quien mandar. Por esa razón, en su casa había más criados de los necesarios y desde muy pronto, nada más que cuarentona, la necesidad de mando excedió de los medios domésticos y aledaños (los aldeanos vecinos de su pazo en Ribadavia, por ejemplo, y las autoridades locales de cuatro o cinco ayuntamientos) y comenzó a derramarse en todas direcciones, aunque ella se especializase en el gobierno de los ámbitos religioso y social que coincidían en la Asociación de Damas Carlistas que ella había fundado y que presidía. Era, además, cabeza visible de las siete cofradías más importantes de Santiago, lo cual le permitía intervenir en el régimen interno de tres o cuatro parroquias, y si en la catedral no influía directamente, unos curatos canónigos la obedecían y mantenían sus puntos de vista en cuestiones tan importantes como la provisión de curatos y la de canonjías vacantes. También se interesaba por los puestos municipales, fuesen de guardias, de serenos o de modestos chupatintas, y hacía lo indecible por colocar a sus candidatos, no se sabe si por caridad o por disponer de sus peones en todas partes. Traía mozas jóvenes de la zona de Ribadavia y las empleaba de criadas para todo en casas amigas o prójimas, lo cual le permitía estar bien informada de lo que sucedía aquí y allá, de cómo se comía, de si el dinero abundaba o no. Nadie, seguramente, como ella, conocía las interioridades locales, no sólo las de las casas blasonadas, pariente que era de todas al fin y al cabo, sino de los catedráticos, de los comerciantes, de toda la chusma liberal, cada vez más crecida e influyente. Cuando algún caballero de la cáscara amarga, por recién venido o por *parvenu,* solicitaba el ingreso en el casino, la media docena de bolas negras que nunca faltaban estaban allí porque doña Ernestina lo había ordenado: sabía de antemano que no impediría la admisión, pero que al menos no fuera mollar.

Todos los años, por Pascua de Resurrección, doña Ernestina daba un baile en su casa. Preparar la lista de invitados le llevaba más de un mes, sobre todo porque, era la tradición, en cada uno de esos bailes había invitados nuevos, no más de tres familias los años de mucha generosidad, a las que daba la alternativa, familias que, desde entonces, serían invitadas por todo el mundo. Su selección era lo que le consumía tanto tiempo de información, de investigación, no sólo quiénes eran, sino cómo pensaban, cuáles eran sus costumbres, si tenían o no dinero y podían corresponder. Doña Ernestina daba los espaldarazos sociales, decía éste sí y éste no. Había familias en larga lista de espera y familias relegadas, unas llenas de entusiasmo y esperanza, otras de resentimiento. El haber sido invitadas al baile de doña Ernestina influía mucho en la

Doña Ernestina se casó con un coronel lisiado que le duró poco, pero que la dejó madre de una hija que no tenía nada de su madre: espiritada, enfermiza, melancólica y con tendencia a la mística: se le metió monja en el convento de Belvís y murió joven de una tisis galopante.
(Al fondo, el convento de Belvís.)

141

D. Angel de Saavedra, DUQUE DE RIVAS

DON ALVARO

ó

LA FUERZA DEL SINO

LA NOVELA ILUSTRADA
Oficinas: Olmo, 4
MADRID

Pero donde doña Ernestina se empleaba a fondo era en la censura de las funciones teatrales, fueran de ópera o de verso. Le puso el veto a «El trovador», y «El trovador» no se cantó; le puso el veto a «Don Álvaro, o la fuerza del sino», porque el protagonista se suicidaba y porque el autor era liberal, y «Don Álvaro» no se representó.

seriedad de los noviazgos, que también merecían cierta atención por parte de la dama, hasta el punto de haber enviado a alguna madre recados como éste: «Si su hija se casa con ese estudiante, les cerraré mis puertas.» Y por ese temor se deshicieron noviazgos serios, y alguna muchachita de buen ver quedó para vestir santos.

Pero donde doña Ernestina se empleaba a fondo era en la censura de las funciones teatrales, fueran de ópera o de verso. Le puso el veto a *El trovador,* y *El trovador* no se cantó; le puso el veto a *Don Álvaro, o la fuerza del sino,* porque el protagonista se suicidaba y porque el autor era liberal, y *Don Álvaro* no se representó. Todas las compañías, dramáticas o líricas, que recorrían las plazas del Noroeste, o las del Norte, sabían que, si querían actuar en Compostela, había que presentar un programa al que doña Ernestina no pudiese poner peros. Y esto duró muchos años, los últimos del reinado de Isabel II y los seis o siete que siguieron, hasta que doña Ernestina tuvo su definitivo tropiezo, la derrota que la desalojó de su pedestal, que le impidió, por vergüenza, seguir mandando, la que la retiró al pazo de Ribadavia hasta que, sintiéndose morir, regresó a Compostela para morir en su casa y en su pueblo, a ver si la gente de bien, y todos los que debían estarle agradecidos, iban a su entierro. Fueron todos, por supuesto: un entierro muy lucido, desde la rúa Nueva hasta el panteón familiar en el cementerio del Rosario. Sucedió que una compañía de ópera viajaba desde Vigo a La Coruña, y el empresario de teatro local la contrató para dos funciones, un miércoles y un jueves, ya que el viernes estaba anunciada la presentación en La Coruña. La compañía traía *La Traviata,* y *La Traviata* fue anunciada con antelación, y las entradas puestas a la venta. Doña Ernestina leyó el anuncio en el periódico local, y lo primero que hizo fue preguntarse cómo un periódico serio, fiel a la Iglesia y a la causa, publicaba el anuncio de un espectáculo repugnante, como tenía que ser aquella ópera. Hizo comparecer al director, y el director, que era un infeliz, echó la culpa a la administración, que no se paraba en barras y dejaba que se colasen anuncios inconvenientes. Después, doña Ernestina fue a ver al empresario del teatro, y le dijo que había que suspender la función. El hombre intentó convencerla de que ya no podía ser, porque los tratos estaban hechos y el teatro vendido, y que si suspendía la representación quedaría

142

arruinado y tendría que pegarse un tiro. «Eso es cosa suya, señor, pero le aseguro que esa porquería de ópera no se representará jamás en la ciudad del Apóstol.» El empresario de teatro rogó mientras tuvo paciencia para rogar, pero, ante la actitud decidida de doña Ernestina, acabó por decirle: «Pues, mire, señora: diga usted lo que diga y piense lo que piense, yo no suspenderé la representación si no me lo ordena el gobernador civil, quien, según tengo entendido, ha comprometido un palco en el teatro de La Coruña para él y para su familia.» «¡El gobernador civil es un masón!» «Eso no me importa a mí, señora. El negocio es el negocio.» Doña Ernestina se fue inmediatamente a ver al arzobispo, cuya autoridad recabó, pero el arzobispo le hizo ver que ya no mandaba como antes, que la mayoría de la sociedad ya no obedecía más que a las autoridades civiles, y que mientras no viniesen mejores tiempos, o volviesen los antiguos, había que tener paciencia. Le prometió, sin embargo, que, al día siguiente, un canónigo se ocuparía del asunto desde el púlpito; pero la perorata del canónigo no fue tenida públicamente en cuenta más que por un catedrático de Literatura que se atrevió a sostener en el periódico que las obras de arte no eran morales ni inmorales, sino buenas o malas, y que *La Traviata* era una ópera excelente, escrita por un genio sobre la novela de otro genio. El canónigo replicó que la novela en cuestión, *La dama de las camelias,* figuraba en el *Índice,* y que se suponía que la versión musical de aquel engendro conservaría las malas cualidades del original; pero el catedrático de Literatura no se dignó responderle, de modo que no hubo polémica, con gran disgusto del empresario del teatro, a quien hubiera favorecido. *La Traviata* se representó dos tardes, a teatro lleno y con gran éxito. Doña Ernestina fue a esconder su fracaso al pazo de Ribadavia, del que no salió hasta que, tiempo después, se sintió próxima a la muerte, como ya se dijo, y quiso morir en su casa de la rúa Nueva.

**Plano actual
de
Santiago de Compostela**

Bibliografía sobre Santiago de Compostela

Casares Mouriño, Carlos, *Todo bajo el sol. Santiago de Compostela,* Novatex Ediciones, Madrid, 1988.

Cebrián Franco, José, *Guía de Santiago de Compostela,* Follas Novas Edicions, Santiago de Compostela, 1980.

Conant, Kenneth John, *Arquitectura románica da Catedral de Santiago de Compostela,* Colegio oficial de Arquitectos de Galicia, Santiago de Compostela, 1983.

Chamoso Lamas, Manuel, *Pórtico de las Platerías de Santiago de Compostela,* Consejo Superior de Investigaciones Científicas, Madrid, 1964.

Chamoso Lamas, Manuel, *Santiago de Compostela,* Sílex Ediciones de Arte, Santiago de Compostela, 1982.

Fraguas Fraguas, Antonio, *Santiago de Compostela,* Publicaciones Españolas, Madrid, 1977.

Franco Taboada, Arturo, *Los orígenes de Santiago de Compostela,* Diputación Provincial de la Coruña, La Coruña, 1987.

López Alsina, Fernando, *La ciudad de Santiago en la Alta Edad Media,* Aldecoa Ediciones, Burgos, 1988.

Lozoya, Juan de Contreras, Marqués de, *Santiago de Compostela: la Catedral.*

Mellini, Gian Lorenzo, *El maestro Mateo en Santiago de Compostela,* Albaicín, Granada, 1968.

Pérez de Urbel, Justo, *Santiago de Compostela,* Consejo Superior de Investigaciones Científicas, Madrid, 1977.

Salvador Conde, José, *El libro de las peregrinaciones a Santiago de Compostela,* Guadarrama, Madrid, 1971.

Torrente Ballester, Gonzalo, *Compostela y su Ángel,* Destino. Barcelona, 1977.

Varela González, Isaura, *Universidad de Santiago de Compostela (1898-1936),* Facultad de Geografía e Historia de Santiago, 1987.

Varela Jácome, Benito, y Rodríguez González, Ángel, *Santiago de Compostela,* Everest, León, 1988.

Vázquez de Parga, Luis, *Peregrinaciones a Santiago de Compostela,* 3 vols., Diputación Provincial de Asturias, Oviedo, 1981.

Vázquez González, Alfredo, *Guía de Santiago de Compostela,* Cobas, Barcelona, 1987.

Bibliografía sobre Rosalía de Castro

Actas del Congreso Internacional sobre Rosalía de Castro, Universidad de Santiago de Compostela, 1986.

Albert Robatto, Matilde, *Rosalía de Castro y la condición femenina,* Partenón, Madrid, 1981.

Azorín, *Rosalía de Castro y otros motivos gallegos,* adaptado por Jesús Alonso Montero, Celta Ediciones, Lugo, 1973.

Baliñas Fernández, Carlos, *Rosalía de Castro entre a poesía e a política,* Casa Museo Rosalía de Castro, Padrón (La Coruña), 1987.

Castro de Díaz, Nidia Altagracia, *La protesta social en la obra de Rosalía de Castro,* Galaxia Editorial, Vigo, 1976.

Lázaro Machado, Ángel, *Rosalía de Castro,* Bibliográfica Española, Madrid, 1966.

Mayoral, Marina, *Rosalía de Castro y sus sombras,* Fundación Universitaria Española, Madrid, 1976.

Rodríguez Sánchez, Francisco, *Analise sociolóxico da obra de Rosalía de Castro,* Ed. As Pg, Santiago de Compostela, 1988.

Índice de nombres y obras

151